Ethical Issues
in the Use of Computers

Ethical Issues
in the Use of Computers

Deborah G. Johnson
Rennselaer Polytechnic Institute

John W. Snapper
Illinois Institute of Technology

Wadsworth Publishing Company   Belmont, California   A Division of Wadsworth, Inc.

Philosophy Editor: Ken King
Production Editor: Gary Mcdonald
Design and Cover Concept: Andrew H. Ogus
Copy Editor: Joan C. Pendleton
Cover Design: Arianne Dickinson
Print Buyer: Karen Hunt

Printed in the United States of America
1 2 3 4 5 6 7 8 9 10——89 88 87 86 85

ISBN 0-534-04257-0

Library of Congress Cataloging in Publication Data
  Main entry under title:

  Ethical issues in the use of computers.

        1. Computers—Moral and ethical aspects—Addresses,
essays, lectures.   I. Johnson, Deborah G., 1945–
II. Snapper, John W.
QA76.9.M65E84   1985   174′.9   84-25681
ISBN 0-534-04257-0

Contents

Introduction   1

PART 3   Privacy and Security   131

PART 4   Computers and Power   241

PART 5   Software As Property   293

Preface

WHILE MUCH HAS been written about computers and their future role in our lives, little attention has been paid to the ethical issues posed by increasing use of computers. What sort of code of conduct should bind computer professionals? Who, if anyone, should be liable for errors in computer programs? How much privacy are individuals entitled to when it comes to data stored in a computer? Do computers cause centralization of power? What sort of property rights should software designers have? This anthology pulls together articles that specifically address these questions together with more general philosophical pieces that broaden understanding of the issues.

The format of the book can easily form the outline of a course on Computer Ethics. We have focused on the most substantive issues and have selected readings that we thought would be accessible to undergraduates. The readings within each part are not aimed at any particular solution to a problem but rather are intended to provide a broad understanding of the complexity of the issue.

We are especially grateful to Kate Schmit for her competent assistance in gathering the permissions for this volume. We would like to thank the publisher's readers for their helpful comments: Robert M. Aiken, Temple University; George Brenkert, University of Tennessee–Knoxville; Anna Mae Walsh Burke, Nova University; Doris K. Liotke, Towson State University; George Lucas, University of Santa Clara; and James Moore, Dartmouth College. We are also grateful for the institutional support that each of us received from our departments: The Science and Technology Studies Department of Rensselaer Polytechnic Institute and the Center for the Study of Ethics in the Professions at the Illinois Institute of Technology.

Deborah G. Johnson and John W. Snapper

Introduction

COMPUTERS ARE NOW a part of our day-to-day activities and will continue their intrusions into our lives. More and more uses will be found for easier-to-use and more sophisticated machines. While researchers have studied the social effects of computers, few have considered the ethical issues posed by this increasing use of computers. Consider the following situations.

1. A computer is given the task of allocating state funds for education. The computer, however, fails to consider certain variables; and, consequently, the allocation of funds is unjust. Who is responsible for the misallocation?
2. A researcher invents a device that can focus a radio antenna to maximize the reception of weak signals. A programmer looks over the device and notes that it can be simulated on a computer that will then perform the same function. Does a computer programmed to simulate the device infringe on the original researcher's claim to own his invention, even though the original invention is not used?
3. Census results are computerized to provide statistics on the makeup of the population. In order to protect the privacy of individuals who participate in a census, publicly available census files are never indexed to individuals. The computer will calculate the average income of 60-year-olds in Lake County but cannot be asked for the income of one G. Washington. Through a computerized, cross-reference attribute search, however, you can discover that there is only one 60-year-old American Indian with five children living in Lake County and that this individual makes $60,000 a year. If you know G. Washington to be this individual, you can discover his income. Has he been injured by the availability of this (usually nonpublic) information, and what should be done about it?

These situations pose problems that are generated by the use of computer technology: either the problem would never have come up were it not for the computer technology, or the computers give an odd twist to a traditional ethical problem, or the computers increase the urgency and significance of already-existing problems.

The first situation illustrates how traditional ethical problems may be given a special

1

twist when they occur in a context of computerized decisions. It is always difficult to assign blame when mistaken actions are taken because a tool does not do what is expected due to poor design, workmanship, incompetent use, or a complicated combination of all three. A very similar sort of problem is posed, for instance, for the medical profession when a patient responds in an unexpected way to a new drug. But there is an important difference between the computer case and other faulty equipment cases. Traditional discussions of blame look at *who* made what decisions and whether those decisions created or placed undue reliance on faulty equipment. We may choose, however, to view the computer not as a tool used by decision makers who, for example, allocate funds, but rather as the decision maker itself. Indeed the language of the first scenario certainly suggests this. If the computer is itself a decision maker, and the allocation is determined by the computer, then the assignment of responsibility will have to be along nontraditional lines. Does it make sense to blame a computer or to hold a computer liable? We will have to decide what aspects of deliberation take place in the machine and which aspects we can attribute to the programmer and which to the user. This will not be a simple matter.

The second scenario highlights a problem almost unique to computer technology. It relates to the well-known difficulty in property law of writing a patent claim with enough precision to identify infringements. Before the advent of computers, however, the problem could not have taken its present form. Our long tradition of recognizing inventors' rights over inventions makes certain assumptions that do not seem to apply to computer hardware and software, because of their relationship to mathematics and because of their versatility. If we must redefine the notion of an invention, we must also reinvestigate the assumption that an inventor has proprietary rights. A comprehensive and philosophically honest response to the second scenario may require a new philosophical justification of the right of a designer to his creative designs. The tradition of granting rights over technical advances as it has developed into present intellectual property law is no longer adequate for modern technology and must be revised with new philosophical underpinnings.

The third case points not so much to a need for a radical revision of our ethical views, as it does to a new heightened significance to old ethical problems. The computer makes it possible to process information in such a way that information perhaps always available in theory is now easily available in fact. Even though the necessary census data may have been available in the past, in practice the attribute search that generated the information about G. Washington requires high-speed computer data processing. The desirability of making information such as census figures public has become a serious problem because it is now easier to generate specific, personal information as an incidental result of otherwise-valid government activity. Concern about this new availability has shifted the focus of recent discussions concerning a supposed right to privacy. In the past, discussions of privacy attempted to distinguish between *activities* that are a matter of personal preference and those that are the proper concern of the state. Today, with computerized records, these discussions attempt to determine what *information* is personal and what is public.

Perhaps because few thinkers are trained in both computer technology and philosophical ethics, very little serious ethical analysis has been done on the problems suggested by the preceding scenarios. This is not to say that the problems have been ignored. There are fine studies of the legal issues. In fact patent law, until recently seen as one of the more boring legal pursuits, has become a vital specialty for both legal scholars and practitioners—largely because of the need to respond to computer technology. Many sociological studies consider the impact of computers on our life and attempt to evaluate the desirability of that impact. Some of these, including Joseph Weizenbaum's popular study *Computer Power and Human Reason* contain ethical proposals for restrictions on computer use. Government studies are directed at the formulation of a legislative response to some of the above problems. Possible invasions of privacy following from an attribute search such as described in the third scenario are, for instance, discussed at length in the 1977 report of the Privacy Study Commission, created by the Privacy Act of 1974. In addition, both the popular press and technical computer journals frequently contain stories that express a deepening concern over possible ethical consequences of new computer technology. What is missing is research by philosophers examining how computer technology changes traditional problems. The present book is an anthology of papers that can provide the basis for that study.

Ethical Issues in the Use of Computers does *not* attempt to define a new area for ethical study, which we may call "computer ethics." Rather it identifies a series of problem areas having little in common except that they are of special importance to those working in the computer field. Each chapter may be the basis of a separate study and may be read in any order, depending on the special interest of the reader. The editors hope that the volume will have several uses. It may be used as a text in a college course on ethical problems in the use of computers. It may be used by researchers seeking an introduction to the issues. And it may be a reference point for computer professionals who actually confront the sorts of issues discussed here. This book can also provide a starting point for the advanced studies and ethical research that the problems demand.

As much as possible, we have included in each section, three sorts of papers: (1) a background study in ethical theory relevant to the issue, (2) an application of the theory to computer technology in particular, and (3) some case studies. Since legal scholars have shown more interest in the problems than have other philosophical ethicists, the editors have had to rely heavily on legal literature in several areas. The legal studies provide good case summaries. It will be unfortunate, however, if the reader is led to think of the problems as simply jurisprudential and best relegated to lawyers and judges. The legal papers in this volume were chosen because they draw attention to the theoretic and ethical basis for the law. The editors hope that the present volume will inspire writers with other backgrounds to make contributions to the subject.

The areas of study are chosen for their significance to the computer industry at the present time. Therefore, although the attempt to predict new ethical concerns inherent in future technology is certainly a worthwhile study, we avoid speculation on emerging problems. Since, for instance, artificial intelligence machines are still highly experimental, we include little discussion of how they may influence future ethical decisions. But since engineers are often puzzled about how much specialized knowledge they may take with them to a new employer without violating a trust, special aspects of this problem for software engineers are discussed.

This book emphasizes the ways in which computer technology itself influences ethical issues. Therefore those problems confronting the computer industry because it is high technology or big business, rather than because of some special aspect of the technology itself, are passed over even though they may be important to computer personnel. Consider, for instance, the conflicts that occur when business customers have inflated expectations for a computerized accounting system or when suppliers lead customers to expect more than can reasonably be provided. So far as this is a question of implied promises in business practice, there is nothing special about it for the computer industry. Indeed the views expressed in the *Uniform Commercial Code* are a good starting point for a study of honesty in the software industry, even though it was written for general purposes. And if there were no special problems for the computer industry here, the issue would be ignored in this text. There are, however, some special twists to the problems in the context of computer use that warrant a new study. For instance a "bug" in a computer may not appear for a long period, well beyond the normal expectations of a supplier's responsibility under the *Commercial Code*. We should, therefore, seriously wonder whether the standard principles of business practice are adequate for the computer industry, and papers bearing on the issue are included here.

Because this text is the first volume to attempt a philosophical overview of ethical problems confronting the computer industry, the editors do not have the advantage of basing their work on earlier attempts. It is certain that this text overlooks some issues and fails to include relevant papers. We hope that it does at least show how some new ethical issues have arisen in the computer industry and how one might start to resolve them.

PART
1

Codes of Conduct for
the Computer Professions

S EVERAL FORMAL CODES of ethical conduct have been written for computer professionals. Included here are the codes of the British Computer Society, the Institute for Certified Computer Professionals, the Data Processing Management Association, and the Association for Computing Machinery. Since many computer professionals are members of the Institute for Electronic and Electrical Engineers, their code is also included.

Important ethical problems are inherent in the notion of an association code. We should question the use of the codes, their implication for professional behavior, the meaning of their ethical demands, and even the reasons an association believes that it needs a code. The associations that adopt codes often leave these questions unsettled. All of the codes, for instance, suggest that ethical considerations are important in the following situation. But it is not at all clear how the codes should be used if the situation were to occur.

John has been working as a systems analyst in a large bank and is familiar with methods for handling large data files. He leaves the bank to work with a software consulting firm. In his new capacity, he is asked to set up a data management system for a trucking firm. Although this is apparently within his field of specialty, his past experience has been on large mainframe computers and the trucking firm wishes to install midsize computers. There are major design differences between mainframe computers and "midis" that present barriers to those who, though familiar with one type of machine, attempt to do systems work on the others. Although John knows himself to be unqualified to carry out the assignment without help from an expert on midi computers, his employers insist that this is the sort of task that an expert in data management is expected to perform. He is confronted with several choices, including refusal to perform the assignment, attempting to learn the material on the job while doing mediocre work at an unprofessionally slow pace, and even telling the trucking firm that they should seek consultation elsewhere.

5

Ignoring the substantial issue of how John should act, let us ask what difference it could possibly make to John's decision that all the ethical codes for computer professionals have clauses that demand that John not represent himself as competent outside his true areas of competence. Is it reasonable for John to base his decision on the code rather than on his personal ethics? Does the code either permit or commit a professional association to act on behalf of one of the parties (perhaps by helping John find new employment, or by censoring the data management firm, or by providing free consultation for the truckers)? Or are the codes not meant to apply directly to particular dilemmas such as John's here, but rather to generally express the ethical ideals of a professional association?

Whether or how a code is intended to apply to a particular situation may be puzzling because it is unclear why an association thinks it needs a code and how it justifies its special ethical demands. We may ask for instance whether the code (1) identifies special duties, responsibilities, rights, or privileges that are distinctive of the profession or (2) demands that members of the profession conform to their ethical duties, even though those duties are not much different from the duties of everyday life. If John were to take one or the other of these views, he would appeal to the codes in different ways.

The first view of codes is exemplified by the codes for the medical, legal, and clerical professions. The codes of conduct that govern medical doctors suggest, for instance, that a doctor is committed to preserve life even in situations where an ordinary citizen need not act to preserve life. On this ground a doctor might argue that although others may sit on a jury deciding a case for capital punishment, doctors are barred from such juries by the special ethics of their profession. Thomas Aquinas argued along similar lines that, although a priest may encourage others to serve in the army, the priest may not himself join an army. Perhaps the organizations that propose codes of conduct for the computer professions do so in the attempt to specify special ethical concerns analogous to the special ethical concerns of doctors and priests. The D.P.M.A. (Data Processing Management Association) code suggests in its preamble that a data processor may be forced to have access to "knowledge of a confidential nature," which may establish a special privilege of confidentiality for some data processors. If this is what the codes are doing, then John should seek in the code of his certifying agency, for instance, some sign of whether his acceptance of certification gives him a status which requires extraordinary ethical consideration.

A code need not be an attempt to define extraordinary ethical considerations. It may instead be an attempt to raise the ethical standards of the computer industry. The view is then not that data processors have a special privilege of confidentiality, but that they should be the sort of person who does indeed strictly keep confidences, whether on or off the job. The I.C.C.P. (Institute for Certification of Computer Professionals) codes apparently take this approach. Its "Code of Ethics" expresses concern for the "reputation and integrity of the computer profession." Its "Code of Good Practice" calls for high standards in "personal life" as well as in professional life. Its "Code of Conduct" is said to be so fundamental that it is independent of any special computer environment. Generally the I.C.C.P. code suggests more concern for the high moral values of its members than it does for any special problems that may confront its members. If John views the codes in this way, then it encourages him to decide what to do on ethical grounds but gives him little help in determining which actions are the morally correct ones.

Whether or not the codes are attempts to discover extraordinary ethical concerns, there remain questions on the force of the codes. Do the codes (1) prescribe requirements for computer professionals that can be used to exclude noncompliers from the profession or (2) express the values of concerned professionals in the hope that others can also be sensitized to those values? Since the A.C.M. (Association for Computing Machinery) code has procedures for its enforcement, it is obviously meant to be viewed in the first way. The B.C.S. (British Computer Society) code, on the other hand, also has an "educational role" and emphasizes "common sense." The possibility of enforcement opens a new controversy on the advisability of a code. When enforced by a private association, a code is clearly an attempt to establish certain practices in the industry as a whole. Such attempts to regulate industry practice, especially through the exclusion of noncompliers, are viewed with suspicion by those who promote free entry into an open industry. In the extreme, the enforcement of a code may bring an association into conflict in the United States with antitrust law.

Included here are two papers that discuss the limits of a professional association to influence professional practice through the use of codes of conduct. The Supreme Court decision in *Fashion Originator's Guild of America* v. *Federal Trade Commission* presents a critique of an organization that overstepped its authority. The case is interesting because of a strong similarity between its background and computer-industry problems. The problem of "style piracy" in the fashion industry, like the problem of "software piracy" in the computer industry is aggravated by the lack of adequate legal protection for creative designs. The Fashion Guild responded by establishing a personal code for design independence and holding its members to that code. The Court decided that the code and its enforcement violated antitrust law by excluding firms that did not have design capabilities from the industry. If the computer industry were to respond to the issues raised here in the chapter on property by establishing guidelines for software design independence enforced through an association code of conduct, then that association would also violate the law. Fay Sawyier's paper "What Professional Societies Should Do About Ethics?" puts the Fashion Guild controversy in a larger perspective and then goes on to say how professional associations may properly encourage the ethical conduct of their members without violating the principles set down in that case.

John Ladd's paper on "The Quest for a Code of Professional Ethics: An Intellectual and Moral Confusion," draws many of the issues together by asking whether a formal code can be viewed as an ethical code, or whether all such codes are really more like *legal* codes. He throws doubt on the view that ethical conduct can be encouraged by the institution of formal codes and even suggests that decisions influenced by codes are (insofar as they are based on those codes) not examples of ethical reasoning. He shows the danger of misreading a code or mistaking the intended use of a code.

We may note finally that although several professional associations describe formal procedures for responding to violations of their codes, the procedures do not seem to be much used. The associations, of course, carefully protect the confidences and reputations of any parties involved in an "ethical dispute," and formal procedures may be more common than the editors of this text know. But to date, the editors know of only one case that proceeded as far as the serious possibility of action by an ethics committee, and that was a notorious case of embezzlement involving legal fraud and theft as well as unethical conduct. Although formal appeals to ethics committees may be rare, the codes may have performed other functions. At least the discussions of the codes within the various associations have contributed to a sense of professional responsibility among the participating members.

1. The Quest for a Code of Professional Ethics: An Intellectual and Moral Confusion

John Ladd

MY ROLE AS A PHILOSOPHER is to act as a gadfly. If this were Athens in the fifth century B.C. you would probably throw me in prison for what I shall say, and I would be promptly condemned to death for attacking your idols. But you can't do that in this day and age; you can't even ask for your money back, since I am not being paid. All that you can do is to throw eggs at me or simply walk out!

My theme is stated in the title: it is that the whole notion of an organized professional ethics is an absurdity—intellectual and moral. Furthermore, I shall argue that there are few positive benefits to be derived from having a code and the possibility of mischievous side effects of adopting a code is substantial. Unfortunately, in the time allotted to me I can only summarize what I have to say on this topic.

(1) To begin with, ethics itself is basically an open-ended, reflective and critical intellectual activity. It is essentially problematic and controversial, both as far as its principles are concerned and in its application. Ethics consists of issues to be examined, explored, discussed, deliberated, and argued. Ethical principles can be established only as a result of deliberation and argumentation. These principles are not the kind of thing that can be settled by fiat, by agreement, or by authority. To assume that they can be is to confuse ethics with law-making, rule-making, policy-making, and other kinds of decision-making. It follows that, ethical principles, as such, cannot be established by associations, organizations, or by a consensus of their members. To speak of codifying ethics, therefore, makes no more sense than to speak of codifying medicine, anthropology, or architecture.

(2) Even if substantial agreement could be reached on ethical principles and they could be set out in a code, the attempt to impose such principles on others in the guise

From *AAAS Professional Ethics Project: Professional Ethics Activities in the Scientific and Engineering Societies,* edited by Rosemary Chalk, Mark S. Frankel, and Sallie B. Chafer (Washington, D.C.: American Association for the Advancement of Science, 1980), pp. 154–159. Reprinted by permission of the American Association for the Advancement of Science.

of ethics contradicts the notion of ethics itself, which presumes that persons are autonomous moral agents. In Kant's terms, such an attempt makes ethics heteronomous; it confuses ethics with some kind of externally imposed set of rules such as a code of law, which, indeed, is heteronomous. To put the point in more popular language: ethics must, by its very nature, be self-directed rather than other-directed.

(3) Thus, in attaching disciplinary procedures, methods of adjudication and sanctions, formal and informal, to the principles that one calls "ethical" one automatically converts them into legal rules or some other kind of authoritative rules of conduct such as the bylaws of an organization, regulations promulgated by an official, club rules, rules of etiquette, or other sorts of social standards of conduct. To label such conventions, rules and standards "ethical" simply reflects an intellectual confusion about the status and function of these conventions, rules, and standards. Historically, it should be noted that the term "ethical" was introduced merely to indicate that the code of the Royal College of Physicians was not to be construed as a criminal code (i.e. a legal code). Here "ethical" means simply non-legal.

(4) That is not to say that ethics has no relevance for projects involving the creation, certification, and enforcement of rules of conduct for members of certain groups. But logically it has the same kind of relevance that it has for the law. As with law, its role in connection with these projects is to appraise, criticize and perhaps even defend (or condemn) the projects themselves, the rules, regulations, and procedures they prescribe, and the social and political goals and institutions they represent. But although ethics can be used to judge or evaluate a disciplinary code, penal code, code of honor, or what goes by the name of a "code of ethics," it cannot be identified with any of these, for the reasons that have already been mentioned.

Some General Comments on Professionalism and Ethics

(5) Being a professional does not automatically make a person an expert in ethics, even in the ethics of that person's own particular profession—unless of course we decide to call the "club rules" of a profession its ethics. The reason for this is that there are no experts in ethics in the sense of expert in which professionals have a special expertise that others do not share. As Plato pointed out long ago in the *Protagoras,* knowledge of virtue is not like the technical knowledge that is possessed by an architect or shipbuilder. In a sense, everyone is, or ought to be, a teacher of virtue; there are no professional qualifications that are necessary for doing ethics.

(6) Moreover, there is no special ethics belonging to professionals. Professionals are not, simply because they are professionals, exempt from the common obligations, duties, and responsibilites that are binding on ordinary people. They do not have a special moral status that allows them to do things that no one else can. Doctors have no special right to be rude, to deceive, or to order people around like children, etc. Likewise, lawyers do not have a special right to bend the law to help their clients, to bully witnesses, or to be cruel and brutal—simply because they think that it is in the interests of their client. Professional codes cannot, therefore, confer such rights and immunities, for there is no such thing as professional ethical immunity.

(7) We might ask: do professionals, by virtue of their special professional status, have

special duties and obligations over and above those they would have as ordinary people? Before we can answer this question, we must first decide what is meant by the terms "profession" and "professional," which are very loose terms that are used as labels for a variety of different occupational categories. The distinctive element in professionalism is generally held to be that professionals have undergone advanced, specialized training and that they exercise control over the nature of their job and the services they provide. In addition, the older professions, lawyers, physicians, professors, and ministers typically have clients to whom they provide services as individuals. (I use the term "client" generically so as to include patients, students, and parishioners.) When professionals have individual clients, new moral relationships are created that demand special types of trust and loyalty. Thus, in order to answer the question, we need to examine the context under which special duties and obligations of professionals might arise.

(8) In discussing specific ethical issues relating to the professions, it is convenient to divide them into issues of *macro-ethics* and *micro-ethics*. The former comprise what might be called collective or social problems, that is, problems confronting members of a profession as a group in their relation to society; the latter, issues of micro-ethics, are concerned with moral aspects of personal relationships between individual professionals and other individuals who are their clients, their colleagues and their employers. Clearly the particulars in both kinds of ethics vary considerably from one profession to another. I shall make only two general comments.

(9) Micro-ethical issues concern the personal relationships between individuals. Many of these issues simply involve the application of ordinary notions of honesty, decency, civility, humanity, considerateness, respect, and responsibility. Therefore, it should not be necessary to devise a special code to tell professionals that they ought to refrain from cheating and lying, or to make them treat their clients (and patients) with respect, or to tell them that they ought to ask for informed consent for invasive actions. It is a common mistake to assume that *all* the extra-legal norms and conventions governing professional relationships have a moral status, for every profession has norms and conventions that have as little to do with morality as the ceremonial dress and titles that are customarily associated with the older professions.

(10) The macro-ethical problems in professionalism are more problematic and controversial. What are the social responsibilities of professionals as a group? What can and should they do to influence social policy? Here, I submit, the issue is not one of professional roles, but of *professional power*. For professionals as a group have a great deal of power; and power begets responsibility. Physicians as a group can, for instance, exercise a great deal of influence on the quality and cost of health care; and lawyers can have a great deal of influence on how the law is made and administered, etc.

(11) So-called "codes of professional ethics" have nothing to contribute either to micro-ethics or to macro-ethics as just outlined. It should also be obvious that they do not fit under either of these two categories. Any association, including a professional association, can, of course, adopt a code of conduct for its members and lay down disciplinary procedures and sanctions to enforce conformity with its rules. But to call such a disciplinary code a code of *ethics* is at once pretentious and sanctimonious. Even worse, it is to make a false and misleading claim, namely, that the profession in question has the authority or special competence to create an ethics, that it is able authoritatively to set forth what the

principles of ethics are, and that it has its own brand of ethics that it can impose on its members and on society.

I have briefly stated the case against taking a code of professional ethics to be a serious ethical enterprise. It might be objected, however, that I have neglected to recognize some of the benefits that come from having professional codes of ethics. In order to discuss these possible benefits, I shall first examine what some of the objectives of codes of ethics might be, then I shall consider some possible benefits of having a code, and, finally, I shall point out some of the mischievous aspects of codes.

Objectives of Codes of Professional "Ethics"

In order to be crystal clear about the purposes and objectives of a code, we must begin by asking: to whom is the code addressed? Although ostensibly codes of ethics are addressed to the members of the profession, their true purposes and objectives are sometimes easier to ascertain if we recognize that codes are in fact often directed at other addressees than members. Accordingly, the real addressees might be any of the following: (a) members of the profession, (b) clients or buyers of the professional services, (c) other agents dealing with professionals, such as government or private institutions like universities or hospitals, or (d) the public at large. With this in mind, let us examine some possible objectives.

First, the objective of a professional code might be "inspirational," that is, it might be used to inspire members to be more "ethical" in their conduct. The assumption on which this objective is premised is that professionals are somehow likely to be amoral or submoral, perhaps, as the result of becoming professionals, and so it is necessary to exhort them to be moral, e.g. to be honest. I suppose there is nothing objectionable to having a code for this reason; it would be something like the Boy Scout's Code of Honor, something to frame and hang in one's office. I have severe reservations, however, about whether a code is really needed for this purpose and whether it will do any good; for those to whom it is addressed and who need it the most will not adhere to it anyway, and the rest of the good people in the profession will not need it because they already know what they ought to do. For this reason, many respectable members of a profession regard its code as a joke and as something not to be taken seriously. (Incidentally, for much the same kind of reasons as those just given, there are no professional codes in the academic or clerical professions.)

A second objective might be to alert professionals to the moral aspects of their work that they might have overlooked. In jargon, it might serve to sensitize them or to raise their consciousness. This, of course, is a worthy goal—it is the goal of moral education. Morality, after all, is not just a matter of doing or not doing, but also a matter of feeling and thinking. But, here again, it is doubtful that it is possible [to] make people have the right feelings or think rightly through enacting a code. A code is hardly the best means for teaching morality.

Thirdly, a code might, as it was traditionally, be a disciplinary code or a "penal" code used to enforce certain rules of the profession on its members in order to defend the integrity of the professional and to protect its professional standards. This kind of function is often referred to as "self-policing." It is unlikely, however, that the kind of disciplining that is in question here could be handled in a code of ethics, a code that would set forth in detail criteria for determining malpractice. On the contrary, the "ethical" code of a profession is usually used to discipline its members for other sorts of "unethical conduct," such as stealing a client away from a colleague, for making disparaging remarks about a colleague in public, or for departing from some other sort of norm of the profession. (In the original code of the Royal College of Physicians, members who failed to attend the funeral of a colleague were subject to a fine!) It is clear that when we talk of a disciplinary code, as distinguished from an exhortatory code, a lot of new questions arise that cannot be treated here; for a disciplinary code is quasi-legal in nature, it involves adjudicative organs and processes, and it is usually connected with complicated issues relating to such things as licensing.

A fourth objective of a code might be to offer advice in cases of moral perplexity about what to do: e.g. should one report a colleague for malfeasance? Should one let a severely defective newborn die? If such cases present genuine perplexities, then they cannot and should not be solved by reference to a code. To try to solve them through a code is like trying to do surgery with a carving knife! If it is not a genuine perplexity, then the code would be unnecessary.

A fifth objective of a professional code of ethics is to alert prospective clients and employers to what they may and may not expect by way of service from a member of the profession concerned. The official code of an association, say, of engineers, provides an authoritative statement of what is proper and what is improper conduct of the professional. Thus, a code serves to protect a professional from improper demands on the part of employer or client, e.g. that he lie about or cover up defective work that constitutes a public hazard. Codes may thus serve to protect "whistle-blowers." (The real addressee in this case is the employer or client.)

Secondary Objectives of Codes—Not Always Salutory

I now come to what I shall call "secondary objectives," that is, objectives that one might hesitate always to call "ethical," especially since they often provide an opportunity for abuse.

The first secondary objective is to enhance the image of the profession in the public eye. The code is supposed to communicate to the general public (the addressee) the idea that the members of the profession concerned are service oriented and that the interests of the client are always given first place over the interests of the professional himself. Because they have a code they may be expected to be trustworthy.

Another secondary objective of a code is to protect the monopoly of the profession in question. Historically, this appears to have been the principal objective of a so-called code of ethics, e.g. Percival's code of medical ethics. Its aim is to exclude from practice those who are outside the professional in-group and to regulate the conduct of the members of the profession so as to protect it from encroachment from outside. Sometimes this kind of professional monopoly is in the public interest and often it is not.

Another secondary objective of professional codes of ethics, mentioned in some of the literature, is that having a code serves as a status symbol; one of the credentials for an occupation to be considered a profession is that it have a code of ethics. If you want to make your occupation a profession, then you must frame a code of ethics for it: so there are codes for real estate agents, insurance agents, used car dealers, electricians, barbers, etc., and these codes serve, at least in the eyes of some, to raise their members to the social status of lawyers and doctors.

Mischievous Side-effects of Codes of Ethics

I now want to call attention to some of the mischievous side-effects of adopting a code of ethics:

The first and most obvious bit of mischief, is that having a code will give a sense of complacency to professionals about their conduct. "We have a code of ethics," they will say, "So everything we do is ethical." Inasmuch as a code, of necessity, prescribes what is minimal, a professional may be encouraged by the code to deliver what is minimal rather than the best that he can do. "I did everything that the code requires. . . ."

Even more mischievous than complacency and the consequent self-congratulation, is the fact that a code of ethics can be used as a cover-up for what might be called basically "unethical" or "irresponsible" conduct.

Perhaps the most mischievous side-effect of codes of ethics is that they tend to divert attention from the macro-ethical problems of a profession to its micro-ethical problems. There is a lot of talk about whistle-blowing. But it concerns individuals almost exclusively. What is really needed is a thorough scrutiny of professions as collective bodies, of their role in society and their effect on the public interest. What role should the professions play in determining the use of technology, its development and expansion, and the distribution of the costs (e.g. disposition of toxic wastes) as well as the benefits of technology? What is the significance of professionalism from the moral point of view for democracy, social equality, liberty, and justice? There are lots of ethical problems to be dealt with. To concentrate on codes of ethics as if they represented the real ethical problems connected with professionalism is to capitulate to *struthianism* (from the Greek word *struthos* = ostrich).

One final objection to codes that needs to be mentioned is that they inevitably represent what John Stuart Mill called the "tyranny of the majority" or, if not that, the "tyranny of the establishment." They serve to and are designed to discourage if not suppress the dissenter, the innovator, the critic.

By way of conclusion, let me say a few words about what an association of professionals can do about ethics. On theoretical grounds, I have argued that it cannot codify an ethics and it cannot authoritatively establish ethical principles or prescribed guidelines for the conduct of its members—as if it were *creating* an ethics! But there is still much that associations can do to promote further understanding of and sensitivity to ethical issues connected with professional activities. For example, they can fill a very useful educational function by encouraging their members to participate in extended discussions of issues of both micro-ethics and macro-ethics, e.g. questions about responsibility; for these issues obviously need to be examined and discussed much more extensively than they are at present—especially by those who are in a position to do something about them.

2. Excerpts from The British Computer Society Code of Practice and Code of Conduct

British Computer Society

[Practice]

Foreword

ANY CODE MAY be considered as a formalisation of experience into a set of rules. A code is adopted by a community because its members accept that adherence to these rules, including the restrictions this implies, is of benefit to all, inside and outside the community alike. A code has an educational role, by setting out what is required of those wishing to join the community.

It may be said that everything contained in an acceptable code is obvious and merely commonsense. This, however, does not lessen its worth. The conscious selection and emphasis of a group of 'commonsense' items on the basis of experience is by itself a worthwhile exercise.

The Code of Practice deals with the ways in which all members of the Society are expected to exercise their professional competence and thereby complements its companion, the Code of Conduct, which deals with behavior. The two codes apply to all members of the Society. Because they are the distillation of considerable experience they set standards for all engaged in the computing profession. At a time when computing is playing an ever-increasing part in national life, whether in business, industry or social affairs, it is important for the profession to state clearly what its rules are.

Introduction

This Code of Practice is directed to all members of The British Computer Society. It consists, essentially, of a series of statements which prescribe minimum standards of practice, to be observed by all members.

The Code is concerned with professional responsibility. All members have responsibilities; to clients, to users, to the State and society at large. Those members who are employees also have responsibilities to their employers and employers' customers and, often, to a Trade Union. In the event of an apparent clash in responsibilities, obligations or prescribed practice the Society's Secretary-General should be consulted at the earliest opportunity.

From the British Computer Society, *Code of Practice,* pp. 1–3, and *Code of Conduct* (Manchester, England: NCC Publications, 1983), pp. 1–12. Reprinted by permission of The British Computer Society.

The Code is to be viewed as a whole: Individual parts are not intended to be used in isolation to justify errors of omission or commission.

The Code is intended to be observed in the spirit and not merely to the word. The BCS membership covers all occupations relevant to the use of computers and it is not possible to define the Code in terms directly relevant to each individual member. For this reason the Code is set out in two levels to enable every member to reach appropriate interpretations.

Level One: a series of brief statements which define the elements of practice to be observed.

Level Two: the rationale for the Level One statements.

Level Two is not intended as guidance on *how* to carry out the Code of Practice, but only to provide an explanation of its meaning and the reason for including the statement at Level One. Where examples are given of how to apply the Code, these are simply to clarify the meaning. Many of the clauses may seem to state the obvious, but much that goes wrong in computer use does so because the obvious has been overlooked. . . .

Level One

In the practice of his profession the member will, to the extent that he is responsible:

1 *Personal Requirements*

1.1 Keep himself, and subordinates, informed of such new technologies, practices, legal requirements and standards as are relevant to his duties.

1.2 Ensure subordinates are trained in order to be effective in their duties and to qualify for increased responsibilities.

1.3 Accept only such work as he believes he is competent to perform and not hesitate to obtain additional expertise from appropriately qualified individuals where advisable.

1.4 Actively seek opportunities for increasing efficiency and effectiveness to the benefit of the user and of the ultimate recipient.

Level Two

1.1 Others will expect you to provide special skills and advice and, in order to do so, you must keep yourself up-to-date. This is true for members of all professions, but particularly so in computing which is developing and changing rapidly. You must also encourage your staff and colleagues to do the same, for it is impossible to retain your professional standing by relying only on the state of your knowledge and competence at the time you achieved professional status.

1.2 Take action to ensure that your hard-won knowledge and experience are passed on in such a way that those who receive them not only improve their own effectiveness in their present positions but also become keen to advance their careers and take on additional responsibilities.

1.3 You should always be aware of your own limitations and not knowingly imply that you have competence you do not possess. This is of course distinct from accepting a task the successful completion of which requires expertise additional to your own. This point is central to the BCS Code of Conduct; you cannot possibly be knowledgeable on all facts but you should be able to recognize when you need additional expertise and information, and where to find it.

1.4 Whatever the precise terms of your brief, you should always be aware of the environment surrounding it and not work solely towards completion of the defined task and no more. You must regard it as part of your duty to make your client aware of other needs that emerge, unsatisfactory procedures that need modification and benefits that might be achieved. You, as an innovator, should take into account the relevance of new methods and should always be looking for the possibility of additional benefits not foreseen when the project was planned. You must also look beyond the immediate requirements to the needs of the ultimate user. For example: the invoice your system produces may be right for company accounting procedures but confusing for the person who is being asked to pay against it. . . .

[Conduct]

Principles

A Professional Member of the BCS

1. Will behave at all times with integrity. He will not knowingly lay claims to a level of competence that he does not possess and he will at all times exercise competence at least to the level he claims.
2. Will act with complete discretion when entrusted with confidential information.
3. Will act with impartiality when purporting to give independent advice and must disclose any relevant interest.
4. Will accept full responsibility for any work which he undertakes and will construct and deliver that which he purports to deliver.
5. Will not seek personal advantage to the detriment of the Society.

Notes for Guidance

The five principles set out [above] make up the BCS Code of Conduct and each professional member of the Society, as a condition of membership, undertakes to adhere to these principles. The principles are clear but have an inevitable appearance of generality and in the following pages each principle is supported by a number of notes for guidance which will help in specific interpretation. Members of the Society will readily appreciate that continued evidence of the determination to abide by the Code will ensure the public trust and confidence in computer professionals which is so necessary to the continuing effective use of computers.

Integrity

He will behave at all times with integrity. He will not knowingly lay claim to a level of competence that he does not possess, and he will at all times exercise competence at least to the level he claims.

Integrity implies wholeness, soundness, completeness: anything he does should be done competently. Where necessary he should obtain additional guidance or expertise from properly qualified advisers.

While claims to competence should not be made lightly, a member will not shelter behind this principle to avoid being helpful and co-operative; any guidance or advice that he can provide from his experience should be readily given.

He should act in a manner based on trust and good faith towards his clients or employers and towards others with whom his work is connected.

He should express an opinion on a subject in his field only when it is founded on an adequate knowledge and honest conviction, and will properly qualify himself when expressing an opinion outside his professional competence.

He should not deliberately make false or exaggerated statements as to the state of affairs existing or expected regarding any aspect of the construction or use of computers.

He should comply with the BCS Code of Practice and any other codes that are applicable and ensure that his clients are aware of the significance of their work.

He should do his best to keep himself aware of relevant developments in his technology.

Confidentiality

He will act with complete discretion when entrusted with confidential information.

He should not disclose, or permit to be disclosed, or use to his own advantage, any confidential information relating to the affairs of his present or previous employers or customers without their prior permission. This principle covers the need to protect confidential data.

Many kinds of information can be considered by a client or employer to be confidential. Even the fact that a project exists may be sensitive. Business plans, trade secrets, personal information are all examples of confidential data.

Training is required for all staff on measures to ensure confidentiality, to guard against the possibility of a third party intentionally or inadvertently misusing data and to be watchful for leaks of confidentiality arising from careless use of data or indiscretions.

Impartiality

He will act with strict impartiality when purporting to give independent advice and in so doing will disclose any relevant interests.

This principle is primarily directed to the case where the member or his relatives and friends may make a private profit if the client or employer follows his advice. Any such interest should be disclosed in advance.

A second interpretation is where there is no immediate personal profit but the future business or scope of influence of his department depends on a certain solution being accepted. Whereas a salesman is assumed to have a bias towards his own company, an internal consultant should always consider the welfare of the organization as a whole and not just the increased application of computers.

Responsibility

He will accept full responsibility for any work which he undertakes and will construct and deliver that which he purports to deliver.

Trust and responsibility are at the heart of professionalism. A member should seek out responsibility and discharge it with integrity. He should complete the work he accepts on time and within budget. If he cannot achieve what he promised then he must alert the client or employer at the earliest possible time so that corrective action can be taken.

He should have regard to the effect of computer based systems, insofar as these are known to him, on the basic human rights of individuals, whether within the organization, its customers or suppliers, or among the general public.

Subject to the confidential relationship between himself and his customer, he is expected to transmit the benefit of information which he acquires during the practice of his profession, as a result of his technical knowledge, to illuminate any situation which may harm or seriously affect a third party.

He should combat ignorance about his technology wherever he finds it and in particular in those areas where application of his technology appears to have dubious social merit.

Relationship to the Society

He will not seek personal advantage to the detriment of the Society.

It is necessary to write this principle into the Code of Conduct to prevent misuse of the considerable influence that a professional society can have. Nevertheless, its impact is largely internal and the points that have been made should be read in that light.

He should not bring the Society into disrepute by personal behavior or acts when acknowledged or known to be a representative of the Society.

He should not misrepresent the views of the Society nor represent that the views of a segment or group of the Society constitutes the view of the Society as a whole.

When acting or speaking on behalf of the Society he should, if faced with conflict of interest, declare his position. He should not serve his own pecuniary interests or those of the company which normally employs him when purporting to act in an independent manner as representative of the Society, save as permitted by the Society following a full disclosure of all the facts.

He is expected to apply the same high standard of behavior in his social life as is demanded of him in his professional activities insofar as these interact. Confidence is at the root of the validity of the qualifications of the Society and conduct which in any way undermines that confidence (e.g. a gross breach of a confidential relationship) is of deep concern to the Society.

He should conduct himself with courtesy and consideration towards all with whom he comes into contact in the course of his professional work.

He should have regard to the great extent that professional and other bodies depend on voluntary effort and should consider what personal contribution he can make both to the Society and to the public generally.

Disciplinary Procedure

All members of the Society undertake to abide by the Society's Code of Conduct. It will sometimes happen, however, that someone (member or non-member) wishes to lay a complaint against a member for infringement of the Code, and this note explains the Society's procedures.

First the complaint is laid by letter with the Secretary-General. In many cases, because of the knowledge and experience that is available to members of the Society in the several areas of computer practice, the grievance can be settled there and then avoiding the time and effort of formal enquiry. These discussions are conducted in strict confidence.

When a more difficult problem is presented an Investigation Committee can be nominated to look into the grievance and make a case to the Disciplinary Committee. The Disciplinary Committee will set a date for a hearing and invite the complainant and the respondent to be heard giving due notice to both parties. Legal assistance may be retained. Sanctions which can be applied include Admonishment, Suspension and Expulsion from membership. In addition, the Disciplinary Committee has power to make public the result of its findings.

There is an appeal procedure.

The Code of Conduct is administered by a representative group, and a number of members of the Investigation Committee retire and are replaced each year. Members of the Disciplinary and Appeals Committees will be specifically appointed by Council for each case to ensure that no member of any of the three committees serves on either of the other committees for that case. Further, the Chairmen of the Disciplinary and Appeals Committees will be advised by lawyers retained by the Society.

The Articles of Association of the Society do not differentiate between professional and non-qualified members. An Institutional Member is regarded as being on the same footing as an Affiliate. A professional worker exercises not only the skills which he has learned in his formal education and training, but also mature personal judgment developed from the use of those skills, in the varying situations of his day-to-day working life. The level of a member's professional objectives will be dependent on, amongst other things, his seniority, his position, and his type of work.

Consultants carry special professional obligations. A senior executive in charge of a major computer application or computer project is responsible for the accuracy of the information produced by the installation and for ensuring that those for whom it is prepared are fully aware of its limitations in relation to the purpose for which they intend to use it; he cannot, however, be held responsible if it is used for a purpose of which he is unaware or for which it was not intended. The responsibility of senior systems analysts and programmers is also heightened because their work is so little understood by others and failures can have serious consequences. It must, however, be borne in mind that the more responsibility a member carries, the higher will be the standard expected of him and the more rigorously may the Society's sanctions have to be applied. In the interest of the public, the highest standard will be expected of those in public practice who by nature of their work accept personal responsibility for what they undertake.

The Society has no legal standing as between a member and his employer, whether an individual or a company. Its remedy lies in giving, where appropriate, fullest support for the stand taken by a member who loses his job, or is in danger of doing so, and of censuring the employer who seeks to place the member in a position which could cause him to violate the ethical code of his profession.

The Society cannot consider a complaint against a member where that member's conduct is the subject of legal proceedings—the Society has no power to take evidence on oath, nor compel the production of documents. In these circumstances a view expressed by any member in his official capacity on behalf of the Society could improperly influence the course of justice. The complaint could only be considered when the legal action is completed, or it is established that no legal proceedings will take place. This does not prevent a member appearing in the courts as an "expert witness."

The Code as Applied to a Consultant

Advice given to a client can come from:

a. outside an organization, either for a fee or as part of supplier's marketing effort or after-sales support;
b. within the organization from business analysts or systems designers working directly or indirectly for a user.

Irrespective of conditions of employment, consultants are expected to give sound advice and honest opinions, and to help the client to a successful planned conclusion. The following points amplify the notes for guidance in respect of consultancy work.

He should hold himself accountable for the advice given to his client, and should ensure that all known limitations of his work are fully disclosed, documented and explained.

He should not attempt to avoid the consequences of poor advice by making the language of his report incomprehensible to the layman by the use of computer jargon.

He should ensure that his client is aware of all significant contingencies and risks which could adversely affect his plans and the scale of the costs he may incur as a result of embarking on any particular DP strategy.

During the course of the work he should bring to the client's attention, at the earliest possible time, any risk that the stated objectives may not be achievable; and if the solution lies in an extension of contract he should use his best efforts to make the necessary time available at an equitable fee.

Where it is possible that decisions may be made as a result of his efforts which could adversely affect the social security, work or career of an individual, he should ensure that his clients are aware of their responsibilities to mitigate the effects of their decisions.

He should always have regard to any factors arising during his professional assignment which might reflect adversely upon his integrity and objectivity.

He should declare to his client, before accepting instructions, all interests which may affect the proper performance of his functions. For example:

a. a directorship or controlling interest in any business which is in competition with his clients;
b. a financial interest in any goods or services recommended to his client;
c. a personal relationship with any person in a client's employment who might influence, or be directly affected by, his advice.

When undertaking consultancy work, he must provide a written agreement clearly stating the basis or amount of remuneration before undertaking the assignment. He is expected not to structure his fees in any way so as to offset his impartiality; examples which have in the past been regarded as suspect include fee splitting, and many cases of payment by results.

He should not invite any employee of a client to consider alternative employment without the prior consent of that client. (An advertisement in the press is not considered to be an invitation to any particular person for the purpose of this rule.)

The Code as Applied to a Salesman

Almost everyone in computing is from time to time in the position of salesman—either in direct contact with clients and customers, or with members of the public (who are themselves often potential customers) or with those who, because they are dependent on results from computing, are in the position of clients. Salesmen are normally direct employees of their companies, and it is implicit that whatever they promise to a customer should be delivered by the company. A salesman must therefore act loyally and honestly as an employee and should declare his status as a representative of his company.

Payment by results in the form of commission to a salesman is an accepted business practice; but in the selling of a continuing system it is probably desirable that some or all of such commission be tied to the proper performance of the work and the long term satisfaction of the customer. He should act in a manner based on trust and good faith towards his customer, to ensure that he receives lasting and profitable enjoyment of his purchase. For example:

he should accept only such work as he believes that his organization can produce and deliver;

he should ensure that any agreement with his customer is explicit, unambiguous and complete;

he should obey the spirit as well as the letter of any contract and of the law;

he should secure an after-sales service where appropriate, commensurate with the kind of product supplied and the price paid;

he should ensure that the customer is aware of any contingencies under which supplementary charges may be payable and the basis of such charges;

he should ensure that the customer is aware of any significant risks which could adversely affect his plans, and of any additional work or expense he will or may incur in using the service or product which is being sold;

he should subcontract only to responsible practitioners and organizations;

he should avoid illegal 'informal' price fixing, market sharing arrangements tending to falsify the process of tendering and open competition;

he should not be party to any practice which could lead to commercial or other corruption;

he should not use products commissioned and paid for by one client for another client, without the knowledge and agreement of the original client;

he should not denigrate the honesty or competence of a fellow professional or competitor with intent to gain unfair advantage;

he should not maliciously or recklessly injure or attempt to injure, directly or indirectly, the professional reputation, prospects or business of others;

he should not exploit customer relations by using either the existence of any contract or any identifiable precis or work done in any advertising or publicity material without the permission of the client.

3. DPMA Code of Ethics, Standards of Conduct and Enforcement Procedures

Data Processing Management Association

Code of Ethics

I ACKNOWLEDGE:

That I have an obligation to management, therefore, I shall promote the understanding of information processing methods and procedures to management using every resource at my command.

That I have an obligation to my fellow members, therefore, I shall uphold the high ideals of DPMA as outlined in its International Bylaws. Further, I shall cooperate with my fellow members and shall treat them with honesty and respect at all times.

That I have an obligation to society and will participate to the best of my ability in the dissemination of knowledge pertaining to the general development and understanding of information processing. Further, I shall not use knowledge of a confidential nature to further my personal interest, nor shall I violate the privacy and confidentiality of information entrusted to me or to which I may gain access.

That I have an obligation to my employer whose trust I hold, therefore, I shall endeavor

From *DPMA Code of Ethics, Standards of Conduct and Enforcement Procedures*. This code includes documents approved at the 1981 and 1982 International Board of Directors meetings and enforcement procedures effective January 1, 1983. Reprinted by permission of the Data Processing Management Association.

to discharge this obligation to the best of my ability, to guard my employer's interests, and to advise him or her wisely and honestly.

That I have an obligation to my country, therefore, in my personal, business and social contacts, I shall uphold my nation and shall honor the chosen way of life of my fellow citizens.

I accept these obligations as a personal responsibility and as a member of this association. I shall actively discharge these obligations and I dedicate myself to that end.

Standards of Conduct

These standards expand on the Code of Ethics by providing specific statements of behavior in support of each element of the Code. They are not objectives to be strived for; they are rules that no true professional will violate. It is first of all expected that information processing professionals will abide by the appropriate laws of their country and community. The following standards address tenets that apply to the profession.

In Recognition of My Obligation to Management I Shall:

Keep my personal knowledge up-to-date and insure that proper expertise is available when needed.

Share my knowledge with others and present factual and objective information to management to the best of my ability.

Accept full responsibility for work that I perform.

Not misuse the authority entrusted to me.

Not misrepresent or withhold information concerning the capabilities of equipment, software or systems.

Not take advantage of the lack of knowledge or inexperience on the part of others.

In Recognition of My Obligation to My Fellow Members and the Profession I Shall:

Be honest in all my professional relationships.

Take appropriate action in regard to any illegal or unethical practices that come to my attention. However, I will bring charges against any person only when I have reasonable basis for believing in the truth of the allegations and without regard to personal interest.

Endeavor to share my special knowledge.

Cooperate with others in achieving understanding and in identifying problems.

Not use or take credit for the work of others without specific acknowledgement and authorization.

Not take advantage of the lack of knowledge or inexperience on the part of others for personal gain.

In Recognition of My Obligation to Society I Shall:

Protect the privacy and confidentiality of all information entrusted to me.

Use my skill and knowledge to inform the public in all areas of my expertise.

To the best of my ability, insure that the products of my work are used in a socially responsible way.

Support, respect and abide by the appropriate local, state, provincial and federal laws.

Never misrepresent or withhold information that is germane to a problem or situation of public concern nor will I allow any such known information to remain unchallenged.

Not use knowledge of a confidential or personal nature in any unauthorized manner or to achieve personal gain.

In Recognition of My Obligation to My Employer I Shall:

Make every effort to ensure that I have the most current knowledge and that the proper expertise is available when needed.

Avoid conflict of interest and insure that my employer is aware of any potential conflicts.

Present a fair, honest and objective viewpoint.

Protect the proper interests of my employer at all times.

Protect the privacy and confidentiality of all information entrusted to me.

Not misrepresent or withhold information that is germane to the situation.

Not attempt to use the resources of my employer for personal gain or for any purpose without proper approval.

Not exploit the weakness of a computer system for personal gain or personal satisfaction.

Enforcement Procedures

1. **Filing a Complaint**
   1.1 Any complaint against any Regular or Honorary Member of the Association shall be in writing, signed by the complainant, properly notarized and submitted by certified or registered mail to the Executive Director at International Headquarters. At a minimum, the complaint must include:
   - 1.1.1 a concise statement of the facts on which the complaint is based;
   - 1.1.2 citations to the section of the Code of Ethics and Standards of Conduct that were allegedly violated;
   - 1.1.3 a statement that the facts are true to the best of the complainant's knowledge and belief;
   - 1.1.4 a statement that the complainant is willing to appear at the expense of DPMA at a hearing with the accused, if requested.
   1.2 Charges may be initiated only by a Regular or Honorary member in good standing of the Association.
   1.3 If the accused is a Chapter president or an Individual member the complaint will be referred to the International President.

2. **Initial Action**
   2.1 The complaint shall be immediately reviewed by the Executive Director to determine whether it complies with Section 1. If the complaint is defective in any respect, International shall return it to the complainant with a letter citing the deficiency and a copy of these Rules and Regulations.
   2.2 Notification of complaints that meet the requirements of Section 1 shall be forwarded with all documentation to the Chapter President, Chapter International

Director, Region Vice President, and the International President within 10 days.

2.3 The Chapter President or International President shall appoint a Hearing Committee composed of not less than four members of the Chapter, or the Executive Council, as appropriate, and chaired by the Executive Vice President or appropriate Chapter/International Officer to perform the functions specified in these procedures. No member of this committee can be directly involved in the complaint in any way. The Region Vice President shall appoint a Region Hearing Committee representative to be included as a voting member of the Hearing Committee. The representative must be a member of the Region but not from the Chapter involved.

3. Preliminary Determination

3.1 The Hearing Committee shall within 10 days send the person against whom allegations have been made, hereafter known as the respondent, a copy of the complaint and these Rules and Regulations by certified or registered mail to be delivered to addressee only, return receipt requested, or by personal delivery to the respondent.

3.2 The notification to the respondent will inform him or her that he/she may file a written reply to the Hearing Committee within 60 days of receipt of the complaint. The respondent shall be further notified that, if he/she fails to file a response, the action against him/her will proceed. The Hearing Committee will make a minimum of two attempts to contact the respondent before continuing the process. Failure to respond will not be taken as proof of guilt. The Hearing Committee will proceed with facts available to them.

3.3 The respondent may elect to refute the allegation. This refutation should directly address the facts alleged in the complaint and must state that the response is true to the best of his/her knowledge and belief.

3.4 A copy of the response shall be sent by the Hearing Committee to the complainant.

3.5 Upon receipt of the response, the Hearing Committee shall, within 30 days, determine whether to dismiss the complaint as unworthy of further consideration or proceed with formal hearing.

3.6 The complainant and the respondent shall be notified of the Hearing Committee's preliminary determination by certified or registered mail within 10 days of the action.

3.7 There shall be no right to appeal the preliminary determination of the Hearing Committee.

3.8 All documentation concerning the case will be returned to International for retention and protection as covered in Section 11. In the case of a dismissed or withdrawn complaint, all documentation shall be sealed and returned to the International Executive Director. The Chapter President, Chapter International Director, Region Vice President, and International President shall be notified of the disposition of the complaint.

4. The Hearing

4.1 At its discretion, the Hearing Committee will interview the complainant, the respondent, and other individuals who have knowledge of the facts alleged. The International Association shall bear the expense of travel, lodging and meals for such interviews. The complainant and the respondent may have access to information obtained in these interviews.

4.2 The Chairperson shall prescribe any procedures for the hearing not consistent with the provisions of this section.

4.3 After a complaint has reached the formal hearing stage, it may be withdrawn by the complainant only with the Hearing Committee's approval.

4.4 The complainant or respondent may be represented by legal counsel. If the Hearing Committee desires, legal counsel for the International Association may give assistance by way of counsel or participation in the proceedings of any hearing or by way of counsel at times other than hearings.

4.5 A transcript of the hearing will be made by DPMA. Participants in the hearing may have access to the transcript. DPMA will pay for the cost of transcripts for the complainant and respondent and will provide them at reproduction cost to other participants if requested.

4.6 The Hearing Committee shall appoint a time and place for the hearing of the complaint and shall notify the complainant and respondent personally or by certified or registered mail at least 60 days before the hearing. Depositions are acceptable in the event that individuals cannot appear at the hearing.

4.7 The Hearing Committee shall be the sole judge as to the character of evidence to be received and the procedures to be followed. Parties, their legal counsel (if any), counsel for the International Association, or any member of the Hearing Committee may question and cross-examine any witness.

4.8 The Hearing Committee may adjourn the hearing from time to time as, in its judgment, justice or expediency requires.

4.9 The specific witness to be called shall be at the discretion of the Hearing Committee. DPMA will pay for travel, lodging, and meals for these witnesses, if necessary. Witnesses called beyond those scheduled by the Hearing Committee will be at the expense of the interested party.

4.10 When any member of the Association receives written notification from the Hearing Committee, the complainant or the respondent, to appear and testify as a witness at such hearing, it shall be the member's duty to testify or to submit a properly notarized affidavit.

4.11 Members appointed to a Hearing Committee shall serve until the matter is disposed of. Committee members who shall resign or be discharged for whatever reason shall be replaced under the same conditions as in 2.3 above.

5. Decision of the Hearing Committee

5.1 The decision of the Hearing Committee shall be rendered within 60 days of the hearing and shall be by two-thirds affirmative vote of the committee members present. It shall be in writing and contain findings of fact and a statement of the recommended disciplinary action, if any.

5.2 The decision concerning the respondent shall be:

    5.2.1 to dismiss the complaint; in which case all records of the proceedings will be sealed and returned to the International Executive Director.

      5.2.2 to censure; in which case a letter of censure will be written to the respondent.

      5.2.3 to suspend; in which case all privilege of membership will be revoked.

      5.2.4 to expel; in which case the privilege of membership will be revoked.

      5.2.6 Adverse action (5.2.2, 5.2.3 and 5.2.4) will be taken only after the process of appeal has been exhausted.

5.3 The Hearing Committee, in its sole discretion, may also reopen the hearing within 30 days of the first hearing for additional evidence to be provided either in person or in writing. Such action would not extend the rendering of the decision for more than 30 days.

5.4 In the event the respondent is found in violation, the Committee may, in its discretion, consider in determining discipline all past records in the DPMA file of previous, relevant determinations of violations.

5.5 The Chairperson shall, within 10 days, send a copy of the decision to the International Headquarters' Corporate Operations Committee and to the International Legal Counsel for their review for consistency with the DPMA bylaws. They shall have 10 days to accomplish their review.

5.6 After their review, the Chairperson shall, within 10 days, submit copies of the decision to the complainant and the respondent by certified or registered mail. If the decision is adverse to the respondent (i.e., censure, suspend, expel), he/she shall have 30 days from the time that the Notice of Decision is received to file a Notice of Appeal.

6. The Appeals Committee

6.1 The International President shall appoint an Appeals Committee of not less than three members of the Executive Council to hear the case on appeal provided that no person:

      6.1.1 who has been involved in the facts underlying the complaint;

      6.1.2 who is a member of the Region involved; or

      6.1.3 who is a member of the Hearing Committee

may hear the same case on appeal.

6.2 Appeals may be taken to the Appeals Committee only from decisions of the Hearing Committee adverse to the respondent.

6.3 If Notice of Appeal is not filed within 30 days of the receipt of the Notice of Decision, the decision of the Hearing Committee shall become final, binding and effective at the beginning of the day after the appeal could have been properly filed.

7. The Appeal Process

7.1 The Notice of Appeal must be in writing, signed by the appellant and contain a statement with sufficient specificity and argument to set forth the grounds upon which the appeal is taken. It shall be sent to the International President by certified or registered mail, and must include the reasons why the decision of the Hearing Committee should be modified, reversed or remanded for further proceedings. Only those arguments advanced in the written Notice of Appeal shall be allowed to be presented to the Appeals Committee at its hearing, except for good cause shown as to why the Appeals Committee should allow additional oral argument.

7.2 The International President shall send a copy of the Notice of Appeal to all members of the Hearing Committee and the Appeals Committee, the Executive Director, legal counsel for the International Association, and to all parties. If within 20 days after receipt of the Notice of Appeal, the International President and the Chairperson of the Hearing Committee, after consultation with legal counsel, agree, the appeal may be stayed pending further action by the Hearing Committee relative to the matters raised in the Notice of Appeal. In such event, all parties shall be notified of the action by certified mail. The Hearing Committee shall take such action as may be necessary to cure any procedural matter raised, including, but not limited to, rehearing the matter. If the appeal is not stayed by such action, the appeal will proceed to hearing in accordance with these Rules and Regulations.

8. Procedures for Hearing the Appeal

8.1 The Appeals Committee shall hear the appeal within 30 days from the date that the Notice of Appeal is issued unless stayed as in Section 7.

8.2 Copies of the Notice of Appeal, supporting materials, and written transcript and exhibits, if any, shall be presented in advance of the meeting to sitting members of the Appeals Committee.

8.3 The International President shall serve as Chairperson of the Appeals Committee. In his/her absence, he/she may designate any other member of the Executive Council to serve as Chairperson consistent with Section 6.1.

8.4 The parties to the appeal may be represented by legal counsel. The services of the International Legal Counsel shall be available to the Appeals Committee.

8.5 The Chairperson shall determine whether a quorum is present and, if so, shall convene the meeting at the time set. If a quorum is not present, the Chairperson may adjourn the hearing until such time as a quorum is present. A quorum shall be a majority (i.e., more than half) of the members of the Appeals Committee.

8.6 The Chairperson shall introduce each person present at the meeting and give the parties the opportunity to challenge the participation of any Appeals Committee member present.

8.7 If objection is raised and the individual challenged chooses not to withdraw, the Chairperson, in his/her discretion, may determine whether the person objected to should participate further in the proceedings.

8.8 The Chairperson may dismiss any person from the meeting who fails to conduct himself/herself in a manner conducive to a fair and expeditious hearing of the appeal.

8.9 Each party to the appeal shall have a maximum period of 20 minutes to initially present his/her case to the Appeals Committee.

8.10 The Chairperson shall not permit any additional evidence to be presented to the Appeals Committee. No written evidentiary material may be presented to the Appeals Committee unless such material was presented to the Hearing Committee at the time of its deliberations.

8.11 A representative of the Hearing Committee shall proceed first by presenting a summary of the case and the reasons for the Hearing Committee's decision.

8.12 Members of the Appeals Committee and the International Legal Counsel shall have the opportunity to question the representative of the Hearing Committee.

8.13 The appellee shall have the right to state his/her position as to why the decision should be upheld.

8.14 Members of the Appeals Committee and the International Legal Counsel shall have the opportunity to question the appellee.

8.15 The appellant, or his/her counsel, shall then present his/her case to the Appeals Committee, stating specifically why the decision should be modified, reversed, or remanded.

8.16 Members of the Appeals Committee and the International Legal Counsel shall have the opportunity to question the appellant.

8.17 Each party shall have the opportunity to summarize his/her position.

    8.17.1 The representative of the Hearing Committee shall have 10 minutes to summarize the Hearing Committee's position and to rebut any statement made by the appellant.

    8.17.2 The appellee shall have 10 minutes to summarize his/her position and to rebut any statement made by the appellant.

    8.17.3 The appellant shall have 10 minutes to summarize his/her position and to rebut any statements made by the appellee or by the representative of the Hearing Committee.

8.18 Appeals Committee members and the International Legal Counsel shall have a final opportunity to question the parties.

8.19 The Chairperson shall dismiss the parties and recess the Appeals Committee meeting.

8.20 The Appeals Committee may, in its sole discretion, alter or waive any procedural requirements, including time limitations except that each party must be granted a minimum of 10 minutes to summarize his/her position as in Section 8.17.

9. Appeals Committee Deliberation

9.1 The Chairperson shall immediately reconvene the Appeals Committee in Executive Session for the purpose of rendering a decision on the appeal.

9.2 The Chairperson shall permit each Appeals Committee member to discuss his/her views on the disposition of the appeal. International Legal Counsel, the Executive Director or his/her designee may also attend such session. They will be present to offer advice and counsel if called upon to do so.

9.3 The Appeals Committee's review shall be limited to the review of the action of the Hearing Committee and the determination of whether the action has been proper or if procedural error has been committed by the Hearing Committee.

9.4 The Appeals Committee shall, by two-thirds affirmative vote of members present, affirm, reject, or modify the decision of the Hearing Committee, or shall request the Hearing Committee to take further action, including, but not limited to, rehearing the case.

9.5 The decision of the Appeals Committee shall be final and binding. Each member of the Association by becoming, or continuing as a member, agrees not to seek review of the decision of either the Hearing Committee, or the Appeals Committee in any court of law or equity or by any governmental body.

10. Notification of Decisions

10.1 The Chairperson of the Hearing or Appeals Committee shall, by certified or registered mail, notify the appellant, the complainant, and the Hearing Committee of the decision of the Appeals Committee within 10 days of the decision.

10.2 Final decisions will be sent to all participants in the hearing and/or appeal process within 10 days after all possible avenues of appeal have been exhausted. The Hearing and/or Appeals Committee will prepare a summary of the case that discusses the situation, the findings, and the reasons for the findings. There shall be no reference to any of the individuals or organizations involved by name. These summaries will be published in DATA MANAGEMENT Magazine for educational purposes and to create a body of knowledge of ethical behavior and to support the refinement of the Code, Standards and procedures.

10.3 All formal actions taken on the appeal by the Appeals Committee shall be made a matter of record in its minutes.

10.4 The Appeals Committee shall also notify the Executive Council of its decision.

11. Record Retention and Availability

11.1 The International office shall maintain a record of all Hearing Committee formal action received and all documentation pertaining to each case. In the event that a determination to take no action is made, the records will be sealed and may be used only in accordance with these regulations. Records of cases which shall have been dismissed shall be maintained only for a period of seven years from the date of dismissal and shall thereafter be destroyed by the International Executive Director.

11.2 The records of the Hearing Committee and the Appeals Committee on a particular case and all pertinent documentation relating thereto shall be retained by the International Association.

11.3 Requests for information on a specific case must be in writing and signed by the person making the request. Information may be released if the Corporate Operations Committee and the original parties, if not deceased, approve such release in advance in writing.

11.4 Requests for general information on ethical proceedings may be responded to by release of statistical information prepared by the staff, provided that the approval of the Corporate Operations Committee is obtained in advance.

4. ACM Code of Professional Conduct and Procedures for the Enforcement of the ACM Code of Professional Conduct

Association for Computing Machinery

[Code]

Preamble

RECOGNITION OF PROFESSIONAL status by the public depends not only on skill and dedication but also on adherence to a recognized code of Professional Conduct. The following Code sets forth the general principles (Canons), professional ideals (Ethical Considerations), and mandatory rules (Disciplinary Rules) applicable to each ACM Member.

The verbs "shall" (imperative) and "should" (encouragement) are used purposefully in the Code. The Canons and Ethical Considerations are not, however, binding rules. Each Disciplinary Rule is binding on each individual Member of ACM. Failure to observe the Disciplinary Rules subjects the Member to admonition, suspension or expulsion from the Association as provided by the Procedures for the Enforcement of the ACM Code of Professional Conduct, which are specified in the ACM Policy and Procedures Guidelines. The term "member(s)" is used in the Code. The Disciplinary Rules of the Code apply, however, only to the classes of membership specified in Article 3, Section 4, of the Constitution of the ACM.

Canon 1

An ACM member shall act at all times with integrity.

Ethical Considerations

EC1.1 An ACM member shall properly qualify himself when expressing an opinion outside his areas of competence. A member is encouraged to express his opinion on subjects within his area of competence.

EC1.2 An ACM member shall preface any partisan statements about information processing by indicating clearly on whose behalf they are made.

EC1.3 An ACM member shall act faithfully on behalf of his employers or clients.

From *ACM Code of Professional Conduct* and *Procedures for the Enforcement of the ACM Code of Professional Conduct.* Courtesy of the Association for Computing Machinery, Inc.

Disciplinary Rules

DR1.1.1 An ACM member shall not intentionally misrepresent his qualifications or credentials to present or prospective employers or clients.

DR1.1.2 An ACM member shall not make deliberately false or deceptive statements as to the present or expected state of affairs in any aspect of the capability, delivery, or use of information processing systems.

DR1.2.1 An ACM member shall not intentionally conceal or misrepresent on whose behalf any partisan statements are made.

DR1.3.1 An ACM member acting or employed as a consultant shall, prior to accepting information from a prospective client, inform the client of all factors of which the member is aware which may affect the proper performance of the task.

DR1.3.2 An ACM member shall disclose any interest of which he is aware which does or may conflict with his duty to a present or prospective employer or client.

DR1.3.3 An ACM member shall not use any confidential information from any employer or client, past or present, without prior permission.

Canon 2

An ACM member should strive to increase his competence and the competence and prestige of the profession.

Ethical Considerations

EC2.1 An ACM member is encouraged to extend public knowledge, understanding, and appreciation of information processing, and to oppose any false or deceptive statements relating to information processing of which he is aware.

EC2.2 An ACM member shall not use his professional credentials to misrepresent his competence.

EC2.3 An ACM member shall undertake only those professional assignments and commitments for which he is qualified.

EC2.4 An ACM member shall strive to design and develop systems that adequately perform the intended functions and that satisfy his employer's or client's operational needs.

EC2.5 An ACM member should maintain and increase his competence through a program of continuing education encompassing the techniques, technical standards, and practices in his fields of professional activity.

EC2.6 An ACM member should provide opportunity and encouragement for professional development and advancement of both professionals and those aspiring to become professionals.

Disciplinary Rules

DR2.2.1 An ACM member shall not use his professional credentials to misrepresent his competence.

DR2.3.1 An ACM member shall not undertake professional assignments without adequate preparation in the circumstances.

DR2.3.2 An ACM member shall not undertake professional assignments for which he knows or should know he is not competent or cannot become adequately competent without acquiring the assistance of a professional who is competent to perform the assignment.

DR2.4.1 An ACM member shall not represent that a product of his work will perform its function adequately and will meet the receiver's operational needs when he knows or should know that the product is deficient.

Canon 3

An ACM member shall accept responsibility for his work.

Ethical Considerations

EC3.1 An ACM member shall accept only those assignments for which there is reasonable expectancy of meeting requirements or specifications, and shall perform his assignments in a professional manner.

Disciplinary Rules

DR3.1.1 An ACM member shall not neglect any professional assignment which has been accepted.

DR3.1.2 An ACM member shall keep his employer or client properly informed on the progress of his assignments.

DR3.1.3 An ACM member shall not attempt to exonerate himself from, or to limit his liability to clients for his personal malpractice.

DR3.1.4 An ACM member shall indicate to his employer or client the consequences to be expected if his professional judgment is overruled.

Canon 4

An ACM member shall act with professional responsibility.

Ethical Considerations

EC4.1 An ACM member shall not use his membership in ACM improperly for professional advantage or to misrepresent the authority of his statements.

EC4.2 An ACM member shall conduct professional activities on a high plane.

EC4.3 An ACM member is encouraged to uphold and improve the professional standards of the Association through participation in their formulation, establishment, and enforcement.

Disciplinary Rules

DR4.1.1 An ACM member shall not speak on behalf of the Association or any of its subgroups without proper authority.

DR4.1.2 An ACM member shall not knowingly misrepresent the policies and views of the Association or any of its subgroups.

DR4.1.3 An ACM member shall preface partisan statements about information processing by indicating clearly on whose behalf they are made.

DR4.2.1 An ACM member shall not maliciously injure the professional reputation of any other person.

DR4.2.2 An ACM member shall not use the services of or his membership in the Association to gain unfair advantage.

DR4.2.3 An ACM member shall take care that credit for work is given to whom credit is properly due.

Canon 5

An ACM member should use his special knowledge and skills for the advancement of human welfare.

Ethical Considerations

EC5.1 An ACM member should consider the health, privacy, and general welfare of the public in the performance of his work.

EC5.2 An ACM member, whenever dealing with data concerning individuals, shall always consider the principle of the individual's privacy and seek the following:

To minimize the data collected.

To limit authorized access to the data.

To provide proper security for the data.

To determine the required retention period of the data.

To ensure proper disposal of the data.

Disciplinary Rules

DR5.2.1 An ACM member shall express his professional opinion to his employers or clients regarding any adverse consequences to the public which might result from work proposed to him.

[Procedures]

I. Initiation of Proceedings Under the Code of Professional Conduct

The Executive Director of the Association shall receive complaints against members of the Association arising under the Code of Professional Conduct (hereinafter referred to as the Code).

The Executive Director shall request that the individual(s) submitting a complaint [hereinafter referred to as the complainant(s)] prepare a written Statement of Complaint signed by the complainant(s) which shall set forth the facts of the situation, as perceived by the complainant(s), and specify those provisions of the Disciplinary Rules of the Code which are believed to have been violated.

II. Notification of a Complaint

Upon the receipt of the Statement of Complaint, the Executive Director shall deliver personally or by certified mail, return receipt requested, a copy of the Statement of Complaint to the member(s) who is alleged to have violated the Code [hereinafter referred to as the charged member(s)]. The Executive Director shall notify the charged member(s) of the possibility of a hearing before the Council of the ACM under these Procedures. Copies of the Code and these Procedures shall be provided along with the Statement of Complaint.

III. PreCouncil Meeting

After transmission of the Statement of Complaint, the Executive Director shall attempt to arrange a meeting between the complainant(s) and the charged member(s). At this meeting there shall be an attempt to resolve the situation complained about to the mutual satisfaction of all of the participants. The President shall appoint one to three disinterested ACM members who are not members of Council to participate in this meeting and shall designate one of these individuals to chair the meeting. The Executive Director or his delegate shall attend and shall keep the minutes of the meeting. The complainant(s), the charged member(s) and the Association shall each have the right to have counsel present and to designate other persons whose presence is relevant to the meeting to attend subject to the approval of the Chairman. The meeting shall be closed to everyone not specified in Section III.

IV. Presentation of a Complaint Before the ACM Council

If the complaint is not resolved to the satisfaction of the complainant(s) and the charged member(s) by a PreCouncil meeting, the President shall at the request of the Chairman of the PreCouncil meeting, place an executive session hearing of the complaint on the agenda of the next regularly scheduled Council meeting or the meeting after the next regularly scheduled meeting, if the later meeting is more convenient to the charged member(s). Such agenda item shall be designated "Code of Professional Conduct Disciplinary Hearing."

The Council members shall be provided with a copy of the Statement of Complaint. The charged member(s) shall have the right to submit a memorandum responding to the Statement of Complaint, which memorandum shall be submitted at least ten (10) days prior to the Council meeting. Such memorandum shall be provided to the Council members and the complainant(s). These materials shall be held in confidence.

The Council hearing of the complaint shall be conducted in executive session.

At the Council hearing the complainant(s) shall appear. The charged member(s) shall have the right to appear before the Council in person and to respond to the Statement of Complaint as set forth, to question the complainant(s) and witnesses appearing in behalf of the complainant(s), to enter objections to material offered in evidence and to call witnesses and enter evidence in his behalf. The complainant(s) shall also have the right to call witnesses in his behalf, to question the charged member(s) and to respond and object to material offered in evidence in behalf of the charged member(s).

Both parties and the Association shall have the right to be represented by counsel and to have such counsel present at the Council hearing. The Executive Director or his delegate shall attend the Council hearings.

The members of the Council and counsel for the Association may question the complainant(s), the charged member(s) and any witnesses. Should the complainant(s), the charged member(s) or a witness fail to appear at the hearing, the Council may, in its discretion, proceed with, dismiss or suspend the hearing.

V. Council Decision

After hearing the statements and questioning by both parties and/or by counsel, and any statement which might be made upon the behalf of the Association itself, the Council, acting under its usual rules of procedure, shall entertain motions, question any of the parties, conduct discussion and vote by secret written ballot. Motions for disciplinary action shall be entertained as follows:

    A. The Council shall first determine by affirmative vote of at least three-fourths of all of the members of the Council which Disciplinary Rules (if any) of those stated in the Statement of Complaint were violated by the charged member(s).

    B. If the Council finds one or more of the Disciplinary Rules to have been violated, it shall determine the action to be taken as follows:

        1. The first vote taken shall be for expulsion. Expulsion shall require the affirmative vote of at least three-fourths of all members of the Council.

        2. If the motion for expulsion does not pass, the second vote taken shall be for suspension from membership for a stipulated period. Suspension shall require the affirmative vote of at least three-fourths of all of the members of the Council.

        3. If neither expulsion nor suspension is approved, a third vote shall be taken for the issuance of a letter of admonishment. Admonishment shall require the affirmative vote of at least three-fourths of all members of the Council.

    C. The published Minutes of the Council shall record the motions and action taken but not the name of the charged member(s) or any details.

    D. The Secretary shall forthwith communicate in writing the action of Council to the complainant(s) and the charged member(s).

VI. Confidentiality of Proceedings

It is the policy of the ACM that disciplinary matters shall be held in confidence by all concerned and not disclosed to those not involved in the proceeding hereunder. Specifically: The Executive Director shall retain in confidence the records pertaining to every complaint submitted; the meeting described in Section III shall be closed; and the hearing described in Section IV shall be conducted in executive session and attendance shall be limited to members of the Council, the charged member(s), the complainant(s), and witnessess, if any (and their counsel, if any).

Violation of the confidentiality of any proceedings under this Bylaw may constitute grounds for proceedings against a member for demonstrating a lack of integrity or for violation of the Code.

VII. Participation in Disciplinary Proceedings

Any member of Council who is a party to a disciplinary action either as the complainant(s) or the charged member(s) shall not be permitted to vote on any decision to be made by the Council pursuant to Section V of this Bylaw. Any officer of the Association who is a party to a disciplinary action either as the complainant(s) or as the charged member(s) shall not participate as an officer of ACM in such disciplinary proceeding under this Bylaw.

If the complainant(s) or the charged member(s) in a disciplinary proceeding is an officer of the Association to whom duties are assigned under the procedures, the following officers shall perform the duties of the officer in question: The duties of the President shall be performed by the Vice President; if the Vice President is also a party to the proceeding, the duties of the President hereunder shall be performed by the Secretary; if the Secretary is also a party to the proceeding, the duties of the President hereunder shall be performed by the Treasurer; if the Treasurer is also a party to the proceeding, the duties of the President hereunder shall be performed by the immediate Past President; if the Past President is also a party to the proceeding, the members of Council who are not parties to the proceeding shall elect one of their numbers to perform the duties of the President hereunder. If either the Executive Director or the Secretary is a party to the proceeding, the President or the person who is performing the duties of the President hereunder shall appoint a member of Council to perform the duties of the Executive Director or the Secretary, as the case may be, under this Bylaw.

5. IEEE Code of Ethics

Institute of Electrical and Electronics Engineers

Preamble

ENGINEERS, SCIENTISTS AND technologists affect the quality of life for all people in our complex technological society. In the pursuit of their profession, therefore, it is vital that IEEE members conduct their work in an ethical manner so that they merit the confidence of colleagues, employers, clients and the public. This IEEE Code of Ethics represents such a standard of professional conduct for IEEE members in the discharge of their responsibilities to employers, to clients, to the community and to their colleagues in this Institute and other professional societies.

Article I

Members shall maintain high standards of diligence, creativity and productivity and shall:

1. Accept responsibility for their actions.
2. Be honest and realistic in stating claims or estimates from available data.

From *IEEE Spectrum*, Vol. 12, No. 2 (February 1975), p. 65. © 1975 IEEE. Reprinted by permission of the Institute of Electrical and Electronics Engineers, Inc.

3. Undertake technological tasks and accept responsibility only if qualified by training or experience, or after full disclosure to their employers or clients of pertinent qualifications.
4. Maintain their professional skills at the level of the state of the art, and recognize the importance of current events in their work.
5. Advance the integrity and prestige of the profession by practicing in a dignified manner and for adequate compensation.

Article II

Members shall, in their work:

1. Treat fairly all colleagues and co-workers, regardless of race, religion, sex, age or national origin.
2. Report, publish and disseminate freely information to others, subject to legal and proprietary restraints.
3. Encourage colleagues and co-workers to act in accord with this Code and support them when they do so.
4. Seek, accept and offer honest criticism of work, and properly credit the contributions of others.
5. Support and participate in the activities of their professional societies.
6. Assist colleagues and co-workers in their professional development.

Article III

Members shall, in their relations with employers and clients:

1. Act as faithful agents or trustees for their employers or clients in professional and business matters, provided such actions conform with other parts of this Code.
2. Keep information on the business affairs or technical processes of an employer or client in confidence while employed, and later, until such information is properly released provided such actions conform with other parts of this Code.
3. Inform their employers, clients, professional societies or public agencies or private agencies of which they are members or to which they may make presentations, of any circumstance that could lead to a conflict of interest.
4. Neither give nor accept, directly or indirectly, any gift, payment or service of more than nominal value to or from those having business relationships with their employers or clients.
5. Assist and advise their employers or clients in anticipating the possible consequences, direct and indirect, immediate or remote, of the projects, work or plans of which they have knowledge.

Article IV

Members shall, in fulfilling their responsibilities to the community:

1. Protect the safety, health and welfare of the public and speak out against abuses in these areas affecting the public interest.
2. Contribute professional advice, as appropriate, to civic, charitable or other nonprofit organizations.
3. Seek to extend public knowledge and appreciation of the profession and its achievements.

6. Codes of Ethics and Good Practices
Institute for Certification of Computer Professionals

Code of Ethics for Certified Computer Professionals

CERTIFIED COMPUTER PROFESSIONALS, consistent with their obligation to the public at large, should promote the understanding of data processing methods and procedures using every resource at their command.

Certified computer professionals have an obligation to their profession to uphold the high ideals and the level of personal knowledge certified by the Certificate held. They should also encourage the dissemination of knowledge pertaining to the development of the computer profession.

Certified computer professionals have an obligation to serve the interests of their employers and clients loyally, diligently, and honestly.

Certified computer professionals must not engage in any conduct or commit any act which is discreditable to the reputation or integrity of the computer profession.

Certified computer professionals must not imply that the Certificates which they hold are their sole claim to professional competence.

Codes of Conduct and Good Practice for Certified Computer Professionals

The essential elements relating to conduct that identify a professional activity are:

A high standard of skill and knowledge
A confidential relationship with people served
Public reliance upon the standards of conduct and established practice
The observance of an ethical code.

Therefore, these Codes have been formulated to strengthen the professional status of certified computer professionals.

1. Preamble

1.1 The basic issue, which may arise in connection with any ethical proceedings before a Certification Council, is whether a holder of a Certificate administered by that Council has acted in a manner which violates the Code of Ethics for certified computer professionals.

From *Codes of Ethics, Conduct and Good Practice for Certified Computer Professionals* (Chicago, IL: Institute for Certification of Computer Professionals, 1977), pp. 2–9. Reprinted by permission of the Institute for Certification of Computer Professionals.

1.2 Therefore, the ICCP has elaborated the existing Code of Ethics by means of a Code of Conduct, which defines more specifically an individual's professional responsibility. This step was taken in recognition of questions and concerns as to what constitutes professional and ethical conduct in the computer profession.

1.3 The ICCP has reserved for and delegated to each Certification Council the right to revoke any Certificate which has been issued under its administration in the event that the recipient violates the Code of Ethics, as amplified by the Code of Conduct. The revocation proceedings are specified by rules governing the business of the Certification Council and provide for protection of the rights of any individual who may be subject to revocation of a Certificate held.

1.4 Insofar as violation of the Code of Conduct may be difficult to adjudicate, the ICCP has also promulgated a Code of Good Practice, the violation of which does not in itself constitute a reason to revoke a Certificate. However, any evidence concerning a serious and consistent breach of the Code of Good Practice may be considered as additional circumstantial evidence in any ethical proceedings before a Certification Council.

1.5 Whereas the Code of Conduct is of a fundamental nature, the Code of Good Practice is expected to be amended from time to time to accommodate changes in the social environment and to keep up with the development of the computer profession.

1.6 A Certification Council will not consider a complaint where the holder's conduct is already subject to legal proceedings. Any complaint will only be considered when the legal action is completed, or it is established that no legal proceedings will take place.

1.7 Recognizing that the language contained in all sections of either the Code of Conduct or the Code of Good Practice is subject to interpretations beyond those intended, the ICCP intends to confine all Codes to matters pertaining to personal actions of individual certified computer professionals in situations for which they can be held directly accountable without reasonable doubt.

2. Code of Conduct

2.1 **Disclosure** Subject to the confidential relationships between oneself and one's employer or client, one is expected not to transmit information which one acquires during the practice of one's profession in any situation which may harm or seriously affect a third party.

2.2 **Social Responsibility** One is expected to combat ignorance about information processing technology in those public areas where one's application can be expected to have an adverse social impact.

2.3 **Conclusions and Opinions** One is expected to state a conclusion on a subject in one's field only when it can be demonstrated that it has been founded on adequate knowledge. One will state a qualified opinion when expressing a view in an area within one's professional competence but not supported by relevant facts.

2.4 **Identification** One shall properly qualify oneself when expressing an opinion outside of one's professional competence in the event that such an opinion could be identified by a third party as expert testimony, or if by inference the opinion can be expected to be used improperly.

2.5 **Integrity** One will not knowingly lay claims to competence one does not demonstrably possess.

2.6 **Conflict of Interest** One shall act with strict impartiality when purporting to give independent advice. In the event that the advice given is currently or potentially influential to one's personal benefit, full and detailed disclosure of all relevant interests will be made at the time the advice is provided. One will not denigrate the honesty or competence of a fellow professional or a competitor, with intent to gain an unfair advantage.

2.7 Accountability The degree of professional accountability for results will be dependent on the position held and the type of work performed. For instance:

A senior executive is accountable for the quality of work performed by all individuals the person supervises and for ensuring that recipients of information are fully aware of known limitations in the results provided. The personal accountability of consultants and technical experts is especially important because of the positions of unique trust inherent in their advisory roles. Consequently, they are accountable for seeing to it that known limitations of their work are fully disclosed, documented, and explained.

2.8 Protection of Privacy One shall have special regard for the potential effects of computer-based systems on the right of privacy of individuals whether this is within one's own organization, among customers or suppliers, or in relation to the general public.

Because of the privileged capability of computer professionals to gain access to computerized files, especially strong strictures will be applied to those who have used their positions of trust to obtain information from computerized files for their personal gain.

Where it is possible that decisions can be made within a computer-based system which could adversely affect the personal security, work, or career of an individual, the system design shall specifically provide for decision review by a responsible executive who will thus remain accountable and identifiable for that decision.

3. Code of Good Practice

3.1 Education One has a special responsibility to keep oneself fully aware of developments in information processing technology relevant to one's current professional occupation. One will contribute to the interchange of technical and professional information by encouraging and participating in education activities directed both to fellow professionals and to the public at large. One will do all in one's power to further public understanding of computer systems. One will contribute to the growth of knowledge in the field to the extent that one's expertise, time, and position allow.

3.2 Personal Conduct Insofar as one's personal and professional activities interact visibly to the same public, one is expected to apply the same high standards of behavior in one's personal life as are demanded in one's professional activities.

3.3 Competence One shall at all times exercise technical and professional competence at least to the level one claims. One shall not deliberately withhold information in one's possession unless disclosure of that information could harm or seriously affect another party, or unless one is bound by a proper, clearly defined confidential relationhip. One shall not deliberately destroy or diminish the value or effectiveness of a computer-based system through acts of commission or omission.

3.4 Statements One shall not make false or exaggerated statements as to the state of affairs existing or expected regarding any aspect of information technology or the use of computers.

In communicating with lay persons, one shall use general language whenever possible and shall not use technical terms or expressions unless there exist no adequate equivalents in the general language.

3.5 Discretion One shall exercise maximum discretion in disclosing, or permitting to be disclosed, or using to one's own advantage, any information relating to the affairs of one's present or previous employers or clients.

3.6 Conflict of Interest One shall not hold, assume, or consciously accept a position in which one's interests conflict or are likely to conflict with one's current duties unless that interest has been disclosed in advance to all parties involved.

3.7 Violations One is expected to report violations of the Code, testify in ethical proceedings where one has expert or first-hand knowledge, and serve on panels to judge complaints of violations of ethical conduct.

Procedural Requirements for Revocation of Certificate Awarded

I. A Certification Council, on behalf of the Institute for Certification of Computer Professionals, has the right to revoke any Certificate which has been administered by it in the event that the recipient violates the Codes or engages in conduct which is a discredit or disgrace to the computer profession.

II. The grounds for revocation will be based upon the opinion of at least two-thirds of the members of the Council.

III. Procedure for handling revocation:

1. A formal written statement of charges alleging facts which constitute the grounds for revocation will be prepared.

2. A copy of said charges will be forwarded to the person accused, fixing a time within which such person may file with the Council answers to the charges.

3. If the charges are denied in the answer, the Council will fix a time for the hearing and give notice of the time and place of the hearing to the person accused.

4. Presentation of evidence in support of the charges will be made by the secretary (a non-voting member) of the Certification Council.

5. Presentation of evidence in defense of the charges will be made by the accused or the designated representative of the accused.

6. Ample opportunity for both sides to present facts and arguments will be allowed at the hearing.

7. At the conclusion of the hearing, the Council will determine whether or not the charges have been sufficiently established by the evidence and whether the Certificate should be revoked or should not be revoked.

8. The accused will be notified of the decision by registered mail.

9. The accused has the right to request review of the decision by the Executive Committee of ICCP, provided an appeal in writing is submitted to the President, ICCP, within 30 days of the accused's receipt of the Council's decision.

7. What Should Professional Societies Do about Ethics?

Fay H. Sawyier

I

IN THINKING ABOUT the word "should," several items come to mind. For instance, if there is something that you *should* do, then it follows (logically) that you must be able to do it. One cannot have a duty to do something which it is impossible to do. But the word "impossible" can take on a range of meanings; for instance it can mean physically impossible or intellectually or even psychologically and perhaps even socially. Another related idea is "forbidden"; an act might be considered to be impossible because it is forbidden. By whom? In our society the authorized "forbidders" are the Legislature and the Courts, laws and their interpretations. It is with this meaning of "impossible" that I propose to begin, remembering always that the point of starting with an inspection of those classes of actions which are legally *im*permissible is intended primarily to clarify the domain of morally obligatory or desirable actions, inasmuch as such must, of necessity, also be permissible.

Sociologists have studied the motives for and the socio-economic results of the formation of professional societies and found, as one might expect, that both contained large elements of self-interest in addition to generous concern for the well-being of the public. But the Courts have come to take a very hard and critical look at the claims and attempts by professional societies to enforce certain presumably "ethical" standards. Examples of such standards which come readily to mind are Code prohibitions on advertising, fee-fixing schedules, Code criteria for client-contact, etc. It is, or was, concerning this area of Code standards which were intended (in part, at least) to protect the public from the presumably dangerous consequences of unrestrained competition among professionals that the saga of Court decisions becomes significant.

As everyone knows, the Sherman Act, passed in 1898, forbids "every combination in restraint of trade." Inasmuch as every contract is, in some sense, a combination in restraint of trade, the Court held (in the Standard Oil case, 1911) that only those combinations that "unreasonably" restrained trade were illegal. This, of course, raised the problem of how "reasonableness" was to be construed. Furthermore during at least the next thirty years (until the Fashion Designers Case of 1941) and effectively until the Goldfarb Case of 1975, professionals and their societies argued that those restrictions upon trade (i.e. on competition) on which they insisted were eminently "reasonable" inasmuch as their intention (motive) was not to restrain trade but to protect the public. The Fashion Designers Case

From *Journal of Professional Issues in Engineering,* Vol. 110, No. 2, (April 1984), pp. 88–99. Reprinted by permission of the American Society of Civil Engineers.

involved the effort of a professional organization (still called the guild) totally to control the industry by boycotting any retailer who sold products whose design had been copied (even where the copying was acknowledged) and by imposing severe fines on any members of the Guild who dealt with any such retailers. The Court found, in addition to the manifestly restrictive practice this involved, that "this combination is in reality an extra-governmental agency, which prescribes rules and regulation and restraint of interstate commerce, and provides extra-judicial tribunals for determination and punishment. . . ."[1] Although the above case constituted an initial assault on professional autonomy and inviolability, it was the Goldfarb Case in 1975 that effectively removed the "professional exemption" to the Sherman Act. There the Court held that a bar association's rule prescribing minimum fees for legal services violated Section 1 of the Sherman Act. Now in connection with fee-setting, one might imagine that although *minimum* fees may not be stipulated, *maximum* ones may. Yet a 1982 Court ruling (in Arizona v. Maricpoa Country Medical Society, 73 L.Ed. 2d) rejected this proposition as well. There are two more famous anti-trust cases to consider: the N.S.P.E. Case in 1978 and the Mardirosian Case in 1979. In each of these a professional organization had prescribed and attempted to enforce a particular mode of client-professional interaction and contact. In the former instance, the rule was that no engineer could discuss price (fees) with a potential client until after he or she had been selected for the job. In Mardirosian, no professional was supposed to bid on a contract (or seek a commission) for which another professional had been selected, even though the contract had not yet been signed or was terminable at will. In both cases the Court ruled that the particular element of the professional code was unenforceable. In the case of Mardirosian, the Court awarded large damages to him, since he had been "expelled" by his professional association. So much, then, for Court action forbidding professional organizations to stipulate and enforce at least these anti-competitive standards.

Before leaving the law, however, there are two other and older decisions to which it is fitting to turn. In the first case, I quote not from the majority opinion, but from a dissent by Mr. Justice Black in Lathrop v. Donahue (367 U.S. 821). The case involved what is known as the "integrated bar." Contrary to the most immediate mental associations to and images of this expression, it refers to a situation in which the State enforces and requires membership in the legal professional society. One involuntary member of this association sued, holding that the collection of dues upheld by the state, which dues were used in part to promote legislation which he abhorred, interfered with his First Amendment rights of freedom of speech and assembly. The majority denied his appeal, but Justice Black had this to say: ". . . the loss inflicted upon our free way of life by invasion of First Amendment freedoms brought about by the powers conferred upon the Wisconsin integrated bar far outweighs any state interest served by the exercise of those powers by that association. At stake here is the interest of the individual lawyers of Wisconsin in having full freedom to think their own thoughts, speak their own minds, support their own causes and whole-heartedly fight whatever they are against, as well as the interest of the people of Wisconsin and, to a lesser extent, the people of the entire country in maintaining the political independence of Wisconsin lawyers."[2]

Finally, there is the case that contains what is known as the "Noerr Defense" against charges of anti-trust violation. At issue here was whether or not a combination of presidents of railroads could work together *to try to influence legislation* which, if passed, would be to their own advantage and would—doubtless intentionally—damage the trucking industry. This surely has the ring of a "combination in restraint of trade," but is protected, ultimately, by another fundamental Constitutional right, that of petition. Here is a part of the language in this decision. "In a representative democracy such as this is, these branches (legislative and executive) of government act on behalf of the people, and, to a very large extent, the whole concept of representation depends upon the ability of the people to make their wishes known to their representatives. To hold that the government retains the power to act in this representative capacity and yet hold, at the same time, that the people cannot freely inform the government of their wishes would impute to the Sherman Act a purpose to regulate, not business activity, but political activity, a purpose which would have no basis whatever in the legislative history of that Act. Secondly, and of *at least* equal significance, such a construction of the Sherman Act would raise important constitutional questions. The right of petition is one of the freedoms protected by the Bill of Rights. . . ."[3]

II

The justifications for the restrictions on the possible actions of professional associations typically involve elements from three sorts of principles, which I am somewhat arbitrarily isolating. The first principled justification stems from the 17th century English legal and political philosopher Thomas Hobbes and was repeated by Zachariah Chafee in a 1930 Harvard Law Review article, by the Court in its language (which I have already quoted) in the Fashion Designers Case in 1941 and by my colleague, John Snapper, in a . . . paper concerned with proprietary rights in software. Essentially this principle states that the powers to legislate and to adjudicate are political, that is public, and may not attach to private bodies.

A rather distinct line of justification (of the trend in interpretation of Sherman) is that advanced by Justice Stevens, by (then) Professor Robert Bork and by a member of the Bar of Illinois now litigating a case involving a specialized association of physicians. Here is Justice Stevens: "We are faced with a contention that a total ban on competitive bidding is necessary because otherwise engineers will be tempted to submit deceptively low bids. Certainly the problem of professional deception is a proper subject of an ethical canon. But once again the equation of competition with deception, like the similar equation with safety hazards, is simply too broad; we may assume that competition is not entirely conducive to ethical behavior, but that is not a reason cognizable under the Sherman Act, for doing away with competition."[4] And Bork, ". . . in the decision of anti-trust cases . . . the main tradition is *the maximization of wealth or consumer want satisfaction*."[5] Underlying this posture is the Utilitarian, Free-Market view that ceteris paribus, the more competition, the greater the "maximization of wealth" and that such "maximization" is the ultimate (or at least the only practicable) value by which to judge action, in particular action with economic consequences. "Price is the central nervous system of the economy."

The third line followed in supporting the trend in Sherman decisions is suggested by Justice Black's dissent quoted earlier and in the reasoning in the Noerr case, also above. It is that there are fundamental rights, notably those in the Bill of Rights, which are in principle inviolate. These rights themselves may be seen as resting upon a certain conception of the human being, and therefore the client *or* professional, as autonomous. Profound theoretic arguments to this point have been made by John Stuart Mill and more recently by John Rawls. But a homely illustration is this: recently the Courts, the legislatures and the various Institutional Review Boards (for experiments involving human subjects) have taken a very hard look at professional (medical) postures supposedly protecting the patient from a comprehensive accounting of disease or experimental procedures "for his or her own good." One does not cease to be a person worthy of respect just because one is a patient (or a client). Therefore, so this line goes, strategies by professional organizations designed to "protect" the clients or the public by restricting access to information or to other professionals, etc. are attacks on the dignity and autonomy of said client, and attacks, moreover, which may invade fundamental rights protected by the First Ten Amendments to the Constitution.

Any one of the above three lines of reasoning seems to me to constitute significant support for anti-trust restrictions on professional associations' actions, and collectively, these lines make a very powerful statement.

III

Now that the boundaries of the permitted have been sketched and the area within which action is possible is clearer, we should inquire about some of the things that professional societies *should* do. Here I offer only sample suggestions, some of my own and some explicitly coming from other sources. Stephen Unger, himself an engineer, has said, "Engineers in ethical quandaries should be able to get advice. An ethics committee should, when appropriate, be prepared to speak informally with parties to a disagreement. . . . Awards may be made in cases where engineers show exceptional zeal in upholding ethical principles in the face of risks to their careers. These cases should be widely publicized for their educational effects."[6] And Michael Bayles, "Professional ethics . . . should develop sensitivity to ethical problems and help one better understand the role of professions in contemporary society."[7] Or again, Jean Mayer, President of Tufts, "Excessively high wages, union work rules and unreasonable governmental regulations are usually offered as reasons for the difficulties of these (steel, automotive, energy and mass transportation) industries. I argue that the quality of management and the quality of engineering are at the root of some of our most serious problems. . . . An excessive proportion of executives are products of business schools and are not technically oriented, and an excessive proportion of engineers just are not adequately trained."[8] These three proposals are that the societies should offer moral support, a forum for open discussion, "sensitizing" to moral issues, and pressure on the schools (and later, on continuing education) to upgrade their training as well as on management either to acquire or more frequently to heed technical judgment. To these proposals I add a further sampling of my own. Professional associations should make clear that lobbying and appeals to legislatures in behalf, say, of the environment or of highway safety, etc. are not only appropriate but legally protected actions. Again, it is fitting for these societies regularly to remind their membership that reporting to the proper governmental agency on false advertising or on safety defects, etc., even when relating to a competing individual or firm, is also protected. That is, although one may be sued, one nearly always has a perfect defense. Again, especially for those engineering societies intimately involved in work for governmental institutions, regular and open discussion of the network of bribery and pressure possibilities not only presents a "forewarned is forearmed" aid but also *by the mere fact of being discussed* and condemned, cuts some of the ground from under the unfortunate tough guy riposte that "everyone does it." That is false; everyone does *not* accept or offer bribes, *nor* is it only the corrupt who prosper. Just reciting this helps. I would like to see much more discussion of the criteria entering into the specifications in contracts of the supervisory and inspecting responsibilities, and of the dissemination of and technical justifications for various standards (such as the standards with respect to boilers and A.S.M.E. which reached the Court in 1980). In using the word "dissemination" just now, I had in mind not only the communication to other fellow professionals, but at least the conveyance of this information (regarding standards, contract specifications, etc.) to the general public. I incline, rather, to the view that this "general public" might well and regularly be an auditor and perhaps an active participant at those debates leading up to standard-setting, etc. It is far more tempting to cut corners or to gloss over unethical maneuvers if one's deliberations are never exposed and are always confined to fellow members of "the fraternity" as it were. This leads me to my last suggestion, with which the above is linked. The professional associations should be leaders in desegregation (racially, sexually and with regard to age) and do this publicly. The linkage with the earlier point about including laypersons is this: the chances that a group committed to effecting a given result or product will not identify and respond to any errors in its own judgment escalate rapidly in proportion as the group is homogenous or is insulated from "outside" comment and criticism. In my 1975 paper concerning the DC-10 crash near Paris, I wrote of the industry, "it has taken on paranoid characteristics. Exclusiveness and privacy have contributed to this, and an attempt at rationalization of such behavior has been sought in the rubric that the laity cannot possibly understand (and a fortiori, judge) matters so highly technical. Consequently the whole issue of professional or peer review, insofar as it means that no one outside of the engineering profession is competent to judge, has excluded not only those who might have pirated trade-secrets etc. *but also the objective input of the consuming public.* This exclusiveness has been aggravated by the similarity of background and training of the relevant persons . . . and it has been alarmingly enhanced by the cultivated stance of loyalty to an embattled super-person, the company."[9]

IV

I have been calling attention to projects that others and I myself feel are appropriate and morally desirable for professional associations to undertake (relevant to ethical concerns). The movement of the paper was from a consideration of "should" in terms of what is not possible, to "should" as a somewhat unanalyzed list of "possible actions." But mere possibility is not enough, of course, to merit "should." The obvious further question is "why should we?" Here it is fitting to note that the obligatory (the imperative) element, the "should" of morality is ultimately grounded in fairness and in respect for persons or in that combination of these which has been called the Golden Rule. These fundamentals underlying all particular "moralities" are entrenched in the inner experience of each of us; the function of great moral philosophers has been, in large part, only to *show* that these principles are indeed at the heart of morality (i.e. are presupposed by all the more detailed moral rules and ideals) and to try to show why it is these principles that do, indeed, take pride of place. The latter philosophical task I entirely omit from this paper, remarking simply that it is the sort of enterprise in which John Rawls was engaged in his great work on justice and Bernard Gert in his systematic defense of a set of ten moral rules. Instead I shall simply quote a sentence or two from the *Grounding of the Metaphysics of Morals* by Immanuel Kant and then make a very brief comment on it. Kant says that the moral command (the "should" of ethics) is "Act in such a way that you treat humanity, whether in your own person or in the person of another, always at the same time as an end and never simply as a means." "The principle of autonomy is the sole principle of morals." "We must be able to will that a maxim of our action becomes a universal law; that is the canon for morally estimating any of our actions."[10] The factor of fairness is shown in this latter, in *not* making exceptions in our own case or favor. It is shown also in the principle of "universalization" which involves explicitly taking account of how a proposed action of yours would seem to (all) others, taken as equally significant to yourself. Respect is already here too, for *taking* "others" as equally significant with yourself *is* considering them to be worthy of your concern and respect. (A history of morality might be written on how certain groups of "others" have finally come to be considered as persons.) Respect is always also for the other's freedom and autonomy. And since as children we learned morality largely through being restrained from engaging in certain actions (beating up small sisters) *and concurrently* being told "how would you like it if someone did that *to you?*" we can easily track the emergence of the Golden Rule, which goes "Do Unto Others as you would have Them Do Unto You."

These are the source of all morally relevant uses of "should." Application to particular cases requires, of course, examining what is in fact particular about the case. The issue is always one of judgment, of how and when to apply the rule. What is particular, then, about professional societies? They have quite specific power: they have, for one thing, the sheer power of numbers (their members as a collectivity), the power of status and influence and, until recently, quite a few other powers such as determining who could and who could not practice, what products met standards, what educational institutions were up-to-grade, etc. Furthermore, there is an incremental power accruing to these organizations from the specialized knowledge and training of its membership (actual and potential). It seems straightforward that with added power goes increased responsibility; whenever you know that what you do (or fail to do) will have, owing to your power, extended and ramified results, then it is incumbent upon you to think carefully and reflectively about the possibly injurious consequences of these results. (By the way, it does *not* follow that the converse holds; it is not an adequate excuse for failure to act on what you reflectively consider to be right, that you are just an insignificant, minor figure and your conduct will make no difference. This position is not only false—consider its self-fulfilling potential—but also a failure of self-respect which in turn is intimately connected with fully moral behavior.) And with regard to the specialized knowledge and training of individual members of these professions, again the inference to increased responsibility holds. The responsibility, besides not to harm, is essentially to warn. Coming from the basic injunctions not to harm or injure others and, where possible, to prevent their being harmed or injured, we have with engineers, for example, a tremendous increase in the capacity to harm and in the knowledge of the potential for harm embedded in objects, processes, structures and gadgets with which the public lives.

In a word, it is crucial to think about what one is doing, not just to do it. Hannah Arendt in a beautiful paper called "Thinking and Moral Considerations" (in which she discussed Eichmann's apparently unthinking behavior) suggested that failure to reflect consciously on the meanings of one's actions and on their consequences is itself a moral shortfall and may, indeed, be that habit which supports all or nearly all misdeeds.

In conclusion, I would like to present a conflicted example and a solution which is, I believe, in keeping with the positions argued for in this paper and with the movement of the Courts respecting professional associations.

1. Both legal reasoning and a Utilitarian approach to morality would have it that competition and the free market best protect the consumers from harm. This position is bolstered (among its adherents) by pointing out that the consumer has, now, two powerful weapons for (threatening) prior restraint: suits for product liability and suits for malpractice. The conjoint force of competition and of these legal threats are supposed to be adequate to protect the consumer and to reinforce that (supposedly) ultimate value, "maximization of wealth or consumer want satisfaction," i.e. utility.

2. However, we all know that this just doesn't work. Not only is it the case that the ideally free-market does not exist, but some harms are so great that neither threatened nor actual "compensation" is adequate. "Rights are violated when the harms imposed are so severe that we do not allow additions of lesser utilities (damages, compensation, etc.) to override. . . . Morality cannot always be made congruent with self-interest and the illusion that it can is dangerous to moral character and action."[11]

Thus, if we cannot rely on the free-market (competition, etc.) to do the job of protection for us and if, moreover, even the weapons of liability and malpractice lawsuits fail somehow to relieve us of a sense of anguish and responsibility when we observe, say, dangerous structures or products or processes, what can we do?

I suggest that professionals and their societies take far more seriously the task of "informing" or "telling on," that they make it a practice (and encourage others to do likewise) to report to the relevant governmental authorities known or suspected cases of danger, fraud, etc. I am well aware that this suggestion runs counter to a very long "old boy" tradition in the professions: "telling on" each other is far worse, it is thought, than "competing with" each other and even that was long held to be very wrong. Moreover many of us were brought up with the idea that being a "tattle tale" was intrinsically bad. A social history of this curious pseudomorality would be interesting, but I shall not inaugurate it here. Suffice it to end by saying that authorized informing does seem to me the only and the obligatory move in these cases.

Notes

1. Fashion Originators' Guild of America, Inc. et al v. Federal Trade Commission, 312 U.S. Supreme Court Reporter, page 707.
2. Lathrop v. Donahue, 367 U.S. Supreme Court Reporter, page 874.
3. Eastern Railroads Presidents' Conference, et al, v. Noerr Motor Freight, Inc., et al, 365 U.S. Supreme Court Reporter, page 137.
4. National Society of Professional Engineers v. United States, 435 U.S. Supreme Court Reporter, page 696.
5. "The Rule of Reason and the Per Se Concept," Robert Bork, Yale Law Journal, v. 74, #5, April 1965, page 830.

6. Stephen Unger, "How Engineering Societies Can Bolster Professional Ethics," page 165, in *AAAS Professional Ethics Project*.
7. Michael D. Bayles, *Professional Ethics*, page 13.
8. Jean Mayer, "Decline in Industrial Engineering," editorial in *Science*, v. 218, #4577, December 1982.
9. Fay Sawyier, "The DC-10 Case and Discussion," page 396, *Engineering Professionalism and Ethics*.
10. Immanuel Kant, *Grounding for the Metaphysics of Morals*, pages 33, 36, 45.
11. Alan Goldman, *The Moral Foundations of Professional Ethics*, pages 262, 267.

8. *Fashion Originators' Guild of America v. Federal Trade Commission*

MR. JUSTICE BLACK delivered the opinion of the Court.

The Circuit Court of Appeals, with modifications not here challenged, affirmed a Federal Trade Commission decree ordering petitioners to cease and desist from certain practices found to have been done in combination and to constitute "unfair methods of competition" tending to monopoly. Determination of the correctness of the decision below requires consideration of the Sherman, Clayton, and Federal Trade Commission Acts.

Some of the members of the combination design, manufacture, sell and distribute women's garments—chiefly dresses. Others are manufacturers, converters or dyers of textiles from which these garments are made. Fashion Originators' Guild of America (FOGA), an organization controlled by these groups, is the instrument through which petitioners work to accomplish the purposes condemned by the Commission. The garment manufacturers claim to be creators of original and distinctive designs of fashionable clothes for women, and the textile manufacturers claim to be creators of similar original fabric designs. After these designs enter the channels of trade, other manufacturers systematically make and sell copies of them, the copies usually selling at prices lower than the garments copied. Petitioners call this practice of copying unethical and immoral, and give it the name of "style piracy." And although they admit that their "original creations" are neither copyrighted nor patented, and indeed assert that existing legislation affords them no protection against copyists, they nevertheless urge that sale of copied designs constitutes an unfair trade practice and a tortious invasion of their rights. Because of these alleged wrongs, petitioners, while continuing to compete with one another in many respects, combined among them-

312 U.S. 705–708.

selves to combat and, if possible, destroy all competition from the sale of garments which are copies of their "original creations." They admit that to destroy such competition they have in combination purposely boycotted and declined to sell their products to retailers who follow a policy of selling garments copied by other manufacturers from designs put out by Guild members. As a result of their efforts, approximately 12,000 retailers throughout the country have signed agreements to "cooperate" with the Guild's boycott program, but more than half of these signed the agreements only because constrained by threats that Guild members would not sell to retailers who failed to yield to their demands—threats that have been carried out by the Guild practice of placing on red cards the names of noncooperators (to whom no sales are to be made), placing on white cards the names of cooperators (to whom sales are to be made), and then distributing both sets of cards to the manufacturers.

The one hundred and seventy-six manufacturers of women's garments who are members of the Guild occupy a commanding position in their line of business. In 1936, they sold in the United States more than 38% of all women's garments wholesaling at $6.75 and up, and more than 60% of those at $10.75 and above. The power of the combination is great; competition and the demand of the consuming public make it necessary for most retail dealers to stock some of the products of these manufacturers. And the power of the combination is made even greater by reason of the affiliation of some members of the National Federation of Textiles, Inc.—that being an organization composed of about one hundred textile manufacturers, converters, dyers, and printers of silk and rayon used in making women's garments. Those members of the Federation who are affiliated with the Guild have agreed to sell their products only to those garment manufacturers who have in turn agreed to sell only to cooperating retailers.

The Guild maintains a Design Registration Bureau for garments, and the Textile Federation maintains a similar Bureau for textiles. The Guild employs "shoppers" to visit the stores of both cooperating and noncooperating retailers, "for the purpose of examining their stocks, to determine and report as to whether they contain . . . copies of registered designs. . . ." An elaborate system of trial and appellate tribunals exists, for the determination of whether a given garment is in fact a copy of a Guild member's design. In order to assure the success of its plan of registration and restraint, and to ascertain whether Guild regulations are being violated, the Guild audits its members' books. And if violations of Guild requirements are discovered, as, for example, sales to red-carded retailers, the violators are subject to heavy fines.

In addition to the elements of the agreement set out above, all of which relate more or less closely to competition by so-called style copyists, the Guild has undertaken to do many things apparently independent of and distinct from the fight against copying. Among them are the following: the combination prohibits its members from participating in retail advertising; regulates the discount they may allow; prohibits their selling at retail; cooperates with local guilds in regulating days upon which special sales shall be held; prohibits its members from selling women's garments to persons who conduct businesses in residences, residential quarters, hotels or apartment houses; and denies the benefits of membership to retailers who participate with dress manufacturers in promoting fashion shows unless the merchandise used is actually purchased and delivered.

If the purpose and practice of the combination of garment manufacturers and their affiliates runs counter to the public policy declared in the Sherman and Clayton Acts, the Federal Trade Commission has the power to suppress it as an unfair method of competition. From its findings the Commission concluded that the petitioners, "pursuant to understandings, arrangements, agreements, combinations and conspiracies entered into jointly and severally," had prevented sales in interstate commerce, had "substantially lessened, hindered and suppressed" competition, and had tended "to create in themselves a monopoly." And paragraph 3 of the Clayton Act, 15 U.S.C. § 14, 15 U.S.C.A. § 14, declares "It shall be unlawful for any person engaged in commerce . . . to . . . make a sale or contract for sale of goods . . . on the condition, agreement or understanding that the . . . purchaser thereof shall not use or deal in the goods . . . of a competitor or competitors of the . . . seller, where the effect of such . . . sale, or contract for sale . . . may be to substantially lessen competition or tend to create a monopoly in any line of commerce." The relevance of this section of the Clayton Act to petitioners' scheme is shown by the fact that the scheme is bottomed upon a system of sale under which (1) textiles shall be sold to garment manufacturers only upon the condition and understanding that the buyers will not use or deal in textiles which are copied from the designs of textile manufacturing Guild members; (2) garment manufacturers shall sell to retailers only upon the condition and understanding that the retailers shall not use or deal in such copied designs. And the Federal Trade Commission concluded in the language of the Clayton Act that these understandings substantially lessened competition and tended to create a monopoly. We hold that the Commission, upon adequate and unchallenged findings, correctly concluded that this practice constituted an unfair method of competition.

Not only does the plan in the respects above discussed thus conflict with the principles of the Clayton Act; the findings of the Commission bring petitioners' combination in its entirety well within the inhibition of the policies declared by the Sherman Act itself. Section 1 of that Act makes illegal every contract, combination or conspiracy in restraint of trade or commerce among the several states; Section 2 makes illegal every combination or conspiracy which monopolizes or attempts to monopolize any part of that trade or commerce. Under the Sherman Act "competition, not combination, should be the law of trade." National Cotton Oil Co. v. Texas, 197 U.S. 115, 129, 25 S.Ct. 379, 381, 382, 49 L.Ed. 689. And among the many respects in which the Guild's plan runs contrary to the policy of the Sherman Act are these: it narrows the outlets to which garment and textile manufacturers can sell and the sources from which retailers can buy . . . ; subjects all retailers and manufacturers who decline to comply with the Guild's program to an organized boycott . . . ; takes away the freedom of action of members by requiring each to reveal to the Guild the intimate details of their individual affairs . . . ; and has both as its necessary tendency and as its purpose and effect the direct suppression of competition from the sale of unregistered textiles and copied designs. . . . In addition to all this, the combination is in reality an extra-governmental agency, which prescribes rules for the regulation and restraint of interstate commerce, and provides extra-judicial tribunals for determination and punishment of violations, and thus "trenches upon the power of the national legislature and violates the statute."

Nor is it determinative in considering the policy of the Sherman Act that petitioners may not yet have achieved a complete monopoly. For "it is sufficient if it really tends to that end, and to deprive the public of the advantages which flow from free competition."

United States v. E. C. Knight Co., 156 U.S. 1, 16, 15 S.Ct. 249, 255, 39 L.Ed. 325. It was, in fact, one of the hopes of those who sponsored the Federal Trade Commission Act that its effect might be prophylactic and that through it attempts to bring about complete monopolization of an industry might be stopped in their incipiency.

Petitioners, however, argue that the combination cannot be contrary to the policy of the Sherman and Clayton Acts, since the Federal Trade Commission did not find that the combination fixed or regulated prices, parcelled out or limited production, or brought about a deterioration in quality. But action falling into these three categories does not exhaust the types of conduct banned by the Sherman and Clayton Acts. And as previously pointed out, it was the object of the Federal Trade Commission Act to reach not merely in their fruition but also in their incipiency combinations which could lead to these and other trade restraints and practices deemed undesirable. In this case, the Commission found that the combination exercised sufficient control and power in the women's garments and textile businesses "to exclude from the industry those manufacturers and distributors who do not conform to the rules and regulations of said respondents, and thus tend to create in themselves a monopoly in the said industries." While a conspiracy to fix prices is illegal, an intent to increase prices is not an ever-present essential of conduct amounting to a violation of the policy of the Sherman and Clayton Acts; a monopoly contrary to their policies can exist even though a combination may temporarily or even permanently reduce the price of the articles manufactured or sold. For as this Court has said, "Trade or commerce under those circumstances may nevertheless be badly and unfortunately restrained by driving out of business the small dealers and worthy men whose lives have been spent therein, and who might be unable to readjust themselves to their altered surroundings. Mere reduction in the price of the commodity dealt in might be dearly paid for by the ruin of such a class and the absorption of control over one commodity by an all-powerful combination of capital."

But petitioners further argue that their boycott and restraint of interstate trade is not within the ban of the policies of the Sherman and Clayton Acts because "the practices of FOGA were reasonable and necessary to protect the manufacturer, laborer, retailer and consumer against the devastating evils growing from the pirating of original designs and had in fact benefited all four." The Commission declined to hear much of the evidence that petitioners desired to offer on this subject. As we have pointed out, however, the aim of petitioners' combination was the intentional destruction of one type of manufacture and sale which competed with Guild members. The purpose and object of this combination, its potential power, its tendency to monopoly, the coercion it could and did practice upon a rival method of competition, all brought it within the policy of the prohibition declared by the Sherman and Clayton Acts. For this reason, the principles announced in Appalachian Coals, Inc. v. United States, 288 U.S. 344, 53 S.Ct. 471, 77 L.Ed. 825, and Sugar Institute v. United States, 297 U.S. 553, 56 S.Ct. 629, 80 L.Ed. 859, have no application here. Under these circumstances it was not error to refuse to hear the evidence offered, for the reasonableness of the methods pursued by the combination to accomplish its unlawful object is no more material than would be the reasonableness of the prices fixed by unlawful combination. . . . Nor can the unlawful combination be justified upon the argument that systematic copying of dress designs is itself tortious, or should now be declared so by us. In the first place, whether or not given conduct is tortious is a question of state law, under our decision in Erie Railroad Co. v. Tompkins, 304 U.S. 64, 58 S.Ct. 817, 82 L.Ed. 1188, 114 A.L.R. 1487. In the second place, even if copying were an acknowledged tort under the law of every state, that situation would not justify petitioners in combining together to regulate and restrain interstate commerce in violation of federal law. . . . The decision below is accordingly Affirmed.

Issues of Responsibility

W HEN A NEW technology is created, marketed, and used, there is almost always an interval of uncertainty about the rights and responsibilities of the persons creating, selling, or using the technology. The uncertainty arises because we are not sure just which legal and moral rules apply to the new technology and how. Indeed, sometimes new laws must be created or precedents set via court cases that interpret the meaning of old laws for the new technology. In this book we consider two different issues that might be characterized in this way. The first, to be dealt with in Part 2, concerns who is responsible for and should be held liable for defects or malfunctions in computer software. While there is an abundance of law dealing generally with faulty products and negligent behavior, it is not at all clear how the law applies or "should" apply to computer software. The second issue, to be dealt with in Part 5, concerns the property rights of those who create software. Here again we have an abundance of laws giving different kinds of ownership rights to inventors, but it is not at all clear how these laws apply or should apply to computer software. Both issues are of great importance because they affect the computer industry, the activities of computer professionals, and ultimately the way in which computer technology will develop and be used in our society.

In Part 2 we provide a set of readings that will examine the problem of assigning liability for defects or malfunctions in computer software. Computer software is now used in many varied contexts or sectors of our society and in many cases the quality of the software can have an enormous impact on the activities of the user. For example, a good billing and accounting system used in a small retail business may enhance the operations of the company such that they are more efficient and more effective. On the other hand, a poorly designed system that continuously breaks down can be an enormous burden to the company. It could interfere with customer relations by making errors in individual billings. It could use up valuable time of employees who are repairing the problems in the system rather than doing other work. The potential harmful effects of defective software are even more dramatic if we think about software used to regulate industrial processes or software used in airplanes or nuclear power plants. Here the defects can result in serious harm to individuals or the environment.

To begin to understand this issue, imagine the following hypothetical situation.

Acme Software, Inc., spent several years developing a computerized medical diagnosis system and began to sell it to hospitals. Sales representatives explained the benefits of the system but also mentioned its limitations. Acme never claimed that the system was 100 percent accurate. General Hospital bought the system and made it available to all doctors on the staff. Dr. Jones used the system in diagnosing Peter Smith. The computerized system diagnosed Mr. Smith as having renal failure, and Dr. Jones prescribed the appropriate treatment. The treatment didn't work and after several months Dr. Jones did more tests and determined that Mr. Smith was suffering from something else. In the meantime, however, Mr. Smith developed a serious infection as a result of the treatment he had received, and he lost many days of work both because of the infection and because the treatment for renal failure involved many in-hospital hours each week. There is even some indication that Mr. Smith's kidney function has been weakened from the treatment. He feels that he has been harmed by the misdiagnosis and wants to sue for compensation and damages.

Who is responsible for the harm to Mr. Smith? Who should be liable to pay compensation and damages? the doctor? the company that created the diagnosis system? the hospital that purchased the system? Should Mr. Smith have to bear the risk of misdiagnosis himself? Could one party be held liable for Mr. Smith's harm and turn around and sue another party—that is, Mr. Smith sues Dr. Jones, Dr. Jones sues the hospital, the hospital sues Acme? If Acme is liable, can it turn around and blame or sue the employees who worked on the system? Did Acme give the hospital sufficient warning about the unreliability of the system such that it is not at fault?

At first thought, the matter might seem simple enough. The people who design the software are responsible for what it is and for what it isn't. When there is a defect, they are at fault and should be held liable. Unfortunately, however, there is much more than this involved, as we will see in the readings. For one thing, it is just not possible with some software to test all the ways in which it may ultimately be used. Thus, a programmer may do a reasonable amount of testing and may in good conscience release a piece of software and yet it may still contain defects. For another thing, it is not clear how we should treat disclaimers made by software vendors. Suppose, for example, that a software vendor sells a program but states explicitly that the software is not error free and that the buyer must take the risk. Should this be allowed? In effect, it allows vendors to avoid liability. On the other hand, insisting that the inventors of software bear liability may adversely affect the development of computer technology. Many beneficial programs may never reach the public if they cannot be sold until they are error free.

There are a myriad of questions here and we have tried to select a set of readings that will help to sort them out. The first three readings provide an introduction to the law regulating the buying and selling of software and suggest the complex and difficult issues in the law. In many ways, these readings are redundant but the law is complex enough that we thought the redundancy would be helpful. Brannigan is primarily concerned with liability for personal injury caused by defective medical computer programs. This builds on the hypothetical case we introduced above and briefly introduces the relevant law sorting the issues into matters of strict liability and negligence. Susan Nycum's paper covers the entire expanse of the law, while Marvin Benn and Wayne Michaels focus more on the problem of representation of a product by a vendor and the use of disclaimers.

One of the important fundamental questions here is whether computer software should be treated as a product or a service. If it is treated as a product, then the *Uniform Commercial Code* applies and vendors of computer software may be held strictly liable for defects in programs. Strict liability is liability without fault and is somewhat a controversial issue in the law because it means that an individual or company may be held liable even though they did everything reasonable to prevent the defect. On the other hand, if the sale of software is treated as provision of a service, then those who buy defective software must sue on grounds of negligence. This approach also raises hard questions, for establishing negligence requires showing that the person who supplied the software failed to perform a procedure or failed to meet some standard of care which is recognized in the industry. In a fairly new and rapidly changing field like software design, it is difficult to establish what adequate testing is or what reasonable care is.

Jim Prince sheds some light on these issues by offering a set of policy considerations to use in distinguishing what a product is. He then applies these considerations to software and finds that software distributed to the public through mass merchandising should be treated as a product. Strict liability should be imposed in such cases. However, when software is developed for and distributed only to an individual user, "public policy considerations do not mandate that strict liability be imposed on the supplier."

The next two readings are theoretical in nature. We have included them to help the reader in understanding what is involved in making judgments about responsibility, liability, and fault. H. L. A. Hart distinguishes several senses of responsibility and helps us to see how these various types of responsibility are connected. Joel Feinberg focuses on the notion of being "at fault" and helps us to understand the basis for making the judgment that someone is "at fault."

With the final reading in this chapter we turn to a somewhat different issue. In none of the previous readings about liability does anyone suggest that a computer or computer program itself be considered liable for an outcome, though clearly computers are often causally responsible for an outcome. In "Are There Decisions Computers Should Never Make?" James Moor does not specifically argue that computers should be held responsible, but he does argue that computers can be decision makers; and, because of this, we must ask the important question of whether there are some decision-making tasks that should never be assigned to computers. Moor believes that nobody really knows whether computers can match or exceed human decision-making ability, and he argues that this is an empirical question. He concludes by expressing some concern about what could happen to responsibility as computers take on decision-making tasks.

9. Liability for Personal Injury Caused by Defective Medical Computer Programs

Vincent M. Brannigan J.D.

Introduction

THE USE OF computer systems in medicine has increased dramatically over the last 10 years. There are several different types of systems, performing a wide variety of operations. Many of these systems, either acting alone or in conjunction with medical personnel, have the potential to injure patients. Under the American legal system, a person who is injured by the wrongful act of another may attempt to shift to the responsible party some or all of the costs of the injury. This paper will address the types of legal actions which may be brought against those who create, own, use, buy, sell or rely on computer systems which injure patients. It will focus on hospital based systems. To date, no such case appears in the literature, so that this article is a preview of the issues a court must consider.

The area of law which addresses recovery for personal injury is tort law. Unfortunately, the concept of a tort describes the legal action, not the conduct of the parties. Any discussion of tort concepts must begin with an understanding of our tort liability system. In the common law, as developed in England and adopted in the U.S., the judiciary controls the process of defining what conduct is sufficiently wrongful to require the defendant to compensate the plaintiff; there is no fixed list of wrongful acts. In each case brought before a judge, he determines what "facts" are proved and consults past cases to determine what law applies.

Over the past 700 years, judges have decided thousands of cases in the medical area. While judges, in general, follow past decisions under the doctrine of precedent or stare decisis, they are alert to changes in the world which undercut the basis for previous decisions and often must adapt to changes in human knowledge. For example, at one time, isolated rural doctors were considered significantly more "backward" than urban doctors, who had access to medical schools, libraries, and learned colleagues. This gave rise to the "locality" rule under which a physician was only held to the standard of other physicians in his area. The rise of state licensing, easier transportation and communication, a wide-spread distribution of medical literature, and increased demands for accountability on the part of professionals has led the courts to abandon the "locality" doctrine and generally to hold all physicians to a standard of care based on their level of training and specialty. This ability to change the law gives the court great power to insure justice in individual cases, but it also means that the law is in constant flux. In a new area such as computer

From a paper presented at the Fourth Annual Symposium on Computer Applications in Medical Care, Washington, D.C., November 4, 1980. Reprinted by permission of Vincent M. Brannigan. The issues of this paper are discussed in greater detail in Vincent Brannigan and Ruth Dayhoff, "Liability for Personal Injuries Caused by Defective Medical Computer Programs," *American Journal of Law and Medicine*, Vol 7, No 2.

programs, it is necessary to determine what cases are most analogous to the new situation. The slow buildup of cases in each area of law causes a problem when a new situation develops which does not fit neatly into a particular set of older cases. There is often great tension in the law which may take years to sort out. Defective computer programs are a problem for the law.

Liability for defective computer programs involves two entirely different streams of cases, depending upon whether computer programs are considered goods or services. The two areas are: Product Liability which involves recovery for injuries caused by defective products and Professional Liability (malpractice) which covers injuries caused by inadequate professional services. These two areas have significantly different standards of liability.

In most parts of the United States, liability for a defective product is determined by the standard of "strict liability." If the product is defective when it leaves the "manufacturer," even if the defect could not be prevented, the manufacturer will be held liable. Services are treated differently;[1] liability for professional malpractice is based on a negligence theory in which liability is imposed only if the producer of the service failed to meet an appropriate standard of care. He would not be liable for injuries which occur despite the exercise of reasonable care.[2] Thus, it is of crucial importance to determine: (1) whether computer programs are products or services, (2) what type of defect has occurred, and (3) who is responsible.

Service or Product

Service—Negligence, Malpractice

The earliest development of negligence law was in the area of "public calling including carriers, innkeepers, blacksmiths and surgeons."[3] These professionals were expected to give their "clients" a reasonable standard of professional competence. Eventually the courts evolved the action of "negligence" to deal with inadequate performance of a public calling.

Negligence has several elements:

1. A duty must exist which binds the defendant to act in a reasonable manner. Duties do not exist "in the air."

   Duties are the product of public policies which define who must use reasonable care to protect another. The issue of "duty" is not normally a problem in medical care, since the undertaking to provide care does imply a duty. However, the complex process for production of a computer program does raise the issue. Does a programmer, working as a consultant to a hospital, owe a patient at that hospital a duty of care? Even more important, does a hospital employee owe a personal duty of care? Suppose the hospital sells its operating system to another hospital or allows other hospitals to copy it. Does the programmer owe a duty to the other hospital? Does a researcher presenting his program to a conference such as the Symposium on Computer Applications in Medical Care owe a duty of care to anyone injured by a user of his research? The ease with which computer programs are copied makes these duty issues complex. There are few clear cut answers to this question.

2. The second element required in a negligence case is that the defendant's conduct must have been below that of a "reasonable man" in performing the service. The defendant is not liable merely because the product is defective; it must be defective because of a lack of care and skill on his part. Failure to meet the standard of care is normally proved by expert testimony of what a reasonable man of the defendant's level of expertise would have done in the defendant's position. In addition the jury must consider the role of

the negligent party. Is he an experienced expert consultant or a beginning student worker? Each would have a different standard of care.

There may be several levels of negligence. For example, negligence may be present when a hospital fails to use reasonable care in selecting a programmer, or in buying a program. Therefore, even if the programmer is not negligent, the hospital can be negligent for having entrusted him with the assignment. In any case, there must be conduct below the appropriate standard of care.

3. The next element of negligence is causation. Causation is the required legal connection between the accident and the injury. Those familiar with the children's poem . . . "For want of a nail the shoe was lost. . . ." etc. have a working concept of causation. However, in negligence law, causation normally requires that it be "foreseeable" that failure to conform to the standard of care will cause injury. It is foreseeable that a medical records program could cause injury if names are erased. But was it foreseeable that a computer program which records lab tests for billing purposes will cause injury when it is used as a substitute for a lab order sheet?

A program must not only be safe for its intended use, it must be safe for any reasonable foreseeable misuse, that is, the improper use of a program which can be foreseen even if not intended. Foreseeable misuse can include: using the system in an inappropriate manner, or modifying the system. This could arise when a frustrated user finds an unintended way of using the program to accomplish a task for which it is not designed. If the misuse is foreseeable, it is up to the producer to anticipate the misuse and make reasonable attempts to prevent it. Whether efforts such as warnings, instructions, or security measures built into the program are sufficient will be decided by the jury, whose knowledge of the system will be entirely derived from expert testimony in court.

Product—Strict Liability, Products Liability

Strict products liability flows from an entirely different history. Classically, Caveat Emptor prevented the buyer from suing the seller for negligence, particularly if the defect in the goods was discernable by the buyer. Third parties were barred by the doctrine of Privity of Contract which required a contractual relationship between the injured party and the defendant. In the classic case, the repairer of a wagon owned by another party owed no duty to a bystander to properly repair the wagon and was not liable for injury to the bystander. The doctrine of privity began collapsing in the 20th Century, and by the early 1960's a manufacturer of a product was responsible to anyone injured by the product.

The second major difference is the basis of liability. Under strict products liability there is no concept of a standard of care. The product itself is examined; and if it is defective and unreasonably dangerous, recovery is allowed even if no amount of care could have prevented injury. In the words of 402A of the Second Restatement of Torts,

1. One who sells any product in a defective condition unreasonably dangerous to the user or consumer or to his property is subject to liability for physical harm thereby caused to the ultimate user or consumer, or to his property, if

a. the seller is engaged in the business of selling such a product, and

b. it is expected to and does reach the user or consumer without substantial change in the condition in which it is sold.

2. The rule stated in Subsection 1 applies although

a. the seller has exercised all possible care in the preparation and sale of his product, and

b. the user or consumer has not bought the product from or entered into any contractual relation with the seller.[4]

In other words, in a products liability trial the computer program itself would be on trial, not the programmer or hospital.

Strict liability was developed both to relieve the plaintiff of the burden of proving negligence, and to shift to the defendant the cost of defects in his product. It was a change in the basic responsibility of a manufacturer. This was a policy judgment, of the type courts make regularly.

This characteristic of the courts, their ability to make policy, must be understood. It means that aggressive counsel will try to stretch the law by bringing novel cases. Predicting what the courts will do in a particular case is very difficult. They need not strictly follow analysis of past cases; they can come out with a new doctrine of law, when faced with a novel question. The question to be addressed in this paper is "Should the courts use strict liability or negligence concepts to determine recovery for defective medical computer programs?" The question will be addressed in two parts.

1. Analysis of computer programs as services or products and
2. Analysis of the policy implications of each classification.

The primary task is to define criteria which differentiate services from products and to determine whether those criteria are relevant to computer programs.

Tangible Format

Most products are tangible items with intrinsic value. Products exist in a corporeal form. Each item has a value based on its characteristics, apart from any ideas incorporated in the item. Services do not have a tangible existence. However, services are often rendered by expressing an idea in writing or other tangible form. Writings expressing an idea are not normally thought of as having intrinsic value since any copy of the expressed idea is equivalent to the original even if the copy is not tangible. The value rests in the idea, not in the expression of the idea in any particular item. Intrinsic value and corporeal existence are the usual hallmarks of products.

Computer programs are difficult to describe in this context. They are ideas committed to tangible form, either as punch cards, printed output, programmed chips or as the ordered arrangement of a magnetic field in a computer. However, the "value" rests in the underlying ideas not in the tangible item. As tangible expression of ideas, they are not dissimilar from books and architectural drawings.

In this analysis, a program appears more like a service expressed in tangible form, than like a product. It should be emphasized that the reduction of a service to a tangible reproducible form is not a trivial step to the courts. Some courts could consider it vital to the case, particularly if the program, directing a machine, actually inflicts an injury. It is similar to a defective camshaft in an automobile. A camshaft is merely a tangible representation of the designer's instructions to the pistons. Once the instructions are reduced to a reproducible tangible form, they appear more like a product than a service. The reduction to tangible form is significant if the tangible form is part of the item which injures the consumer.

Besides computer programs, there are other exact writings such as architectural drawings and machinery blueprints. However, these are usually turned into a final product; they

61

do not of themselves constitute the final product. Computer programs may be part of the final product which inflicts injury. This is significant both for the privity concept in negligence law and the requirement that the product, in its "defective" form "reach" the user or consumer, which is a requirement of products liability. It will be necessary to examine whether the program "reaches" the consumer.

Ownership

A second criteria for dividing services from products is the concept of ownership. Only "property" can be owned. Property can be either tangible or intangible (licenses, patents etc.). A service can produce an intangible property, which can be reduced to ownership, such as a program.

A person who owns a particular item can do anything [he or she wants] with that item. It can be destroyed, incorporated into another product, or improved. That item can then be sold to someone else. Ownership has been crucial in product liability by making each seller of a product in the course of business liable to an injured consumer. One of the advantages of strict liability is that it makes no difference who the defendant is. Both retailer and manufacturer will be liable to the consumer if the product is defective, on the same terms. Once a computer program is in a form where it can be owned, it has become an article of commerce, rather than a service. All sellers of that article, including the creator can be treated alike. Services not reduced to tangible form, such as a symphony concert, do not become articles of commerce.

In contrast, under a negligence theory there would be widely differing standards of care for various manufacturers or sellers. The philosophy of strict liability would seem to apply to any tangible item which can be owned since once the program has become an article of commerce, there is no way to distinguish it from products, such as automobiles or dishwashers which at one time existed only as intangible design ideas.

In fact some writers have suggested that programmers keep control of their programs by owning the programs and licensing them to users to prevent alteration. This emphasizes the significance of the ownership of the program, since what is owned is not the "service" of producing the program but the tangible output.

Process of Correcting Defects

One further difference between products and services can be described. Inadequate services are not normally thought of as having correctable defects. Since services are performed at a particular point in time, defective services are not normally "correctable." While the effect of a defective service can be counteracted by additional services, the original service cannot be adjusted since it no longer exists. Products such as machines, can be adjusted or fixed, even long after production. The process of debugging a program is very similar to the process of adjusting and tinkering with a machine. In addition, the program can be handed over to others besides the designer for debugging. In this functional comparison a program is very similar to a product.

On policy grounds it is possible to argue that the rationale of product liability ought to be expanded to cover tangible output capable of ownership. The ability to own tangible items is an easily used point at which to attach liability. This would serve to reduce uncertainty and promote responsible action by the "manufacturers." The person who originally "owned" the program would be treated as the "manufacturer" of the program in strict liability. Other "owners" who obtain and resell the program from the manufacturer would be treated as middlemen.

One reason that strict liability is considered acceptable for products but not services is that the manufacturer/seller is in a better position than the consumer to bear the risk and spread it across an entire production or use of the item. Computer programs can be reproduced in quantity, like automobiles, and used repeatedly. The person who *owns* the rights to reproduce the program is in the best position to spread the risk across many users.

In the end, trying to decide whether medical computer programs are a service or a product is reminiscent of the early 20th Century debate over whether light is a wave or a particle. Quantum mechanics says it is neither, and both. In the end, after gnawing the legal bones, the courts will make essentially a policy judgment. In my personal opinion, that judgment will declare medical computer programs to be products, subject to strict liability. The commercial user would be treated as the seller to the ultimate consumer. All sellers and the final user would be equally liable for a defective program.

This result is tempered by two key factors:

1. Strict liability is primarily focused on manufacturing defects as opposed to design defects.
2. The injury must be caused by the product "reaching" the consumer in its defective form.

What Type of Defect?

Design Defects vs. Production Defects

Many writers in products liability have noted that it is much easier to apply strict liability for manufacturing defects than for design defects. A product with a manufacturing defect fails to measure up to the designer's own expectation or specification, and often there are nondefective models of the same product for comparison. This makes proof of the defect easy. In a design defect case, the plaintiff must prove that a design without the defect was "reasonably" available. This requires expert testimony comparing options available to a reasonable designer. Most writers have acknowledged that this introduces a "negligence" orientation to strict liability for design defects since it requires testimony of what a "reasonable designer" would do. Some writers and the Uniform Product Liability Act[5] claim that there is no true "strict" liability for design defects, that it is identical to negligence.

For most products, there is a clear differentiation between the "design" and construction phases. Normally, the designer starts from ideas and reduces the ideas to tangible form. They are then incorporated into a prototype, which is tested to see whether it conforms to the designer's original idea and will function as the designer intended. The prototype is then described in a set of production instructions, which will reproduce the prototype for sale.

The design phase of a product can be used to describe two very different concepts.

The first is the set of conscious choices made by the designer, of which he has full knowledge. The McDonnell Douglas DC 10 aircraft has three independent hydraulic control systems, instead of the four found on the Lockheed L 1011 jets. This is a conscious design choice.

The second concept is to describe any feature of the product which is present in all items of a production, even if no conscious choice was made to include the feature. For example, the defective door on the DC 10 was the inevitable result of a particular material chosen for the door latches, but there was no conscious acceptance of the possibility of door failure. Most of the criticism of strict liability for design defects has focused on the conscious choices made by the designer.

In computer programs, there are two significant related problems: (1) In many systems, it is unclear when the design phase stops and the production phase begins, and (2) it is usually unclear whether a particular program characteristic is the product of conscious design choice.

Computer programs are normally perfected by an iterative process known as "debugging." This normally occurs before the program is released for use, but it is widely accepted that complex computer programs often contain significant programming errors that cannot be discovered until the system is operating in its intended location. Debugging a major system can be a permanent process, since the system may be under constant modification. On the other hand, programs may be sold as "turnkey" systems which are expected to work properly when installed. Two possible points for dividing the design from production stages are: (1) any system used to perform patient related functions is a production system. This would discourage premature use of a still defective system. (2) The entire debugging/modification process is in the design phase, and production phase is limited to "turnkey" and "locked-up" systems. The courts' choice between these two depends a great deal on the courts' weighing of the advantages of technological development vs. a concern for patient welfare.

Defining Defects

Since liability for design choices turns on whether the choice was unreasonable, defendants normally try to emphasize that the feature claimed to be defective was inherent in the desirable attributes of the product. For example, in *Dreisenstock vs. Volkswagenwerk* an injured driver sued Volkswagen because the minibus design gave the driver no protection against a collision.[6] The cause of the injury was a feature which also made the bus desirable, so the court held that in such a case, the car was not defective as a matter of law.

One of the most useful tests to determine whether a product has a design defect or not was stated in *Roach*.[7] "Would a reasonable manufacturer, with actual knowledge of the alleged defect, have put the program into use?" All strict liability supplies is the substitution of constructive knowledge for actual knowledge. Such a test would be easy to apply to computer programs. It would render all ordinary bugs, manufacturing defects, but allow the system designer freedom to make any reasonable choices for the system. Under this definition ordinary mistakes by programmers in carrying out the system designer's instructions would be considered manufacturing defects.

Does the Product Reach the Consumer?

The second requirement for strict liability is that the product "reach" the consumer in its defective condition. At least three categories of computer programs are involved.

1. Programs which control direct interaction with the patient, such as machinery operations, patient education, and intensive care monitoring. In these cases courts would be inclined to find that the product interacts directly with the patient and thus "reaches" him. Such cases are most similar to current product liability lawsuits.[8]
2. Programs which are ordinarily relied on by medical personnel who do not question the correctness of the output. This type of program is typified by a medical records program. The users of a medical record do not normally challenge or discuss the truth of the record. While the question is less clear, courts have tended to expand strict liability when no independent human intervention is expected.
3. Physician support programs, which supplement the medical library or act in place of a consultant. In either case they expand the physician's medical knowledge. It is unlikely that courts would consider these programs as "reaching" the patient. The physician is expected to use his support materials in a critical way, and does not rely on them in the same way as a nurse in an ICU relies on a warning buzzer. He has discretion to ignore them and is expected to evaluate their accuracy. In this case liability to the patient would be based on negligence.

Who Is Responsible?

The final problem courts must cope with is allocating the responsibility of the parties. Normally the parties can be divided into three classes.

1. Hospitals who contract with the patient.
2. Medical personnel who contract with the patient.
3. Support services which contract with the hospital or physician, but not the patient.

Hospital

Traditionally hospitals were the physicians' workshop, and the patient relied on the physician's care and skill. As medicine has evolved, patients rely to a greater extent on hospitals to provide a safe environment. For the purpose of this paper, the question is "would a court hold a hospital liable in strict tort for a defective medical computer program which injures a patient?" It should be noted that there are few cases which attempt to hold hospitals in strict liability for any type of product, and none at all for computer programs.[9]

In most of the early cases, courts rejected strict liability for medical products supplied by hospitals, on the grounds that they were "incidental" to the services of providing medical care. The rationale for these cases is not supported by the Restatement, which includes as a consumer a customer in a beauty shop injured by a permanent wave solution. However, it is clear that the courts prefer to hold the manufacturer of the product liable rather than the hospital.

Unfortunately, the hospital is often the "manufacturer" of the computer system. Should it make any difference if the patient is injured by the hospital's own system, or one it buys from a manufacturer as a "turnkey" operation? It is perhaps unfortunate that most of the cases dealing with hospital liability have arisen in the area of hepatitis-infected blood used for transfusion. Blood is a very special product, so unique as to be "sui generis," unlike anything else. It is not "manufactured," but donated. Courts strained to avoid putting responsibility on hospitals for defective blood and often declared the transaction to be one of providing a service rather than selling a product. A better view would have been that blood is an "unavoidably unsafe" product under the Restatement and thus requires only an appropriate warning. Unfortunately, the blood cases have confused the issue and left hospitals and patients in a state of uncertainty.

A few recent cases have addressed the issue. In *Dubin vs. Michael Reese Hospital*,[10] X-rays were held to be a "product" subjecting the hospital to strict liability, and Albert Einstein Medical Center was held liable for supplying a defective bone cutter in a surgical operation.[11] When the hospital itself is the manufacturer of the product, there is no inherent reason why it should not be treated as any other manufacturer.

Physicians

The policy judgments that tended to limit the liability of a hospital for a defective program are applied even more strongly to a physician using a program. Ordinarily the physician does not own or create the program, and does not furnish it for the patient's use. His reasonable reliance on the functioning of a program is all that can normally be required. If he unreasonably relies on a program, liability would be based on negligence.

Supplier to the Hospital and Physicians

It is clearly the policy of products liability law to put the greatest burden on the person who manufactures a "product" and introduces it into commerce. Once a clearly defined "sale" or other introduction into commerce (lease, gift, trade) has taken place, courts will allow any injured party to sue the seller or manufacturer, usually in strict liability. This is the case even if the commercial purchaser accepts the product without warranty. Those who "manufacture" programs for sale or other introduction into commerce can expect to be held liable for defects, if they are selling the program rather than their services. It will often be a very close question. This poses a number of special problems for hospitals or medical personnel, since hospitals may buy their systems from other hospitals.

1. Is the hospital the manufacturer or the purchaser of the program? This is determined by the jury after a consideration of the entire process of putting the program together. In general, if the hospital purchases the programmers' time, on an hourly basis, the hospital is more like a manufacturer. If they buy "rights" to a particular piece of work, they are more like purchasers.
2. Does the hospital sell the program? If a hospital, attempting to recoup the cost of developing a system, sells the system to another user, they will probably be treated as the manufacturer of the system.

Conclusion

Liability for personal injury caused by defective medical computer programs is a novel issue both factually and legally. The highly decentralized court system in the United States makes development of a single concrete answer impossible. A paper such as this is an attempt to structure the discussion of the problem so that both courts and computer specialists can understand the types of decisions and the responsibilities that await them in this area.

Notes

1. Application of Rule of Strict Liability in Tort to Person Rendering Service, 29 ALR 3rd 1425.
2. *Hoven v. Kelble*, 256 N.W.2d 379 (1977).
3. Prosser, W. L., *The Law of Torts*, p. 139, 4th Edition, 1971, West Pub., St. Paul, Minn.
4. Section 402A *Restatement (Second) of Torts*, 1965, American Law Institute, St. Paul, Minn.
5. Uniform Product Liability Act, 44 *Federal Register* 62721, Sec 104, October 31, 1979.
6. *Dreisenstock v. Volkswagenwerk*, 489, Fd. 2d, 1055, (1974).
7. *Roach v. Kononen*, 525 P2d 125 (1974) Oregon.
8. *Ethicon Inc. v. Parten*, 520 S.W. 2d 527, (1975).
9. Morris, C. Physician and Hospital Liability for Defective Products Used in the Treatment of Patients, 46 *Insurance Council Journal* 566, 1979.
10. *Dubin v. Michael Reese Hospital and Medical Center*, 393 N.E. 2d 588 (1979).
11. *Grubb v. Albert Einstein Medical Center*, 387 A 2d 480 (1979).

10. Liability for Malfunction of a Computer Program

Susan Nycum

I. Introduction

THREE DEVASTATING ACCIDENTS had occurred. First, an air traffic controller, relying on his instruments, had directed two passenger jets onto an intersecting course. The jets had crashed and all aboard were killed. Second, a subway train, following directions from the central controller, had switched onto a track only to discover another train on that track rushing from the other direction. In the collision dozens had died. Third, industrial workers had found themselves being spattered with molten steel poured from the automated machinery above them. In this, as in the other accidents, investigators eventually traced the fault to errors in the computer programs which had directed the operations. At that point hundreds of plaintiffs filed suits against the computer software houses which had developed the programs.

From *Rutgers Journal of Computers, Technology, and the Law* 7 (1979), pp. 1–22. Notes deleted. Reprinted by permission of Susan Nycum.

These hypothetical examples illustrate the potential for catastrophic harm which erroneously programmed computers can cause. But because computers now control so many facets of modern society, it is easy to uncover instances of programming error causing damage. In a recent case the Arkansas Supreme Court cancelled a note and mortgage in the amount of $28,000 because a computer error caused the mortgage company to charge a usurious rate of interest, even though the company had no actual usurious intent.

This article gives an overview of the different legal theories under which the computer programmer or his company may be liable for such errors. It assumes that the programmer, a potential defendant, possessed average skill and had no actual intent to cause harm, and that his company, another potential defendant, had warranted with the program's purchaser, a potential plaintiff, that the program would be free from error, but that such warranty period had expired. The contract with the purchaser had limited the liability of the company defendant to the price of the program; such liability did not extend to third party or consequential damages.

Given these facts, a plaintiff might base his case against the programmer or his company on several different theories. They include breach of express warranty, breach of implied warranties, breach of a third party beneficiary contract, negligence, and strict liability. In addition, the programmer might be liable to his employer. Each of these possibilities receives attention below.

II. Contract Theories

A. Violation of Express Warranties

1. The Warranty Involved Here

When a programmer's company agrees to supply a program, it enters into a contract with the customer. Usually the contract sets out the guarantees and express warranties that the company gives as to the quality of the program and as to what the company will do for the customer if the quality falls below that specified. Under the assumed facts the company warranted that the program would be free of errors, but that warranty was good only for a limited time. If errors appeared after the expiration date, as they did disastrously in the hypotheticals, then the company promised no compensation. If the errors appeared before the expiration date, the company promised only to refund to the customer the cost of the program; it refused to compensate anyone for injuries to person or property. The company thereby protected itself to the extent that it could. But this protection might prove insufficient.

2. What Law Applies

At this time no one knows for certain what law would govern a contract for a computer program. If it qualifies as a contract for the sale of goods, then Article 2 of the Uniform Commercial Code (U.C.C.) would apply. This statute is in force in every state, except Louisiana, as well as in the District of Columbia and the Virgin Islands. If the contract qualifies as one for performance of services, then the contract law of the individual state involved would apply.

Article 2 of the U.C.C., the one possibly of relevance here, "applies to transactions in goods." Goods are defined to include "all things (including specially manufactured goods) which are movable at the time of identification to the contract for sale." Several writers have suggested that the U.C.C. should apply to sales of computer programs or software generally. Some even suggest that if a contract for programs is not for the sale of goods, Article 2 should apply to leases and service contracts as well. Whether the U.C.C. applies may depend on what was purchased by the customer. The answer may turn on the extent to which the programmer must custom-design the program for the customer's use under the customer's direction and control and the extent to which the program comes as part of a package with other computer items which are clearly goods, such as hardware. In the computer industry, the first category, which is sometimes known as custom programming, may involve the programmer selling the customer only his time (a service), with all other materials and supplies—including computer time—being provided by the customer. Other special-purpose programs are contracted for in much the same way as are custom-made manufactured goods. The "packaged program" is analogous to off-the-shelf goods.

3. Remedies Under the U.C.C.

If the U.C.C. applies, the customer's remedy includes the difference in the value between the program accepted and the value it would have had if it had been as warranted, plus any consequential damages. The U.C.C. defines consequential damages to include injury to person or property proximately resulting from any breach of warranty. But for goods other than consumer goods, the parties may limit or exclude liability for consequential damages, if such limitation would not be unconscionable. The contract discussed here did exclude this liability, and computer programs are generally not considered consumer goods. (This analysis should change as programs are made available to individuals owning personal computers.) The customer or injured third parties could argue that under the particular circumstances of a computer-caused disaster the exclusion is unconscionable. Even if the customer were to prevail on that point, however, the company should still be protected on a warranty theory because the express warranty had expired.

If the U.C.C. does not apply, the company could probably rely on its expired time limit on the express warranty to protect itself. In an analogous situation, accountants have been able to restrict the scope of their liability for errors by clearly giving only a limited certification.

Conceivably the customer might have an action for breach of contract on two bases other than the express warranty referred to above. By describing the program's capacity or by advertising, the company may have unwittingly given an additional express warranty that the program would conform with the description or advertisement. The time limit and consequential damages disclaimer might not apply to this additional warranty. In addition, the company may have promised to test the program adequately and failed to do so. If the error ("bug") which led to the crash probably would have been caught and corrected by adequate testing, then the customer may have a cause of action for breach of the contract with consequential damages. Many contracts now include a requirement that the customer perform acceptance tests. In the event that the program passes such customer tests, the customer may be estopped to complain of damages caused by patent error.

If either of these two theories is sustained, the company still may be liable for injuries to persons other than the customer. The old requirement that plaintiffs be in privity of contract with defendants for actions for breach of express warranty is fast disappearing. At least this is true for persons in a direct chain of distribution. Whether bystanders such as workmen in an automated steel plant would be able to sue depends on the various state laws. The U.C.C. offers the states a choice on the degree to which privity should be irrelevant. At a minimum, injured third parties could make a strong case that the contract's provision excluding liability for damage done to third parties has no validity as to them. It could, however, serve as an agreement between the computer company and the customer that the customer will reimburse the company for any payments the company may have to make to third parties. This is one form of an indemnity agreement. Customers should be alert to such possibilities, however remote the likelihood may appear, and structure the contract to preclude such interpretation.

4. Review

In summary, the company would probably escape liability for consequential damages to both the customer and third parties under an express warranty, but only because the time limit on the express warranty has expired. It may face suits based on other express guarantees to which the time limit and third party limitation may not apply. But even if it does escape all liability for breach of an explicit provision of the contract, the company may still face attacks based on other legal theories. Against these it would have fewer defenses.

B. Violation of Implied Warranties

An implied warranty is one imposed by law on the basis of public policy. The contract need not refer to the warranty for it to be effective. In most cases, however, the contract can expressly exclude all implied warranties. Whether without such exclusion a contract would contain implied warranties depends for the most part on whether the U.C.C. applies.

If computer programs are held to constitute services, then the U.C.C. will not apply. Under this interpretation, public policy or statutory law in some states may lead to the imposition of implied warranties. In practice, however, such warranties arise infrequently.

If the U.C.C. does apply, however, the plaintiffs may be able to sue for breach of two implied warranties: those of merchantability and of fitness for intended use. Merchantability means that the program is fit for the ordinary purposes for which programs are used. Fitness for intended use means that the program is fit for the particular use intended for it by the customer. This warranty has particular relevance where the programmer has worked closely with the customer in adapting the program to the customer's specific needs.

Even if the warranties are in effect, the company may have several defenses. The contract may have excluded all implied warranties. The plaintiffs may not have given timely notice of defect. They may have misused the program, or been contributorily negligent in some other way. Finally they may have assumed the risk of accident.

If implied warranties do arise, third parties as well as the customer can probably sue for damage. The landmark case of *Henningsen v. Bloomfield Motors, Inc.* was the first to attack the privity of contract doctrine. This decision and its progeny have led to the virtual elimination of the privity requirement for actions based on implied warranties.

C. Violation of a Third Party Beneficiary Contract

Persons other than the customer might argue that, since the program was ultimately written for their benefit, they should be able to sue directly for breach of contract without regard to the privity limitations as still remain. That is, the courts should construe the agreement between the company and the customer as a third party beneficiary contract. This theory, however, holds little promise of success for such third parties. The mere fact that the breach of a contract between two parties injures a third does not make the contract one for the benefit of the third party. For the other plaintiffs to be able to sue, the company and the customer must have intended for those third parties to receive a benefit enforceable by them in court. The use of the program by the plaintiffs must have been "the end and aim of the transaction." While the parties to the contract undoubtedly intended that the other plaintiffs benefit from the program, they would not have intended that the third parties actually use it. Hence, this theory of liability appears hollow.

With the decline of privity requirements in other theories, however, the injured plaintiff still has an ample supply of other weapons in his legal arsenal without this one. Of all of these, negligence seems most clearly available if the facts accommodate it.

III. Tort Theories

A. Negligence

1. Cause in Fact

The first question in any negligence suit is this: Did anything the defendants do or omit to do contribute to the harm sued on? If not, then the case stops immediately. Here the program gave erroneous output. The reason may be erroneous input not the fault of the company: "garbage in, garbage out." Or, the problem may have been a hardware failure, a power failure, or a failure on the part of the system operator. The error may have been a typical or obvious error such that both parties expected the air traffic controller to catch and correct it. Such possibilities must be explored, for they may block liability.

2. Existence and Nature of a Duty of Care Owed to the Plaintiff

Under common law principles of negligence, the company and probably the programmer as well owe a duty of care at least to the customer for writing the program. Just what standard of care is owed remains a source of controversy.

Given that a computer program can, under the wrong circumstances, cause airplanes to collide, trains to slam into each other, and industrial machinery to spill hot liquids, courts might classify computer programs as inherently dangerous instrumentalities requiring the highest degree of care. This reasoning seems weak, however, since, like a painter's scaffold, the program becomes dangerous only when improperly constructed or used.

A more likely standard is that of a professional. At least one judge has found a programmer to have committed malpractice. Similarly, some commentators have concluded that computer programmers should be held to a professional standard of care. These opinions emphasize that a programmer holds himself out as a professional with special expertise. Indeed, the programmer may belong to a technical or professional organization that has a canon of ethics he is required to follow. As a professional, he would be held to the level of care exercised by a reasonable member of the profession under similar circumstances.

The programmer may not qualify as a professional, however. To date, no states have enacted legislation regulating the conduct of personnel in the computer industry or requiring that they be licensed. Absent classification as a professional, a programmer would be judged as are other expert laymen, according to his skill and experience. This standard, however, is greater than that of the reasonable layman.

The company and the programmer would owe this duty of care to the customer regardless of the potential harm. But for duty owed to third persons, the law equivocates somewhat. For negligent manufacture of a product, a company may be liable to third persons for whose use the product was intended. With defective products, however, the amount of damage possible resulting from the defect tends to reach a limit as to physical harm. The author of *MacPherson* (Justice Cardozo) switched sides on the question of duty owed to third parties when this ceiling of injury by physical harm was removed. There the court worried about "a liability in an indeterminate amount for an indeterminate time to an indeterminate class." Liability so unrestricted could be uninsurable, which would discourage the continuance of the occupation. A computer programmer might fall into the same category as an accountant. Certainly a program could lead to an incalculable amount of physical damage as well as financial damage to a class of indeterminate size. The program may run for an extended period before a particular combination of circumstances arises which reveals too late the fatal bug. Like accountants, lawyers, and other professionals who continue to benefit from the *Ultramares* decision, where Justice Cardozo held that accountants owe no liability for negligence to creditors and investors who relied on their certification, computer programmers deal with abstractions not necessarily subject to physical limitation. Thus, programmers might not owe a duty of care to third persons harmed by their negligence.

But the chances are that either at present or within a few years programmers will owe such a duty of care. Already airlines accept liability for huge air crashes. Private utilities have managed to insure up to the $560,000,000 limitation on liability for nuclear accidents under the Price-Anderson Act. Although financial resources differentiate the independent programmer from the airline or power utility, the same principle of responsibility should apply.

Moreover, even in its core applications the *Ultramares* case is losing its force. An important California case dealing with the liability of attorneys articulated a balancing test to determine whether professionals should be held responsible for their negligence to third persons not in privity. The factors to be considered included "the extent to which the transaction was intended to affect the plaintiff, the foreseeability of harm to him, the degree of certainty that the plaintiff suffered injury, the closeness of the connection between the defendant's conduct and the injury, and the policy of preventing future harm." Those considerations appear to call for imposition of liability in this case.

3. Violation of the Duty of Care

Once a duty and a standard of care are established, the next question to be asked is whether the defendants violated that duty. It may not be easy to determine this since the industry has relatively few standards. Both hardware and software are continually changing; new applications and techniques become available regularly; and the particular usage, such as air traffic control, may be difficult for a programmer to handle, or at least novel. With this much uncertainty as to the standard of care, violations may be difficult to prove.

A possible shortcut for plaintiffs, *res ipsa loquitur,* probably would not apply. This doctrine, which means literally "the act speaks for itself," can apply in cases where the fact that a particular harm occurred establishes a presumption that the duty of due care has been violated. Those cases deal with injuries which usually do not occur in the absence of negligence; hence a jury could find the defendant negligent even without much evidence beyond the fact of the accident itself. Given the complexities of computers and the state of the art of computer science and the computer industry, one cannot say that errors usually do not occur in the absence of negligence. On the other hand, should programming for particular applications become so commonplace and straightforward that errors usually arise only in the case of negligence, then the doctrine might apply. The doctrine now applies to trains and to planes.

In determining whether the defendants violated the standard of care, a court will look at the adequacy of the testing and debugging. The contract should spell out the relative responsibilities for these functions; if the programmer satisfied the contract specifications for them, he may not be negligent. But because of his greater expertise, he may have a duty to test beyond minimal specifications for such an important project. Not only must the programmer test the program sufficiently, he must test it correctly. He may be responsible for insuring that when he wrote the program he had sufficient knowledge of the usage of the program. Of course, gross mistakes would create liability. But under the negligence test the programmer is not an insurer. Because of the fallibility of men and machines, the mere presence of some error would not prove negligence. This is especially true when the error is latent, defying discovery by test or practical application until the fatal moment.

The programmer may have a duty to warn the client as to the limitations of the program, including the possibility of error. This may be especially true here, where the company warranted that the program was totally free of errors. Accountants, in issuing limited certifications, warn their clients and the public of the reliability of their opinions, and it is this warning which leads courts to accept the disclaimers as legally effective against liability in tort as well as in contract. This warning must be specific and explicit, particularly since the customer may have insufficient expertise to evaluate on his own the reliability of the program. Courts have pierced limited certifications by accountants to impose on them liability for negligence when the warning simply cautioned that the reports were "unaudited."

In addition, the programmer may have a duty to provide adequate safeguards against error in the program or machine malfunction. Failure to provide these protections may be a violation of the duty of care.

4. Absence of Affirmative Defense

Where the application is novel and complex, as it may be for air traffic control, use of a computer at all by the customer may be an assumption of the risk. One writer has so suggested. But such a rule would tend to discourage the introduction of computers to new and potentially useful areas of endeavor. Where the computer's role has been planned carefully, use of a computer would probably not amount to an assumption of risk.

Contributory negligence offers more promise to the defendant company. The customer may have failed to inform the programmer completely and accurately as to his particular needs, and this failure may have caused a deficiently designed program to be produced. He may have neglected to notify the programmer of material changes in conditions that would warrant revision of the program. The data which he supplied the programmer may be erroneous or out of date. He may have relied insufficiently on computers in doing his work, so that his human capabilities were pushed too far for him to catch the program error before it could cause harm. He may have relied on computers to too great a degree, so that the essential human traits of judgment, intuition, and abstract reasoning were negligently underemployed. He may not have fulfilled his duty to have backup systems, and he may have negligently ignored an obvious error before acting on it. The company need not warn about obvious errors, but the customer may have no duty to inspect for latent errors. If the company can establish any of these sets of facts, it may be able to block or reduce its liability.

5. Proximate Cause

Liability for negligence is predicated upon a causal connection between the negligence alleged as the wrong and the injury of which complaint is made. Except where the requirement is abrogated or modified by statute, the common law refers the alleged injury to the proximate cause in determining tort liability for negligence. The existence of merely some causal relation or connection between a negligent act and an injury is not sufficient to satisfy the legal requirements for negligence liability. Negligence, regardless of its form, will not give rise to a right of action unless it is the proximate cause of the injury in question. Delineating the contours of proximate cause is a difficult task. What is said to be perhaps the best, as well as the most widely quoted definition is that the proximate cause of an injury is that cause which, in natural and continuous sequence, unbroken by any efficient, intervening cause, produces the injury, and without which the result would not have occurred.

The programmer's error may be too remote for imposition of liability on him if the negligent acts of others intervene before the crash occurs. The customer's contributory negligence may be a sufficient intervening cause in an action by victims of the crash. In addition, it is conceivable that government regulation could intervene. This argument seems particularly weak here, for no governmental entity appears to regulate the transaction of air traffic control itself. In *Goldberg v. Kollsman Instrument Corp.*, a court imposed strict liability in tort on an airplane manufacturer despite substantial FAA regulation of parts. The opinion did not even refer to governmental regulation.

The programming error could be the proximate cause of the deaths of the passengers and of the destruction of the planes, yet because of independent intervening causes not serve as the proximate cause of death and destruction on the ground.

B. *Strict Liability*

1. Meaning of Strict Liability

The programmer could conceivably satisfy both the reasonable care standard for negligence and the merchantability and fitness for use standards for implied warranties. Yet, an accident may still occur due to the uncertainties of computers and their use. With explicit warranties having lapsed, potential plaintiffs may have available to them only one theory of recovery: strict liability in tort, in its products liability aspect.

Strict liability, if it applies, would render the programmer liable to the user even though he exercised all possible care in the writing and debugging of the program. It is liability without fault. The concept finds its justification in three main ideas. First, since the person responsible for producing a product can reduce his hazards better than can those persons affected by it, public policy suggests that he should have every incentive to reduce the hazards. Second, to the extent that some irreducible chance of harm remains, the producer can more efficiently insure against the harm than can individuals, because he can distribute the cost of insurance among the public as a cost of doing business. Third, strict liability greatly eases the litigation burden of an injured consumer who may be powerless to prove negligence.

2. Would Strict Liability Apply to Programming?

A widely used formulation of the law of products liability is that of the Restatement of Torts:

1. One who sells any product in a defective condition unreasonably dangerous to the user or consumer or to his property is subject to liability for physical harm thereby caused to the ultimate user or consumer, or to his property, if
   a. the seller is engaged in the business of selling such a product, and
   b. it is expected to and does reach the user or consumer without substantial change in the condition in which it is sold.
2. The rule stated in Subsection (1) applies although
   a. the seller has exercised all possible care in the preparation and sale of his product, and
   b. the user or consumer has not bought the product from or entered into any contractual relation with the seller.

This formulation raises the question of whether computer programming is a product or a service, for if it is a service, strict liability would probably not apply. A similar question arose in regard to whether Article 2 of the U.C.C. (sale of goods) applies to computer programming. The tort context involves additional considerations.

In arguing that products liability should apply to programs, one can rely on both policy and analogy. The policies underlying products liability seem fully relevant to defective computer programs. The programmer is usually the only person who can prevent errors, and he can best warn the user of possible problems and the need for backup systems. If he faced strict liability for his mistakes, he would have every incentive to act so as to avoid accidents, and he would have to insure sufficiently to cover the remaining risk. The airline passenger, subway rider, or industrial worker who depends for his safety on the quality of the computer program may not even realize that a computer is controlling his environment. He certainly has no capacity to avoid the harm, and he is an inefficient insurer. Use of a computer in the control of transportation or industrial processes does not represent an unavoidably unsafe activity such as would make strict liability inappropriate. However complex, predictable mechanical operations such as these lack the inherent inexactitude of medical diagnosis, for example, in which context computer programs might not be subject to strict liability.

Analogy, too, provides a rationale for imposing strict liability on programmers. A defective program, it can be said, suffers from defective design. When unreasonably dangerous, a defective design can serve as a basis for imposing strict liability. The "unreasonably dangerous" requirement of Section 402a of the Restatement means that the programmer would not guarantee that his program is capable of causing harm, but rather that it is reasonably safe for its intended use.

After originally endorsing the analogy of defective design, one writer now rejects it. He regards a program not as a product but as a process—something intangible, and therefore an inappropriate subject for imposition of strict liability. But a design is itself intangible. A design for an automobile is as independent of the paper on which it is drawn as is a computer program of the magnetic tape on which it is stored; yet a defective design for a car can clearly serve as a basis for applying strict liability against the designer. The distinction comes in that an automobile design achieves concrete embodiment in the car itself. A computer program has no such physical realization. Whether this difference has sufficient significance to constitute programs a service rather than a product remains for the courts to determine.

On the other hand, computer programming resembles the rendition of services more than it does the manufacture of products. With programming there is no mass production or large body of distant consumers practically unable to trace their injuries to the programmer. Even though ultimately many people may rely on the program indirectly, this fact alone would not necessarily call for strict liability. Many people rely on the reports of accountants, for example, yet accountants are liable to these third persons, if at all, only for their negligence. If a program cannot be taxed as a product usually is, presumably it should not be considered a product for the purposes of strict liability.

This distinction between goods and services has created disagreements in at least one other context as well. Different jurisdictions have reached opposite conclusions on whether a blood transfusion is the sale of goods (blood) or a service for the purpose of imposing strict liability. In some respects software is more like goods than a transfusion; in others it has less resemblance to goods than a transfusion. For example, the operation of transferring a program between buyer and seller signifies the chief business of the seller, while with a transfusion the transaction is merely incidental to the chief business of a hospital, which is clearly the rendition of health care services. On the other hand, with respect to a program, no physical object except the medium on which the product resides changes ownership, as it does with blood. The different facets make the two contexts directly incomparable. The similarities suggest that courts could have a difficult time resolving the question of whether strict liability should apply to programming, and there may indeed be a split in their decisions.

In summary, because a programmer cannot know whether or not strict liability could be applied, he would be well advised to proceed as if it could indeed be imposed. This includes performing the programming with the greatest care and securing maximum insurance coverage.

3. Duty to Warn

Defective design may not be the only possible basis for imposing strict liability on the programmer, assuming it can be imposed at all. Failure to warn or instruct the user with respect to potential damage as to the use of the program may also serve as a ground, even if no bugs remain. To protect himself, the programmer must advise the user both as to the possibility and the impact of errors and as to the limitations of the program. The warnings must go beyond mere notification that at some point something might go wrong. They must serve to keep the program from being unreasonably dangerous by making clear its safe and proper use.

4. Privity

As in other areas of the law, with respect to strict liability the requirement of privity is in the process of disappearing. Thus the programmer or his company may be liable to the persons actually injured as a result of the computer error, as well as to the program's purchaser. In some jurisdictions, however, a distinction still exists between persons for whose use the product was intended and bystanders. The Restatement of Torts states that it expresses no opinion on whether strict liability would protect persons other than users or consumers. Thus a programmer who makes an error in an air traffic control program might be liable for injuries to the passengers but not to the persons on the ground who were also hurt. Nevertheless the trend is toward embracing even bystanders.

IV. Individual Liability of the Programmer

Up to this point the discussion of tort liability has assumed that the programmer and his employer are equally liable. This may not be true. The company may face liability not shared with the programmer, and the programmer may be liable to his company for all the damages it has had to pay because of his error.

An employer is responsible for the tortious acts of its employee committed within the scope of employment under the settled principle of *respondeat superior*. This is vicarious liability imposed by law without regard to the employer's wrongful acts, if any. It applies to suits for strict liability as well as for negligence. Hence, the programming company would be liable to injured plaintiffs for the programmer's error.

If he were negligent, the employee himself may be directly liable to the plaintiffs for his error as well. This liability rests on the common law duty incumbent upon every person to use due care so that he does not negligently injure another. Since the duty is merely one of due care, the employee presumably would not be directly liable to the plaintiffs under a theory of strict liability.

In negligence cases, a critical question is whether the programmer owes a duty of care to anyone but his employer. If he owes none to the client or the passengers, then he has no liability for their losses. In general, he cannot assume a task and fail to give attention to the necessary consequences of its execution without incurring liability. Courts would probably conclude that where the programmer has independence, has worked closely with the customer, knows the use to which the program will be put and the damages of error, the programmer owes a duty of due care at least to the customer, and probably to injured third persons as well. Hence, he could be liable for negligence. Since his personal assets would probably be small compared to the damages, however, the plaintiffs might seek their whole remedy against his employer instead.

In one situation the plaintiffs might want to sue the programmer along with his company even if they knew he had no assets with which to pay a judgment. By making him a party, the plaintiffs would be able to admit in evidence his statements, if any, under the party admissions exception to the hearsay rule. Without this joinder, the plaintiffs might have difficulty overcoming the hearsay rule in some jurisdictions.

The company itself may choose to implead the programmer, that is to say, bring him into the suit as a third party defendant, in order to sue him for indemnity. Indemnity is a right which inures to a person who has discharged a duty owed by him but which, as between himself and, another, should have been discharged by the other. Unless the programmer has explicitly provided otherwise in his contract with the company, he may be liable for the payments made by the company to the plaintiffs as a result of his negligence. Under common law an employee owes his employer the duty of exercising a reasonable degree of skill, care, and judgment in the performance and discharge of the duties of his employment. If he violates that duty he has to compensate his employer, even if the damage to the employer is in the form of a judgment against it for injuries sustained by a third person on account of the employee's negligence. Again, since the duty is one of reasonable care, the employee may not be liable under a strict liability theory. In either case, if the employee-programmer is liable, the amount of the liability may be considerable. Hence, the programmer may wish to bargain with his employer at the outset of employment or assignment to a specific task for a limitation on his obligation to indemnify his employer for damages resulting from errors in the programs he writes.

V. Conclusion

Persons who supply computer programs or programming services to others have become increasingly concerned about their exposure to liability when such programs fail to function properly. It appears inevitable that eventually a program will malfunction causing harm and that suit will be brought. This article has set forth a number of approaches to ascertaining legal responsibility for such harm. It has also suggested some means to specifically allocate the risks of such occurrence among the parties at the outset of the transaction or relationship.

11. "Multi-Programming" Computer Litigation

Marvin N. Benn and Wayne H. Michaels

THE COMPUTER IS a recent phenomenon. The first digital computer was completed just forty years ago; the first commercially built system, the Univac I, was delivered to the Bureau of the Census in 1951. Originally, computers were considered to be tools for large bureaucracies and, even throughout the 1960s, they were so mammoth, complex and expensive that only the largest corporations were able to use them.

During the last two decades, advances in logic, storage and microtechnologies have engendered a new breed of computers that are smaller, simpler, more versatile and much less expensive. Consequently, electronic data processing has reached a vast new market— that of small businesses. Computer sales and the entire computer industry have grown exponentially.

An adjunct of this expansion has been the phenomenal rise in the number of suits brought against computer vendors by disgruntled customers. This is due partly to the sheer increase in the number of computer users but is also attributable to the psychology of the small computer purchaser, who usually has had little, if any, first-hand experience with computers and who views them as unfathomable alien creatures.

Because the typical buyer cannot conceptualize the uses of the computer to his or her particular business, the buyer is almost totally dependent upon the computer manufacturer. The purchaser places inordinate reliance upon the computer system vendor, who instills in the purchaser the belief that the entire system will plug together and operate like a sophisticated home stereo system. The purchaser not only fails to comprehend the capabilities and limitations of the equipment, but also neglects to consider the consequences of equipment malfunction.

Thus, there exists a situation in which vendors in a young, extremely competitive industry are attempting to market highly sophisticated new equipment to customers who hardly understand what they want or need, except that they need a computer. The problem is exacerbated because the vendor must turn over the equipment quickly before further technological advances make it obsolete and valueless.

The new hardware may be marketed before its reliability is established. The software may be unproven, especially since each customer's software package is, to some extent, unique. The inevitable result has been a proliferation of disenchanted, frustrated customers and a concomitant flood of law suits involving the electronic data processing industry.

Not every case of computer error or buyer dissatisfaction is necessarily the fault of the vendor or the equipment; it simply may be the product of the purchaser's unrealistic expectations or carelessness in purchasing. Nevertheless, presuming the likelihood, or at least the possibility, of vendor fault, this article will examine how the unhappy computer

---

From *Chicago Bar Record* 64, 1 (July–August 1982), pp. 32–47. Notes deleted. Reprinted by permission of the Chicago Bar Association and Marvin N. Benn and Wayne H. Michaels.

system user can "multi-program" computer litigation—that is, maximize the potential for recovery by taking advantage of all the available causes of action.

Scenario

This scenario is typical of the situation that ends in litigation. A small merchant watches the company grow to the point where the manual bookkeeping system has become cumbersome and inadequate. The merchant decides it is time to invest in a small computer that will keep pace with, and even contribute to, the company's growth.

Some preliminary investigation reveals the exciting potential of electronic data processing. The merchant discovers that the computer system can not only maintain a general ledger, but also keep track of the accounts payable and accounts receivable and perform all billing functions. When the sale of an item is entered into the computer, it can simultaneously create a bill of lading, warehouse packing slip and invoice, adjust the inventory and update the customer's account and accounts receivable. The system also can manage the payroll for fifty employees, maintain customer lists and generate almost any type of sales summary or other report or analysis the merchant desires. When several terminals are used, various functions can be performed simultaneously. While one person enters sales orders, another can do the payroll and other billing. Thus, in computer terminology, the merchant can have an "on-line," "interactive," "multi-programmable" system.

After talking with several computer system vendors, the merchant selects one manufacturer which has represented that the merchant's computer needs can be handled quickly and easily by modifying Computer Company's existing base software programs. Without considering the risks of computer failure, and without consulting an attorney, the merchant decides to purchase the equipment recommended by the vendor and promptly signs standard form contracts for the hardware, firmware and application software programs.

The hardware is delivered, along with the first two programs. The merchant sends two employees to the manufacturer for training in the system's operation. They have had no previous experience with computers .but the manufacturer assures them that if they can type they will be able to operate the system after the preparatory course. They return to their company and for the next several months they convert and enter data into the computer system. Meanwhile, the manufacturer's salesman has convinced the merchant to "de-activate" each parallel manual system as the corresponding accounting function is brought "on-line."

Things begin to go wrong. Only one terminal works at a time. Response times degrade from a few seconds to five minutes. Data entered into the machine vanishes. Hours of work are wasted. Sales reports take eight hours of computer time to generate and do not balance or correspond with the general ledger. The merchant is forced to add office personnel to operate the computer. The inventory software package does not work at all. The payroll package is often inaccurate. Some of the software is never delivered at all.

Since the parallel manual recording methods have been discontinued the consequences are disastrous. The data entered into the computer cannot be retrieved, or if it can, it is not dependable. Having lost track of the inventory, the merchant has difficulty shipping goods. Some customer payments are lost, and customer billing cannot be done accurately. Inventory skyrockets. The business begins to lose customers who are upset because of unsatisfactory service. Receivables begin to rise. The employees spend most of their time trying to get the computer to work. They become overworked and disenchanted, and some quit. The business deteriorates and, perhaps, even goes under.

The merchant is disillusioned and angry. The vendor's sales and service personnel, along with its programmers, have worked diligently with the merchant in an attempt to get the machine to operate properly. The vendor has persuaded the merchant to purchase additional hardware and software items to solve the problems.

Nevertheless, the problems continue and new ones appear. The vendor still insists that there is nothing wrong with the system, and contends that the fault lies with the operators. The merchant, however, no longer believes it. Realizing the computer simply does not work, the merchant refuses to pay any more money on the contract and the vendor threatens to sue for nonpayment. Finally, the merchant calls an attorney. What options are available?

Caveat

Although litigation is not necessarily to be avoided at all costs, generally it is a last resort. The old adage that an ounce of prevention is worth a pound of cure holds true here. The two most effective safeguards against disaster are: care in purchasing the system, including sufficient education to enable the merchant to develop realistic expectations regarding what the computer will and will not be able to do; and care in negotiating a favorable contract. If a dispute later arises, it may be resolved by an agreement for a partial refund or trade-in, or by arbitration.

This article assumes that all options have been considered and the best, and perhaps only, available alternative is a law suit, and considers the potential causes of action available to the dissatisfied customer.

Fraudulent Misrepresentation

The major advantage to bringing an action for fraudulent misrepresentation is that it avoids many of the limitations normally imposed by the parties' contract. Whereas potential contractual remedies may be thwarted by limitations of liability and disclaimer clauses in the contract, such clauses will not defeat an action for fraudulent misrepresentation.

For instance, an integration clause disavowing all prior representations not incorporated into the written agreement will not relieve the vendor of liability if those representations fraudulently induced the buyer to enter into the contract.

A cause of action for fraud, or deceit, will lie if the following elements are present:

A material misrepresentation, usually of fact, made by the vendor
Vendor's knowledge that the representation was false, or lack of a sufficient basis of information to have made the statement, i.e., the vendor should have known that the representation was false
Intent to induce the plaintiff to rely upon the misrepresentation
Justifiable reliance by the plaintiff upon the representation of the vendor, and
Resulting damage to the plaintiff.

This cause of action presupposes that the computer system vendor's agent knowingly made material false representations to induce the buyer to enter into a purchasing contract. Fraud in the inducement is not committed by mere statements of opinion or sales "puffing," but requires material misrepresentations of fact.

For example, the vendor may represent that the computer system has certain qualities or capabilities that in fact it does not have. In *Clements Auto Company v. Service Bureau Corporation*, a Minnesota district court found the following to be actionable false statements by the vendor's sales representative: the only way that the purchaser could obtain inventory control was by automating the business' accounting; controls built into the automated accounting system were adequate to prevent all but a minimum number of errors; and ironclad controls insured accurate reports.

The vendor may represent that the customer's needs can be met easily by simple modifications of existing vendor software programs when in fact the programs do not exist, or, if they exist, do not work. The vendor may falsely represent that the computer is capable of performing to certain specifications of response time, multi-programmability, or storage capacity.

The misrepresentation may consist of an omission of material fact. For example, a court might find fraud in a vendor's failure to disclose that other customers have had serious problems with the operation of computer systems substantially similar to that proposed for this customer.

In *Strand v. Librascope, Inc.*, a Michigan district court held that the computer vendor committed deceit by not completely disclosing the state of development of a new product. The *Strand* court stated that fairness required complete disclosure by the manufacturer to avoid misimpressions, particularly where the plaintiff was forced to rely on the expertise of the vendor, which had necessary information in its exclusive possession.

Another important advantage to the cause of action for deceit is the avoidance of any statute of limitations imposed by written agreement. Whereas the statutory limitations period for an action on a written contract may run as long as ten years, the vendor's contract normally will provide for a much shorter period, ordinarily two years, within which the user must bring an action based upon the written agreement. This clause will be upheld by the courts.

The cause of action will be deemed to have accrued at the time of breach, which may be regarded as the time of delivery. The purchaser, encouraged by the vendor, believes that the system must work and may spend many months, perhaps years, attempting to get the system to function properly. By the time the futility of this attempt becomes apparent, the limitations clause may bar any suit on that contract. A tort action may not be precluded, since it does not arise out of the agreement itself. In Illinois the statute of limitations for fraud is five years.

An action for fraudulent misrepresentation also has significant advantages with respect to recoverable damages. Whereas the vendor contract inevitably will impose severe limitations upon the type and amount of damages recoverable by the customer in an action on the contract, no such limitations will apply to the deceit action. Moreover, even if the contract does not effectively limit the amount of damages, contract law restricts recovery to damages that were reasonably foreseeable.

A judgment in tort for fraud, however, permits an award of all proximately caused damages, which increases the possibility of recovering speculative damages. For example, in *Consolidated Data Terminals v. Applied Digital Data Systems, Inc.*, a federal district court, finding a consequential damages provision inapplicable to design defects, awarded the plaintiff three years worth of lost profits.

In preparation for litigation, the plaintiff should estimate all damages. All payments to vendors or lessors under the contract are covered, including interest, penalties and other financing charges. Additionally, the plaintiff should consider the following as damages:

The cost of the equipment's environment and site preparation, including space rental, electricity, electrical wiring, air conditioning units, power filters, and humidifiers

Labor and management costs, including employee training time, preparation of the system, conversion of procedures, time spent attempting to program the system, make it work, correct defects, rewrite defective reports and run parallel systems

Wasted expenditures for supplies, consultants

Business losses, including lost profits, loss of goodwill, loss of anticipated savings in office time and labor, loss of disgruntled personnel

Unfavorable tax consequences of early disposition of the equipment.

If the court finds especially onerous misconduct, it may award punitive damages. This can be the most substantial portion of the plaintiff's recovery. In *The Glovatorium, Inc. v. NCR Corp.*, a California district court characterized the defendant's conduct as "utter and knowing and in deliberate disregard of its responsibility" to its customer, whose company's very survival depended on the defendant's product. The court awarded the plaintiff three days worth of the defendant's profits ($2 million) as punitive damages. This award was eight times the award for compensatory damages.

Finally, in the proper case, the plaintiff also may recover attorney's fees, which are not inconsequential in these cases.

The defendant's risk of incurring such substantial penalties for losing an action for fraud has the advantage to the plaintiff of encouraging a favorable settlement. At the least, it adds force to the plaintiff's claim and increases the psychological strength of its position.

Naturally, the fraud is not likely to be discovered by the purchaser until long after the equipment problems surface. However, if there is reasonable justification for believing that the defendant has misrepresented its products, a fraud count should be included in the plaintiff's complaint. If actual proof of fraud exists, it should be discoverable by an attorney who has an understanding of data processing systems and vendors. Conversely, although fraud may not be alleged initially, discovery may reveal enough evidence of fraud to justify amending the complaint.

Negligent Misrepresentation

The vendor's false representations may be merely negligent rather than fraudulent. Plaintiff can bring action for negligent misrepresentation if there is insufficient evidence of fraud or as an alternative to a fraud count. A representation may be negligent, although made with an honest belief in its truth "because of lack of reasonable care in ascertaining the facts, or in the manner of expression, or absence of the skill and competence required by a particular business or profession."

The success of this cause of action may vary from state to state. Some states do not acknowledge the doctrine at all. Although Illinois recognizes a cause of action for negligent misrepresentation, it is not certain that economic damages, as opposed to compensation for personal injury, are recoverable on this claim.

Illinois appellate courts are divided on the issue. In *Moorman Manufacturing Co. v. National Tank Co.*, the fourth district court of appeals recently held in a products liability case that economic losses are recoverable under the tort theories of strict liability, misrepresentation and negligence. On the other hand, the first and second district appellate courts have reached the opposite conclusion. The conflict may soon be resolved by the Supreme Court of Illinois, which is now reviewing the appellate court decision in *Moorman*.

If an action for negligent misrepresentation is allowed for economic loss, then the plaintiff will be entitled to all consequential damages, both special and general, as in any other negligence case. However, because negligence lacks the requisite element of aggravation, wantonness or evil motive, punitive damages will not be recoverable.

Deceptive Business Practices

In addition to the common law, certain statutory remedies may be available to the disgruntled buyer. Illinois, for example, has enacted the Consumer Fraud and Deceptive Business Practices Act, which prohibits:

> [u]nfair methods of competition and unfair or deceptive acts or practices, including but not limited to the use or employment of any deception, fraud, false pretense, false promise, misrepresentation or the concealment, suppression or omission of any material fact, with intent that others rely upon the concealment, suppression or omission of such material fact. . . .

The protection afforded by this statute is quite broad and will be available to most dissatisfied computer users who entered into agreements in reliance upon vendor misrepresentations. The statute merely requires that the misrepresentation be made with the intent that the customer rely upon it. It does not require that the vendor knew or should have known that the representation was false. Furthermore, such misrepresentation is actionable "whether any person has in fact been misled, deceived or damaged thereby."

Since consumer fraud statutes vary among states, the buyer's attorney is advised to carefully examine the statutes of each potential forum to determine their applicability to the particular case. In Montana, the plaintiff must have purchased the goods for personal use to be availed of the statute, whereas in Illinois, merchants and businessmen are embraced by the Act.

Moreover, statutes of limitations vary, usually between one and three years. Certain state statutes also contain additional provisions or requirements with which the plaintiff must comply. In Texas, for example, the plaintiff must provide the defendant with thirty days written notice of complaint prior to filing suit as a precondition to recovering treble damages and attorney's fees.

The elements of recoverable damages also vary from state to state, but generally actual damages can be recouped. The Illinois consumer fraud statute authorizes the court in its discretion to award actual damages "or any other relief which the court deems proper." Attorney's fees also may be available to the plaintiff or the statute can authorize the court in the proper case to award attorney's fees and costs to the defendant.

On the whole, an action under a consumer fraud and deceptive business practices statute is probably the best option available. Misrepresentations may be actionable under such a statute although no deceitful intent is attributable to the vendor. Contractual limitations can be bypassed without having to produce the degree of proof necessary to establish fraud. Although punitive damages may not be available, the plaintiff potentially can recover all actual damages and reasonable attorney's fees and costs.

Breach of Contract

The most obvious, but perhaps least helpful, legal theory of liability against the computer system vendor is that of breach of contract. In evaluating this theory of liability (and that of breach of warranty, discussed below), initial consideration must be given to the applicability of the Uniform Commercial Code (UCC).

Assuming that the transaction is a sale and not a lease, there remains the question of whether the subject matter of the contract is "goods" within the meaning of Article 2. Clearly, a sale of computer hardware is embraced by the statute. On the other hand, a transaction concerning software services alone would not be governed by the UCC, although the products of those services, such as computer tapes and reports, may constitute goods. Where the transaction involves the sale of software in conjunction with the sale of hardware, the courts generally have viewed the agreement as a sale of a complete "turn-key" system, and have applied Article 2.

If the equipment delivered does not work at all, or hardly works, the customer may claim that there has been a material breach of contract and sue for rescission. The breach must be significant, amounting to substantial lack of consideration or fraud. Because rescission normally is accompanied by restitution on both sides, the user must shut down the system and tender all of the equipment back to the vendor. He or she then should be able to recover, in addition to all monies paid for the equipment, incidental and consequential damages. Thus rescission is an attractive remedy.

Unless the computer system is virtually useless from the beginning, however, rescission may not be a viable option. In most cases, the system's operational defects only reveal themselves with time. Typically, the user and vendor attempt to correct the problems as they are discovered over a period of months. The user frequently does not recognize that the system is substantially defective and expects the bugs to be ironed out shortly. By the time the extent of the system's failure becomes apparent, it is difficult for the user to free the business from dependence on the system.

Moreover, since the user often has such a substantial emotional investment in the system, there is a reluctance to pull the plug. Additionally, the user may not be satisfied merely with recovery of consequential damages, particularly if fraud is evident. Finally, rescission may be precluded altogether by the presence of a third-party financing agent, whose contract may strictly impair the user's contractual remedies.

Alternatively, the dissatisfied user may wish to affirm the contract and bring an action for damages for breach of contract. Under the UCC, the user may recover the loss from the breach, including incidental and consequential damages. It is extremely likely, however, that a written contract, particularly a vendor's form contract, will severely restrict such recovery.

Breach of Warranty

The dissatisfied customer may have two distinct warranty actions under the Uniform Commercial Code, one for breach of an express warranty, the other for breach of an implied warranty.

An express warranty can be created by written statements contained in the contract, and by any affirmation of fact or promise, description of the goods, sample or model that is made part of the basis of the bargain. There need be no intent to create a warranty. An oral representation will suffice, so long as the statement is not merely the seller's opinion or commendation or an affirmation of the value of the goods.

Unfortunately, the vendor's contract typically will contain an integration clause effectively nullifying any prior commitments or representations of the vendor and its agents, and making the written contract the entire and exclusive agreement between the parties. Generally the purchaser will find few express warranties in the written agreement itself other than a provision warranting that the equipment will be installed in good working order and will be free from defects in material and workmanship for a period of one year.

Most likely, even this warranty will be mitigated by an additional provision such as: "Vendor does not guarantee that the programs will operate in the combinations selected by the purchaser, or will meet the purchaser's requirements." The contract may contain something like: "The purchaser agrees to accept responsibility for the equipment's selection to achieve the purchaser's intended results, its use, and the results obtained therefrom." Thus, any express warranties very likely will be narrowly circumscribed by other contractual provisions.

The unhappy customer can have an action for breach of an implied warranty of merchantability which ordinarily rests upon the equipment's lack of fitness for the "*ordinary* purpose for which such goods are used."

Breach of this warranty may be found in a system's repeated failures and unreliable operation or its inability to withstand normal shocks. The warranty can be repudiated, however, as long as the disclaimer is conspicuous and mentions merchantability.

The warranty of fitness for a particular purpose usually applies as well. The data processing equipment vendor is well aware of the particular purposes for which the equipment will be used, since such specificity is necessary to assemble an appropriate data processing package. The vendor recognizes "that the buyer is relying on the seller's skill or judgment to select or furnish suitable goods." The warranty is breached by the system's failure to perform its intended functions, or merely by sufficient unreliability. This warranty also may be disavowed by a written, conspicuous disclaimer.

The vendor contract undoubtedly will contain such disclaimer clauses that will undermine any potential action for breach of warranty. A typical vendor agreement will provide:

> There are no other warranties, express or implied, including, but not limited to, the implied warranties of merchantability or fitness for a particular purpose.

Combined with the contract's integration clause, this can effectively eliminate all express and implied warranties. Generally, the courts will enforce these provisions.

Furthermore, the agreement is likely to contain a provision that the customer's exclusive remedy for nonperformance is repair or replacement of the defective equipment. The vendor can further provide that if the vendor cannot put the equipment in working order, then the user shall recover its actual damages—limited, however, to a specific dollar amount. The limit usually is the cost of the equipment, which is clearly insufficient to compensate a user if its business has become insolvent. The user also is likely to find a further limitation of damages such as the following:

> In no event will the vendor be liable for any lost profits or savings or other indirect, special, consequential, or other similar damages arising out of any breach of this agreement or obligations under this agreement.

The limitations clause can go so far as to exclude consequential damages regardless of the form of action, whether in contract or in tort, including negligence. Such disclaimers, limitations of liability and exclusive remedy clauses are permissible under the UCC.

These provisions can be avoided if they can be proven unconscionable under UCC sections 2-302 and 2-719(3). Courts seldom strike such clauses for unconscionability, however, and the plaintiff's burden of proof is particularly high in cases of business users. Courts generally regard them as commercially sophisticated, despite their inexperience with computers.

It is possible to sidestep certain disclaimer and limitation clauses by using UCC section 2-719(2). This section provides that notwithstanding an exclusive or limited remedy provision in the sales contract, other UCC remedies can become available to the plaintiff if the limited remedy provision "fails of its essential purpose." For example, if the vendor cannot cure the system's defects within a reasonable time, then the "repair or replace" provision may be avoided, and the user should recover incidental and consequential damages.

However, if the contract contains separate clauses disclaiming warranties and limiting liability for consequential damages, then the failure of the exclusive remedy provision will not automatically nullify the other disclaimers and limitations clauses.

Lanham Act

A new, still unproven theory of recovery that nevertheless deserves consideration by the unhappy computer user is a claim arising out of section 43(a) of the Lanham Act. Section 43(a) creates a federal statutory cause of action for false designations of origin and false descriptions of goods and services in interstate commerce.

To state a claim under section 43(a), there must be a false designation of origin or a false description or representation used in connection with one's goods or services. It is not necessary to prove intent to deceive. The misrepresentation must be material, but need not be literal—the creation of a false impression is actionable. The description or representation must be likely to cause confusion or to deceive. Actual public deception also is a prerequisite to the recovery of monetary damages.

Section 43(a) closely parallels the state statutory action for deceptive business practices. The purchaser should allege that the vendor's false representations or descriptions of its goods and services deceived him or her and caused damage by inducing him or her to enter into a contract for the defective goods and services.

One possible advantage of this action is that it opens the door to federal court if the plaintiff otherwise would be restricted to state court because of a lack of diversity. Note that although section 43(a) is part of the federal Trademark Act, this section does not require that the vendor have a trademark. This section is, in effect, a federal fraud statute.

Another advantage to a section 43(a) claim is that there is no statute of limitations. However, the action might be barred under the equitable doctrine of laches.

The remedies available under this statute are diverse. In the proper case, the plaintiff may obtain an injunction against further violations. More applicable here, the plaintiff also may recover any damages sustained, the defendant's profits from the sale of the misrepresented goods or services, and costs of the action. The court, in its discretion, can also award treble damages and attorney's fees. Obviously, section 43(a) could be a powerful weapon in computer litigation.

There is an important drawback to this cause of action. As mentioned above, it is unproven against data processing vendors. Section 43(a) has been used primarily by competitors who have been harmed by the false advertising of others, and the statute traditionally has been so limited. Although the courts generally have construed section 43(a) broadly, they have had difficulty with the clause that confers standing upon "any person who believes that he is or is likely to be damaged by such false description or representation."

A literal reading of the statute would mean that consumers have standing to sue under this section. However, although the issue has not been addressed often, the weight of authority has been to preclude consumer standing to sue under section 43(a). Some commentators have criticized the courts' denial of consumer standing, arguing that the legislative and judicial history of the statute indicates an intent to grant standing to consumers. To date only one court specifically has held that consumers have such standing. The applicability of section 43(a) to claims against the computer industry is now just being tested in courts throughout the country.

Conclusion

There are numerous causes of action potentially available to the dissatisfied computer system user. Remedies may be afforded by common law contract and tort doctrines, the Uniform Commercial Code, and state and federal deceptive practices statutes. As in any case, the user's attorney should be aware of all potential remedies, and should analyze the facts of each case to determine which causes of action are applicable and available.

It is most helpful if the attorney already has a thorough understanding of computer components, operations and vernacular. This knowledge enables the attorney to come to a deeper understanding of the basis of the lawsuit, i.e., what was promised, what went wrong and why. Familiarity with the technical aspects of the subject matter of the litigation will allow the attorney to intelligently and productively question witnesses and experts, examine documentation and evidence, and present the case at trial.

There are, of course, other litigation decisions to be made besides selecting causes of action. For example, the advisability of demanding a jury, the desirability of expert testimony, and the most advantageous forum all must be considered. Even before filing suit, discovery and settlement strategies must be decided. In an extreme case, the consequences of bankruptcy should be explored.

Whatever decisions are made must be made quickly. Unlike most lawsuits filed after the fact, a user's difficulties with a computer system are likely to continue while relief is sought. Computerization of a small business has been likened to a heart transplant; the result is the company's dependence upon the computer for its very life. If the computer does not work, and relief is not obtained quickly, the business may die.

It is hoped that the computer industry, like some emerging industries of the past, will soon be self-regulating. Meanwhile, it is up to the consumers to protect themselves. If a law suit becomes necessary, the consumer should use every available remedy.

12. Negligence: Liability for Defective Software
Jim Prince

THE COMPUTER HAS come of age in the land of the consumer. The use of electronic data processing continues to grow not only in traditional applications but also in areas not previously considered. As the use of computers becomes more widespread, more injuries will be caused by defects in the computers and the related computer programs. For example, it is foreseeable that computers will be used by consumers in a variety of ways, such as controlling the environment within a home. A defect in the program controlling the humidity within a home could cause the humidifier to fill the house with excess moisture, thereby damaging it.

The typical computer system consists of three elements: the hardware, the data, and the software. The hardware is the machine, the actual computer. The data is the information to be processed. In the case of a computer system to control the humidity in a home, the data would include the humidity level at which the home is theoretically to be kept and input from sensors informing the system of the actual humidity in the home. The software is the computer program that tells the machine what to do with the data. A defect in any of the elements of the system could cause the system to damage the home as described. Injuries resulting from defective computer systems have already arisen. However, no court has yet considered the imposition of strict liability in tort against a supplier of defective software.

Section 402A of the *Restatement [Second] of Torts* provides: "One who sells any product in a defective condition, unreasonably dangerous to the user or consumer or to his property . . ." shall be subject to liability regardless of the amount of care the seller has exercised. The definition of the word "product" is a limitation on the doctrine of strict tort, *i.e.*, strict tort should be applied to suppliers of products but should not be applied to suppliers of items that are not products.

This note will discuss the propriety of applying strict liability in tort to a case of injury

From *Oklahoma Law Review* 33 (1980), pp. 848–855. Notes deleted. Reprinted by permission of the *Oklahoma Law Review*.

caused by defective computer software. This will be accomplished by defining the basic public policy considerations that underlie the imposition of strict liability to any product; then, based on these policy considerations, determining whether strict liability should be imposed on the supplier of defective software. This note will not discuss the possibility of imposing liability for injuries caused by defective hardware. It also will not include any analysis of the current state of the law of products liability regarding economic loss caused by defective products.

What Is a "Product"?

There is a tendency to assume that the word "product" refers only to chattels. This inference results because the theory of strict liability in tort arose from the combined areas of negligence and contractual warranty. Section 402A of the *Restatement [Second] of Torts* is found under the chapter headed "Liability for Suppliers of Chattels." If the definition of "product" is confined to chattels, this note could be concluded at this point. Intangible items are not chattels and computer programs in the form in which they are used are electronic impulses which, of course, are not tangible. The only tangible evidence of the program is the media in which the program is transported, *i.e.*, the punched cards, magnetic tape, or magnetic discs on which the program is stored. If such a restricted definition of "product" is used, the result is that since computer software is not a chattel, strict liability in tort should not be applied. However, a review of recent decisions indicates that the courts have expanded the definition of "product" beyond chattels. For example, application of the doctrine of strict liability in tort has been expanded to such nonchattels as real property, leases of real property, leases of personal property, energy, and certain service transactions. Indeed, the Oklahoma Supreme Court, in electing to adopt the doctrine of strict liability, stated that the doctrine should be referred to as manufacturer's products liability and should be imposed on all manufacturers, processors, assemblers, and all who were similarly situated. The proper conclusion to be drawn from these results is that the application of the doctrine of strict liability in tort should not be based on a dictionary definition.

A definition of "product," consistent with the case law applying strict liability to suppliers, can be developed by analyzing the policy considerations that underlie the application of strict liability to the supplier of any item. Generally, when courts are required to determine the scope of strict liability in tort, *i.e.*, when the court is asked to expand the scope, they consider the following policies.

1. The stream of commerce policy. The supplier must have placed the product in the stream of commerce and made it available for use by the general public in order to come within this rationale. When the supplier places his product in the stream of commerce, he should be liable for any injury caused by a defect in the product. There are two reasons for placing liability on the supplier. The first reason is that he has placed the product in the stream of commerce in order to earn a profit. Public policy requires that because the supplier has placed the product in the market to earn a profit, he should bear the risk of loss of injury. The second reason for holding the supplier strictly liable when he places his product in the stream of commerce is that the supplier has invited the public to use his product by making it available to the public in general. Implicit in this invitation is an assurance that the product is safe. Public policy requires that the consumer's expectation regarding the product's safeness be protected.

2. The position to control risks rationale. The supplier, because of his association with the product and his presumed knowledge of the product, is in a better position to anticipate and control the risks of harm. As a result, the supplier is in a better position to determine if the product is safe enough for use by the public. Because of this presumed judgmental capacity of the supplier, public policy requires that he be held liable for any injury that results when the product is not safe.

3. The cost-spreading rationale. The supplier of a product should be held strictly liable when he is in a better position than the user to spread the cost of the injury. The supplier is able to spread the cost of an injury when the product is sold to a number of users and the supplier is able to adjust the price at which he sells the product to cover the cost of the injury. In effect, the cost of the injury is made a cost of the product. In this way the cost of the injury is spread over all the buyers of the product.

This list of policy considerations is not totally inclusive, but it does include the rationales commonly used by courts considering the expansion of the scope of strict liability beyond chattels. In effect, these policy considerations answer the question: On whom and for what reasons should strict liability be imposed? The previously cited cases that expand the scope of strict liability illustrate this consideration of the underlying public policy rationales. For example, the New Jersey Supreme Court, in *Schipper v. Levitt & Sons, Inc.*, found a mass-produced home builder strictly liable for an injury to the plaintiff caused by a defectively designed home built by the defendant. The reason given for extending strict liability in this case is that the pertinent overriding policy considerations are the same for a mass producer of homes as they are for a mass producer of automobiles. Similarly, in *Cintrone v. Hertz*, a lessor of automobiles was held liable for a breach of an implied warranty when a defect in a leased vehicle caused an injury to the plaintiff. The reason given for imposing liability was that the defendant/lessor had placed the product in the stream of commerce. The defendant had, by placing the product in the stream of commerce, created the risk of harm and reaped a profit from so placing the product. In *Ransome v. Wisconsin Electric Power Co.*, the supplier of electricity was held strictly liable when electricity it furnished was defective and caused injury. The Supreme Court of Wisconsin stated that the policy considerations underlying the rule of strict liability mandate that electricity be considered a product.

Moreover, in addition to these cases expanding the scope of strict liability in tort, the rationales of courts refusing to expand the scope also justify the use of the underlying policy considerations as a basis for defining "product." For example, in *La Rossa v. Scientific Design Co.*, the court refused to hold the defendant strictly liable for a defectively designed chemical plant because the defendant's action was highly specialized and there was no impact on the public at large. The Scientific Design Company engineered the design of the chemical plant; its design was produced specifically for La Rossa's employer and was not made available to the public at large. Similarly, in *Immergluck v. Ridgeview House, Inc.*, the Illinois Supreme Court cited the lack of a basis for the underlying policy consideration as its reason for refusing to apply strict liability to a nursing home operator. In *Dwyer v. Skyline Apartments*, the New Jersey Superior Court refused to hold a landlord liable in strict tort for a defective dwelling because he was not engaged in the mass production of such dwellings and was not in a better position than the plaintiff/consumer to know about and correct the condition. These cases show that it is the underlying policy considerations that should be used to define the items to which strict liability in tort should be applied.

Therefore, a proper definition of "product" for purposes of imposing strict liability in tort must be based on policy considerations. That is, any item to which the policy considerations apply is a "product" within the purview of strict liability in tort.

The criteria common to each of the public policy considerations is that each is concerned not with the product itself but with the manner in which the product reaches the consumer. In other words, the policies are concerned with the manner in which the supplier is situated in the market. For instance, the stream of commerce consideration requires that the seller make his product available to the general public. The seller then is situated as a supplier to the general public. The position to control risks theory presumes that the supplier is in a better position to have knowledge of and to control the risks created by his product. This presumption is made because the seller is situated in a position of control over the product. Finally, the loss-spreading theory requires that the seller of the product be in a better position to bear the cost of any injury caused by his product. A seller would be in a favorable position to bear such costs because of the place in which he is situated in the market. His position as seller allows him to set the price at which his product is offered. As a result, he can set the price at a level that will enable him to spread the cost of injury over all buyers of the product. Therefore, in determining if strict liability in tort should be imposed on a supplier, emphasis must be placed on examining the relationship of the supplier and the user in the marketplace, in effect, the manner in which the product is distributed.

Is Software a Product?

Should strict tort liability be applied to suppliers of defective software? This determination will be based on the applicability of the underlying policy considerations to the methods by which computer software is supplied. A general application of the policy considerations to computer software can be achieved by analyzing the relationship between the supplier, the market, and the consumer.

The manner in which computer software is distributed is analogous to the market for a suit of clothing. There are generally three modes by which the item reaches the consumer. First, the consumer may have a suit specifically tailored to fit his exact measurements. Second, the consumer may buy a suit that is already made but which will be altered or modified for him. Finally, the consumer may buy a suit that is ready to wear and to which no alterations will be made. In all three situations the end result is a consumer with a suit of clothing, but the actions of the supplier are quite distinguishable. Likewise, the market for computer software can be analyzed by separating the market into three categorical situations. The first situation is parallel to the purchase of clothing that is completely tailored. In this situation, the software is designed and implemented by the supplier specifically for the customer. Typically, the supplier will make a detailed study of the user's needs, much like a tailor will take detailed measurements of a customer buying a tailored suit. The software is then developed based on the specific needs of the user as determined by the study. Because the software is so specifically tailored to the peculiar needs of the user, it is generally usable only by that user. It is at least limited in application to situations with nearly identical requirements.

The second method of distributing software is the same as the purchase of a ready-to-wear suit. In this situation, no tailoring to the particular user's needs is performed. The same software is sold to any user who wishes to buy it without regard to the peculiarities of the user's needs. An example of such ready-to-use software, sometimes referred to as "canned software," is a software program developed to account for the receivables of a business entity. When the business entity buys the canned software, it fits its procedures, such as the form in which it inputs sales information, to meet the requirements of the software. This is directly opposed to the first situation where the software was tailored to fit the user's requirements. It is similar to the purchase of an automobile where the consumer conforms his actions to the constraints inherent in the car.

A computer program completely tailored to meet a particular user's needs is analogous to a chemical plant designed by an engineer for one particular user, as in *La Rossa v. Scientific Design Co.* In such a situation the item, be it a computer program or a chemical plant, is not really placed in the stream of commerce because it is distributed to only one customer. Also, because the product is only sold to one user, the supplier is not in a better position than the user to bear the costs. Since the supplier is not selling the product en masse, he cannot spread the cost of a defect over a number of consumers. Finally, the supplier may have more expertise and knowledge regarding the tailored program because the supplier wrote the program. However, in these situations the user is normally very heavily involved in the design stage of the program because the user must tell the supplier what the program is to do. Because the underlying policy considerations are not applicable for the most part to programs designed and tailored to meet one particular user's specific needs, strict liability in tort should not be applied to the supplier of these products.

Software that is sold "ready to use," *i.e.*, canned software, represents a method of distribution analogous to the mass distribution of any product. In this situation, the objective is not to design a program for one particular user but to sell the same program to as many consumers as possible. The marketing of home-use computers and the necessary programs is an example of such a method of distribution. The supplier develops a product, a computer program, which can be used by a large number of consumers without any tailoring or modification required. This method of distribution is the same as the mass production and sale of homes to which strict liability in tort was applied in *Schipper v. Levitt & Sons, Inc.* In these situations, the supplier is placing the program into the stream of commerce. If the program is defective, the supplier is creating a risk of harm by placing the program in the stream of commerce, and at the same time, the supplier is earning a profit. Also, the user in this situation typically has very little knowledge of the program. He relies on the supplier's expertise. As a result of the user's lack of knowledge, the supplier is in a better position to anticipate and control the risks. Finally, the supplier is in a better position than the user to bear the cost of an injury caused by the program. The supplier can increase the price for which he sells the program to all consumers and thereby cover the cost of the isolated injury. In effect, all the consumers would bear a part of the cost of the product's defect. Should the cost of the injury require the supplier to raise the price above that at which consumers will buy the product, the product will not be distributed. In this way, the marketplace helps the public determine those risks it is willing to pay for in order to use the product that creates the risk. The underlying policy considerations require that the supplier of computer software be subject to strict liability when the software is distributed through some sort of mass production and selling.

The third method of distributing software may be referred to as a hybrid of the first two. This method consists of the use of generic, *i.e.*, canned, software, which is partially modified for a particular user's needs. This method does not represent a totally individualized design for each user and is similar to products which fit the so-called sales/service transaction. Much discussion has occurred regarding the so-called sales/service transaction, where the transaction consists of two parts: (1) the sale of a product, and (2) the performance of a service. The distribution of partially modified software falls into this category because the providing of the generic software would be the sale of a product and the modification would be the performance of a service. Such a situation is analogous to the sale of prescription contact lenses discussed in *Barbee v. Rodgers*. In that case, the Texas Supreme Court segregated the product from the service, the product being the lenses themselves and the service being the professional acts required to fit the lenses to the individual patient. Since the defect arose from the service portion, which was not a finished product offered to the general public in the regular channels of trade, the policy considerations did not mandate an imposition of strict liability. This kind of reasoning applied to computer software marketed as a hybrid would mean that the policy considerations mandate an imposition of strict liability if a defect is found in the generic software, but if the defect occurred in the modifications made to the generic software, then strict liability should not be imposed.

Conclusion

In summary, it is proper to say that the definition of "product" as it is used in imposing strict liability on suppliers should not be based on the arbitrary definition of "chattels." Rather, as court decisions which have considered expanding the scope of strict liability beyond chattels indicate, the definition of "product" should be based on the public policy considerations that underlie the imposition of strict liability on a supplier. These public policy considerations indicate that it is the manner in which a product is distributed to the user rather than the nature of the product that should control the decisions to impose strict liability. In terms of software, this analysis specifically means that when software is distributed to the public through mass merchandising, strict liability in tort should be an available theory for a consumer who is injured because of a defect in the software. When, however, the software is developed for and distributed only to an individual user, public policy considerations do not mandate that strict liability be imposed on the supplier.

13. Punishment and Responsibility

H.L.A. Hart

Part One: Responsibility

A WIDE RANGE of different, though connected, ideas is covered by the expressions "responsibility," "responsible," and "responsible for," as these are standardly used in and out of the law. Though connections exist between these different ideas, they are often very indirect, and it seems appropriate to speak of different *senses* of these expressions. The following simple story of a drunken sea captain who lost his ship at sea can be told in the terminology of responsibility to illustrate, with stylistically horrible clarity, these differences of sense.

> As captain of the ship, X was responsible for the safety of his passengers and crew. But on his last voyage he got drunk every night and was responsible for the loss of the ship with all aboard. It was rumored that he was insane, but the doctors considered that he was responsible for his actions. Throughout the voyage he behaved quite irresponsibly, and various incidents in his career showed that he was not a responsible person. He always maintained that the exceptional winter storms were responsible for the loss of the ship, but in the legal proceedings brought against him he was found criminally responsible for his negligent conduct, and in separate civil proceedings he was held legally responsible for the loss of life and property. He is still alive and he is morally responsible for the deaths of many women and children.

This welter of distinguishable senses of the word "responsibility" and its grammatical cognates can, I think, be profitably reduced by division and classification. I shall distinguish four heads of classification to which I shall assign the following names:

a. Role-Responsibility
b. Causal-Responsibility
c. Liability-Responsibility
d. Capacity-Responsibility.

I hope that in drawing these dividing lines, and in the exposition which follows, I have avoided the arbitrary pedantries of classificatory systematics, and that my divisions pick out and clarify the main, though not all, varieties of responsibility to which reference is constantly made, explicitly or implicitly, by moralists, lawyers, historians, and ordinary men. . . .

Role-Responsibility

A sea captain is responsible for the safety of his ship, and that is his responsibility, or one of his responsibilities. A husband is responsible for the maintenance of his wife; parents for the upbringing of their children; a sentry for alerting the guard at the enemy's approach; a clerk for keeping the accounts of his firm. These examples of a person's responsibilities

Abridged from H.L.A. Hart, "Postcript: Responsibility and Retribution," in *Punishment and Responsibility: Essays in the Philosophy of Law* (New York: Oxford University Press, 1968), pp. 210–229. Notes deleted. © Oxford University Press 1968. Reprinted by permission of Oxford University Press.

suggest the generalization that, whenever a person occupies a distinctive place or office in a social organization, to which specific duties are attached to provide for the welfare of others or to advance in some specific way the aims or purposes of the organization, he is properly said to be responsible for the performance of these duties, or for doing what is necessary to fulfill them. Such duties are a person's responsibilities. As a guide to this sense of responsibility this generalization is, I think, adequate, but the idea of a distinct role or place or office is, of course, a vague one, and I cannot undertake to make it very precise. Doubts about its extension to marginal cases will always arise. If two friends, out on a mountaineering expedition, agree that the one shall look after the food and the other the maps, then the one is correctly said to be responsible for the food, and the other for the maps, and I would classify this as a case of role-responsibility. Yet such fugitive or temporary assignments with specific duties would not usually be considered by sociologists, who mainly use the word, as an example of a "role." So "role" in my classification is extended to include a task assigned to any person by agreement or otherwise. But it is also important to notice that not all the duties which a man has in virtue of occupying what in a quite strict sense of role is a distinct role, are thought or spoken of as "responsibilities." A private soldier has a duty to obey his superior officer and, if commanded by him to form fours or present arms on a given occasion, has a duty to do so. But to form fours or present arms would scarcely be said to be the private's responsibility; nor would he be said to be responsible for doing it. If on the other hand a soldier was ordered to deliver a message to H.Q. or to conduct prisoners to a base camp, he might well be said to be responsible for doing these things, and these things to be his responsibility. I think, though I confess to not being sure, that what distinguishes those duties of a role which are singled out as responsibilities is that they are duties of a relatively complex or extensive kind, defining a "sphere of responsibility" requiring care and attention over a protracted period of time, while short-lived duties of a very simple kind, to do or not do some specific act on a particular occasion, are not termed responsibilities. Thus a soldier detailed off to keep the camp clean and tidy for the general's visit of inspection has this as his sphere of responsibility and is responsible for it. But if merely told to remove a piece of paper from the approaching general's path, this would be at most his duty.

A "responsible person," "behaving responsibly" (not "irresponsibly"), require for their elucidation a reference to role-responsibility. A responsible person is one who is disposed to take his duties seriously; to think about them, and to make serious efforts to fulfil them. To behave responsibly is to behave as a man would who took his duties in this serious way. Responsibilities in this sense may be either legal or moral, or fall outside this dichotomy. Thus a man may be morally as well as legally responsible for the maintenance of his wife and children, but a host's responsibility for the comfort of his guests, and a referee's responsibility for the control of the players is neither legal nor moral, unless the word "moral" is unilluminatingly used simply to exclude legal responsibility.

Causal-Responsibility

"The long drought was responsible for the famine in India." In many contexts, as in this one, it is possible to substitute for the expression "was responsible for" the words "caused" or "produced" or some other causal expression in referring to consequences, results, or outcomes. The converse, however, is not always true. Examples of this causal sense of responsibility are legion. "His neglect was responsible for her distress." "The Prime Minister's speech was responsible for the panic." "Disraeli was responsible for the defeat of the Government." "The icy condition of the road was responsible for the accident." The past tense of the verb used in this causal sense of the expression "responsible for" should be noticed. If it is said of a living person, who has in fact caused some disaster, that he *is* responsible for it, this is not, or not merely, an example of causal responsibility, but of what I term "liability-responsibility"; it asserts his liability on account of the disaster, even though it is also true that he is responsible in that sense *because* he caused the disaster, and that he caused the disaster may be expressed by saying that he was responsible for it. On the other hand, if it is said of a person no longer living that he was responsible for some disaster, this may be either a simple causal statement or a statement of liability-responsibility, or both.

From the above examples it is clear that in this causal sense not only human beings but also their actions or omissions, and things, conditions, and events, may be said to be responsible for outcomes. It is perhaps true that only where an outcome is thought unfortunate or felicitous is its cause commonly spoken of as responsible for it. But this may not reflect any aspect of the meaning of the expression "responsible for"; it may only reflect the fact that, except in such cases, it may be pointless and hence rare to pick out the causes of events. It is sometimes suggested that, though we may speak of a human being's action as responsible for some outcome in a purely causal sense, we do not speak of a person, as distinct from his actions, as responsible for an outcome, unless he is felt to deserve censure or praise. This is, I think, a mistake. History books are full of examples to the contrary. "Disraeli was responsible for the defeat of the Government" need not carry even an implication that he was deserving of censure or praise; it may be purely a statement concerned with the contribution made by one human being to an outcome of importance, and be entirely neutral as to its moral or other merits. The contrary view depends, I think, on the failure to appreciate sufficiently the ambiguity of statements of the form "X *was* responsible for Y" as distinct from "X *is* responsible for Y" to which I have drawn attention above. The former expression in the case of a person no longer living may be (though it *need* not be) a statement of liability-responsibility.

Legal Liability-Responsibility

Though it was noted that role-responsibility might take either legal or moral form, it was not found necessary to treat these separately. But in the case of the present topic of liability-responsibility, separate treatment seems advisable. For responsibility seems to have a wider extension in relation to the law than it does in relation to morals, and it is a question to be considered whether this is due merely to the general differences between law and morality, or to some differences in the sense of responsibility involved.

When legal rules require men to act or abstain from action, one who breaks the law is usually liable, according to other legal rules, to punishment for his misdeeds, or to make compensation to persons injured thereby, and very often he is liable to both punishment and enforced compensation. He is thus liable to be "made to pay" for what he has done in either or both of the senses which the expression "He'll pay for it" may bear in ordinary usage. But most legal systems go much further than this. A man may be legally punished on account of what his servant has done, even if he in no way caused or instigated or even knew of the servant's action, or knew of the likelihood of his servant so acting. Liability in such circumstances is rare in modern systems of criminal law; but it is common in all systems of civil law for men to be made to pay compensation for injuries caused by others, generally their servants or employees. The law of most countries goes further still. A man may be liable to pay compensation for harm suffered by others, though neither he nor his servants have caused it. This is so, for example, in Anglo-American law when the harm is caused by dangerous things which escape from a man's possession, even if their escape is not due to any act or omission of his or his servants, or if harm is caused to a man's employees by defective machinery whose defective condition he could not have discovered. . . .

The question whether a man is or is not legally liable to be punished for some action that he has done opens up the quite general issue whether all of the various requirements for criminal liability have been satisfied, and so will include the question whether the kind of action done, whatever mental element accompanied it, was ever punishable by law. But the question whether he is or is not legally responsible for some action or some harm is usually not concerned with this general issue, but with the narrower issue whether any of a certain range of conditions (mainly, but not exclusively, psychological) are satisfied, it being assumed that all other conditions are satisfied. Because of this difference in scope between questions of liability to punishment and questions of responsibility, it would be somewhat misleading, though not unintelligible, to say of a man who had refused to rescue a baby drowning in a foot of water, that he was not, according to English law, legally responsible for leaving the baby to drown or for the baby's death, if all that is meant is that he was not liable to punishment because refusing aid to those in danger is not generally a crime in English law. Similarly, a book or article entitled "Criminal Responsibility" would not be expected to contain the whole of the substantive criminal law determining the conditions of liability, but only to be concerned with a specialized range of topics such as mental abnormality, immaturity, *mens rea*, strict and vicarious liability, proximate cause, or other general forms of connection between acts and harm sufficient for liability. These are the specialized topics which are, in general, thought and spoken of as "criteria" of responsibility. They may be divided into three classes: (1) mental or psychological conditions; (2) causal or other forms of connection between act and harm; (3) personal relationships rendering one man liable to be punished or pay for the acts of another. Each of these three classes requires some separate discussion.

Mental or Psychological Criteria of Responsibility

In the criminal law the most frequent issue raised by questions of responsibility, as distinct from the wider question of liability, is whether or not an accused person satisfied some mental or psychological condition required for liability, or whether liability was strict or absolute, so that the usual mental or psychological conditions were not required. It is, however, important to notice that these psychological conditions are of two sorts, of which the first is far more closely associated with the use of the word responsibility than the second. On the one hand, the law of most countries requires that the person liable to be punished should at the time of his crime have had the capacity to understand what he is required by law to do or not to do, to deliberate and to decide what to do, and to control his conduct in the light of such decisions. Normal adults are generally assumed to have these capacities, but they may be lacking where there is mental disorder or immaturity, and the possession of these normal capacities is very often signified by the expression "responsible for his actions." This is the fourth sense of responsibility which I discuss below under the heading of "Capacity-Responsibility." On the other hand, except where responsibility is strict, the law may excuse from punishment persons of normal capacity if, on particular occasions where their outward conduct fits the definition of the crime, some element of intention or knowledge, or some other of the familiar constituents of *mens rea*, was absent, so that the particular action done was defective, though the agent had the normal capacity of understanding and control. Continental codes usually make a firm distinction between these two main types of psychological conditions: questions concerning general capacity are described as matters of responsibility or "imputability," whereas questions concerning the presence or absence of knowledge or intention on particular occasions are not described as matters of "imputability," but are referred to the topic of "fault" (*schuld, faute, dolo*, etc.). . . .

Causal or Other Forms of Connection with Harm

Questions of legal liability-responsibility are not limited in their scope to psychological conditions of either of the two sorts distinguished above. Such questions are also (though more frequently in the law of tort than in the criminal law) concerned with the issue whether some form of connection between a person's act and some harmful outcome is sufficient according to law to make him liable; so if a person is accused of murder the question whether he was or was not legally responsible for the death may be intended to raise the issue whether the death was too remote a consequence of his acts for them to count as its cause. If the law, as frequently in tort, is not that the defendant's action should have caused the harm, but that there be some other form of connection or relationship between the defendant and the harm, e.g. that it should have been caused by some dangerous thing escaping from the defendant's land, this connection or relationship is a condition of civil responsibility for harm, and, where it holds, the defendant is said to be legally responsible for the harm. No doubt such questions of connection with harm are also frequently phrased in terms of liability.

Relationship with the Agent

Normally in criminal law the minimum condition required for liability for punishment is that the person to be punished should himself have done what the law forbids, at least so far as outward conduct is concerned; even if liability is "strict," it is not enough to render him liable for punishment that someone else should have done it. This is often expressed in the terminology of responsibility (though here, too, "liability" is frequently used instead of "responsibility") by saying that, generally, vicarious responsibility is not known to the criminal law. But there are exceptional cases; an innkeeper is liable to punishment if his servants, without his knowledge and against his orders, sell liquor on his premises after hours. In this case he is vicariously responsible for the sale, and of course, in the civil law of tort there are many situations in which a master or employer is liable to pay compensation for the torts of his servant or employee, and is said to be vicariously responsible.

It appears, therefore, that there are diverse types of criteria of legal liability-responsibility: the most prominent consist of certain mental elements, but there are also causal or other connections between a person and harm, or the presence of some relationship, such as that of master and servant, between different persons. It is natural to ask why these very diverse conditions are singled out as criteria of responsibility, and so are within the scope of questions about responsibility, as distinct from the wider question concerning liability for punishment. I think that the following somewhat Cartesian figure may explain this fact. If we conceive of a person as an embodied mind and will, we may draw a distinction between two questions concerning the conditions of liability and punishment. The first question is what general types of outer conduct (*actus reus*) or what sorts of harm are required for liability? The second question is how closely connected with such conduct or such harm must the embodied mind or will of an individual person be to render him liable to punishment? Or, as some would put it, to what extent must the embodied mind or will be the author of the conduct or the harm in order to render him liable? Is it enough that the person made the appropriate bodily movements? Or is it required that he did so when possessed of a certain capacity of control and with a certain knowledge or intention? Or that he caused the harm or stood in some other relationship to it, or to the actual doer of the deed? The legal rules, or parts of legal rules, that answer these various questions define the various forms of connection which are adequate for liability, and these constitute conditions of legal responsibility which form only a part of the total conditions of liability for punishment, which also include the definitions of the *actus reus* of the various crimes.

We may therefore summarize this long discussion of legal liability-responsibility by saying that, though in certain general contexts legal responsibility and legal liability have the same meaning, to say that a man is legally responsible for some act or harm is to state that his connection with the act or harm is sufficient according to law for liability. Because responsibility and liability are distinguishable in this way, it will make sense to say that because a person is legally responsible for some action he is liable to be punished for it. . . .

Capacity-Responsibility

In most contexts, as I have already stressed, the expression "he is responsible for his actions" is used to assert that a person has certain normal capacities. These constitute the most important criteria of moral liability-responsibility, though it is characteristic of most legal systems that they have given only a partial or tardy recognition to all these capacities as general criteria of legal responsibility. The capacities in question are those of understanding, reasoning, and control of conduct: the ability to understand what conduct legal rules or morality require, to deliberate and reach decisions concerning these requirements, and to conform to decisions when made. Because "responsible for his actions" in this sense refers not to a legal status but to certain complex psychological characteristics of persons, a person's responsibility for his actions may intelligibly be said to be "diminished" or "impaired" as well as altogether absent, and persons may be said to be "suffering from diminished responsibility" much as a wounded man may be said to be suffering from a diminished capacity to control the movements of his limbs.

No doubt the most frequent occasions for asserting or denying that a person is "responsible for his actions" are cases where questions of blame or punishment for particular actions are in issue. But, as with other expressions used to denote criteria of responsibility, this one also may be used where no particular question of blame or punishment is in issue, and it is then used simply to describe a person's psychological condition. Hence it may be said purely by way of description of some harmless inmate of a mental institution, even though there is no present question of his misconduct, that he is a person who is not responsible for his actions. No doubt if there were no social practice of blaming and punishing people for their misdeeds, and excusing them from punishment because they lack the normal capacities and understanding and control, we should lack this shorthand description for describing their condition which we now derive from these social practices. In that case we should have to describe the condition of the inmate directly, by saying that he could not understand what people told him to do, or could not reason about it, or come to, or adhere to any decisions about his conduct.

Legal systems left to themselves may be very niggardly in their admission of the relevance of liability to legal punishment of the several capacities, possession of which are necessary to render a man morally responsible for his actions. So much is evident from the history sketched in the preceding chapter of the painfully slow emancipation of English criminal law from the narrow, cognitive criteria of responsibility formulated in the M'Naghten Rules. Though some continental legal systems have been willing to confront squarely the question whether the accused "lacked the ability to recognize the wrongness of his conduct and to act in accordance with that recognition," such an issue, if taken seriously, raises formidable difficulties of proof, especially before juries. For this reason I think that, instead of a close determination of such questions of capacity, the apparently coarser-grained technique of exempting persons from liability to punishment if they fall into certain recognized categories of mental disorder is likely to be increasingly used. Such exemption by general category is a technique long known to English law; for in the case of very young children it has made no attempt to determine, as a condition of liability, the question whether on account of their immaturity they could have understood what the law required and could have conformed to its requirements, or whether their responsibility on account of their immaturity was "substantially impaired," but exempts them from liability for punishment if under a specified age. It seems likely that exemption by medical category rather than by individualized findings of absent or diminished capacity will be found more likely to lead in practice to satisfactory results. . . .

14. Sua Culpa

Joel Feinberg

I

IT IS COMMON enough for philosophers to analyze moral judgments and for philosophers—usually other philosophers—to analyze causal judgments. But statements to the effect that a given harm is some assignable person's fault, having both moral and causal components, import the complexities of judgments of the other two kinds. They are, therefore, especially challenging. Yet they are rarely considered by analytical philosophers. This neglect is to be regretted, because "his fault" judgments (as I shall call them) are important and ubiquitous in ordinary life. Historians employ them to assign blame for wars and depressions; politicians, sportswriters, and litigants use them to assign blame for losses. The disagreements they occasion are among the most common and intensely disputed in all "ethical discourse."

It may seem that most of those who quibble and quarrel about "his fault" are either children or lawyers; and even lawyers, therefore, can seem childish when they are preoccupied with the question. But investigators, editorialists, and executives must assign blame for failures and thereby judge the faults of their fellows. (Indeed, their inquiries and debates are most childish when they do *not* carefully consider fault and instead go scapegoat-hunting.) My assumption in what follows is that the faults that concern nonlawyers, both children and adults, are faults in the same sense of the word as those that concern the lawyer, that the concept of "his fault" is imported into the law from the world of everyday affairs. On the other hand, "proximate cause" (to pick just one of a thousand examples) is a technical term of law invented by lawyers to do a special legal job and subject to continual refashioning in the interests of greater efficiency in the performance of its assigned legal task. To explain this term to a layman is precisely to explain what *lawyers* do with it; if it should ever happen that a child, or a sportswriter, or an historian should use the expression, that fact would be of no relevance to its proper analysis. But to explain the concept of "his fault," we must give an account that explains what both lawyers and laymen do with it and how it is possible for each to understand and to communicate with the other by means of it.

An equivalent way of saying that some result is a man's fault is to say that he is *to blame* for it. Precisely the same thing can also be said in the language of *responsibility*. Of course, to be responsible for something (after the fact) may also mean that one did it, or caused it, or now stands answerable, or accountable, or liable to unfavorable responses from others for it. One can be responsible for a result in all those senses without being to blame for it. One can be held liable for a result either because it is one's fault or for

From Joel Feinberg, *Doing and Deserving: Essays in the Theory of Responsibility* (Princeton: Princeton University Press, 1970), chapter 8, pp. 187–221. Notes deleted. © 1970 by Princeton University Press. Adapted by permission of Princeton University Press.

some quite different kind of reason; and one can be to blame for an occurrence and yet escape all liability for it. Still, when one is to blame for a harm, one can properly be said to be "responsible for it *really*"; that is, there is a sense of "responsible for" that simply means "chargeable to one as one's fault." One of the commonest uses of the expression "*morally* responsible for" is for being responsible for something in this sense. (Another is for chargeability to a fault of a distinctively moral kind. Still another is for being *liable* to responses of a distinctively moral kind.)

II

The word "fault" occurs in three distinct idioms. We can say of a man that *he has a fault*, or that he is (or was) *at fault*, or that he is "to blame" for a given harm, which is to say that the harm is (or was) *his fault*. In this essay I shall be directly concerned only with the last of these idioms, except to make some necessary preliminary remarks about the other two.

To Have a Fault

A fault is a shortcoming, that is, a failure to conform to some norm or standard. Originally, perhaps, the word "fault" gave emphasis to failures through deficiency; but now any sort of failure to "measure up" is a fault, and we find no paradox in "falling short through excess." Not all defective human properties are faults. Evanescent qualities are hardly around long enough to qualify. To be a fault, a defective property must be sufficiently durable, visible, and potent to tell us something interesting about its possessor. A fault can be a durable manifestation almost constantly before the eye; but, more typically, human faults are latencies that manifest themselves only under special circumstances. Flaws of character are tendencies to act or feel in subpar ways, which, as tendencies, are *characteristic* of their possessor, that is, genuinely representative of him. Moreover, faults, like virtues, are commonly understood as comparative notions. An irascible man, for example, is not merely one who can become angry, for on that interpretation we may all be considered irascible. Rather, he is one who is more prone than most to become angry, either in the sense that he becomes angry on occasions when most men would not or in the sense that he gets angrier than most men on those occasions when most men would be angry. Equally commonly, however, we interpret a tendency-fault as a failure to satisfy not merely a statistical norm, but a norm of propriety: an irascible man has a tendency to get angry on occasions when he *ought* not to. And even when the implied norm is a statistical one, the fault predicate does more than describe neutrally. A fault word always expresses derogation.

The concept of fault has a close relation to that of harm, but it would be an overstatement to claim that all human faults create the risk of harm. David Hume was closer to the mark when he divided faults into four categories: those that cause displeasure or harm to self or others. Immediate displeasure, however, is only one of the diverse negative reactions that, quite apart from harmfulness, can be the sign of a fault. I would also include, for example, offense, wounded feelings, disaffection, aversion, disgust, shock, annoyance, and "uneasy sensations"—reactions either of the faulty self or of others. If we use the word "offensiveness" to cover the provoking of this whole class of negative responses, and if we assume that everything that is offensive to self, in this broad sense, is likely also to be offensive to others, we can summarize Hume's view by saying that it is either harmfulness or social offensiveness that makes some characteristics faults. Hume notwithstanding, there are some (though perhaps not many) faults that neither harm nor offend but simply fail to benefit, such as unimaginativeness and various minor intellectual flaws. We can modify Hume's account of the offensive faults further, perhaps in a way Hume would not have welcomed, by adding that it is not the mere *de facto* tendency of a trait to offend that renders it a fault. Normally when we attach the fault label to personal characteristics—that is, when we speak as moralists expressing our own judgments, and not merely as sociologists describing the prevailing sentiments of our communities—we are not simply predicting that the characteristics will offend; we are instead (or also) endorsing offense as an appropriate reaction to them. Most of those faults that do not harm, we think, are traits that naturally, or properly, or understandably offend (in the widest sense of "offend").

Often we speak as if a man's fault can enter into causal relations with various outcomes external to him. These assertions, when sensible, must be taken as elliptical forms of more complex statements. To say that a man's faulty disposition, his carelessness or greed, caused some harm is to say that the man's action or omission that did the causing was of the type that he characteristically does (or would do) in circumstances of the kind that in fact were present, or that the act or omission was of the sort he has a predominant tendency to do in circumstances of that kind. (He may, of course, also have a countertendency to restrain himself by an act of will, or the like.) To cite a man's character flaw as a cause of a harm, in short, is to *ascribe* the cause to an act or omission and then to *classify* that act or omission in a certain way—as characteristic of the actor. (It is just the sort of thing he *would* do, as we say.) It is also, finally, to *judge* the manifested characteristic as substandard and thereby to derogate it.

One can be *at fault* on a given occasion, however, even though one does not act in a characteristic way. Even very careful men sometimes slip up; even the most talented make mistakes; even the very calm sometimes lose their tempers. When these uncharacteristic failures cause harm, it is correct to say that a *faulty aspect* of some act or omission did the causing, but incorrect to ascribe the cause to some faulty characteristic of the actor, for that would be to imply, contrary to the hypothesis, that he is a generally careless, irascible, or inept person. This is the kind of faulty doing (as opposed to "faulty being") that could happen, as we say, to anyone; but in the long run it will be done more often by those who have serious character faults than by those who do not.

"Being at fault," even in one's perfectly voluntary and representative conduct, is in a sense partly a matter of luck. No one has complete control over what circumstances he finds himself in—whether, for example, he lives in times of war or peace, prosperity or depression, under democratic or autocratic government, in sickness or health, and so on. Consequently, a man may, by luck merely, escape those circumstances that would actualize some dreadful latency in him of which he is wholly unaware. It may even be true of *most* of us virtuous persons that we are to some small degree, at least, "lucky" in this sense. (We do not, however, normally refer to the mere absence of very bad luck as "good luck.") Not only can one *have a fault* and "luckily" escape *being at fault* in one's actions (on analogy with the hemophiliac who never in fact gets cut); one can also have a small fault (that is, a disposition very difficult to actualize) and unluckily stumble into those very rare circumstances that can actualize it. (The latter is "bad luck" in a proper sense.) Both of these possibilities—the luckily unactualized and the unluckily actualized latencies—follow from the analysis of faults as dispositions and, if that analysis is correct, should be sufficient at least to temper anyone's self-righteousness about the faulty actions of others.

To Be at Fault

When a man is "at fault" on a given occasion, the fault characterizes his action itself and not necessarily the actor, except as he was during the performance of the action. There is no necessary relation between this kind of fault and general dispositions of the actor—though, for all we know, every faultily undertaken or executed action *may* exemplify extremely complicated dispositions. When we say that a man is at fault, we usually mean only to refer to occurrent defects of acts or omissions, and only derivatively to the *actor*'s flaw as the doer of the defective deed. Such judgments are at best presumptive evidence about the man's general character. An act can be faulty even when not characteristic of the actor, and the actor may be properly "to blame" for it anyway; for if the action is faulty and it is also *his* action (characteristic or not), then he must answer for it. The faultiness of an action always reflects *some* discredit upon its doer, providing the doing is voluntary.

One standard legal classification divides all ways of being at fault into three categories: intentional wrongdoing, recklessness, and negligence. The traditional legal test of intentional doing has been a disjunctive one; there is intentional wrongdoing if either one acts with a wrongful conscious objective or one knowingly produces a forbidden result even incidentally as a kind of side-effect of his effort to achieve his objective. When the occurrence of the forbidden or undesirable side-effect is not certain, but nevertheless there is a known substantial likelihood of its coming about as an incidental byproduct of one's action, its subsequent production cannot be called "intentional" or "knowing" but verges into *recklessness*. What is known in recklessness is the existence of a *risk*. When the actor knowingly runs the risk, when he is willing to gamble with his own interests or the interests of others, then, providing the risk itself is unreasonable, his act is reckless.

One can hardly escape the impression that what is called "negligence" in the law is simply the miscellaneous class of faulty actions that are not intentional (done purposely or knowingly) or reckless; that in this classification of faults, once wrongful intentions and reckless quasi-intentions have been mentioned, "negligence" stands for everything else. This would leave a class of faults, however, that is *too* wide and miscellaneous. Humorlessness (to take just one example) is a kind of fault that is not intentional; yet we would hardly accuse a man of being "negligent" in failing to be amused or to show amusement at what is truly amusing. The point, I think, is that inappropriate failures to be amused are not the sorts of faults likely to cause *harm*. There is no great risk in a blank stare or a suppressed giggle. Negligence is the name of a heterogeneous class of acts and omissions that are unreasonably *dangerous*. Creation of risk is absolutely essential to the concept, and so is fault. But the fault is not merely conjoined coincidentally to the risk; rather, the fault consists in creating the risk, however unintentionally. When one knowingly creates an unreasonable risk to self or others, one is reckless; when one unknowingly but faultily creates such a risk, one is negligent.

There are a large number of ways of "unintentionally but faultily" creating an unreasonable risk. One can consciously weigh the risk but misassess it, either because of hasty or otherwise insufficient scrutiny (rashness), or through willful blindness to the magnitude of the risk, or through the conscientious exercise of inherently bad judgment. Or one can unintentionally create an unreasonable risk by failing altogether to attend either to what one is doing (the manner of execution) or to the very possibility that harmful consequences might ensue. In the former case, best called *carelessness* or *clumsiness* (in execution), one creates a risk precisely in virtue of not paying sufficient attention to what one is doing; in the latter case, which we can call *heedlessness* (in the very undertaking of the action), the risk is already there in the objective circumstances, but unperceived or mindlessly ignored.

There are still other faults that can render a given act or omission, unknown to its doer, unreasonably dangerous. Overly attentive drivers with the strongest scruples and the best intentions can drive as negligently as inattentive drivers and, indeed, a good deal more negligently than experienced drivers of strong and reliable habits who rely on those habits while daydreaming, their car being operated in effect by a kind of psychic "automatic pilot." Timidity, excitability, organic awkwardness, and slow reflexes can create unreasonable risks too, even when accompanied by attentive and conscientious advertence; and so can normal virtues like gallantry when conjoined with inexperience or poor judgment. (Imagine stopping one's car and waving a pretty pedestrian across the street right into the path of a speeding car passing on the right, unseen because momentarily in the "blind spot" of one's rear view mirror.) Almost any defect of conduct, except the likes of humorlessness, can be the *basis* of negligence, that is, the fault in virtue of which a given act or omission becomes, unknown to its actor, unreasonably dangerous. "Negligence" in the present sense is the name of a category of faulty acts. The negligence of any particular act or kind of act in the general category is always a consequential fault, a fault supervenient upon a fault of another kind that leads to an unreasonable risk in the circumstances.

It is worth emphasizing that this analysis applies to *legal negligence* only, which is negligence in a quite special sense. In ordinary nontechnical discourse, the word "negligence" is often a rough synonym for "carelessness" and as such refers to only one of the numerous possible faults that can, in a given set of circumstances, be the faulty basis of negligent conduct in the legal sense.

III

We come now to the main business at hand: the analysis of the concept of "his fault." It should be clear at the outset that, in order for a given harm to be someone's fault, he must have been somehow "at fault" in what he did or omitted to do, and also that there must have been some sort of causal connection between his action or omission and the harm. It is equally obvious that neither of these conditions by itself can be sufficient. Thus a motorist may be at fault in driving with an expired license or in exceeding the speed limit by five miles per hour, but unless his faulty act is a cause of the collision that ensues, the accident can hardly be his fault. Fault without causally determining action, then, is not sufficient. Similarly, causation without fault is not sufficient for the caused harm to be the causer's fault. It is no logical contradiction to say that a person's action caused the harm yet the harm was not his fault.

The Triconditional Analysis

It is natural at this point to conclude that a harm is "his fault" if and only if (1) he was at fault in acting (or omitting) and (2) his faulty act (or omission) caused the harm. This analysis, however, is incomplete, being still vulnerable to counterexamples of faulty actions causing harm that is nevertheless not the actor's fault. Suppose that *A* is unlicensed to drive an automobile but drives anyway, thereby "being at fault." The appearance of him driving in an (otherwise) faultless manner causes an edgy horse to panic and throw his rider. His faultily undertaken act caused a harm that cannot be imputed to him because the respect in which his act was faulty was causally irrelevant to the production of the harm. (When we come to give a causal explanation of the harm, we will not mention the fact that the driver had no license in his pocket. *That* is not what scared the horse.) This example suggests that a further condition is required to complete the analysis: (3) the aspect of the act that was faulty was also one of the aspects in virtue of which the act was a cause of the harm.

The third condition in the analysis is especially important when the fault in question falls under the general heading of negligence. Robert Keeton in effect devotes most of a book to commentary on a hypothetical example which illustrates this point:

> The defendant, proprietor of a restaurant, placed a large unlabelled can of rat poison beside cans of flour on a shelf near a stove in a restaurant kitchen. The victim, while in the kitchen making a delivery to the restaurant, was killed by an explosion of the poison. Assume that the defendant's handling of the rat poison was negligent because of the risk that someone would be poisoned but that the defendant had no reason to know of the risk that the poison would explode if left in a hot place.

The defendant's action, in Keeton's example, was faulty, and it was also the cause of the victim's death; but, on the analysis I have suggested, the death was nevertheless not his fault. The defendant's conduct was negligent because it created a risk of *poisoning*, but the harm it caused was not within the ambit of *that* risk. The risk of *explosion* was not negligently created. Hence the aspect of the act in virtue of which it was faulty was not the cause of the harm. Keeton puts the point more exactly: the harm was not "a result within the scope of the risks by reason of which the actor is found to be negligent." Keeton's concern is with a theory of liability for negligence, not with an analysis of the nontechnical concept of "his fault"; but, liability aside, the analysis I have given entails that the death, in Keeton's example, was *not* the defendant's fault.

We can refer to this account as "the triconditional analysis" and to its three conditions as (in order) "the fault condition," "the causal condition" (that the act was a cause of the harm), and "the causal relevance condition" (that the faulty aspect of the act was its causal link to the harm). I shall conclude that the triconditional analysis goes a long way toward providing a correct account of the commonsense notion of "his fault" and that its three conditions are indeed necessary to such an account even if, in the end, they must be formulated much more carefully and even supplemented by other conditions in an inevitably more complicated analysis. The remainder of this section discusses difficulties for the analysis as it stands which, I think, it can survive (at least after some tinkering, modifying, and disclaiming). One of these difficulties stems from a heterogeneous group of examples of persons who, on our analysis, would be blamed for harms that are clearly not their fault. I try to sidestep these counterexamples by affixing a restriction to the fault condition and making corresponding adjustments in the formulation of the relevance condition. The other difficulties directly concern the causal condition and the relevance condition. Both of these can involve us quickly in some fundamental philosophical problems.

Restrictions on the Fault Condition

There are some exceptional cases (but readily accessible to the philosophical imagination) in which a person who is clearly not to blame for a given harm nevertheless is the sole person who satisfies the conditions of the tripartite analysis. These cases, therefore, constitute counterexamples to that analysis if it is taken to state not only necessary but sufficient conditions for blame. Nicholas Sturgeon has suggested an especially ingenious case:

> A has made a large bet that no infractions of the law will occur at a certain place in a certain period of time; but B, at that place and time, opens a pack of cigarettes and fails to destroy the federal tax seal thereby breaking the law. A, seeing B's omission, is so frustrated that he suffers a fatal heart attack on the spot. (To simplify matters, we may suppose that no one has any reason to suppose A is endangering his health by gambling in this way.)

Clearly, A's death is not B's fault. Yet (1) B was at fault in acting contrary to law; (2) his faulty act frustrated A, causing the heart attack; and (3) the aspects of B's act (omission) that were faulty (the illegality of his omission to destroy the tax stamps) were also among the aspects of it in virtue of which there was a causal connection between it and the harm. A similar example is provided by John Taurek:

> C is so programmed (by hypnosis, perhaps C is a clever robot, whatever) that if A lies in answering B's question, C will harm D. B asks A her age and she lies. C harms D. A's action seems to be a causal factor in the production of harm to D, and just in virtue of its faulty aspect. Yet who would hold that D's harm was A's fault?

Perhaps it is possible to add further conditions to the analysis to obviate this kind of counterexample, but a more likely remedy would be to restrict the kinds of faults that can be elements of "his fault" judgments. Sometimes a man can be said to be at fault in acting (or omitting to act) precisely because his action or omission will offend or fail to benefit himself or others, or because it is a violation of faith (even a *harmless* instance of promise-breaking, such as a secret breaking of faith to a person now dead), or simply and precisely because it breaks an authoritative legal rule. Most intentional wrongdoing, on the other hand, and all recklessness and negligence are instances of being at fault for another (perhaps additional) reason—either because "they make a certain kind of harm or injury inevitable, or because they create an unreasonable risk of a certain kind of harm." We can attempt to avoid counterexamples of the sort Sturgeon and Taurek suggested by tampering with the first condition (the fault condition). We can say now (of course, only tentatively and not without misgiving) that, for the purpose of this analysis, the way of being at fault required by the fault condition is to be understood as the harm-threatening way, not the nonbenefiting, offense-threatening, harmless faith-breaking, or law-violating ways. The fault condition then can be reformulated as follows (in words suggested by Sturgeon): a given harm is A's fault only if (1) A was at fault in acting or omitting to act and "the faultiness of his act or omission consisted, at least in part, in the creation of either a certainty or an unreasonable risk of harm. . . ." Now the faulty smoker in Sturgeon's example and the liar in Taurek's example are no longer "at fault" in the requisite way, and the revised analysis no longer pins the blame for coincidental harms on them. To open a cigarette package in an overly fastidious fashion is not to endanger unduly the health of others; nor is lying about one's age (except in very special contexts) to threaten others with harm.

In the light of this new restriction on the fault condition, we can formulate the causal relevance condition in an alternative way, along the lines suggested by Keeton's account of harm caused by negligence. We can now say that the (harm-threatening) "faulty aspect" of an act is a cause of subsequent harm when the risk or certainty of harm in virtue of which the act was at fault was a risk or certainty of "just the sort of harm that was in fact caused," and not harm of some other sort. The resultant harm, in other words, must be within the scope of the risk (or certainty) in virtue of which the act is properly characterized as faulty. This is more than a mere explication of the original way of putting the third condition. It is a definite modification designed to rule out cases of *coincidence* where the faulty aspect of an act, even when it is of the harm-threatening sort, may be causally linked to a subsequent harm via such adventitious conditions as standing wagers and programmed robots. Under the revised formulation, the very same considerations involved in the explanation of *why* the act is faulty are also involved, essentially and sufficiently, in the explanation of *how* the harm was caused.

We have not even considered, of course, the crucial question of how reasonable risks are to be distinguished from unreasonable ones; and there are still other problems resulting from the fact that a "sort of harm" (crucial phrase) can be described in either more or less full and determinate ways. These problems, like several other closely related ones, are too complicated to be tackled here.

Fault and Cause: Dependent and Independent Determinations

Can we tell whether an act caused a given harm independently of knowing whether the actor was at fault in acting? The answer seems to be that we can determine the causal question independently of the fault question in some cases but not in others. Part of our problem is to explain this variation. Consider first some examples. A blaster takes every reasonable precaution, and yet by a wildly improbable fluke his explosion of dynamite sends a disjarred rock flying through the window of a distant isolated cabin. He was not at fault, but whether he was or not, we are able to say independently that his setting off the blast was the cause of the broken window. Similarly, the motorist in our earlier example, by driving (whether with or without fault is immaterial to this point) along a rarely traveled stretch of country road, caused a nervous horse to bolt. That is, it was his activity as he conducted it then and there, with its attendant noise and dust, that caused the horse to bolt; and we can know this independently of any determination of fault.

Examples provided by J. L. Mackie and William Dray, however, seem to cut the other way. Mackie describes an episode in which a motorcyclist exceeded a speed limit and was chased by a policeman, also on a motorcycle, at speeds up to seventy miles per hour. An absentminded pedestrian stepped off a bus into the policeman's path and was killed instantly.

The newspapers for the next few days were full of debates over the question of whose conduct was the "real cause" of the death, debates that seemed to center on the question of whose conduct was the least *reasonable* intrusion into the normal course of events. To express an opinion at all on the causal question seemed to be to take a stand, plain and simple, about the *propriety* of pursuits by police in heavily populated areas.

Dray discusses a hypothetical debate between two historians who argue "whether it was Hitler's invasion of Poland or Chamberlain's pledge to defend it which caused the outbreak of the Second World War." The question they *must* be taken to be trying to settle, he avers, is "who was to blame." "The point," he says, "is not that we cannot hold an agent responsible for a certain happening unless his action can be said to have caused it. It is rather that, unless we are prepared to hold the agent responsible for what happened, we cannot say that his action *was* the cause." Mackie comes to a similar conclusion, embracing what he calls a "curious inversion of utilitarianism," namely, that one often cannot tell whether a given harm is a causal consequence of a given act without first deciding whether the actor was *at fault* in acting the way he did.

To clarify the relations between cause and fault, it will be necessary to digress briefly and remind ourselves of certain features of causal judgments as they are made in ordinary life. That one condition is causally necessary or, in a given context, sufficient for the occurrence of a given event is normally a question simply for empirical investigation and the application of a scientific theory. Normally, however, there will be a plurality of distinguishable causal conditions (often called "causal factors") for any given event, and the aim of a causal inquiry will be to single out one of these to be denominated "the cause" of the event in question. A judgment that cites one of the numerous eligible causal conditions for an event as "the cause" I call a *causal citation*. The eligibility of an event or state as a causal factor is determined empirically via the application of inductive criteria. On the other hand, the citation of one of the eligible candidates as "the cause" is normally made, as we shall see, via the application of what Dray calls "pragmatic criteria." In Dray's convenient phrase, the inductive inquiry establishes the "importance of a condition to the event," whereas the causal citation indicates its "importance to the inquirer."

The point of a causal citation is to single out one of the certified causal candidates that is especially *interesting* to us, given our various practical purposes and cognitive concerns. These purposes and concerns provide a convenient way of classifying the "contexts of inquiry" in which causal citations are made. The primary division is between explanatory and nonexplanatory contexts. The occasion for an explanatory citation is one in which there is intellectual puzzlement of a quite specific kind. A surprising or unusual event has occurred which is a deviation from what is understood to be the normal course of things. A teetotaler is drunk, or an alcoholic sober; a punctual man is tardy, or a dilatory man early; it rains in the dry season, or it fails to rain in the wet season. Sometimes the breach of routine is disappointing, and we wish to know what went wrong this time. But sometimes the surprise is pleasant or, more commonly, simply stimulating to one's curiosity. We ask what caused the surprising event and expect an explanation that will cite a factor normally present but absent this time, or normally absent but present this time, that made the difference. The occasion for explanation is a breach of routine; the explanatory judgment cites another deviation from routine to correlate with it.

Very often one of the causal conditions for a given upshot is a faulty human action.

Human failings tend to be more "interesting" factors than events of other kinds, even for purely explanatory purposes; but it is important to notice that this need not always be the case. Faulty human actions usually do *not* fall within the normal course of events, so that a dereliction of duty, for example, when it is a causally necessary condition for some puzzling breach of routine, being itself a departure from the normal course of things, is a prime candidate for causal citation. But when the faulty conduct of Flavius is constant and unrelieved and known to be such to Titus, it will not relieve Titus's perplexity over how a given unhappy event came about simply to cite Flavius's habitual negligence or customary dereliction of duty as "the cause." What Titus wishes to know is what new intrusive event made the difference *this* time; and it won't help *him* to mention a causal factor that has always been present even on those occasions when no unhappy result ensued.

Not all causal explanations by any means employ causal citations. Especially when we are puzzled about the "normal course of events" itself and wish explanations for standardly recurring regularities (Why do the tides come in? Why do released objects fall? Why do flowers bloom in the spring?), mere brief citations will not do. In such cases we require long stories involving the descriptions of diverse states of affairs and the invocation of various laws of nature. Similarly, not all causal citations are explanatory. Sometimes there is no gap in a person's understanding of how a given interesting event came about, and yet he may seek nevertheless to learn its "real" or "most important" cause. Nonexplanatory citations are those made for some purpose other than the desire simply to put one's curiosity to rest. Most frequently they cite the causal factor that is of a kind that is easiest to manipulate or control. Engineers and other practical men may be concerned to eliminate events of the kind that occasioned the inquiry if they are harmful or to produce more of them if they are beneficial. In either case, when they seek "the cause," they seek the causal factor that has a handle on it (in Collingwood's phrase) that they can get hold of and manipulate. Another of our practical purposes in making causal citations is to *fix the blame*, a purpose which introduces considerations not present when all the leading causal factors are things other than human actions (as they often are in agricultural, medical, or engineering inquiries). Insects, viruses, and mechanical stresses and strains are often "blamed" for harms, but the word "blame" in these uses, of course, has a metaphorical sense.

In summary, causal citations can be divided into those made from explanatory and those made from nonexplanatory standpoints, and the latter group into those made from the "engineering" and those made from the "blaming" standpoints. Explanatory citations single out abnormal interferences with the normal course of events or hitherto unknown missing links in a person's understanding. They are designed simply to remove puzzlement by citing the causal factor that can shed the most light. Hence we can refer to the criterion of selection in explanatory contexts (for short) as *the lantern criterion*. Causal citations made from the "engineering standpoint" are made with a view to facilitating control over future events by citing the most efficiently and economically manipulable causal factor. The criterion for selection in engineering contexts can thus be called (for short) *the handle criterion*. The point of causal citations in purely blaming contexts is simply to pin the label of blame on the appropriate causal factor for further notice and practical use. These judgments cite a causal factor that is a human act or omission "stained" (as an ancient figure of speech would have it) with fault. The criterion in blaming contexts can be called (for short) *the stain criterion*. When we look for "the cause," then, we may be looking for the causal factor that has either a lantern, a handle, or a stain on it.

Purely blaming citations can be interpreted in two different ways. On the first model, to say that a person's act was the cause of the harm is precisely equivalent to saying that he is to blame for the harm, that is, that the harm is his fault. The causal inquiry undertaken from the purely blaming perspective, according to this view, is one and the same as the inquiry into the question of who was to blame or of whose fault it was. On this model, then, causal citation is not a condition for the fixing of blame; it is, rather, precisely the same thing. It is simply a fact of usage, which the examples of Dray and Mackie illustrate, that questions of blame often get posed and answered in wholly causal language. Historians, for example, are said by Dray often to "use expressions like 'was responsible for' [or 'was to blame for'] when they want to put into other words conclusions which they would also be prepared to frame in causal language."

On the second model of interpretation, which is also sometimes *a propos*, the truth of the causal citation "His act was the cause of the harm" is only one of the *conditions* for the judgment that "The harm was his fault." Here we separate cause and fault before bringing them together again in a "his fault" judgment, insisting that the harm was his fault *only if* his action caused it. The causal inquiry, so conceived, is undertaken for the sake of the blame inquiry, but its results are established independently.

Now how do we establish a causal citation on the first model (or, what is the same thing, a "his fault" citation on the second)? Again, we have two alternatives: either we can hold that the person (or his act) was *the cause* of the harm (meaning that he was to blame for it) only if his act was a genuine causal factor in the production of the harm; or we can require that his act be *the cause* of the harm, and not merely a "causal factor." But then we must find a way of avoiding a vitiating circularity. If we mean "the cause" as selected by *the stain criterion*, we have made a full circle; for, on this first model, our *original inquiry* is aimed at citing the cause by a stain criterion, and now we say that the achievement of this goal is a condition of itself. Clearly, if we are going to insist that his act be "the cause" as a condition of its being "the cause for purposes of fixing blame," we have to mean that it must be the cause *as determined by either the lantern or the handle criteria*. A quick examination of cases will show that this is just what we do mean.

When a man sets off a charge of dynamite and the earth shifts, dust rises, and rocks fly, the blasting is conspicuously the cause of these results by the lantern criterion (since it is the abnormal intervention) and equally clearly by the handle criterion (since it is part of the handiest causal recipe for producing results of precisely that kind). We can know, therefore, that the blasting caused the results by these commonsense criteria before we know anything at all about fault. Then we can go on to say, without circularity, that one or another of these causal criteria must be satisfied if those of the results that are harmful are to be charged to the blaster as his fault, but that further conditions of faultiness must also be satisfied.

Should we say that being "the cause" by the other commonsense criteria is *always* a necessary condition of being the cause by the stain criterion? I think this specification would prove to be artificially restrictive, for we sometimes (though perhaps not often) wish to ascribe blame whether or not the blamed action satisfies the lantern and handle criteria, and even in some instances where (allowing for the usual relativity of context) it appears not to. Suppose *A*, an impressive adult figure, offers a cigarette to *B*, an impressionable teenager. *A* is *B*'s original attractive model of a smoker and also one who deliberately seduces him into the habit. Much later, after thirty years of continuous heavy smoking, *B* begins to suffer from lung cancer. Neither the lantern nor the handle criteria in most contexts are likely to lead one to cite *A*'s earlier act as the cause of *B*'s cancer, for *A*'s act is not conspicuously "the cause" of the harm by these criteria (as the blasting was, in the earlier example). Yet we may wish to say that *A*'s seduction of *B* was the cause of his eventual cancer for purposes of fixing blame or as a mode of expressing that blame. Such a judgment may not be morally felicitous, but it can be made without committing some sort of conceptual solecism.

The best way of avoiding both circularity and artificial restriction of expression in our account of blame-fixing citations is to require not that the blamed action be citable as "the cause" (by *any* criteria), but only that it be a genuine causal factor, in the circumstances that obtained, and then to add fault and relevance conditions to the analysis. Most of the time, perhaps, being "the cause" by the lantern or handle criteria will also be required; but being a *causal factor merely* will be required always.

The Causal Relevance Condition: Is It Always Necessary?

Does the analysis of commonsense "his fault" judgments really require a causal relevance condition? Many people, I suspect, are prepared to make "his fault" judgments in particular cases even when they know that a causal relevance condition has not been satisfied; and many puzzling cases are such as to make even most of us hesitate about the matter. Consider, for example, the case of the calamitous soup-spilling at Lady Mary's formal dinner party. Sir John Stuffgut so liked his first and second bowls of soup that he demanded a third just as Lady Mary was prepared to announce with pride to the hungry and restless guests the arrival of the next course. Sir John's tone was so gruff and peremptory that Lady Mary quite lost her composure. She lifted the heavy tureen with shaking arms and, in attempting to pass it to her intemperate guest, spilled it unceremoniously in the lap of the Reverend Mr. Straightlace. Now both Sir John and Lady Mary were at fault in this episode. Sir John was thoughtless, gluttonous, and, especially, *rude* in demanding another bowl in an unsettling tone of voice. Lady Mary was (perhaps forgivably) negligent in the way she executed her action, and, besides she should have known that the tureen was too heavy for her to lift. Furthermore, both Lady Mary's faulty action and Sir John's faulty action were necessary conditions for the ensuing harm. Assuming that we must fix the blame for what happened, whose fault, should we say, was the harm?

Most of us would be inclined to single out Sir John's rudeness as "the cause" for purposes of blaming, partly because it was the most striking deviation from routine, perhaps, but mainly because, of the causal factors with stains on them, his action was the most deeply stained, which is to say that he was the most at fault. Moreover, his action was a causal factor in the production of the harm precisely in virtue of that aspect which was faulty, namely, its unsettling rudeness, which created an unreasonable risk of upsetting the hostess, the very result that in fact ensued. Thus the causal relevance condition is satisfied in this example.

Suppose, however, that the facts had been somewhat different, Sir John, at just the wrong moment (as before), requested his third bowl, but in a quiet and gentle manner, and in a soft and mellifluous tone of voice, perfectly designed to calm its auditor. Sir John this time was not being rude, though he was still at fault in succumbing to his excessive appetites and indulging them in an unseemly public way to the inconvenience of others. In short, his primary fault in this new example was not rudeness, but plain gluttony; and (as before), but for his act which was at fault, the harm would not have occurred. Likewise (as before) the clumsiness of Lady Mary was a causal factor in the absence of which the harm would not have resulted. This case differs from the earlier one in that the causal relevance condition is not satisfied, for gluttony normally creates a risk to the glutton's own health and comfort, not to the interests of others. Unlike rudeness, it is a primary self-regarding fault. Thus that aspect of Sir John's request for more soup that was faulty was an irrelevant accompaniment of the aspects that contributed to the accident. Hence we could conclude that, although Sir John was *at fault* in what he did, the resulting harm was not *his fault*.

It would be sanguine, however, to expect everybody to agree with this judgment. Mr. Straightlace, for example, might be altogether indisposed to let Sir John escape the blame so easily. He and others might prefer to reject the causal relevance condition out of hand as too restrictive and urge instead that the blame always be placed on the person *most at fault*, whether the fault is causally relevant or not, providing his faulty action was a genuine causal factor. This alternative would enable one to pin the blame on Sir John in both versions of the soup-spilling story. It does not commend itself to the intuitive understanding in a quiet reflective hour, however, and seems to me to have no other merit than that of letting the indignation and vindictiveness occasioned by harm have a respectable outlet in our moral judgments. If we really want to keep Sir John on the hook, *we do not have to say* that the harm was "really his fault" and thereby abuse a useful and reasonably precise concept. Rather, if we are vindictively inclined, we can say that to impose liability on a person to enforced compensation or other harsh treatment for some harm does not always require that the harm be his fault. This would be the moral equivalent of a departure from what is called "the fault principle" in the law of torts. It is an attempt to do justice to our spontaneous feelings, without confusing our concepts, and has the merits at least of openness and honesty.

Disinterested parties might reject causal relevance as a condition for being to blame in a skeptical way, offering as an alternative to it a radical contextual relativism. One might profess genuine bafflement when asked whose fault was the second soup-spilling, on the grounds that the question cannot be answered until it is known for what purpose it is asked. Is the person singled out for blame the one to be punished, forced to make compensation, expected to apologize? What is the point of narrowly pinning blame? We could, after all, simply tell the narrative as accurately as possible and decline to say whose fault, on balance, the harm was, although that evasive tactic might not be open to, say, an insurance investigator. The point, according to this skeptical theory, is that, after all the facts are in, we are still not committed by "the very logic of the everyday concept" to saying anything at all about whose fault it was. The blame-fixing decision is still logically open and will be determined in part by our practical purposes in raising the question. This skeptical theory, however, strikes me as a combined insight and *non sequitur*. The insight is that we are not *forced* to pinpoint blame unless some practical question like liability hinges on it and that it is often the better part of wisdom to decline to do so when one can. But it does not follow from the fact that "his fault" judgments can sometimes be avoided that it is logically open to us to make them in any way we wish when we do make them. I hold, therefore, to the conclusion that, in fixing the blame for harm, we are restricted by our very concepts to the person(s) whose faulty act was a causal factor in the production of the harm in virtue of its causally relevant faulty aspect.

There often is room for discretion in the making of "his fault" judgments, but it comes at a different place and is subject to strict limitations. The person whose fault the harm is said to be *must* satisfy the conditions of the triconditional analysis (and perhaps others as well); but when more than one person is so qualified, the judgment-maker may sometimes choose between them on "pragmatic grounds," letting some of them off the hook. When this discretion is proper, the three conditions of our analysis must be honored as necessary, but they are no longer taken to be sufficient. Suppose one thousand persons satisfy the three conditions of our analysis in respect to harm X, and they acted independently (not in concert) over a period of many years. To say simply that the harm is (all) *their* fault, or part his, and part his, and part his, and so on, would be to defeat altogether the usual point of a "his fault" judgment, namely, to fix more narrowly, to single out, to focus upon. When fixings of blame become too diffuse, they can no longer perform this function. They might still, of course, be *true*, but just not very useful. It is not exactly false to say of the first soup-spilling example that it was the fault of *both* Lady Mary and Sir John; but "practical purposes" may dictate instead that we ignore minor or expectable faults and confer all the blame on the chief culprit. At any rate, if it is given that we must, for some practical purpose, single out a wrongdoer more narrowly, then we have discretion to choose among those (but only those) who satisfy the necessary conditions of the tripartite analysis.

Fault and Tort Liability

Suppose we accept the revised triconditional analysis of "his fault" but jettison the causal relevance condition as a requisite for tort *liability*, so that we can get the likes of Sir John on the hook after all, even though we admit he is not to *blame* for the harm. The prime consequence of dropping the causal relevance condition is to downgrade the role of causation as a ground for liability and to increase the importance of simply being at fault. If causal relevance is not required, it would seem that being at fault is the one centrally important necessary condition for liability, and indeed so important as to render the causal condition itself a mere dispensable formality. To upgrade the fault condition to that extent is most likely to seem reasonable when the fault is disproportionately greater than the harm it occasions. Imagine a heinously faulty act that is a necessary causal condition for a relatively minor harm. Suppose that A, a matricidal fiend, in the cruelest way possible sets himself to shoot his mother dead just as B, the lady across the street, is fondling a delicate and fragile art object. The sound of the revolver shot startles B, causing her to drop the art object which shatters beyond repair. Is its loss A's fault? Let us assume (for the sake of argument) that the murderous act was at fault in at least two ways: (1) it created a certainty of death or severe injury to the actor's mother (the primary way it was at fault); and (2), in making a loud report, it created an unreasonable risk to (among other things) the art objects of neighbors. Thus, in virtue of (2), A is at fault in the manner required for his being to blame for breaking the neighbor's glass vase. His act caused the breaking and did so in virtue of its faulty aspect (2); hence it was his fault. But even if he had (thoughtfully) used a silencer on the gun, and nevertheless the very slight noise caused by his act had startled a supernervous vase-fondling neighbor, causing the dropping and breaking, we might find it proper to charge him for the damage *even though the loss was not his fault.* (The "faulty aspect" of his act—its heinousness—was causally irrelevant to that loss.) It is precisely this kind of case where common sense seems most at home without the causal relevance condition; for no question of "fairness" to the faulty one is likely to trouble us when his fault is so great. Any number of minor harms of which his act was a necessary condition can be charged to his moral bill without disturbing us—at least so long as we remain "spontaneous" and unreflective.

It is another matter, however, when the harm is disproportionately greater than the fault, when a mere slap causes an unsuspected hemophiliac to bleed to death, or a clumsy slip on the sidewalk leads one to bump an "old soldier with an egg shell skull," causing his death. Hart and Honoré suggest that even here commonsense considerations can help justify abandonment, in some cases at least, of the causal relevance condition by mitigating its apparent harshness:

> The apparent unfairness of holding a defendant liable for a loss much greater than he could foresee to some extent disappears when we consider that a defendant is often negligent without suffering punishment or having to pay compensation. I may drive at an excessive speed a hundred times before the one occasion on which my speeding causes harm. The justice of holding me liable, should the harm on that occasion turn out to be extraordinarily grave, must be judged in the light of the hundred other occasions on which, without deserving such luck, I have incurred no liability.

This argument is reminiscent of the Augustinian theory of salvation. We are all sinners; therefore, no one really deserves to be saved. Hence if anyone at all is saved, it can only be through God's supererogatory grace. The others are (relatively) unlucky; but, being undeserving sinners, they can have no just complaint. All of us are negligent, goes the parallel argument; so none of us really deserves to escape liability for great harm. That majority of us who do escape are lucky, but the others who fall into liability in excess of their fault on the occasion have no just complaint, since they have accumulated enough fault on other occasions to redress the disproportion.

If justice truly requires (as the Hart-Honoré argument suggests) that blame and liability be properly apportioned to *all* a person's faults as accumulated in the long run, causal linkage to harm aside, why not go all the way in this direction and drop the "causal factor" condition altogether in the interest of Aristotelian "due proportion" and fairness? To say that we are all negligent is to say that on other occasions, at least, we have all created unreasonable risk of harms, sometimes great harms, of one kind or another, to other persons. Even in circumstances where excessive harm actually results, we may have created other risks of a different kind to other individuals, risks which luckily failed to eventuate in harm. Robert Keeton foresees the consequences for the law of torts of taking all such faults seriously in the assignment of liability for particular harms:

> . . . if it is relevant to take into account defendant's fault with respect to a risk different from any that would include the harm plaintiff has suffered, then would it not also be relevant to take into account his other faults as well? And would it not seem equally

relevant to consider plaintiff's shortcomings? Shall we fix legal responsibility by deciding who is the better and who the worse person? An affirmative answer might involve us, and quickly too, in the morality of run-of-the-ranch TV drama, where the good guys always win.

In effect Keeton challenges those who would drop the causal relevance condition to explain why they would maintain any causal condition at all. If the existence of fault of one kind or another, on one occasion or another, is the controlling consideration, why do we not simply tally up merits and demerits and distribute our collective compensation expenses in proportion to each person's moral score?

Why not indeed? This is not an unthinkable alternative system. We could, in principle, begin with the notion of a "compensable harm" as one caused by fault. (Other harms could be paid for out of tax funds or voluntary insurance.) Then we could estimate the total cost of compensable harms throughout the country for a one-year period. We would have to acquire funds equal to that amount by assigning demerits throughout the year to persons discovered to be "at fault" in appropriate ways in their conduct. Those who fail to clear their sidewalks of ice and snow within a reasonable period after the finish of a storm would be given so many demerits per square foot of pavement. Those convicted of traffic offenses would be assigned demerits on a graduated scale corresponding to the seriousness (as compounded out of unreasonableness and dangerousness) of their offense. Then, at the end of the year, the total cost of compensable harms would be divided by the total number of assigned demerits to yield the dollar value per demerit, and each person would be fined the dollar equivalent of the sum of his demerits. These fines would all go into a central fund used to compensate all victims of faulty accidents and crimes. Such a system would impose on some persons penalties disproportionately greater than the harm they actually caused; others would pay less than the harm they caused; but as far as is practically possible, everyone would be fined in exact proportion to the unreasonable risks he created (as well as certain and deliberate harms) to others.

The system just described could be called a system of "liability without *contributory* fault," since it bypasses a causation requirement. It is a system of liability based on fault simply, whether or not the fault contributes to harm. It thus differs sharply from the traditional system of liability based in part upon what is called *the fault principle*, which requires that accidental losses be borne by the party whose fault the accident was. This is liability based on "his fault" ascriptions, rather than "at fault" imputations. In contrast, the principle underlying a system of liability based on fault without causation might well be called the *retributive theory of torts*. It surely deserves this name drawn from the criminal law more than the so-called fault principle does, since it bases liability *entirely* upon fault purged of all extraneous and fortuitous elements. To be sure, what is called retributivism in the criminal law is a principle that would base (criminal) liability entirely on *moral fault*, and most retributivists would oppose punishing nonmoral faults, including much negligence, as ardently as they would oppose punishing the wholly faultless. A retributive principle of reparation *could* take this very moralistic form. As we have seen, legal negligence is always supervenient upon a fault of some other kind, sometimes "moral" (callousness, inconsiderateness, self-centeredness), sometimes not (timidity, excitability, awkwardness). A moralistic principle would issue demerits to negligence only when it is supervenient upon a fault judged to be a *moral* failing. In a sense, the more inclusive version of the theory is more "moralistic" still, since it treats even nonmoral failings as essentially deserving of penalty, that is, just *as if* they were moral failings. We can safely avoid these complications here.

One way to understand the retributive theory of torts is to relate it to, or derive it from, a general moral theory that bears the name of retributivism. In treating of this more general theory, it is very important to distinguish a strong from a weak version, for failure to do so has muddled discussions of retributivism in criminal law and would very likely do the same in discussions of principles of tort liability. According to the strong version of the general retributive principle, *all* evil or, more generally still, all *fault* deserves its comeuppance; it is an end in itself, quite apart from other consequences, that all wrongdoers (or faulty doers) be made to suffer some penalty, handicap, or forfeiture as a requital for their wrongdoing. Similarly, it is an end in itself, morally fitting and proper irrespective of other consequences, that the meritorious be rewarded with the means to happiness. Thus the best conceivable world would be that in which the virtuous (or faultless) flourish, the wicked (or, more generally, the faulty) suffer, and those in between perfect virtue and perfect wickedness enjoy happiness or suffer unhappiness in exact proportion to their virtuous and faulty conduct. Both a world in which everyone suffers regardless of moral condition and a world in which everyone flourishes regardless of moral condition would be intrinsically inferior morally to a world in which all and only the good flourish and all and only the bad suffer. If everyone without exception is a miserable sinner, then it is intrinsically better that everybody suffer than that everybody, or even anybody, be happy. There may be intrinsic goods other than the just apportionment of reward and penalty to the virtuous and the faulty respectively; but insofar as a state of affairs deviates from such apportionment, it is intrinsically defective.

Note that this way of putting retributivism makes it apply only to apportionments of a noncomparative kind, where to give to one is not necessarily to take from another and where to take from one is not necessarily to give to another. It is not, therefore, a principle of distributive justice, telling us in the abstract how all pies are to be cut up or how all necessary burdens are to be divided. Indeed, for some situations it would decree that no one get any pie, and in others that no one should suffer any burdens. It is concerned with deserving good or deserving ill, not with deserving one's fair share relative to others. To be sure, the world in which the good suffer and the evil are happy it calls a moral abomination, but not because of the conditions of the parties relative to one another, but rather because the condition of each party is the opposite of what *he* deserves, quite independently of the condition of the others. A world in which every person is equally a sinner and equally very happy would also be a moral abomination, on this view, even though it involves no social inequality.

The weaker version of general retributivism, on the other hand, is essentially a comparative principle, applying to situations in which it is given that someone or other must do without, make a sacrifice, or forfeit his interest. The principle simply asserts the moral priority, *ceteris paribus*, of the innocent party. Put most pithily, it is the principle that *fault forfeits first*, if forfeit there must be. If someone must suffer, it is better, *ceteris paribus*, that it be the faulty than the meritorious. This weaker version of retributivism, which permeates the law, especially the criminal law, has strong support in common sense. It commonly governs the distribution of that special kind of benefit called "the benefit of the doubt," so that, where there is doubt, for example, about the deterrent efficacy of a particular mode of punishment for a certain class of crimes, the benefit of that doubt is given to potential victims instead of convicted criminals.

I find the weaker version of retributivism much more plausible intuitively than the stronger, though even it is limited—for example, by the values of intimacy and friendship. (If I negligently spill your coffee cup at lunch, will you insist that I pay for a new cup, or will you prefer to demonstrate how much more important my friendship is to you than the forfeiture of a dime?) The weaker principle allows us to say, if we wish, though it does not require us to say, that universal happiness, if it were possible, would be intrinsically better than happiness for the good only, with the wicked all miserable. (Indeed, what would wickedness come to if its usually negative effect on the happiness of others was universally mitigated or nullified?) The weak principle also permits but does not require us to say that, even though it is better than the faulty forfeit first where there is no alternative to *someone's* forfeiting, it is better still that some other alternative be found.

Now let us return to our tort principles. What is called the "fault principle" (or, better, the "his fault" principle) does not derive from, and indeed is not even compatible with, the strong version of general retributivism. As we have seen, the causal component of "his fault" ascriptions introduces a fortuitous element, repugnant to pure retributivism. People who are very much at fault may luckily avoid causing proportionate harm, and unlucky persons may cause harm in excess of their minor faults. In the former case, little or no harm may be a person's fault even though he is greatly at fault; hence his liability, based on "his fault," will not be the burden he deserves, and the moral universe will be out of joint. In the latter case, unhappily coexistent circumstances may step up the normal magnitude of harm resulting from a minor fault, and again the defendant's liability will not do proper justice to his actual fault.

The tort principle that is called for by strong retributivism is that which I have called "the retributive theory of torts." Being at fault gets its proper comeuppance from this principle, whether or not it leads directly to harm; and the element of luck—except for luck in escaping detection—is largely eliminated. Hence fault suffers its due penalty, and if that is an end in itself, as strong retributivism maintains, then the retributive theory of torts is well recommended indeed. But the lack of intuitive persuasiveness of the general theory, I think, diminishes the plausibility of its offshoot in torts. Weak retributivism, which is generally more plausible, in my opinion, than its strong counterpart, does not uniquely favor either the retributive theory of torts or the "his fault" principle. Except in straightforwardly comparative contexts where the necessity of forfeiture is given, it takes no stand whatever about principles of tort liability. If *A* and *B* are involved in an accident causing a loss to *B* only, which is wholly *A*'s fault, and it is given that either *A* or *B* must pay for the loss, no other source of compensation being available, then the weak principle says that *A* should be made to pay, or rather (put even more weakly in virtue of the *ceteris paribus* clause) it holds that, insofar as the loss was *A*'s fault, that is a good and relevant reason why *A* should pay and, in the absence of other relevant considerations, a sufficient reason. In short, if someone has got to be hurt in this affair, let it be the wrongdoer (other things being equal). But where there is no necessity that the burden of payment be restricted to the two parties involved, weak retributivism has no application and, indeed, is quite compatible with a whole range of nonfault principles.

One final point remains to be made. If we hold that we are all more or less equally sinners in respect to a certain area of conduct or a certain type of fault—if, for example, we are all as likely, more or less, to be erring defendants as wronged plaintiffs in driving accident suits—then the principle of strong retributivism itself would call for the jettisoning of the "his fault" principle in that area of activity. If fault is distributed equally, the "his fault" principle, in distributing liability *unequally* among a group, will cause a lack of correspondence between fault and penalty. On the assumption of equal distribution of fault, the use of the "his fault" principle would lead to *less* correspondence, *less* exact proportioning of penalty to fault, even than various principles of social insurance that have the effect of spreading the losses as widely as possible among a whole community of persons presumed to be equally faulty. But then these schemes of nonfault liability are supported by strong reasons of their own, principles both of justice and economy, and hardly need this bit of surprising added support from the principle of strong retributivism.

15. Are There Decisions Computers Should Never Make?

James H. Moor

THE POSSIBILITY MAY seem exhilarating or it may seem repugnant, but the possibility should be carefully considered. The possibility is that computers may someday (and perhaps to a limited extent already do) serve not merely as tools for calculation or consultation but as full-fledged decision makers on important matters involving human welfare. In examining this possibility I hope to avoid computerphilia and computerphobia and argue for an empirical approach as a significant component in our assessment of computer activity and its effects. I wish to focus on the issue of decision making because it is in this area that computers have the greatest potential for influencing and controlling our lives. In determining what limits, if any, we should place on the use of computers, we must consider whether there are decisions computers should never make.

Do Computers Make Decisions?

It can be objected that asking whether there are decisions computers should never make begs an important question, i.e., whether computers are the sort of thing which can make decisions at all. Before considering this objection, it is useful to distinguish between two

From *Nature and System* 1 (1979), pp. 217–229. © 1979 by Nature and System, Inc. Reprinted by permission of Nature and System, Inc.

senses of making a decision. In the *narrow* sense "making a decision" refers to the arrival at a decision, i.e., to the selection of a course of action. Processes leading up to the decision are ignored. For example, if one is asked to pick any card during a card trick, then simply selecting a card constitutes making a decision. In the *broad* sense "making a decision" refers not only to the decision but to processes leading up to the decision as well. Thus, in the broad sense making a decision may involve investigating possible courses of action, evaluating alternative strategies and selecting a course of action based on this investigation and evaluation. For example, in playing checkers one makes a decision by considering various possible moves, weighing the advantages and disadvantages of each and finally selecting a move based on this analysis.

Now, the objection above can be put more precisely. Computers might make decisions (or at least be used to make decisions) in the narrow sense of the term, but computers are not the sort of thing which can make decisions in the broad sense. In other words, computers might make decisions in the sense that one can flip a coin to make decisions, but computers are not the sort of thing which can investigate and evaluate alternative strategies in order to select a course of action.

I believe this objection is mistaken. Perhaps its initial plausibility stems from understanding a computer simply as a calculator of arithmetic operations. However, computer activity can be understood in many other ways.[1] One of the most common ways of understanding computer activity is in terms of the execution of an ordinary computer program. In describing this activity, programmers often use decision making language. For instance, a programmer might say that at a certain point in the execution of a program the computer decides whether an inputed string of characters matches another string of characters. Of course, such uses of "decides" and its cognates might be discounted as nothing more than technical jargon. But there are other situations in which computer activity can be understood as a complex analysis of information resulting in the selection of a course of action. In such cases, decision making language often has a very natural application.

As an example, consider A. L. Samuel's now classic program for playing checkers.[2] The computer using Samuel's program not only plays checkers, but improves its game with experience. The computer understood as a checker player is naturally described as a decision maker. When its turn comes, the computer must decide what move to make. Moreover, if the computer is to play checkers well, it must base its decisions upon sophisticated decision making processes. As Samuel points out, "There exists no known algorithm which will guarantee a win or draw in checkers, and the complete explorations of every possible path through a checker game would involve perhaps 10^{40} choices of moves which, at 3 choices per millimicrosecond, would still take 10^{21} centuries to consider."[3] The computer, using Samuel's program, makes its decision not unlike human players in that it looks ahead a few moves and evaluates the possible resulting board positions, but it differs from the human decision maker in the manner in which it evaluates board positions. The computer evaluates a board position in terms of a polynomial each term of which represents a parameter of the game, i.e., some configuration of pieces and squares. By playing lots of games, sometimes with itself as an opponent, the computer learns which parameters are important. By altering the weights of the parameters and trying different parameters from a stockpile of them, the computer's evaluation mechanism becomes better and better. Although the computer played poor checkers initially, through competition the computer's abilities improved to the point that it beat a human checker playing champion.[4]

The fact that the computer uses a polynomial to determine its selection of moves does not show that the computer is not a decision maker, for a human player could make his decisions in the same manner though certainly not as quickly. Indeed, a computer playing checkers is a very clear illustration of a computer making a decision in the broad sense. The computer must analyze the situation, discover what courses of action are available, evaluate the options, and select a course of action based on its information. This is a paradigm of decision making.

One might attempt to buttress the original objection that computers cannot make decisions by assuming that decision making must be done consciously. Certainly we are conscious of much of our decision making, but it is important to realize that we are not conscious of much of it as well. For example, each of us often decides what food to eat or which clothes to wear without being even slightly aware of why a particular decision is made. Much money is invested in marketing research to discover those factors, those "hidden persuaders" as Vance Packard once called them, which can affect our decision making without our being aware of them. Sometimes we can make decisions without even being aware that decisions are being made. For instance, unless we happen to reflect on the situation later, we can make many complex driving decisions in heavy traffic, perhaps while thinking about something else, without being conscious of our own decision making (in the narrow or the broad sense). Since our consciousness of our own decision making can vary from being much aware to completely unaware, consciousness of decision making should not be regarded as an essential feature of decision making.

Finally, it might be argued that it is not computers which make decisions but rather humans who *use* computers to make decisions. But, this point confuses the *power* to make decisions with the *ability* to make decisions. The power to make decisions involves being in the appropriate situation and having the authority to make decisions. For instance, at any time, only one person has the power to make United States presidential decisions although many people may have the ability to make such decisions. The source of this power comes from an election by the people under the Constitution. The fact that we use the president to make decisions is compatible with the president being a decision maker. Similarly, we can delegate decision making power to computers, and the fact that we use computers in this way is compatible with computers being decision makers.

I believe it is important to understand computer activity in some contexts as decision making not only because it is so, but because to see it otherwise tends to minimize our appreciation for the potential impact of computers on our society. To delegate decision making power is to delegate control. Ultimately, the issue is what aspects of our lives, if any, computers should control.

How Competent Can Computer Decision Making Be?

If one grants that at least in principle computers are able to make decisions, it remains a question what kinds of decisions computers can make competently. Since computers are not limited to making random, fixed, or arbitrary decisions, as the checker playing computer illustrates, it may seem that there are no limits to computer decision making. But, the results of logic clearly indicate some limitations. If one accepts Church's thesis that algorithmic computability of a function is equivalent to Turing machine computability of it, then limits of Turing machines are limits of computers. Specifically, the results of the halting problem show that there are decisions even universal Turing machines cannot make effectively, viz., there is no universal Turing machine which can decide for every Turing machine whether or not it will halt. The trouble with this type of limitation is that it seems to apply to humans as well as to computers. Moreover, if one were to seriously set out to decide whether or not sufficiently complex Turing machines would halt, computers, though not infallible, would likely be better at the job than humans.

Therefore, the issue is not whether there are some limitations to computer decision making but how well computer decision making compares with human decision making. In order to make the matter most interesting, I will limit the class of computers to those sorts of electronic and mechanical devices which are ordinarily considered to be computers, i.e., for the purposes of this paper, I wish to specifically rule out considering human beings as computers and considering computers as persons.[5] Are there, then, decisions which (nonperson) computers could never make as well as humans?

I believe the simple, honest answer is that nobody really knows whether computers can possibly match or exceed human ability at decision making. I wish to advocate an empiricist's position on the question of computer decision making and on the question of computer intellectual abilities in general. My claim is:

1. It is essentially an empirical matter what a computer's level of ability is for a given intellectual activity.
2. It is possible to gather evidence to determine a computer's level of ability for a given intellectual activity.
3. For most kinds of intellectual activities it is still unknown whether or not computers will one day match or exceed human levels of ability.

As a corollary of my general empiricist's position, I want to maintain that for most kinds of decision making, it is still a very open empirical question whether computers will ever have levels of ability which match or exceed human levels. I regard my view as nothing more than common sense, but common sense seems to be somewhat uncommon on this matter. For instance, some would challenge my view on the grounds that it is not an empirical matter at all. With regard to decision making, I have already responded to this kind of objection. Others who grant that there is an empirical component involved often suggest that the matter is already settled. For instance, in 1958 Herbert Simon and Allen Newell, prominent artificial intelligence researchers, asserted that "there are now in the world machines that think, that learn and that create. Moreover, their ability to do things is going to increase rapidly until—in the visible future—the range of problems they can handle will be coextensive with the range to which the human mind has been applied."[6] Artificial intelligence workers have clearly demonstrated that computers can possess certain kinds of intellectual abilities. To an amazing extent, today's computers can solve problems, recognize patterns, play games, prove theorems, and use natural language.[7] Nevertheless, it is just a brute fact that computers do not now possess anywhere near the general intelligence of an average human being, and there is no strong evidence that in the visible future the range of problems they will be able to handle will be coextensive with the range to which the human mind has been applied. The enthusiasm of artificial intelligence researchers for their work is commendable, but at this time the results of their labors do not establish that computers will one day match or exceed human levels of ability for most kinds of intellectual activities.

Some of the critics of artificial intelligence research would also disagree with my view. Hubert Dreyfus concludes his analysis of such research by stating: "Thus, insofar as the question whether artificial intelligence is possible is an empirical question, the answer seems to be that further significant progress in Cognitive Simulation or in Artificial Intelligence is extremely unlikely."[8] Dreyfus appeals both to the fact that work in these areas sometimes fails and to a phenomenological analysis which he takes to show that there are nonprogrammable human capacities involved in all forms of intelligent behavior.[9] The argument about failures in early endeavors is not very persuasive since it can be launched against any science in its early stages. The more interesting argument is his phenomenological appraisal which emphasizes, I think correctly, that when we engage in perceptual and intellectual activities, we usually have a global recognition of the situation and can pull out the essential features even in ambiguous contexts. For instance, if I utter the sentence "Christopher Columbus had global recognition which no computer has ever had" we can all immediately grasp several meanings of the sentence and know which are related to this discussion and which are puns; and yet, we are not aware of any extensive analysis leading up to this understanding. Computers clearly lack such facility with language. Although today's computers can handle some perceptual and linguistic ambiguities, on the whole computers are very much inferior to people on such matters. Computers are not good punsters. Nevertheless, these phenomenological and factual points are not adequate to establish Dreyfus' conclusion that there are nonprogrammable capacities involved in all forms of intelligent behavior. What appears unlawlike, even capricious, at one level may be perfectly lawlike at another. It remains a possibility that activities of which we are not aware, but which underlie intelligent behavior, can be expressed in terms of computable functions. If this is the case, then computers might one day carry them out.

A task which may seem unprogrammable is the selection of appropriate hypotheses in science. But for certain families of molecules a computer using the program DENDRAL is an expert in identifying the molecular structure which best explains data produced by mass spectrometers. The computer is an expert in doing this even when compared with the best human performance.[10] On the other hand, for most of chemistry the computer's performance in selecting appropriate hypotheses is at the novice level or worse. The point is that there is enough evidence from artificial intelligence research to be suspicious of dogmatic claims that computers will never be able to accomplish certain feats of intelligence; yet, today there is not nearly enough evidence to support the conclusion that computers will someday match or exceed human intellectual ability in general or human decision making ability in particular.

How Can Computer Decision Making Competence Be Judged?

Empirical investigation will allow us to refine our judgments about the nature of computer abilities, but what sort of evidence counts? Since competence is the ability to perform at a given level of accomplishment, obviously the computer's performance will be one important source of evidence in evaluating competence. With regard to decision making, two features of the performance are relevant: (1) the decision making record and (2) the justifications offered for the decisions. These two types of evidence will carry various weights depending upon the kind of decision making and the cirmcumstances in which it is made.

Specifically, I wish to distinguish two extremes of decision making: decision making under clear standards and decision making under fuzzy standards. Many cases of decision making lie between these two extremes. In making decisions under clear standards every decision (or series of decisions) can be clearly classified as either correct or incorrect. For example, deciding which horse to bet on to win a race is a decision made under clear standards. The horse will either win or not win. After a number of such decisions, preferably made in a variety of situations, the decision maker will have established a clear record of correct decisions vs. incorrect decisions. In the case of decision making under clear standards the justifications offered for decisions are usually not very important in evaluating competence. If the bettor routinely picks winning horses, it hardly matters if he is unable to produce justifications for his decisions. If he cannot pick winning horses, justifications for decisions are small consolation. However, if the decision making record is not available or for some reason is not trusted, then certainly the justifications given for the decisions can be important in evaluating decision making under clear standards.

In decision making under fuzzy standards at least some of the possible decisions (or series of decisions) will be difficult to classify as correct or incorrect. For many people deciding which career to pursue is an example of decision making under fuzzy standards. The fuzzier the standards are the more difficult it is to establish a clear record of correct decisions vs. incorrect decisions, and the more important it is to provide some justifications for the decisions. For instance, it may be impossible to determine how many "correct" and "incorrect" grades a professor gives, but one can evaluate his decision making by checking his justifications for assigning individual grades.

The checker playing computer is making decisions under clear standards in that a series of decisions about moves either leads to a win or it does not. It is impressive that the computer has beaten a checker playing champion; but in order to really establish its competence, the computer would have to establish a substantial record of play against a variety of opponents.

Some computers can make decisions under fuzzy standards and can offer justifications for their decisions. For instance, consider MYCIN, an interactive program that "uses the clinical decision criteria of experts to advise physicians who request advice regarding the selection of appropriate antimicrobial therapy for hospital patients with bacterial infection."[11] Advice of this kind has practical importance because often drug therapy has to be recommended before a positive identification of the bacteria can be made and because not every physician is a specialist in the subject. The computer asks the physician for information about the situation including the results of laboratory tests. The computer will give its conclusions about the identities of the organisms; and upon asking a few more questions about the patient's allergies, renal and hepatic status, the site(s) of the infection, etc., the computer will formulate and recommend therapy. MYCIN contains a set of over 200 production rules each of which states a set of preconditions and a conclusion or action to be taken if the preconditions occur. The production rules not only give the computer a basis for decisions, but allow it to offer justifications for its decisions. The computer can explain either why certain information is important in terms of its goals or how it arrives at its conclusions. Thus, a physician has a check on the computer's competence without knowing the computer's overall decision making record. The decision making record cannot be completely clear since even experts disagree about what is a "correct" or an "incorrect" decision in some cases, e.g., in recommending certain therapies. Nevertheless, in a preliminary evaluation, MYCIN's therapy recommendations were acceptable to the experts in 75% of the cases.[12] The workers on the MYCIN project hope to increase the computer's competence in this type of decision making and to extend the production rule methodology to other areas.[13] But whatever abilities computers may eventually acquire using the production rule approach, the MYCIN program illustrates that a computer's performance can be such that one can evaluate the computer's competence even in decision making under fuzzy standards.

Another kind of evidence about a computer's competence in decision making results from an analysis of the internal operation of the computer, perhaps in terms of a computer program. This kind of evidence is not essential, at least not in principle; for if the performance is good enough, it will provide a sufficient basis for a justified inductive inference about the computer's competence.[14] We often infer that other humans are competent decision makers without having any information about their internal operation except indirectly through performance. Nevertheless, as a practical matter it certainly can be very useful to have such information, e.g., in those situations in which a justification for a decision is an important piece of evidence but which the computer can not provide as part of its performance. Obviously, in the development stage one must pay close attention to the program for even the most novice programmer knows that a well-thought-out program may not result in the performance expected and a performance which is good in general may be the result of a program with hidden "bugs."

Usually it is not very helpful in assessing a computer's competence at decision making to simply ask whether the computer makes its decisions on the same basis (in the sense of internal operation) that humans do. The answer can almost always be "yes" or "no" depending upon how the activity is described. Yes, the computer checker player is like a human checker player in that it looks ahead a few moves. Or no, the computer checker player is not like a human checker player in that it uses a polynomial to evaluate board positions.[15] What is crucial is that the basis be capable of reliably generating a reasonable level of performance (including producing justifications when relevant). Indeed, if a computer does exceed human competence in decision making, it is very likely the basis for its decisions will be different from the human basis.

Are There Decisions Computers Should Never Make?

The empirical position I am advocating undercuts a lot of argumentation about which decisions computers should and should not make. Joseph Weizenbaum states:

> What could be more obvious than the fact that, whatever intelligence a computer can muster, however it may be acquired, it must always and necessarily be absolutely alien to any and all authentic human concerns. The very asking of the question, "What does a judge (or a psychiatrist) know that we cannot tell a computer?" is a monstrous

obscenity. That it has to be put into print at all, even for the purpose of exposing its morbidity, is a sign of the madness of our times.

Computers can make judicial decisions, computers can make psychiatric judgments. They can flip coins in much more sophisticated ways than can the most patient human being. The point is that they ought not be given such tasks. They may even be able to arrive at "correct" decisions in some cases—but always and necessarily on bases no human being should be willing to accept.[16]

Weizenbaum claims that computers are outsiders to human affairs just as humans are sometimes outsiders to other human cultures. Outsiders will have bases for decisions which "must be inappropriate to the context in which the decision is to be made."[17] But this argument confuses lack of information with lack of competence. There may be good reasons not to grant outsiders the power to make some decisions, but there is no reason in principle why an *informed* outsider cannot be a competent decision maker. A physician who is an outsider may be more competent to make medical decisions than anybody in a primitive tribe. A computer which never has a bacterial infection may be very competent in making decisions about them.

Weizenbaum does not make it clear whether by "bases" he means the internal operation of the computer or the sorts of justifications it could give for making its decisions. But for neither case has he demonstrated that they must always and necessarily be such that human beings should not accept them. Weizenbaum's examples—judicial decisions and psychiatric judgments—are cases of decision making under fuzzy standards. It is possible to evaluate a computer's competence in these areas by paying close attention to the sorts of justifications the computer gives for its decisions. It is at least conceivable that the computer might give outstanding justifications for its decisions ranging from detailed legal precedents to a superb philosophical theory of justice or from instructive clinical observations to an improved theory of mental illness so that the competence of the computer in such decision making was considered to be as good or better than the competence of human experts. Empirically this may never happen but it is not a necessary truth that it will not.

Perhaps more importantly, an empirical attitude challenges an uncritical acceptance of computer competence. It is far too easy to try to justify a decision by simply saying "the computer says so." Such a reply should carry no weight unless the computer's competence has been rigorously tested. It is always relevant to raise two competency questions when computer decision making occurs—"What is the nature of the computer's (alleged) competence?" and "How has the competence been demonstrated?" A company spokesman might announce that a computer has decided there should be a 20% layoff when in fact the computer has done nothing more than determine which 20% of the firm's employees has least seniority. The problem is not just that one group might deceive another about the computer's competency but that even immediate users of the computer may take the computer's word too uncritically. In a nuclear age in which some of the decision making about whether to launch missiles is in part made by computers, the possibility of deception about computer competency is a matter of great importance.

Thus, the first step in determining what kinds of decisions computers should and should not make at particular times is to determine what kinds of decisions computers can and cannot make competently at those times. But, there remains a question of values. Even if someday computers are competent to make a wide range of important decisions, should certain kinds of decision making be forbidden to computers? I believe that the proper answer suggests itself when considering why the following three maxims, though initially plausible, are really unsatisfactory.

Dubious Maxim 1

Computers should never make any decisions which humans want to make. This is a somewhat plausible maxim since we obviously enjoy the pleasure and freedom involved in making many of the decisions which affect our lives. A computer could competently decide which shoe a person should put on first in the morning, but clearly such a meaningless intrusion into a person's affairs would greatly reduce the quality of his life. However, this maxim is unsatisfactory in general because there can be other factors which outweigh the benefits of the freedom and pleasure humans derive from doing the decision making. For example, even if humans would like to make certain medical decisions, it might be the case that a computer existed which could make them far better. If the computer's diagnosis and suggestions for treatment would result in a significant savings of lives and reduction of suffering compared with human decision making on the subject, then there is a powerful moral argument for letting computers decide.

Dubious Maxim 2

Computers should never make any decisions which humans can make more competently. This also seems like a very reasonable maxim. We do not want the computer to make life-or-death medical decisions if the computer is less competent than human decision makers. But again the maxim is too limited because it neglects other considerations. Some activities, e.g., certain kinds of factory work or prolonged space travel, may be so boring, time-consuming, or dangerous that it would be morally better to use computers, even if this involved sacrificing some competency in decision making, in order to spare humans from enduring such experiences.

Dubious Maxim 3

Computers should never make any decisions which humans cannot override. This maxim seems most reasonable of all especially if it is set against a background of numerous science fiction tales in which computers take control and humans become their slaves. But there could be situations in which it would be morally better to make it impossible, at least practically speaking, for humans to override computer decisions. Suppose that when people drive cars, tens of thousands of people are killed in automobile accidents, hundreds of thousands are injured, and millions of dollars are lost in property damage. But when computers drive cars, not only are human transportation needs carried out more efficiently but there is a substantial reduction in deaths, injuries, and property damage. Further suppose in those cases in which humans override computer driving decisions, the accident rate soars. Under such circumstances there is a persuasive moral and prudential argument to have computers do the decision making and not to allow humans to override their decisions.

What I am advocating is that we regard computer decision making instrumentally. For particular situations we must determine whether using computer decision makers will better promote our values and accomplish our goals. The maxims above suggest important considerations but are inadequate as general rules because situations may arise in which the consequences are far better if the maxims are violated. This approach is a natural extension of the empiricist's position described earlier. Within the context of our basic goals and values (and the priorities among them) we must empirically determine not only the competence of the computer decision maker but the consequences of computer decision making as well.

This instrumental view of the value of computer decision making leads to the answer to the question what decisions computers should never make. Computers should never decide what our basic goals and values (and priorities among them) should be. These basic goals and values, such as the promotion of human life and happiness, decrease in suffering, search for truth and understanding, etc., provide us with the ultimate norms for directing and judging actions and decision making. By definition there are not further goals and values by which to evaluate these. Since we want computers to work for our ends, we obviously want to prohibit computers from deciding to change these ultimate norms, e.g., promoting computer welfare at the expense of human welfare or taking inconsistency to be the mark of good reasoning.

To prohibit computers from making decisions about basic goals and values (and the priorities among them) is, of course, not to limit computer decision making very much. Our basic goals and values remain fairly constant and humans rarely decide to change them. Thus, there is a wide range of possible decision making which computers one day might justifiably perform. Nevertheless, I believe there is a very legitimate concern that increased computerization of our society will lead to dehumanization of our lives. The proper root of this concern is not that computers are necessarily incompetent or inherently evil. It may be the case that one day computers will make the major decisions about the operations of our society better than humans with the result that the quality of human life is substantially improved. The root of concern about increased computerization should be focused on the issue of responsibility. By assumption, the kind of computers under discussion are not persons; and although they are causally responsible for their decisions, they are not legally or morally responsible for their decisions. One cannot sue a computer. Therefore, humans have not only an initial responsibility, but a continuing responsibility to raise the competency and value questions whenever computer decision making is at issue. First, what is the nature of the computer's competency and how has it been demonstrated? Secondly, given our basic goals and values why is it better to use a computer decision maker in a particular situation than a human decision maker? The danger is that our responsibility can be easily undermined by strong pressures, e.g., economic incentives, not to investigate and answer these questions. The dehumanization which results can either be in the form of computers making decisions which humans should make or vice versa. Of course, if the delegation of decision making power is carried out responsibly, we may be creating a much more humane society. Some of the most humanistic decisions may well come from decision makers which are not human.

Notes

1. On one level a computer is nothing more than a physical system and can be explained as such. For the computer to perform even simple arithmetic calculations, we must interpret its activities symbolically. Obviously, there is a wide range of possible interpretations. See James H. Moor, "Explaining Computer Behavior," *Philosophical Studies,* 34 (1978): 325–27.
2. A. L. Samuel, "Some Studies In Machine Learning Using the Game of Checkers," *Computers and Thought,* ed. Edward A. Feigenbaum and Julian Feldman (New York: McGraw-Hill, 1963), pp. 71–105.
3. Samuel, p. 72.
4. Samuel, pp. 103–105.
5. I want to separate the question of computers being persons from the main issue because I believe interesting results follow about computer decision making without raising matters of civil rights. The set of computers I am considering will have members which may be very good at particular kinds of decision making but no one member of the set will have sufficient variety of decision making abilities (among other things) to be considered a person.
6. H. A. Simon and A. Newell, "Heuristic Problem Solving: The Next Advance in Operations Research," *Operations Research* 6 (1958): 8.
7. For a nice summary of artificial intelligence work see Patrick Henry Winston, *Artificial Intelligence* (Reading, Mass.: Addison-Wesley, 1977).
8. Hubert Dreyfus, *What Computers Can't Do* (New York: Harper and Row, 1972), p. 197.
9. Dreyfus also has an argument based on the digital/analogue distinction. See James H. Moor, "Three Myths of Computer Science," *The British Journal of Philosophy of Science,* 29 (1978): 213–22.
10. E. A. Feigenbaum, B. G. Buchanan and J. Lederberg, "On Generality and Problem Solving: A Case Study Using the DENDRAL Program," *Machine Intelligence,* 6, ed. B. Meltzer (Edinburgh: Edinburgh University Press, 1971), p. 165.
11. Edward H. Shortliffe, Randall Davis, Stanton G. Axline, Bruce G. Buchanan, C. Cordell Green, and Stanley N. Cohen, "Computer-Based Consultations in Clinical Therapeutics: Explanation and Rule Acquisition Capabilities of the MYCIN System," *Computers and Biomedical Research* 8 (1975): 303.
12. *Ibid.,* p. 318.
13. Randall Davis, Bruce Buchanan, and Edward Shortliffe, "Production Rules as a Representation for a Knowledge-Based Consultation Program," *Artificial Intelligence* 8 (1977): 15–45.
14. James H. Moor, "An Analysis of the Turing Test," *Philosophical Studies* 30 (1976): 249–57.
15. The difference between doing artificial intelligence and cognitive simulation is not a sharp distinction. It is a matter of emphasis and level of description of the computer activity.
16. Joseph Weizenbaum, *Computer Power and Human Reason* (San Francisco: W. H. Freeman, 1976), pp. 226–27.
17. Weizenbaum, p. 226.

PART
3

Privacy and Security

OF ALL THE problems discussed in this book, privacy and security are probably the topics that have received the most public attention and have been addressed the most via laws, changes in technology, and so forth.

Our first reading by R. Turn and W. H. Ware ("Privacy and Security Issues in Information Systems") draws the distinction between privacy issues and security issues and gives us a historical perspective on each. For the most part, the readings in Part 3 do not take up the security issues but rather concentrate on privacy. We have limited the discussion of security issues because they are technical in nature; the problem is how to design information systems so that they cannot be tampered with by unauthorized persons. Furthermore, the security problem does not raise a particularly interesting or even complex ethical problem. When unauthorized individuals intentionally get access to data stored in a computer, they know they are doing something wrong. The problem or problems surrounding security are problems of how to rather than what "should" we do or how far "ought" we to go.

On the other hand, the privacy issue is enormously complex from a moral point of view. Even though there has been much public debate the fundamental questions remain: What is privacy? Why is it so important? What is the basis for saying that people have a "right" to privacy?

The computers and privacy issue has to do primarily with the record-keeping capability of computers. Computers do not by themselves pose a threat to privacy. Rather, they make possible an array of activities that mean individuals have lost control over who has what kind of information about them. Of course, records were being kept long before the inception of computers and would, no doubt, continue to be kept if computers were somehow eradicated from the earth. What computers do is make possible a scale of in-

131

formation gathering that was just not possible without the computer. The numer of individuals whose behavior can be monitored increases as well as the amount of information that can be gathered about each individual. What is perhaps more significant is that this information can be exchanged with incredible ease and speed. The use of computers has also meant that information that might have been dropped from a person's record over time, because of the inconvenience of storage and expense of transmission, can follow the person through life and never be dropped. Finally because of the ease and speed of exchange of information, the effects of an error in someone's record can be magnified enormously. The error is transmitted to database after database before it is discovered, and then it is nearly impossible to backtrack and correct the information in each database.

To illustrate the significance of the problem and bring it home we have included a chapter from David Burnham's *The Rise of the Computer State.* Here you will find examples not just of the potential of the computer but of what it has already been used to do.

The interesting and difficult philosophical matter here is to try to understand exactly why we value privacy so much. It is only with such an understanding that we can strongly argue for protections against intrusions of privacy resulting from use of computers. Much to the surprise of many Americans there is no explicit constitutional guarantee to privacy. Rather our right to privacy has evolved from legal interpretations and precedent-setting legal rulings. To get at the problem of understanding why privacy is important we have included three quite different readings. The first is the classic legal work on privacy by Samuel Warren and Louis Brandeis, in which they try to argue that a right to privacy exists. The challenge is to see if what they say applies to computerized record keeping. The second is a broader look at the function of privacy by Alan Westin. But here again it is not obvious that the case Westin makes for privacy applies to computerized records.

The issue pertaining to computers might best be characterized as a struggle between the need for information by organizations and the right of individuals to control that information. When it comes to computerized records, we are really talking about large organizations that make use of personal data—for example, insurance companies, credit agencies, banks, government agencies such as the CIA or the Census Bureau. It may be useful, indeed, to take James Rachels' idea (in "Why Privacy is Important") that control of information allows one to control relationships and extend it to say that, when individuals lose control over information about themselves, they lose control over their relationships with the organizations that have a good deal of power and that use the information to make decisions affecting the individual's life. W. A. Parent is critical of both the Brandeis-Warren approach and theories like Rachels' that stress autonomy. He offers a definition of privacy that applies most directly to computerized records. "Privacy," he claims, "is the condition of not having undocumented personal knowledge about one possessed by others." The questions we must ask about Parent's analysis are these: Does it allow us to understand why privacy is most important, and does it help us to balance the value of privacy against other values?

We conclude this chapter with the introduction to *Personal Privacy in an Information Society,* the report of the Privacy Protection Study Commission (1977). This report focuses on the problem as one involving the relationship between individuals and large organizations and goes on to outline a national policy for protecting the individual against unnecessary intrusions.

16. Privacy and Security Issues in Information Systems

R. Turn and W. H. Ware

I. The Emerging Problems

PRIVACY AND SECURITY are problems associated with computer systems and applications that were not foreseen until well into the second half of the present computer age. *Privacy* is an issue that concerns the computer community in connection with maintaining personal information on individual citizens in computerized record-keeping systems. It deals with the rights of the individual regarding the collection of information in a record-keeping system about his person and activities, and the processing, dissemination, storage, and use of this information in making determinations about him. This last aspect is a long-standing legal and social problem that has become associated with the computer field mainly because computerized record-keeping systems are much more efficient than the manual systems they have replaced, and because they permit linkages between record-keeping systems and correlations of records on a much greater scale than previously possible in manual systems. Thus threats to individual privacy from manual record-keeping systems are potentially amplified in computerized systems.

Computer *security* includes the procedural and technical measures required 1) to prevent unauthorized access, modification, use, and dissemination of data stored or processed in a computer system, 2) to prevent any deliberate denial of service, and 3) to protect the system in its entirety from physical harm. The access control requirements are particularly important in time-shared and multiprogrammed systems in which multiple users are served concurrently—jobs processed concurrently must be prevented from interfering with each other and users must be prevented from gaining unauthorized access to each other's data or programs. When classified defense information is stored or processed in a system, the mutual isolation of users is called the *multilevel security* problem: how can a system permit concurrent processing of information in different security classification categories, and concurrent use of the system by users who have different security clearances, while still guaranteeing that no classified information is leaked, accidentally or deliberately, to those who do not possess appropriate authorizations and security clearances.

Privacy and security emerged separately as problem areas in the computer field in the mid-1960's. The privacy *cause célèbre* was a recommendation in 1965 that a Data Service Center be established within the federal government to be a centralized data base of all personal information collected by federal agencies for statistical purposes [1]. This computerized system, also known as the National Data Bank, was to be used only for obtaining

From *IEEE Transactions on Computers* C-25, 12 (December 1976), pp. 1353–1361. © 1976 IEEE. Reprinted by permission of The Institute of Electrical and Electronics Engineers, Inc. and Rein Turn and Willis H. Ware.

statistics in support of federal programs and decisions. The proposal received a strongly negative reaction from the Congress, news media, the legal community, and the public. Unfortunately, many of its critics have associated the envisioned threats to individual privacy and other freedoms that such a system was claimed to pose directly with the use of computers. Gathering of crib-to-grave dossiers on individuals and establishment of a comprehensive system of data surveillance were perceived to be direct consequences of the computer's presence.

Congressional hearings were held on the National Data Bank [2], [3], and eventually the project was abandoned. Testimony given by computer specialists [4], [5] at these and subsequent hearings exposed legislators, perhaps for the first time, to the potential of computer technology as a force to both cause and drive societal change and to the need for legislative action to surround computer applications that may produce harmful impacts on society with appropriate legal safeguards. Since then, many papers and books have analyzed the privacy problem and offered solutions [6]–[9]; there is now a general consensus that the legislative approach, rather than reliance on self-policing by record-keeping agencies, is a preferred approach to solving the privacy protection problem in the United States. Different solutions have been proposed in other countries where there is a similar concern with threats to individual privacy [10], [11].

Initial steps to solving the privacy problem in record-keeping systems have addressed specific sectors of society: the Fair Credit Reporting Act of 1971 grants certain rights to individuals who are data subjects in their relations with the financial credit reporting industry [12], the Privacy Act of 1974 requires privacy protection in record-keeping systems in the federal government [13], and the Family Educational Right and Privacy Act extends privacy protection to students' records in federally supported educational institutions [14]. Legislation generally similar to the Privacy Act has been enacted in Minnesota, Arkansas, and Utah, and is pending in many others. At the present time, federal privacy bills encompassing the entire private sector and the criminal justice area are pending in Congress. The principles embodied in the already enacted and pending legislation and certain requirements they pose on record-keeping organizations are discussed in detail in Section II.

The first apprehensions about computer security began in the 1950's with concern over degaussing of magnetic tapes and preventing dissemination of classified information via electromagnetic emanations. By the mid-1960's time-sharing and multiprogramming allowed computer systems to serve many users simultaneously, and on-line programming, job execution, and data file manipulations could be performed from remotely located terminals. In such systems, as first discussed at the 1967 Spring Joint Computer Conference [15]–[17], security problems are different; there are many vulnerabilities which can be exploited by maliciously motivated users or by intruders from outside the system to perpetrate a variety of threats. Section III discusses these vulnerabilities and threats. Solutions to the physical security problem are now well in hand, but totally secure software and consequently, totally secure computer systems are still unattainable.

II. Privacy Protection Principles

In the early 1970's, computerization of personal information record-keeping systems maintained by the federal, state, and local governments and in the private sector expanded rapidly. For example, it was emphasized during Congressional hearings on record-keeping systems maintained by the federal government that nearly 2000 such systems existed, containing hundreds of millions of personal records [18]–[20].

Proliferation of record-keeping systems has come to pass partly because of 1) the increasing size of the population plus the complex lives individuals lead; 2) the demand for services that society now makes on the government; 3) the need for improved efficiency in the conduct of government; and 4) the economics realizable in business. Contemporary computer technology provides society with the tool that it needs to accommodate growing information requirements, not only for the conduct of government, but also for industry and commerce.

A study for the National Academy of Sciences [21] has demonstrated that, contrary to earlier beliefs, a great majority of organizations that have computerized their record-keeping systems have not significantly altered the data-collection and data-sharing policies followed in earlier manual systems. In particular, computerized record-keeping is still expensive enough generally to deter excessive collection of personal information

A. Privacy and Record-Keeping

Surrounded by record-keeping systems that contain extensive personal information about him, the citizen finds that he is increasingly in a position of significant disadvantage in the balance of power between himself and the totality of data systems. He has given personal information to a record-keeping system for some purpose, usually because he expects in exchange some right, privilege, benefit, opportunity, or assurance of civil liberty. He expects that this information will be used for the purpose for which he gave it and in his best interest, certainly not in any way to his detriment. He does not expect to be annoyed, pressured, harassed, or harmed by its use.

An organization that holds personal data does so usually for some valid purpose; for example, it must administer a public assistance program, or operate a teaching institution, or maintain an inventory of some group of people such as property holders, customers, or persons wanted by the criminal justice system. Thus the holder of personal information and the individual each have an interest in the proper use of such information. Neither should have unilateral control over its use; mutuality of control is appropriate.

This paper addresses personal privacy as it relates to the interface between an individual and any record-keeping system that holds personal information on him. Invasion of privacy implies that the holder of personal information has misused it to the detriment of one or more individuals, or has exploited it in some fashion other than for the purpose for which it was collected.

A pivotal aspect of the privacy issue is the present one-sided control that the "data owner" has over the use of personal information; in contrast, some argue that data on a given individual should belong to that individual and to no one else. Except in isolated categories of data, an individual has nothing to say about the use of information that he has given about himself or that has been collected about him. In particular, an organization can acquire information for one purpose and use it for another, perhaps for its own bureaucratic end, perhaps for harassment, or perhaps for combining it with other data to create more extensive records on individuals. Moreover, the data owner can do this without consulting or informing the data subject. While recourse is now available to the individual in such sectors as the credit industry, federally controlled record-keeping systems, some educational institutions, and in some state and local governments, generally the private sector is not legislatively constrained.

B. The Code of Fair Information Practices

Privacy is not a right explicitly enumerated in the United States Constitution, although it is in the California and Alaska constitutions. Furthermore, until recently the entire concept of privacy protection as it applies to personal information in record-keeping systems had not been developed. In related areas such as eavesdropping, wiretapping, and use of polygraphs, a series of court interpretations had applied various Amendments of the Constitution, such as the Fourth Amendment's right to security from unreasonable search and seizure. However, these were not readily and naturally applicable to information privacy.

A very different approach to individual privacy *vis-à-vis* record-keeping systems, in the context used in this paper (i.e., the rights of individuals regarding the collection, processing, storage, dissemination, and use of personal information), is the concept of a Code of Fair Information Practices. It was conceived by the Special Advisory Committee on Automated Personal Data Systems to the Secretary of the Department of Health, Education, and Welfare [22], and rested on five principles that had been talked about by many people but not succinctly and comprehensively considered as a whole prior to the HEW Committee.

Both the concept of a Code and its details are now widely used as the foundation of privacy legislation in the United States, and its applicability is being studied in other countries. The five basic principles of the Code are equally applicable to personal information record-keeping systems in the government and in the private sector.

1. There must be no personal data record-keeping systems whose very existence is secret.
2. There must be a way for an individual to find out what information about him is on record and how it is used.
3. There must be a way for an individual to correct or amend a record of identifiable information about him.
4. There must be a way for an individual to prevent information about him that was obtained for one purpose from being used or made available for other purposes without his consent.
5. Any organization creating, maintaining, using, or disseminating records of identifiable personal data must guarantee the reliability of the data for their intended use and must take precautions to prevent misuse of the data.

Legislation based on these principles would deter the misuse of personal information by stipulating that any deviation from the Code would be an abuse of personal information subject to criminal and civil sanctions, recovery of punitive and actual damages, and injunctive relief.

C. Privacy Safeguards

It was intended by the HEW Committee that the Code of Fair Information Practices would be implemented by a series of safeguards which collectively specify the preferred behavior and method of operation of record-keeping systems and which describe the rights and privileges of the individuals relative to them.

One set of safeguards would require an annual public notice that is intended to inform the public at large as to the name of a record system, its nature and purpose, its data sources, the categories of data maintained, the organizational policies and practices regarding data storage, and so forth. It would make visible the record-keeping practices of organizations.

A second set of safeguards would stipulate the behavior of an organization maintaining a personal data record system. The organization would be required 1) to identify a focal point to which complaints could come; 2) to take affirmative action to inform its employees of the safeguards and to specify penalties for any infraction of them; 3) to take precautions against transferring identifiable personal information to data systems that may not include adequate safeguards; and 4) to maintain records with sufficient accuracy, completeness, timeliness, and pertinence as is relevant to their intended use.

A third set of safeguards gives the individual data subject certain rights. 1) When asked to supply personal data, he would be informed whether he is legally required to or may refuse to supply them. 2) He would be informed, upon his request, whether he is a subject in a given data system. 3) He would have the opportunity to inspect the record, to challenge it, and to cause corrections to be made. 4) He would be assured that data about him are used only for the stated purposes of the system.

D. Confidentiality of Statistical Data

In contrast to *privacy*, which refers to the rights of the individual *vis-à-vis* record systems, *confidentiality* implies that the data themselves must be protected, and that their use must be confined to authorized purposes by authorized people. Certain categories of personal information have a confidential status by statute. For example, the personal data gathered in the United States decennial census are required to be kept confidential by federal law [23]; this means that no individually identified census responses may be disseminated to anyone outside the Census Bureau, and even within the Bureau only specifically authorized employees are permitted access.

Most categories of personal information do not enjoy statutory protection. Disclosure of such information may be compelled by legal process, such as a subpoena issued by a court, search warrant, legislative committee, or other official body that has jurisdiction in the locality where the data are kept. Personal information gathered by educational institutions and by research projects in social, political, and behavioral sciences is susceptible to such procedures.

Absence of statutory confidentiality of personal information gathered for research purposes is a serious concern to researchers whose studies require the gathering of sensitive personal information. While the researchers may have the best of intentions as far as preventing any dissemination of identified information (and may even assure his respondents of its confidentiality), if faced with a subpoena he has the choice of either being in contempt and suffering the penalties or of surrendering the data [24]. In either case his research project has been seriously damaged.

The Code of Fair Information Practices addresses this problem by seeking federal legislation to protect statistical reporting or research data against compulsory disclosure through the legal process. Such statutory protection should: 1) be limited to data identifiable with or traceable to specific individuals; 2) be specific enough to qualify for the nondisclosure exemption under the Freedom of Information Act [25]; and 3) be applicable to data in the custody of all statistical reporting and research systems whether supported by federal funds or not. The federal law should be controlling; no state statute should interfere with the protection provided.

Whether or not general statutory confidentiality protection is provided for statistical reporting or research data, the Code would require that the data gathering organization:

1. inform the individual whether he is legally required to supply the data requested or may refuse, and of any specific consequences for him, which are known to the organization, of providing or not providing such data;
2. guarantee that no use of individually identifiable data will be made that is not within the stated purposes of the system as understood by the individual, unless the informed consent of the individual has been explicitly obtained; and
3. guarantee that no data about an individual will be made available from the system in response to a compulsory legal process, unless the individual to whom the data pertains has been notified of the demand and has been afforded full access to the data before they are made available in response to the demand.

E. Privacy Legislation

The principal privacy protection law now in force, the Privacy Act of 1974, applies to record-keeping systems maintained by federal agencies, except that intelligence, criminal justice, and law enforcement agencies and the National Archives either have exemptions or may seek exemption by formal rule-making procedures. The Act embodies the principles set forth in the Code of Fair Information Practices such as: 1) requiring that all agencies publish an annual notice on their record-keeping system; 2) requiring that an agency notify an individual, upon his request, of the existence of any records of personal information on him; 3) granting the individual the right of access to his records and their correction or amendment; 4) requiring that the agency obtain prior approval from the individual concerned for any nonroutine use or dissemination of his records; and 5) providing penalties, both criminal and civil, that can be levied for failure to comply.

In addition, the Privacy Act established a Privacy Protection Study Commission with a charter to study record-keeping systems in governmental and private organizations not yet covered by the Privacy Act, in order to recommend whether the Act, and which of its provisions, should be extended to cover these systems.

Pending in Congress is a bill, H.R. 1984, which would extend the Privacy Act to record-keeping systems in the private sector and would strengthen numerous requirements of the present Act. For example: 1) notices would have to be published in local or regional news media that are most likely to reach the largest number of data subjects; 2) individuals would have to be notified of their records on the agency's own initiative; 3) the use of Social Security numbers, or any other universal identifiers, would be prohibited if not required by statute or unless given permission by Congress; 4) the only exemptions would be active criminal investigation files, data systems maintained by the news media, and certain mailing lists. Penalties for noncompliance would be strengthened, and a Federal Privacy Board would be established to oversee enforcement of the Act.

F. Implementation and Costs

There are a number of procedural and technical ways of implementing the privacy protection requirements of the Privacy Act of 1974, state privacy laws, and pending privacy protection bills. For example, organizations that are in regular correspondence with individuals in their record-keeping systems can use such means for notifying them of the existence of records. Requirements of the Privacy Act to assure that records are "accurate, complete, timely, and relevant for agency purposes," and that the agency "establish the appropriate administrative, technical, and physical safeguards to ensure the security and confidentiality of records" involve three categories of technical safeguards: information management practices, physical security procedures, and data security controls within the system and its communications. No part of a system by itself is likely to offer protection against all risks of privacy violation, but by careful selection of safeguards that reflects the needs of the data system being considered, the level of protection can usually be improved significantly at reasonable cost [26]. Safeguards for data security are discussed briefly in the following section.

The cost of implementing privacy safeguards depends on the details of the record-keeping system and the implementation [27], [28]. Initial cost includes the analysis, design, and implementation of the protection system safeguards; acquisition of protection-oriented equipment; improvement of data handling practices and generation of the necessary software; conversion of the data bases to make provisions for protection-oriented data fields; and management adjustments. The operational costs include salaries of employees performing protection-oriented tasks, the cost of computer resources for protection-oriented processing and communication task, and the administrative cost of privacy protection.

Other protection-related costs may be less visible. For example, protection requirements may reduce the availability of a record-keeping system to other users, as well as reducing the system's throughput and efficiency. If such reductions are significant, the record-keeping system may be unable to meet its peak inquiry-handling or processing demands, and may need additional or faster processors or additional storage configuration capacity. In this respect, privacy protection may be in conflict with the usual goals of a system's manager and users.

No information is yet available on the cost experience of federal or state agencies under the Privacy Act of 1974; but it has been estimated that the initial costs are approximately $100 million and the recurring costs $200 million. On a per-capita basis, these costs are quite reasonable—roughly a dollar for each person in the country. However, much higher costs have been estimated for the private sector, and certainly the basis over which to spread the costs is much smaller. Clearly, legislatures must take care not to specify protection requirements that would entail unreasonable implementation costs or that may even be technically infeasible.

III. Computer Security

In addition to supporting legally mandated privacy protection requirements, there are other compelling reasons for maintaining computer and data security. Computers in the federal government process classified information on national defense policies, systems, and plans. In business and industry, valuable information on new product development, marketing, finances, and planning are kept in computer systems. The financial community is automating banking and funds transfer systems; Electronic Funds Transfer Systems (EFTS) will eventually replace a large percentage of financial documents with electronic signals and magnetization patterns.

A. Computer Abuse

Computerization of daily business operations has provided new opportunities and new means for such white-collar crimes as embezzlement, falsification of records, fraud, and larceny. Case histories demonstrate that employees who manage or design data systems, write application programs, or operate the equipment have recognized opportunities for criminal acts [29], [30]. Abuses that the computer makes especially easy are payments for fictitious purchases or to fictitious employees, manipulation of credit levels, and deposits of unauthorized payments into various accounts. Consolidation of record-keeping systems into computerized systems creates highly centralized, easily identifiable targets for disruption, sabotage, or fraudulent manipulation. Table 1 summarizes a history of computer abuse incidents.

As previously noted, computer security includes safeguards to 1) protect a computer-based system, including its physical hardware, personnel, and data against deliberate or accidental damage; 2) protect the system against denial of use by its rightful owners; and

TABLE 1: Reported Cases of Computer Abuse[a]

Year	Financial Fraud	Theft of Information	Unauthorized Use	Vandalism	Total
1969	3	6	2	4	15
1970	10	5	10	8	33
1971	23	19	6	6	54
1972	16	17	18	15	66
1973	26	20	11	11	68
1974	25	15	12	7	59
1975	26	7	4	6	43
Totals	129	89	63	57	338

[a]As of January 1976. Data for 1974 and 1975 are still incomplete. Personal communication from Don Parker, Stanford Research Institute, Menlo Park, CA.

3) protect information or data against divulgence to unauthorized recipients. Threats that must be averted include natural disasters, riots, equipment failures, negligent or maliciously motivated employees and users, and external intruders.

Although manual record-keeping systems and data files are subject to similar threats, certain characteristics of information storage and processing in computer systems make threats to them more serious. First, information is stored in forms not directly readable by users, e.g., magnetization, voltage levels. They can be changed without a trace of evidence unless comprehensive audit trails have been incorporated into the design system. Computerized records do not have signatures or seals to verify authenticity or to distinguish copies from originals, and they can be manipulated electronically from terminals remote from the physical storage of the data. Transactions can be performed automatically at high speed without human monitoring or intervention. Finally, processing rules are expressed as programs stored in the same devices and in the same manner as the data; they too can be changed without trace. While processing programs are difficult to validate, a properly designed and implemented computerized information system can control errors and manage access to the records much more effectively than can any manual record-keeping system, provided such controls have been included in the design specifications.

B. Security Safeguards

How to provide computer security is now reasonably well understood [15], [16], [31]. In particular, it is understood that:

1. Physical safeguards such as locks, fire protection, water protection, and so forth are necessary to prevent physical damage to the equipment and its associated information.
2. Computer hardware safeguards such as memory protect, are essential to implement an access control mechanism between user and computer file and to isolate users from one another.
3. Software safeguards such as a file access control scheme must be provided to create, in conjunction with hardware, a protective barrier between a user and data files to which he is not authorized while permitting his access to those to which he is.
4. Communication safeguards must be provided when necessary to assure secrecy of information when in transit over communication channels.
5. Personnel safeguards such as background checks, bonding, training, and disciplinary actions are required to deter potential leakage of information due to an individual's actions.
6. An administrative and management overlay must be created that oversees all aspects of the security safeguard system, inspects, tests, and audits them, and controls movement of people, magnetic discs, magnetic tapes, paper, etc.

Thus, within a conceptual security fence one finds the computer with its software and application programs, communication circuits, terminals, data files, and support personnel.

The techniques for providing physical security to the computer system are in hand [32], [33]. A variety of equipment and techniques exist for controlling fires in computer rooms, preventing unauthorized physical access, providing safe storage, and the like. Nevertheless, their application in a given system requires careful analysis of the threat and engineering. For example, a ceiling water sprinkler system may not be appropriate in a computer room; and although a tear gas dispensing system may deter a rioting mob, it can also corrode computer circuitry.

A different set of techniques deals with protection of programs and data within the computer system against unauthorized access or modification. Such access may be obtained accidentally due to hardware or software errors, or by intent as a result of a preplanned penetration operation. In the latter case the ability of a penetrator to gain access to protected resources depends on the sophistication of the security safeguards employed, as well as on the structure of the computer system and the services it provides to its users. For example, a remotely accessible, time-shared system which permits users to submit their own assembly language programs offers more opportunities for penetration than a system in which users cannot submit programs and are limited to performing a fixed set of trans-actions. Security tests have demonstrated that at present there exist no resource-sharing computer systems that do not yield to sustained penetration attempts [34].

Data security techniques are intended to counter threats that can be reasonably ex-pected to be directed against the system or, if absolute prevention is impossible or im-practical, at least to increase the cost of penetration and the risk to the penetrator to levels where the possible profit from penetration is no longer advantageous. The methodology for performing threat analyses, assessing the level of the system's security, and designing a cost-effective security system is still being developed, but guidelines are available [26], [33].

The objectives of implementing security techniques in computer hardware and software include the following:

1. isolation of users and their processes (programs in execution) from each other and from the system's supervisory programs to prevent interference with each other or with the supervisor and to prevent a user from capturing control of the system
2. positive identification of all users and authentication of their identities; attachment of unforgeable identifiers to all programs being processed
3. total control by the system's supervisory program over all shared system resources (mem-ory space, data files, subroutines, input-output devices, communications, etc.) and overall processes
4. concealment of information on removable storage media and in communication channels by encryption techniques, and
5. implementation of effective integrity controls and auditing procedures to assure that security safeguards operate correctly and that users follow security procedures.

Techniques for implementing security objectives are briefly discussed below; details can be found in recent literature [35].

C. Isolation and Identification

A conceptually simple way to isolate users is to process their programs one at a time, completely erasing any portion of memory that has been used before processing the next job. This approach is still practiced in processing classified government data, but it is unnatural, wasteful in modern resource-sharing systems, and does not exploit third-gen-eration capabilities. An elementary isolation technique is to bound the memory space as-signed to a user and test each memory reference for compliance with the bounds.

A major advantage of contemporary computer systems is the ability of users to share programs and data among themselves. However, the owners of shared resources must be able to specify to the system who is to access data and what processing actions each may take. In return, the system must be able to enforce rigid rules, not only under static predetermined conditions, but also under dynamic conditions when authorization changes occur frequently. In a dynamic situation, an authorized user may generate new processes and data files and wish to pass selected access rights to others, to retract previously granted rights, or to specify the rights-passing conditions within the new processes themselves. Clearly, management of access rights is a complicated task that must be implemented in the operating system software. Techniques for this are discussed in [35].

No access control technique can work effectively without an ability to identify users and authenticate the identification. Commonly used identification techniques include a user name, person number, or account number as supplied by the user. Authentication may be based on something the user knows, is, or has. The first category includes passwords, combinations to locks, or some facts from a person's background. Passwords are widely used and can be quite effective if they are properly chosen, managed, and safeguarded. They should not be (1) easy to guess, (2) excessively long or complicated, or (3) printed out at terminals; and (4) they should be changed frequently.

Authentication can also be based on automated recognition of some hard-to-forge physical characteristic of the individual (e.g., fingerprints, voice print, signature, or hand dimensions). Automated recognition techniques are still being developed and so far tend to be expensive. In the third category, "something a person has," are computer-readable badges and cards. Typically, they contain authentication information (which should be unknown to the individual) on a magnetic strip part of the card, which can be encrypted to prevent forgeries. If possession by users is mandatory, and penalties are levied for non-compliance, careless handling would be sharply reduced.

D. Encryption

Cryptographic techniques can be used in communication links between computers and between computers and terminals to protect information from interception by wiretapping, or capture and modification at illicit terminals or computers that could be surreptitiously inserted in the system. Such threats are extraordinarily and ominously real in computer networks handling monetary transactions, such as the proposed EFTS. Historically, cryptographic techniques were developed for concealment of natural language messages, but the basic principles are also applicable for protection of computer data [36]–[38]. There are a number of differences, however, between natural language text and computer data which both enhance and diminish the protection provided. For example, data in computers are mostly numerical values, codes, names and addresses of individuals, or statements in artificial programming languages. These tend to have more uniform character frequency statistics than natural languages, thus reducing the effectiveness of such cryptanalytic processes as frequency analyses. On the other hand, computer data and records tend to have rigid formats, follow strict syntactic rules, and larger amounts of encrypted material are available; all tend to help cryptanalytic efforts.

Given such differences and the availability of computers themselves for cryptanalysis, standard cryptographic techniques are not overly effective [39]. Fortunately, rapidly decreasing costs of digital hardware are now making economical new, much more complex and much more effective techniques, such as the standard encryption algorithm recently proposed by the National Bureau of Standards [40]. The NBS algorithm operates on 8-byte blocks of data by applying a long sequence of key-dependent substitutions, transpositions, and nonlinear operations to thoroughly mix the original bits. Its implementation in software is rather inefficient, but it will be acceptably fast and economical if manufactured as a microelectronic hardware chip using large-scale integration (LSI) manufacturing methods. It is to be expected that future computers will use similar cryptographic devices to protect information stored in data bases.

E. Integrity and Auditing

A system of security safeguards is effective only if it is correctly designed and implemented, operates correctly thereafter, and is constantly monitored. A major source of vulnerabilities in resource-sharing systems is the operating system software which may contain hundreds of program modules and hundreds of thousands of instructions. It is impossible to design and implement such systems without risking many design flaws and implementation errors. Although a vast majority of such flaws and errors will be removed in debugging phases, many will remain undetected for long periods; indeed, errors are still being found in operating systems that have been in use as long as ten years. Some flaws may provide a way for disabling or circumventing the security system by knowledgeable penetrators [31], [34] and are, therefore, of special concern.

Software shortcomings are, of course, a general problem in producing reliable systems, but security requirements add a new dimension. Not only should programs correctly perform all tasks they are designed for, but they should not do anything they are not intended to do. Verifying that a program satisfies such a stringent requirement is very difficult, and may be possible only by formal correctness proofs. Unfortunately, very little progress has been made in developing practical program proving techniques, or of exhaustive testing or verification.

In the absence of totally effective security safeguards in contemporary computer systems, various auditing procedures are used to discourage the curious or slightly larcenous users—the expert penetrators will not be thwarted—and to maintain control over the system [41]. Typically, records are made of all jobs processed in the system, all log-ons at on-line terminals, accesses to files, exception conditions detected by the system, and the like. If an audit log is properly designed, it can permit tracing anomalous user actions in the system and, thus, establish accountability through *ex post facto* analysis; moreover, active and dynamic audits can intercept a penetration effort in progress.

In present systems, real-time threat monitoring is implemented at a very primitive level. For example, counts are made of the number of consecutive times a user fails to provide a correct password and, if a preset threshold is exceeded, the user is automatically disconnected. More sophisticated threat monitoring requires an ability to characterize security violations in terms of measurable system variables, an ability to distinguish penetration attempts from other unusual but legitimate data processing activities, and the ability to instrument the system to collect needed information without unacceptable increases in the system's overhead.

IV. Concluding Remarks

We have presented a broad overview of privacy and security in computer systems—two topics important in the design, operation, and use of contemporary computer systems that will become even more important in the future. Space did not permit detailed treatment of technical aspects; these are available in the cited literature.

A ten-year period of alerting the American public to the latent dangers posed to their individual rights and freedoms by computerization of record-keeping systems has ended with the enactment of the Privacy Act of 1974. With this landmark legislation, we entered an era of active resolution of the privacy problem. Extension of privacy protection to record-keeping systems maintained by criminal justice and law enforcement agencies by state and local governments, and by private industry and institutions is the next order of business.

We must recognize, however, that the right of privacy vis-à-vis record-keeping systems is not more important than other individual rights that may be supported and strengthened by the same record-keeping systems. In many cases the objectives in providing privacy are in consonance with other rights, but at times they conflict. There is a central conflict between the legitimate need of public and private institutions for information about people and the need of individuals to be protected against harmful uses of information. There is also a conflict between an individual's desire for privacy and society's collective need to know about and to oversee government's operations. Furthermore, since privacy safeguards can delay access to information needed for making determinations about an individual or can increase the associated costs, privacy can be in conflict even with the individual's own interests. Yet it has been said that "freedom is what privacy is all about," and that without privacy protection the very existence of massive record systems in the government will have a chilling effect on citizens' exercise of their rights and freedom of expression and of petitioning the government. Thus, it will not be easy to strike the right balance among the many dimensions of this issue. The Privacy Act of 1974 is a starting point on a learning curve which through amendments, court decisions, and new privacy laws, will hopefully lead toward such a balanced solution. Numerous organizations, study groups, and especially the Privacy Protection Study Commission established by the Privacy Act of 1974 are working toward this end.

Techniques for providing data security are evolving rapidly, but much research and development remains to be carried out. At present these efforts are concentrating on software—the design of provably secure operating systems or operating system kernels for implementing the access control function. Attention is also being focused on hardware approaches to security—new architectures that reduce the need for resource sharing and that provide special access control hardware. Concepts such as data base machines and security machines are already emerging. It is almost certainly clear that a balanced approach between hardware, software, and procedures will provide the most effective security safeguards.

Legal provisions already exist to require data security in personal information record-keeping systems. Valuable organizational assets are increasingly represented by records in computer data bases rather than by hardcopy documents; systems such as the Electronic Fund Transfer offer high-payoff opportunities for computer crime of various kinds. As statistics on computer abuse show, the perpetrators of criminal acts are rapidly moving upward on a learning curve of their own; thus, in this environment it is a serious challenge for the computer profession to devise effective solutions now. We cannot wait for a leisurely sojourn through the next 25-year segment of the computer era.

References

[1] *Report of the Committee on the Preservation and Use of Economic Data to The Social Science Research Council* (R. Ruggles, Chairman), Washington, DC, 1965.

[2] *Special Inquiry on Invasion of Privacy,* Hearings, House Committee on Government Operations, Special Subcommittee on Invasions of Privacy, 89th Congress, Parts 1 and 2, U.S. Government Printing Office, Washington, DC, 1966.

[3] *Computer Privacy,* Hearings, Senate Committee on the Judiciary, Special Subcommittee on Administrative Practice and Procedure, U.S. Government Printing Office, Washington, DC, Part I: 1967, Part II: 1968.

[4] P. Baran, *Communications, Computers and People.* The Rand Corporation, Santa Monica, CA, P-3235, Nov. 1965.

[5] P. Armer, *Privacy Aspects of the Cashless and Checkless Society.* The Rand Corporation, Santa Monica, CA, P-3822, Apr. 1968.

[6] A. F. Westin, *Privacy and Freedom.* New York: Atheneum, 1967.

[7] A. R. Miller, *Assault on Privacy: Computers, Data Banks and Dossiers.* Ann Arbor, MI: University of Michigan Press, 1971.

[8] A. Harrison, *The Problem of Privacy in the Computer Age: An Annotated Bibliography.* The Rand Corporation, Santa Monica, CA, vol. I: RM-5495-PR/RC, Dec. 1967; vol. II: RM-5495/1-PR/RC, Dec. 1969.

[9] M. K. Hunt and R. Turn, *Privacy and Security in Databank Systems: An Annotated Bibliography, 1970–1973.* The Rand Corporation, Santa Monica, CA, R-1361-NSF, Mar. 1974.

[10] F. W. Hondius, *Emerging Data Protection in Europe.* Amsterdam, The Netherlands: North-Holland, 1975.

[11] *Privacy and the Computers, A Report by Department of Communications and Department of Justice.* Ottawa, Ont. Canada: Information Canada, 1972.

[12] *Fair Credit Reporting Act of 1971,* Title 15, U.S. Code, sec. 1681.

[13] *Privacy Act of 1974,* Title 5, U.S. Code, sec. 557a (P.L. 93-579, Dec. 31, 1974).

[14] *Family Educational Rights and Privacy Act,* Title 5, P.L. 93-380, 1974.

[15] W. H. Ware, "Security and privacy in computer systems," in *Spring Joint Comput. Conf., AFIPS Conf. Proc.,* vol. 30, 1967, pp. 279–282.

[16] H. E. Petersen and R. Turn, "System Implications of Information Privacy," in *Spring Joint Comput. Conf., AFIPS Conf. Proc.,* vol. 30, 1967, pp. 291–300.

[17] B. Peters, "Security considerations in a multi-programmed computer system," in *Spring Joint Comput. Conf., AFIPS Conf. Proc.,* vol. 30, 1967, pp. 283–290.

[18] *Federal Data Banks, Computers and The Bill of Rights,* Hearings, Senate Committee on the Judiciary, Constitutional Rights Subcommittee, 92nd Congress, 1st Session, 1971.

[19] *Federal Data Banks and Constitutional Rights, A Study in 6 Volumes,* Senate Committee on the Judiciary, Subcommittee on Constitutional Rights, 93rd Congress, 2nd Session, 1974.

[20] *Privacy—The Collection, Use and Computerization of Personal Data,* Joint Hearings, Ad Hoc Subcommittee on Privacy and Information Systems, Senate Committee on Government Operations, and Subcommittee on Constitutional Rights, Senate Committee on the Judiciary, 93rd Congress, 2nd Session, 1974.

[21] A. F. Westin and M. A. Baker, *Databanks in a Free Society.* New York: Quadrangle, 1972.

[22] *Records, Computers and the Rights of Citizens, A Report of the Secretary's Advisory Committee on Automated Personal Data Systems* (W. H. Hare, Chairman), U.S. Department of Health, Education, and Welfare, Washington, DC, 1973.

[23] U.S. Code, Title 13, sec. 9.

[24] R. Nejelski and L. M. Lerman, "A researcher-subject testimonial privilege: What to do before the subpoena arrives?", *Wisconsin Law Review,* 1971, pp. 1085–1148.

[25] U.S. Code, Title 5, sec. 552.

[26] *Computer Security Guidelines for Implementing the Privacy Act of 1974,* FIPS Publication no. 41, National Bureau of Standards, Washington, DC, May 30, 1975.

[27] R. Turn, "Cost implications of privacy protection in Databank systems," *Data Base,* vol. 6, pp. 3–9, Spring 1975.

[28] R. C. Goldstein, *The Cost of Privacy.* Brighton, MA: Honeywell Information Systems, 1975.

[29] D. B. Parker, "Computer abuse perpetrators and vulnerabilities of computer systems," in *Nat. Comput. Conf., AFIPS Conf. Proc.* vol. 45, pp. 65–73, 1976.

[30] B. Allen, "Embezzler's guide to the computer," *Harvard Business Review,* vol. 41, pp. 79–89, July–August 1975.

[31] J. P. Anderson, "Information security in a multi-user computer environment," in *Advances in Computers,* vol. 12. New York: Academic, 1972, pp. 2–36.

[32] *Guidelines for Automatic Data Processing: Physical Security and Risk Management,* FIPS Publication no. 31, National Bureau of Standards, Washington, DC, 1974.

[33] *AFIPS System Review Manual on Security.* Montvale, NJ: AFIPS Press, Montvale, NJ, 1974.

[34] T. Alexander, "Waiting for the great computer rip-off," *Fortune,* vol. 41, pp. 143–150, July 1974.

[35] J. H. Saltzer and M. C. Schroeder, "Protection of information in computer systems," *Proc. IEEE,* vol. 63, pp. 1278–1308, Sept. 1975.

[36] R. Turn, "Privacy transformations for databank systems," in *Nat. Comput. Conf., AFIPS Conf. Proc.,* vol. 42, pp. 289–601, 1973.

[37] H. Feistel, W. A. Notz, and J. L. Smith, "Some cryptographic techniques for machine-to-machine data communications," *Proc. IEEE,* vol. 63, pp. 1545–1554, Nov. 1975.

[38] H. S. Bright and R. L. Enison, "Cryptography using modular software elements," in *Nat. Comput. Conf., AFIPS Conf. Proc.,* vol. 45, pp. 113–123, 1976.

[39] B. Tuckerman, *A study of the Vigenere-Vernam single and multiple loop enciphering systems,* Rep. RC-2879, IBM Research Lab., Yorktown Heights, NY, 1970.

[40] "National Bureau of Standards encryption algorithm," *Federal Register,* Mar. 17, 1975.

[41] E. G. Jancura and A. H. Berger, Ed., *Computers: Auditing and Control.* Philadelphia, PA: Auerbach, 1973.

17. Data Bases

David Burnham

IT IS A truism that we live in a world radically different from that of our grandparents. One way to measure the great distance we have traveled during this microsecond of human history is to compare the records that documented the life of an American before the turn of the century with the records that document our individual lives today. One hundred years ago, the few records that existed could tell us when a child was born, when a couple were married, when a man or woman died and what the boundaries of the land purchased by a family were. In those days, of course, only a handful of the American people went to college. Social security, income taxes and life insurance did not exist. Three-quarters of the population was self-employed.

Today fewer than 5 percent of the American people work for themselves. And of the remaining 95 percent, almost half are employed by large corporations that collect detailed information about the education, health, family and work habits of their employees. Today two out of three Americans have life insurance and nine out of ten are covered by health insurance plans. Insurance companies usually collect large amounts of information about their customers—revealing information such as whether they are seeing a psychiatrist, what drugs they use and whether they have a drinking problem. Today 60 million students are enrolled in schools and colleges that generally collect detailed personal and financial histories about both the student and his or her parents.

The vast scale of information collected by government agencies, private corporations and institutions such as hospitals and universities would not be possible without large centralized computers or, alternatively, linked series of smaller computers. It is also true, however, that some of these organizations did in fact collect some of this information before the computer. With armies of meticulous clerks, there were a few industries and a few countries like Germany and Chile that did compile massive handwritten records about the lives of an amazing number of people.

The computer, however, has powers well beyond that possessed by human scribes, no matter how numerous, and thus has fundamentally altered the nature of society's records.

The first important change is that the computer mass-produces what has come to be called transactional information, a new category of information that automatically documents the daily lives of almost every person in the United States. Exactly when did you leave your home? Exactly when did she turn on the television? Exactly when did he deposit the check? Exactly when were the calls made from their telephone? How many times have you driven your automobile? In the centuries before the computer, transactional information answering these kinds of questions was almost never collected. And in those very few instances where

---

it was collected, it was not easily available for later inspection.

With the computerized filing systems now available, the larger organizations of our society can easily collect and store this new kind of information. Equally important, they can combine it with automated dossiers containing the traditional kinds of information such as a person's age, place of birth and the material contained in school and work records.

There is one more important development made possible by the computer: the incredible maze of electronic highways that can move the new and old information about the country in a matter of seconds at an astoundingly low cost. The automatic exchange of information between different data bases was not seriously considered in the first years of the computer age. But as the technology has become more subtle and sophisticated, it gradually is reducing the barriers between these giant repositories, increasing their ability to "talk" with each other.

The contributions of these linked data bases to our daily lives are enormous. The swift granting of lines of credit to a substantial number of American people would not be possible without the computerized data bases maintained by credit reporting companies like TRW and Equifax. The hundreds of millions of checks written each year by tens of millions of Americans could not be processed and cleared without the computerized data bases maintained by the separate banks and the Federal Reserve System. Easy movement about the United States would be far harder without the computerized reservation systems of the airlines and car rental agencies. The collection each year of nearly $500 billion in federal taxes from almost 100 million individuals and corporations would be extraordinarily difficult without the computerized data bases of the Internal Revenue Service and the large corporations who each year employ more and more Americans.

There are a variety of reasons why understanding the true significance of all of these changes is very hard. First there is the fundamental difficulty of putting anecdotal flesh on the bones of the abstract truth that information is power and that organizations increase their power by learning how to swiftly collect and comprehend bits and pieces of information.

This difficulty is greatly multiplied by the sheer force of the tools of the new information age: the machines that can locate a single item of a file of millions in the blink of an eye or that can swiftly develop statistical trends by massing these single items and the communication links that can shuttle the collected information about the world at almost the speed of light.

When thinking about the impact of these technical achievements, allow your mind to wander beyond the traditionally narrow boundaries of the computer debate. Consider how the technology is altering the power of large organizations. Consider how the technology is affecting our social values such as the notion of checks and balances, the role of work and the importance of spontaneity. Consider the far-reaching changes it is bringing to the nation's economy.

What does it mean, for example, that the officials and clerks of the U.S. government, each year armed with more and more computers, have collected 4 billion separate records about the people of the United States, seventeen items for each man, woman and child in the country? What does it mean that an internal communication network serving just one multinational corporation now links more than five hundred computers in over a hundred cities in eighteen countries and has been growing at a rate of about one additional computer a week in recent years? What does it mean that ten thousand merchants all over the country are able to obtain a summary fact sheet about any one of 86 million individual Americans in a matter of three or four seconds from a single data base in southern California? What does it mean that a handful of federal agencies, not counting the Pentagon, have at least thirty-one separate telecommunication networks stretching all over the United States?

Two of the world's largest and most complicated systems of linked data bases are controlled by the American Telephone and Telegraph Company and the Federal Bureau of Investigation. AT&T's gigantic network was deliberately developed by the company's scientists, engineers and businessmen. The FBI system, which seeks to link the computerized data bases operated by a majority of the fifty states, has developed in a more haphazard fashion.

Because the information collecting and distributing systems of both the telephone company and the FBI began to function long before the birth of the computer, they illustrate the important point that the new tools of information processing usually are extensions of old bureaucracies, not shiny stand-alone machines that can be considered on their independent merit.

A second trait shared by these two very different systems is that neither has been subject to much outside scrutiny during much of their development. AT&T is a private company regulated by fifty state utility bodies of widely varying quality and a federal commission that never had the staff to adequately monitor the company's interstate operations. And very few congressional committees or state legislatures have taken the time or possess the perspective to consider the impact of the gradually growing network linking the FBI to the states.

First a little background about the two organizations that have developed computerized data bases and communication systems for their very different purposes.

For many years the American Telephone and Telegraph Company has been the largest and most powerful corporation in the history of the world. With more than 1,044,000 employees, 3.5 million stockholders and property and equipment worth $119 billion—that's more than the *combined* assets of General Motors, Ford, Chrysler, General Electric and IBM—AT&T has been a formidable force in the economic life of the United States.

But AT&T is much more than a commercial giant. Simply put, the telephone company has become the central nervous system of the American society, as essential to the functioning of the nation's political, cultural and social activities as the circuitry of neurons in the body are to our ability to move, eat and breathe.

As the result of an antitrust suit initially brought by the U.S. government in 1974, AT&T has agreed to reorganize itself. Under the proposal accepted by the Justice Department in 1982, the long-distance, research and manufacturing arms of AT&T will remain a single company, while the local operating companies that provide telephone service to different areas of the country will be spun off and reestablished as seven independent regional companies. Whatever the final outcome of these complex negotiations, however, the system's incredible network of computerized data bases and complex overlapping webs of fiber optic cable, microwave towers, coaxial cable and satellite hookups must remain connected. The system, as AT&T television advertisements proclaim, is the solution.

The Federal Bureau of Investigation is the primary law-enforcement agency of the federal government. The FBI has 19,421 agents and other employees and an annual budget of $739 million, not counting a separate secret account for money spent on counterintelligence. The bureau is responsible for investigating violations of federal law concerning such problems as espionage, official corruption, organized crime and some kinds of white-collar crime. During the mid-1970s the FBI encountered a strong wave of public criticism because of a variety of illegal activities it had engaged in under J. Edgar Hoover. The FBI, however, is not just one more law-enforcement agency. As the result of an intense public relations campaign and extensive educational and technical assistance programs for state and local police agencies, the FBI continues to enjoy a powerful mystique among both the public and many police officials.

The primary purpose of the many computerized data bases of AT&T is to facilitate the operation of the national telephone network by such activities as automatically routing and switching calls, automatically identifying and correcting technical problems, and automatically compiling and mailing monthly bills to the system's 72 million customers. But AT&T does not just transmit telephone calls. More and more it is moving a much broader range of data, including business reports, production plans and television images.

The FBI's National Crime Information Center (NCIC) is a computerized network designed to directly or indirectly link the more-than-1,100,000 policemen, prosecutors, judges, probation officers and correctional officials who together work for about 57,000 different federal, state and local criminal justice agencies. The primary purpose of the NCIC, as defined by the FBI, is to improve the ability of all levels of government to combat crime by speeding the exchange of information about stolen property and criminal suspects. In many ways the NCIC is the single most complex communication system operated by the federal government. Because of its direct connection to computerized data bases operated by other federal agencies, many states and some foreign countries, the NCIC has an unusually broad reach.

Computers generate transactional information for many purposes and many organizations. Computers allow the construction of huge, speedy and low-cost communication networks to transmit many different kinds of information to thousands of different customers. But the very different information processing systems developed by AT&T and the FBI provide clear examples of how transactional information and mass networks have enhanced the impact of these two pre-computer bureaucracies on all of our lives. First consider AT&T. Through its millions of miles of cables, microwave highways and satellite hookups, the American people make 500 million calls a day—four calls, on the average, for each of the nation's 130 million telephones. Thanks to the computerized data bases that are tied into this massive electronic network at a steadily increasing number of junctures, AT&T has become the largest single holder of transactional information in the world. Buried in the computers of the system are records that can be helpful in drawing an amazingly detailed portrait of any single person, group or corporation who uses the telephone.

The astounding power of these records is not appreciated by the public, the courts or Congress. But for government and industry investigators, they have become an important tool. A few years ago, for example, the Senate created a special committee to investigate a very sensitive and delicate subject, the relationship between President Carter's brother Billy and the government of Libya. After many months of embarrassed maneuvering, the Democratic Senate committee issued a report on the antics of the brother of the Democratic president. Almost every other page of the committee's 109-page final report contains a footnote to the precise time and day of calls made by Billy Carter and his associates from at least ten different telephones operating in three different states.

In describing the somewhat tawdry history of how the Libyan government sought to increase its influence in Washington by giving money to the president's brother, the report said that on November 26, 1979, Billy Carter and an associate began driving to Washington from Georgia. Shortly after beginning the trip, the report said, the two men stopped to telephone the Libyan embassy and request a meeting with a high-ranking official. The assertion was supported by a footnote to telephone company records showing that "a five-minute call at 3:43 was charged to Billy Carter's telephone from [a pay telephone in] Jonesboro, an Atlanta suburb."

Another footnote to telephone records described Billy Carter's many conversations with Libyan officials after a meeting with them on March 4, 1980. The footnote said that calls were made from Carter's office telephone in Georgia to the Libyan embassy in Washington "on March 7, March 10, four times on March 11, twice on March 12, three times on March 13, three times on March 14, March 15 and March 17."

The investigations of the special Senate committee were publicly announced and the telephone records that document the report were obtained by a formal legal process. But this sometimes is not the case. One of the top officials in the Nixon White House, for example, claims that shortly after the automobile accident that claimed the life of Mary Jo Kopechne in Martha's Vineyard, the White House political operatives ordered the FBI to obtain the telephone credit card records of Senator Edward Kennedy. These records, which almost certainly would have revealed who and when Senator Kennedy called immediately after the accident, obviously would have been considered useful to those Nixon advisers who thought Kennedy was a likely opponent in the coming elections. Though reporters for the *New York Times* determined the records in question disappeared from the files of New England Bell shortly after the accident, they never found documentary evidence confirming the account of a top Nixon lieutenant that they were obtained by the White House.

Both the Billy Carter and Teddy Kennedy cases illustrate why investigators are so interested in transactional information. First, the information can be extraordinarily revealing. Only considering the data that can be collected from a telephone computer, investigators can learn what numbers an individual has called, what time of day and day of the week the calls were made, the length of each conversation and the number of times an incorrect number was dialed. Considered as a whole, such information can pinpoint the location of an individual at a particular moment, indicate his daily patterns of work and sleep, and even suggest his state of mind. The information also can indicate the friends, associates, business connections and political activities of the targeted individual.

But there is an even more fundamental consideration at stake. Almost by definition, transactional information is automatically collected and stored in the data bases of the telephone company, the electronic equipment of banks and the computers of two-way interactive television systems. This means that transactional information can be obtained months after the instance when the particular event that is documented by the records actually occurred.

This ability greatly enlarges the scope of any investigator. Before the computer age, it was extremely hard to develop concrete evidence about the activities and whereabouts of an individual unless someone had been assigned to follow him. In most cases, investigators were limited to pursuing the handful of individuals they believed might undertake a forbidden act in the future. Now they can move back in time, easily gathering concrete evidence about any person of interest long after the forbidden act occurred.

An example comes to mind. During the last few years, the FBI at any one time has assigned teams of agents to listen in on the telephone conversations of a few hundred people it thought were about to commit serious crimes. As a result of these taps, the FBI was able to collect substantive information about what was said by the handful of official suspects. But now the FBI can supplement this old kind of information with transactional information. After a suspicious event has occurred, after the initial investigation has been completed, after the bureau has drawn up a list of possible suspects, it now can obtain long-distance telephone records, computerized bank records and other documents to pinpoint the exact location in both geography and time of all of those on the FBI list.

The broad broom of transactional information, however, can sweep up much more than the highly revealing computer tracks of an individual citizen. In at least two instances, for example, evidence has recently come to light where this same kind of computerized information was used by AT&T to track the activities of several large corporations and even the ethnic and economic groups living in a single state.

As long as AT&T enjoyed a near monopoly in the provision of telephone services in the United States, the company was able to project the friendly, protective and faintly patronizing image of Ma Bell. But beginning in the mid-1960s a series of changes in the technology of communications led to a gradual shift in the philosophy of federal and state communication regulators. Because of this shift in perceptions, the regulators slowly began to encourage companies to compete with AT&T.

One company called MCI, for example, built its own network of microwave radio towers and offered businessmen and individual families a way of making long-distance calls at significantly less cost than through the long-lines division of AT&T. What the bargain hunter does is use the local AT&T service to dial the MCI terminal in his city. MCI transmits the call to the desired city via its own microwave networks. Then the call is switched back into the local AT&T network and relayed to the final destination.

AT&T was not amused by this innovation and decided to go on the offensive. For many, the old image of Ma Bell as the friendly, warmhearted and faithful helper underwent a rapid transformation. Washington lawyers and others familiar with the communication industry began sporting bumper stickers and T-shirts saying "Reach Out and Crush Someone," a takeoff of the company's faintly weepy television advertising slogan, "Reach Out and Touch Someone."

The U.S. Justice Department took notice of the changed mood of AT&T and began a lengthy investigation. After six years of shifting through company and industry records, the department formally charged the Bell System with monopolizing the telecommunication service and equipment markets of the United States in violation of the nation's antitrust suit. In response to the request in this suit that the federal courts order the breakup of AT&T, the company agreed to spin off the local telephone operating divisions before the case went to the jury.

About a year before AT&T's offer to settle the matter out of court, the Justice Department lawyers filed a pretrial brief summarizing the company's activities which they believed supported the formal antitrust charges.

One of the activities that AT&T was accused of by the Justice Department harked back to transactional information—specifically, to how AT&T had extracted the data in its computers about telephone usage to keep track of the companies who had decided to hook into the long-distance service offered by MCI.

"AT&T kept extremely close track of the market status of its competitors," the brief charged, "going so far as to create a centralized data base to organize its competitive information. Included were data culled by the operating companies from their customers' confidential billing records and forwarded to AT&T."

The lawyers explained that it was not illegal for one firm to keep abreast of what its competitors are doing by collecting and analyzing publicly available information. "However, the utilization by AT&T of confidential billing records and other information assembled at the local exchange level is an example of AT&T's making use of its monopoly in one market (local telephone service) to reinforce its monopoly position in another market (long-distance service)."

William Caming is a precise and elegant man. His silver hair is parted in the middle. A handkerchief is tucked in the left breast pocket of his suit. His office in the massive AT&T headquarters building in Basking Ridge, New Jersey, has white gauzy curtains, an antique desk, old prints and a thick beige carpet. William Caming is the senior AT&T lawyer responsible for developing and defending AT&T's policies, procedures and legal tactics on all matters relating to protecting the company's data from improper use.

As is appropriate for a company that prides itself on careful businesslike engineering, William Caming seems to hide his genuine concern about the importance of protecting the privacy and freedom of individual Americans behind a businesslike facade. "We feel that privacy of communication is imperative to our business," he said. "If people do not believe they can talk privately, they won't talk or they will talk less."

Given this philosophy, how did AT&T respond to the Justice Department allegations that the company had used its equipment to improperly monitor the activities of its customers?

Neither the AT&T lawyers handling the antitrust action of the Justice Department nor Mr. Caming deny that information was drawn from the operating companies and collated by a high-level company market analysis group. The transactional information in question, the Justice Department said, "included data such as the names of customers, types, usage and numbers of circuits, monthly charges and end links ordered from the operating companies."

But there is disagreement about why the information was collected and what was done with it. In the statement of fact agreed to by both sides in the early stages of the case, AT&T lawyers contended the collection program was undertaken in response to orders from the Federal Communications Commission. The Justice Department, however, rejected this explanation. "No regulatory body ever imposed an obligation on Bell or affirmed the propriety of Bell's decision to exploit its access to confidential customer records for use in planning and executing its responses to competition," the government lawyers said.

Mr. Caming offered this explanation: "When MCI won the right to compete with us, they told the Federal Communications Commission that they would offer new and innovative services. We contended that they were just skimming the cream, providing low-cost high-density services because they did not have to provide telephone links in rural areas. We decided to find out who was right, to determine what happened to the AT&T services when corporations decided to give some of their business to MCI and other carriers."

The lawyer also explained that steps were taken to protect the privacy of the individual corporations. Once the data on each company was collected, it was collated by types of industry, rather than single companies, and the last four digits of the numbers called were removed.

"The information was sent to a market research group at AT&T, not marketing," Mr. Caming said. "The resulting studies were made available to only the chairman of the board and a few top executives, and specific instructions were given that the information was not to be shown to marketing and sales people."

Even taking the company's precautions at face value, the AT&T decision to track the activities of the corporations who chose to leave the fold is a highly revealing example of the great power of transactional information.

The tracking also raises several difficult questions. Was the program a gigantic breach of stated policies and ethical standards of AT&T? The Bell System has gone to great lengths to assure the American people that their telephone records will be protected. Every executive, scientist, secretary and worker coming to work for AT&T, for example, must sign a statement that he or she has read and fully understood a short booklet summarizing the ethical standards required of all employees. One provision of this booklet orders employees never "to engage in industrial espionage." Another provision states that "no transmission, either by voice, data or other non-voice communications, is to be tampered with or intruded upon" and that "communication arrangements with customers, and information about billing records, equipment or circuits, are not to be disclosed to any unauthorized person."

It is very easy, of course, for the chairman of the board and top executives of any organization to decide privately that they are authorized persons. In this particular case, the executives ran the telephone company. But they could just as easily have been the officials directing the Federal Reserve Board, the local bank, the company that won the two-way interactive cable television franchise in your city or any one of the growing number of computer-based businesses.

Private corporations, however, are not the only potential target of tracking by transactional information. A few years ago, for example, Southern New England Bell decided it would like to change the way it charged the people of Connecticut for their telephone service. Instead of a flat rate for local calls, the company wanted to bill customers according to how long they talked. Before acting on the request, the Connecticut Public Utility Control Authority asked the telephone company to use the unusually computerized telephone system in Connecticut to conduct a study determining how the proposed rate change would affect different segments of the state's population.

Without informing the people of Connecticut, scientists from Bell Laboratories helped Southern New England select on a random basis the telephones of 1,600 households. The computers at the necessary locations were then instructed to automatically record every local call made from the selected telephones. What time was each call made? How long was each call? How many calls on each telephone?

After the transactional information had been collected for one year, Southern New England sent each of the 1,600 households a questionnaire that did not explain that the telephones had been monitored. The questionnaires asked a number of detailed questions about the economic, ethnic and educational status of people living in each household. Two-thirds of the questionnaires were returned. Southern New England then combined the information about the financial and social position of the responding households with the information on how they used their telephones.

The study came up with some surprising findings. Poor black families used the phone a good deal more than poor white families. Poor blacks also used the phone more than middle- and upper-income families of both races. Black families earning less than $3,000 a year talked on the average of 723 minutes a month. White families in the same income bracket only talked for 296 minutes. Black families earning $3,000 to $5,000 a year used the phone for 1,532 minutes a month, compared to 254 minutes for their white counterparts. The study found that the more intensive use of the telephone by black families continued up to the income level of $12,500 a year, when the pattern reversed itself. For families earning more than $20,000 a year, for example, blacks were on the phone for only 310 minutes a month, while whites used it for 417 minutes.

Fred Fagel, the now-retired sales executive who directed the research, said in an interview that the study was extremely useful in understanding exactly how the proposed change in billing would impact on the pocketbooks of the people of Connecticut. It is hard to fault Mr. Fagal's analysis. But along with a number of other similar AT&T marketing studies, it suggests how transactional information might some day be used to track the individual members of different groups.

David Watters is a Washington-based communications expert who once worked for the CIA. He is concerned that transactional information collected by the computers of such organizations as AT&T could be used to develop "signatures" of classes of people that would enable a subtle and hard-to-detect form of mass surveillance.

"Let's say one of our powerful federal agencies became worried about the activities of a group of people who share a common interest in stopping the country's involvement in some war or in halting the placement of some new missile system," the tall, slim computer engineer explained. "The organization conducts a detailed study of how the members of the group or organization use the telephone. Then the federal agency instructs the computers to raise a flag any time a series of phone calls are made from a telephone that fits the transactional signature already established as common for members of the group."

As fantastic as the scenario of David Watters sounds, it is worth noting that 30 to 40 percent of the local telephone switches in the United States are now equipped with the ESS computer equipment similar to that installed in Connecticut when Southern New England undertook its survey of the telephone use of 1,600 families. The amount of such equipment varies widely. In the Washington, D.C., area, for example, 70 percent of the equipment is now computerized, while in Massachusetts only 16 percent of the switches operate with the latest technology.

William Caming, the AT&T lawyer, explained the significance of the ESS computer: "We can get local message detail on the ESS for any specific number or small collection of numbers without adding any additional equipment, by just changing the program. To get such detail for every number attached to an ESS, the technicians tell me would require some additional equipment."

A significant characteristic of the transactional information collected by AT&T and other major computer systems is that its reach is universal. Transactional information is collected and stored about the telephone use and banking habits of everyone who lives in America, rich and poor, ethical and unethical, white and black, Republican and Democrat. Though the information ultimately may cast a revealing light on the activities of a single individual, it is collected about the activities of all.

The system of data bases that gradually are being linked by the computerized network of the FBI does not share this universal quality. Instead, it collects and distributes information about one segment of the population, the millions of Americans who are arrested each year in the United States.

The story of the FBI system begins almost a hundred years ago, long before the birth of either the modern computer or the FBI. The occasion was a meeting of reform-minded policemen who decided the time had come to ask Congress to finance an agency in the federal government to maintain a central record of all American criminals. The policemen, who called themselves the National Chiefs of Police Union, argued that the prompt exchange of information about "criminals and criminal cases" made possible by such an agency would improve the ability of their separate departments to control crime.

Nearly nine decades later, in the summer of 1981, a task force appointed by President Reagan's attorney general, William French Smith, acted to bring the original proposal in line with current technology: the panel endorsed a plan to have the FBI make a significant change in its existing communication system to speed up the exchange of the records of millions of people who are arrested each year all over the United States. As was suggested by the police chiefs in St. Louis, the Reagan administration's task force said the adoption of the proposal would help the government curb serious crime.

There is a good deal of plausibility in the belief of both the police chiefs at the turn of the century and the Reagan administration today that the swift exchange of summary information about an individual's past contacts with the criminal justice system will significantly improve the ability of the police, prosecutors and judges to catch and punish criminals. Careful examination of the sources of information that lead a policeman to make an arrest or a judge to decide an appropriate sentence, however, suggests that the nearly instantaneous retrieval of criminal history records may be considerably less useful than is generally thought to the business of crime-fighting.

Furthermore, the gradual computerization of criminal history records in most of the states and the development of a single computerized network to link all these state and local data bases raise questions that go to the heart of democratic institutions of the United States. So profound are these questions, in fact, that they have provided a handful of critical congressmen, working with communication experts of the Nixon, Ford and Carter administrations, with the necessary weapons to stall the construction of the federal network for the last decade.

But now, with the blessing of the attorney general's Task Force on Violent Crime, plans to have such a network constructed by the FBI appear to be nearing fruition. Should the FBI get its way, the single most powerful law-enforcement agency in the United States will control a computerized network linking a system of data bases of almost unimagined size and complexity.

The objections that prompted sober officials such as Attorney General Edward Levi and Attorney General Griffin Bell to order that the system not proceed were generated by three very different concerns.

The first concern focused on questions about the *communication network* itself. Should the control of the proposed network be placed in the hands of the FBI? Or would it be more appropriate to give the network to a separate federal agency not directly involved in law enforcement? Or perhaps it would be best if a consortium of the states took over the operation of the system? Will a network controlled by the federal government alter the relationships between it and the sovereign states? Will a computerized information system that is meant to serve the needs of the judicial branch of government but is controlled by the police agency in the executive branch undermine the system of checks and balances established by our Constitution?

The second concern focused on questions about the *records*. Because of the wide variation in state laws and local arrest policies and the frequently inaccurate or incomplete nature of arrest records, will their wide distribution reduce the chance for a fair trial that our Constitution guarantees every person? Might the increased flow of records to employers, state licensing boards and universities create a situation where individuals turn to crime because they are denied a legitimate opportunity to earn a living?

The third concern focused on questions about the *combined impact* of the proposed communication network and the huge mass of information contained in the frequently computerized criminal history data bases maintained by the states and many local jurisdictions. Could such a system be used to keep track of American citizens who are not criminals?

To comprehend the stakes involved in a decision to grant the FBI authority to build and control what is now called the Interstate Identification Index, it is necessary to learn something about the role of the FBI and the purposes and practices of the state and local institutions that would be linked by the bureau's new computer proposal. It also is necessary to understand the nature of the records that would circulate with increasing frequency and speed because of the creation of this network. How many Americans have records? What information do they contain? How accurate are they? Who has access to them? What are they used for? How effective are the rules intended to limit their improper use?

In almost all cases, a criminal-history record first comes into existence when a city or county law-enforcement officer makes an arrest. Depending upon widely varying law and custom, the officer usually will fingerprint the person who has been arrested because it is the only sure way to identify him. Again, depending upon widely varying law and custom, the record of each arrest may be stored at one or more levels of government. Sometimes the record remains in the shoebox filing drawer of a small-town police department; sometimes the record is stored in the files of the state identification agencies; sometimes it is dispatched to one or both of the two separate criminal file systems maintained by the FBI.

Virtually nothing is known about the number, size, contents and operating procedures of the local institutions holding criminal-history records. Thanks to some recent and very original studies by the research arm of Congress, however, considerably more is now known about the holders of arrest records at the state and federal level.

During the last three years, the Office of Technology Assessment (OTA) has hired researchers to answer a number of key questions about the organizations compiling and holding the records, the rules governing the distribution of the records, the information contained on the records themselves and the ways the records are actually used. A national survey conducted for OTA last year, for example, found that state repositories contain about 34 million criminal-history records, 8 million of which are computerized. Sliced another way, the same survey determined that thirty-four of the forty-nine responding states were then operating computerized criminal-history systems that could provide a policeman or district attorney with either an extensive summary of an individual record or instructions on where the record was located in a manual file.

At the federal level, there are two principal repositories where information is stored about people who have been arrested. Both are located in the FBI. One repository, first established in 1924, is called the Identification Division. The Identification Division contains 77 million fingerprint cards representing approximately 24 million people arrested for a variety of local, state and federal crimes ranging from public drunkenness to espionage. Attached to each fingerprint card is a rap sheet, a list of charges the police have brought against the person in question. There also is room on the rap sheet to record the individual's permanent FBI number, the agency making the arrest and the outcome of the case in the courts.

Upon the receipt of a set of prints from a law-enforcement agency or other authorized organization such as a bank or defense contractor, the FBI searches its records to determine if the person with those particular prints has been arrested before. If he has, the list of previous arrests is sent back to the agency that made the inquiry, usually through the mails. (The Identification Division has an additional 93 million cards representing 42 million people in its *civil* files. These cards contain the prints of all people who have sought to work for the federal government, all who have been in the armed forces and those who have voluntarily submitted their prints to the FBI.)

The second repository of criminal histories within the FBI is now tucked into the NCIC, the very large computerized communication system. The initial use of the data base and massive network of the NCIC was entirely different than the rap sheets of the Identification Division in that it was not established to transmit a list of an individual's past contacts with the law.

Instead, the first purpose of the NCIC was to give policemen a way of quickly determining if a particular person they had detained was wanted at that very moment for committing a crime in another jurisdiction or if a particular car had been reported stolen. To this day, about 90 percent of the millions of messages that move in and out of the NCIC's computers each year are concerned with outstanding arrest warrants and stolen property.

On December 10, 1970, however, a controversial attorney general named John Mitchell made a controversial decision when he authorized the FBI computer to begin providing the states and cities with an entirely new kind of service: almost instantaneous access to a summary of the past criminal records of those they were arresting.

From the very beginning, the new NCIC service ran into a storm of criticism. The service was called CCH, an acronym for "computerized criminal history." Because of the strenuous and repeated objections by some officials in the Justice Department, communication specialists under Presidents Nixon, Ford and Carter and a number of senators and House members, the CCH has yet to be fully implemented eleven years after it first was authorized by John Mitchell.

Partly in response to the stream of criticism, the FBI has substantially changed the design of the CCH. At first the FBI fought for a central repository in Washington that would have stored a summary notation about all arrests throughout the United States except for the most insignificant crimes. Now, with the endorsement of the Reagan administration's

Task Force on Violent Crime, the FBI has proposed a "pointer system" to guide the policemen or other authorized investigators in one state to the records of interest held by other states. The current proposal, the Interstate Identification Index—sometimes called the Triple I—would work like this. A policeman in California wants to determine the past criminal record of a person he is investigating or has arrested. He types out an inquiry to the FBI. Within a few seconds the index reports that a person with the same name, age, sex and race as described by the policeman has arrest records in Florida and New York. At the same time the FBI system sends a message to the criminal-history repositories in Tallahassee and Albany asking them to send a summary of the records about the individual in question to the policeman in California.

The III pointer system design was tested by the FBI and Florida in 1981 and ten more states in 1983. The bureau hopes to offer it to all the states sometime in 1984.

It is the actual development of the computerized criminal-history segment of the NCIC, the forging of a direct electronic link between all the agencies of the crime-fighting system, that has served as the focus of the debate for the last decade. But the issues at stake are far broader. To understand the full dimensions of the controversy, it is necessary to consider the nature of the information that will move through the linked computers and the potential impact of this information on the workings of our government and society—not to mention the lives of millions of individual citizens.

In 1974, J. Edgar Hoover said the bureau's NCIC was the first government computer system that directly linked federal, state and local agencies. This use of the computer to unify three levels of government operating under the separate laws and customs of fifty separate states makes the NCIC significantly different from most of the other large government communication systems created by federal agencies in the last decade. The very large communication net of the Internal Revenue Service, for example, must speak only to a single group of uniformly trained bureaucrats engaged in administering a relatively narrow spectrum of federal law.

But in an uncharacteristic way, Mr. Hoover's 1974 description of the NCIC significantly understated its capabilities. The network does not just link the federal, state and local law-enforcement agencies of this enormous and highly diverse nation. In addition, this federally funded and federally controlled system will provide a new kind of bridge between the police, an arm of the executive branch, and the judiciary.

It was the potential ability of the complex new linkages to undermine and erode the important principle of checks and balances that triggered the outspoken opposition of conservative lawyers like Clay Whitehead, director of the White House Office of Telecommunications under President Nixon, and John Eger, the man who succeeded Mr. Whitehead under President Ford. Mr. Eger, for example, did not mince his words in a letter opposing the FBI plan that he sent the Justice Department in 1974. The computerized criminal-history project, he said, "could result in the absorption of state and local criminal data systems into a potentially abusive, centralized, federally controlled communication and computer information system."

A very similar kind of objection was raised one year later in a study of the FBI plan prepared by the Law Enforcement Assistance Administration. The LEAA, which is now defunct, was then the fund-granting arm of the Justice Department and also happened to be engaged in an intense power struggle with the FBI. The computerized criminal history

160

project raised concerns over "(a) the development of a Big Brother system, (b) reduced state input and control over security, confidentiality and use of state-originated data and (c) dangers from using non-updated, and hence inaccurate, centrally maintained rap sheets."

The impact of the information that would be transmitted through the vast maze of telephone lines, data bases and computer terminals is, however, of even greater concern than the network itself. When FBI officials call for the development of a bureau-controlled network to speed the exchange of criminal-history records—rap sheets—most Americans assume the proposal is designed to reduce the chance that they or members of their family will be the victim of a hardened criminal, an experienced mugger or a drug-crazed rapist.

But the reality of trying to control crime in America is much more ambiguous and complex than is sometimes suggested by advocates of a greatly enlarged computer network for the FBI. For example, only a small portion of the millions of traumatic events logged yearly into the criminal-history records involve what are now called career criminals—professional murderers, robbers and burglars who repeatedly prey on their victims.

The sad truth is that many of the murderers and rapists who terrorize the American people are not marauding strangers. Instead, they are wives who have been driven to kill their husbands in the dark heat of the night. They are uncles who have been asked to babysit for their young nieces. They are old acquaintances who fell to fighting at the end of an all-night bout of drinking.

The question of whether this kind of criminal has a record in another state is not of urgent importance to the family who already knows his flaws. The suspect's record also is of little immediate importance to the police, who frequently "solve" such crimes when the murderer either turns himself in at the local precinct house or is immediately known to the family and neighbors. Contrary to popular belief and what the police sometimes contend, research indicates that very few arrests are the result of any kind of investigation at all. The vast majority of clearances come from a police capture at the scene of the crime or the complete identification of the criminal by victims or witnesses.

But there is another reason why police do not find the existing massed criminal-history records of much assistance in their search for the relatively rare professional criminal. Despite their name, criminal-history records deal with a staggeringly large number of people who may have broken the law at some time in their lives but whom we usually do not consider truly criminal: men who have been arrested for public drunkenness, youngsters who have been arrested for stealing a neighbor's car, college kids who have been arrested for protesting against the construction of a nuclear power plant or the draft.

There is a second reason why many of the individuals whose records are contained in the state and federal criminal-history files cannot be considered criminals: they were never convicted of a crime. Police in the United States are now making more than 10.5 million arrests a year. According to studies done in jurisdictions all over the United States, however, 30 to 40 percent of these arrests are dismissed by the police or the district attorney before the question of guilt or innocence has been resolved.

In a fair number of these millions of cases, it can safely be assumed that the individual involved actually was guilty of the charge for which he was arrested. But common sense and the constitutional principle of innocent until proven guilty strongly argue that millions of those listed in the files because of an arrest did not commit the act of which they are accused.

An astoundingly large number of Americans have at one time or another been arrested. Because some individuals have records in more than one jurisdiction and because millions of those with arrest records have subsequently died, it is not easy to estimate how many people have actually been arrested during the course of their lives. A recent authoritative study done for the Labor Department by Neal Miller, however, concludes that about one out of five living Americans have an arrest record somewhere in the United States.

In the past few years, local, state and federal law-enforcement officials throughout the country have successfully argued that society should provide them with statewide and national computerized communication systems that can instantly inform a policeman on the street whether the individual he has just stopped is currently wanted on suspicion of committing a crime. These systems make sense from the standpoint of protecting both the patrolman who is making the stop and society at large from the possibility of further hurtful activities by the person who is being temporarily detained.

But the acknowledged value of a hot-line system to inform a patrolman that the person he has stopped *currently* is a suspect for another crime does not necessarily justify a parallel system informing the patrolman that his target was arrested for a crime in a distant city at some possibly *distant period of time.*

The computer panders to the natural human instinct to desire more information about everything. But there are some law-enforcement officials who question whether more arrest records are actually going to help them do their work. They contend that the value of the arrest record has been greatly diluted, partly because so many Americans have been arrested for so many insignificant causes that it is hard to separate the wheat from the chaff. They further believe the records are of questionable value because they frequently do not disclose whether the case was immediately dismissed, whether the defendant was found guilty or innocent, and what sentence, if any, was imposed. Beyond the pragmatic judgment about the utility of providing the patrolman instant access to arrest records, they see a larger ethical and constitutional question: Do the American people want their police making arrests for *current* activities partly on the basis of *past* behavior?

"The idea that a national rap sheet system would make an important contribution to our work here is just a bunch of baloney," the skeptical supervisor of a burglary section in a large California city told a congressional consultant recently. "Our problem is not to find out who the guy is. Our biggest problem is once we catch him coming out of a house with the goods, how do we keep him in jail and how do we make sure he stays in jail. If anything, we have over-information-oriented and over-computerized this department. The patrol officer learns to use the vast array of information resources at his command, which means you learn to sit in a car and punch in the numbers of people's license plates and the numbers of people's driver's licenses. What this does is inhibit the development of traditional police skills, of interviewing, interrogating and investigating. We need people to get out of their offices and get out of their cars and talk to people. Most of our leads come from citizens reporting a crime or having heard about a crime. Without these resources, which have nothing to do with computers and criminal histories, we would be dead."

These critical comments are drawn from a 1981 report to the Office of Technology Assessment as part of a congressional effort to determine the impact—positive and negative—of the FBI's proposed system. This particular report was prepared by Dr. Kenneth C. Laudon, a professor at New York's John Jay School of Criminal Justice. During its preparation,

Dr. Laudon interviewed over 140 experienced criminal justice officials working in four states and six cities.

Dr. Laudon found that the prosecutors and judges he talked with were even more doubtful about the utility of the FBI plan than the police.

"We know our local people and we can compensate for the activities of our local law-enforcement agencies," a midwestern judge said. "We know the victims of crime, and in 80 to 90 percent of the cases we know the local criminals. But in a national system it would be virtually impossible to understand rapidly what that out-of-state information was all about."

An assistant district attorney made a somewhat similar point. "The fact that somebody has twenty arrests in Oakland may be understandable to a district attorney here. In any event I can call the arresting officers to check on the nature of these arrests. And I do that. But this would not be the case with a person who had twenty arrests in Bangor, Maine, or Poughkeepsie, New York. These kinds of arrests could not be checked out and they probably would be thought meaningless to a D.A."

Charles Silberman, one of this country's perceptive social commentators, in his book *Criminal Violence, Criminal Justice* summarized the important aspects of a crime that inevitably must go unnoted in a computerized criminal history record.

"In the great majority of criminal cases 'the facts' are not in dispute," he wrote. "What is at issue . . . is the significance that should be attached to the facts. Decisions about the seriousness of the offense and the degree of the offender's culpability involve complex and often highly subjective judgments about such factors as premeditation, intent, force, credibility, negligence, threat, recklessness and harm."

But the complaints of the policemen, prosecutors and judges interviewed by Dr. Laudon went well beyond simply questioning the utility of a summary record that has been lifted out of its original legal and social context. Over and over again the users complained that the records being moved along the experimental criminal-history segment of the FBI's communication network were incomplete and inaccurate. The subjective judgments of the police officials, prosecutors and judges about the poor quality of the information was supported by a second investigation undertaken by Congress's Office of Technology Assessment.

For this second study, the OTA arranged for Dr. Laudon to obtain access to a random sample of the criminal history records that recently had been dispatched to law enforcement and other agencies from five official repositories maintained and operated by three separate states and the FBI. The information in the records from the repositories was then compared with the information in the original records in files of the county courthouses. Procedures were followed that permitted the comparative analysis without disclosing individual names.

The findings are surprising. In North Carolina, only 12.2 percent of the summaries were found to be complete, accurate and unambiguous. In California, 18.9 percent were complete, accurate and unambiguous. In Minnesota, the researchers found almost half the sample—49.5 percent—met the same standards.

The quality of the FBI files, which of course rests on the information submitted by the fifty states, was not noticeably better. Based on a random sample of 400 records dispatched by the Identification Division during a single week in August of 1978, Dr. Laudon found that 25.7 percent of the FBI rap sheets met the standards suggested by federal law.

Assuming the one-week sample was valid for the entire year, the OTA study suggests that 1.75 million of the 2.35 million records sent by the FBI to criminal justice and other institutions all over the country had various failings.

The quality of the much smaller number of records disseminated by the Computerized Criminal History segment of the FBI's National Crime Information Center was somewhat better than that of the Identification Division rap sheets. In the computerized system, the comparison of the sample summary and the original records disclose that 45.9 percent were complete, accurate and unambiguous.

At the request of OTA, Dr. Laudon also checked a sample of 400 arrest warrants from the 127,000 contained in the FBI's "hot file" on a single day in August of 1979. Upon comparing the information on the FBI's warrant notices with the information in the local court records, he found that 10.9 percent of the sample already had been cleared or vacated, 4.1 percent showed no record of the warrant at the local agency and a small additional number of warrants had other problems. Again assuming the validity of the sample, it appears that on that single day in 1979, 17,340 Americans were subject to false arrest because the FBI computer incorrectly showed they were wanted when the warrants in question had been cleared or vacated. Approximately the same number of FBI warrant notices involved cases so old that most district attorneys regarded them as not prosecutable because of the problem of missing or deceased witnesses.

The FBI strongly objected to the OTA research on a number of grounds. "The criteria chosen by OTA to judge the quality of records appear to have been set at levels which criminal-history record systems will never be able to completely achieve because of the limited types of information the systems contain, how the information is compiled, the limited resources available to compile the information," Conrad S. Banner wrote the OTA. Mr. Banner at that time was the FBI official in charge of the Identification Division.

David F. Nemecek, chief of the NCIC, said the OTA report on its research contained "many factural inaccuracies" and "undocumented conclusions which are the basis for ill-founded alternatives." At about the same time Mr. Nemecek addressed his complaints to the OTA, he was asked to testify about the system by the House Subcommittee on Civil and Constitutional Rights.

"We do have serious concerns regarding the draft report in terms of certain study methodologies, certain definitions that were used in terms of what is accurate, what is complete, etc.," he said.

In response to questions from Representative Don Edwards, the chairman of the subcommittee, however, the FBI manager acknowledged that the files have serious flaws and that correcting them raises serious constitutional problems. "It concerns me very much that we don't have disposition data," Mr. Nemecek said, listing several recent steps taken by the bureau to try to improve their quality. "As you are well aware, we are operating a voluntary system, and trying to balance states rights and federal rights."

Despite the documented shortcomings of criminal records, more and more employers around the country seem to be using them to screen new employees. "The most frightening thing about state and federal systems is that they are incredibly difficult to protect from non-criminal justice use," one California judge said.

"The situation in California, where so much of the rap sheet information is really used to keep people unemployed, and hence inherently prone to crime, is absolutely frightening and outrageous. If they build a national system you can be sure that there will be more and more demands by employers, by state and local governments, to use the national resources along with the state and local resources."

The research director of a state legislative committee to revise the state's criminal code made a parallel point. "But the worst consequence would probably be to develop a national caste system of unemployables," he said. "We've already developed a racial caste system, and it would seem that national CCH system would create a parallel caste composed of racial minorities and poor people who would be unemployable in any state of the nation."

Official records, of course, were subject to improper use long before the computer became an important part of every major public and private bureaucracy in the United States. But an executive in a New York State agency explained how the computer has enlarged the opportunity to abuse.

"Technology may not be the only villain, but it is one villain," the official said. "Before high technology, you could actually control information better; at least it could not spread very far because it was impractical to transmit it. With the computer system, you can't control it any more, largely because of the automatic interfacing of the system, which makes it difficult for even us to know who's getting our information."

The Office of Technology Assessment asked a team at the Bureau of Governmental Research and Service at the University of South Carolina to try to determine exactly who was now receiving criminal-history information and to assess the social impacts of computerizing these histories. According to the South Carolina researchers—Lynne Eickholt Cooper, Mark E. Tompkins and Donald A. Marchand—the use of criminal records outside the traditional confines of the criminal justice system is enormous and growing.

All applicants for federal positions, all military recruits, many of the hundreds of thousands of citizens working for private contractors who are doing jobs for the federal government, and all new employees of federally chartered and insured banks are among the millions of persons who have long been subject to criminal-history record checks for many years, the researcher reported.

In addition, with the recent growth in the number of states and cities requiring licenses and permits for almost any kind of job, the population subject to criminal-record checks has further exploded. At last count, more than 7 million Americans must obtain licenses to earn their living. In California, for example, forty-seven separate licensing boards, fifty state agencies and thirty-two out-of-state agencies have access to the criminal-history records stored in the state's computerized record system. In New York, the use of criminal records by law-enforcement agencies has declined in recent years, while its use by private employers has gone up.

Many of the state and local licensing boards that may now rummage through the criminal-history repositories of the nation are not really government organizations. Instead, they are the enforcement arms of quasi-professional trade associations such as barbers, real estate dealers and morticians. Roughly parallel developments exist at the federal level. Just recently, for example, the FBI agreed to give the National Auto Theft Bureau direct access to records maintained by the FBI. The Auto Theft Bureau is a private organization established by the insurance industry to combat the stealing of cars. The FBI is also talking with the

Wackenhut Corporation—a large private detective and security company with government and industry contacts all over the country—about what information in the NCIC files it may examine.

Some states have gone even further, throwing their computerized criminal-history records open to anyone who will pay the necessary search fee. Florida is one of these so-called open-record states. Peggy Horvath, the deputy director of Florida's Division of Criminal Justice Information Systems, said individual corporations such as Jack's Cookie Company and the Winn Dixie Stores are making about 90,000 requests a year for information in the state's computerized files. Ms. Horvath contended, however, that recent computerization of prosecutorial and court records in the state's major urban areas means that in Florida, at least, 80 to 90 percent of the current records now include dispositions.

In addition to giving any individual or private institution access to state criminal history records, Ms. Horvath said the legislature had approved laws granting twelve Florida licensing boards covering such individuals as bankers, mortgage brokers, real estate salesmen, security dealers and liquor dealers access to information kept in the FBI's files in Washington. She noted that requests to the FBI by the twelve licensing boards, which are processed through her agency, are now running about 80,000 a year.

Through a variety of federal and state laws, society has made the collective decision that individuals *convicted* of certain crimes may be properly denied certain privileges. Sometimes such individuals lose the right to vote. Sometimes they may not run for public office. Sometimes they are prohibited from bidding on government contracts.

The United States also pays a good deal of lip service to the principle that an arrest or investigation, *without a conviction,* should not be sufficient grounds to deny an individual an honorable place in the job market. In late 1981, President Reagan provided an eloquent testimonial to this principle when asked why he had not asked three officials in his administration to remove themselves from office after they were accused of illegal activities. The three men were Labor secretary Raymond Donovan, CIA director William Casey and National Security Council director Richard Allen.

"I believe in the fairness of the American people, and I believe that in recent years there has been a very dangerous tendency in this country for some to jump to the conclusion that accusation means guilt and conviction," Mr. Reagan told reporters. "And I think it is high time we recognize that any individual is innocent until proven guilty of a wrongdoing, and that's what we are going to do."

Mr. Reagan's eloquent statement has considerable backing in the laws and regulations of the United States. The Civil Service Reform Act of 1978 includes a provision limiting federal suitability checks to conviction records, and only for those crimes that are reasonably related to job performance. Three states have laws explicitly barring employer discrimination against ex-offenders. Many state and local human relations offices have issued rules barring private employers from requesting arrest information and limiting the use of conviction information.

Despite the various restrictions, however, there is considerable evidence that the president's policy for the high officials of his administration frequently does not obtain for the average job hunter. According to one congressional survey, for example, the fifty states handed out a total of 10.1 million criminal-history records in 1978. Two million of the records—one out of five—went to private corporations and government agencies that were not part of the criminal-history system.

Because of the size of the United States, estimating the number of private employers who try to obtain arrest data about their employees is very hard. From the evidence suggested by several separate surveys and other data, however, Neal Miller concluded in his Labor Department analysis that "the majority of private employers and a preponderance of large employers seek criminal record information."

The Labor Department study that concluded that 40 million Americans have an arrest record also estimated that just under 26 million of them were in the job market. With so many people applying for so many different jobs it is nearly impossible to generalize about the impact of criminal records on their lives. Certainly the bank is on solid grounds when it decides not to hire a convicted bank robber. Certainly no one would argue about a hospital personnel director who decides not to hire a convicted narcotics dealer.

But there is good evidence that some employers assume that any kind of record, no matter what the offense, no matter what the outcome, is a powerful mark against the individual. More than a decade ago, two sociologists named Richard Schwartz and Jerome Skolnick attempted to measure this kind of bias in an experiment in which a number of employers were shown the employment folders submitted by a hundred men who were looking for a menial job in the Catskill area of New York. The applicants were broken down into four groups. The first group had no criminal records. The second group had been arrested for assault and acquitted of the charge with a letter from the judge explaining the presumption of innocence. The third had been arrested for assault and acquitted, but there was no letter from the judge. The fourth group had been convicted.

The employers were asked whether they would be willing to offer the individuals in each group a job. Thirty-six percent said they would hire the men with no record, 24 percent said they would hire the men who had been acquitted and had a letter from the judge, 12 percent said they would hire the men who had been acquitted but had no letter, and 4 percent said they would hire the men who had been convicted.

The findings of this simple study, replicated in a number of subsequent research projects, are a dramatic illustration of the powerful impact of a criminal record, even if the individual under consideration has been acquitted. The implications of these findings—when considered in terms of the number of Americans with records and the accuracy and completeness of these records—are staggering.

There are two broad strategies for reducing crime. One approach is to concentrate on apprehending and punishing the criminal at the time of his crime. The second is to try to eliminate those situations that encourage an individual to become a criminal. The sometimes conflicting goals of these two strategies are dramatically displayed by the computerized data bases and communication facilities that each day are increasing the availability of criminal-history information to both the police and employers. If the computerized records ultimately allow the police and courts to apprehend and punish more criminals, society benefits. If the computerized records work to create a permanent class of people who are unemployed and thus prone to crime, society loses. The complex balance between these two strategies is not clear.

But it does seem clear that the computerized records being rocketed around the country would be a greater help to the police and less damaging to the public if they were accurate and complete. In the pursuit of this worthy goal, after failing to reach a compromise on comprehensive legislation to govern the NCIC, Congress adopted a brief amendment to the Crime Control Act of 1973. The 139-word amendment, which all parties regarded as an interim measure, contained three very simple principles. First, to the maximum extent feasible, criminal-history information disseminated with the help of federal funds should contain disposition, as well as arrest data. Second, procedures would be adopted to require that the information is kept current. Third, the information would be used for law-enforcement, criminal justice and "other lawful purposes." As already noted, the exception for other lawful purposes has become something of a gusher.

The 1973 amendment also offered the citizen an apparent remedy. "An individual who believes that criminal information concerning him in an automated system is inaccurate, incomplete or maintained in violation of this title, shall, upon satisfactory verification of his identity, be entitled to review such information and to obtain a copy of it for the purpose of challenge or correction."

Almost three years later, the government followed up on the 1973 amendment by issuing a vaguely worded regulation that nominally required the states to develop policies and procedures to ensure the privacy and security of criminal-history records. Individual access and review was one of five specific areas the federal government said the states must cover in their regulations.

Ever since the computer became a major force in the administration of large government and business organizations in the mid-1960s, the individual's right to see and correct his own computerized record has been held up as a miracle cure for many of the potential abuses of the computer age. Alan F. Westin, in his pioneering 1967 book *Privacy and Freedom,* was among the first to find wonderful powers in the cure of public access. The principle was subsequently embraced by both the Privacy Act of 1973 and the 1977 report of the Privacy Protection Study Commission.

But the OTA report indicating that more than half of the millions of criminal-history records now circulating in the United States are incomplete, inaccurate or ambiguous is compelling evidence that the remedies prescribed by law and regulation are not very effective. And when the congressional researchers looked at the actual record-keeping practices of four states and six urban areas, they found strong evidence that the promises made in the 1973 Crime Control Act amendment are largely an illusion.

The California criminal justice system, for example, contains more than 3 million records, 1.1 million of which are in computers, the balance in manual files. In a recent year, authorized organizations made 5 million separate inquiries of the system. Despite the huge number of transactions, however, the researchers discovered that only three hundred to four hundred individuals each year ask to see their records, eighty find something they record as incorrect and forty are actually successful in forcing California to make a correction.

Approximately one out of four who check their California records discover what they claim to be discrepancies. Approximately one out of ten who check their records force the state to make a correction. No one believes that the same proportion of errors would be found if a thorough audit was made of all 3 million records held in California. At the same time, however, it seems certain that a very large absolute number of records used to make important decisions about people are flawed.

A second approach to assuring accurate records is to require that the record keepers periodically check their files and dump those that are inaccurate or incomplete. The government, at least in theory, adopted this alternative approach in 1976 when it required that all the states develop plans for regularly auditing and purging their criminal history files.

In 1980 the Office of Technology Assessment sent a questionnaire to the fifty states about how they managed their criminal-history records. One question was whether they checked the accuracy of the records in their files. Four out of five of the forty-nine states answering this question responded that they had never conducted record quality audits. So much for federal regulations.

The astounding finding that only one out of five of the states has ever sought to audit and purge the information in their criminal-history files may explain why so many of the records are inaccurate or incomplete. It also demonstrates how difficult it is for the federal government to force state and local agencies to meet a standard established by Congress.

But it is not only the states that have been unable to assure the accuracy of these records. Despite the 1981 testimony to the House Subcommittee on Constitutional Rights that the FBI is working to improve the records, the bureau has never conducted a systematic audit comparing the information sent to Washington against the information recorded in the nation's courthouses.

Kenneth Laudon, one of the researchers hired by OTA to consider the impact of the FBI plan to enlarge its computer capacity to speed the transmission of criminal-history records, is disturbed by their discoveries. "Systems can be thought of as politically accountable," he said recently, "when they operate under statutory authority and within statutory guidelines, when existing institutions are capable of effective oversight, audit and monitoring, and when such systems are open. By and large, the evidence we found shows that the criminal justice information systems at the local, state and federal levels simply do not meet these criteria."

Even with all the questions about the accuracy of the records, the impact of the records and the inability of Congress and most of the state legislatures to force the record holders to meet certain minimal standards, many policemen, probably a majority, support the FBI drive to enlarge its already dominant hold on an extensive communication system intended to forge the separate data bases into a single entity.

There are some law-enforcement officials and other experts, however, who flatly oppose the FBI's central role. "The bureau is a law-enforcement agency, not a communications agency, and I think it would be better if the federal end of the criminal-history repository was not under the control of the FBI," said Patrick V. Murphy, the former police chief of Washington, Detroit and New York City. Mr. Murphy now heads the Police Foundation, an independent research group.

Representative Don Edwards, chairman of the House Subcommittee on Constitutional Rights, was an FBI agent before he was elected to Congress. "It is bad policy to locate this repository in the FBI," he said recently. "If the federal government should have any role at all, the repository should be placed outside the FBI, outside the Justice Department."

Kenneth Laudon articulated some of the concerns underlying the opposition of Mr.

Murphy and Mr. Edwards to the FBI plan that has won the blessing of the Reagan administration's Task Force on Crime. "The very same technology which law-enforcement officials believe will increase the efficient administration of criminal justice records also creates an instrument of potential subjugation by a victorious foreign power, the internal subversion of the normal democratic process or, by the drift of bureaucratic growth, ever larger instruments of social control. There is no technical difference between instruments of subjugation and instruments of efficient administration. The possibility exists, however remote, that American society is building the tools of its own political demise."

Computer scientists and manufacturers purport to believe their machines are neutral. This is true, of course, as long as the technology remains in the showroom. The neutrality evaporates, however, when powerful officials running powerful bureaucracies harness the computers to achieve their collective goals. Often both the goals and methods of achieving them are in the public interest. History tells us, however, that the organizations of fallible men sometimes lose their way.

During the sixties and seventies the leadership of the FBI and a number of police departments throughout the country came to believe that their responsibilities went beyond arresting those who had committed criminal acts. Their job, some policemen thought, extended to trying to channel the political thoughts and lifestyles of the American people along certain narrow paths. Police departments in such cities as Chicago and Los Angeles enormously expanded their surveillance of individuals who did not share conventional police values. The U.S. Army ordered its intelligence agents to attend all sorts of political rallies. The FBI, with the explicit approval of J. Edgar Hoover, undertook a secret program in which it deliberately sought to have critics of the federal government fired from their jobs or otherwise discredited by mailing false and anonymous reports to their neighbors and colleagues.

The FBI's effort to expand its activities beyond the precise boundaries of criminal law did not stop with the anonymous smearing of thousands of Americans who did not happen to share Mr. Hoover's view of the universe. From 1971 to 1974 the FBI harnessed the computerized data bases of the National Crime Information Center to pick up the movements of persons who were not criminal suspects.

Under the public regulations establishing the NCIC and how it would operate, the FBI declared that only the names of persons who had been formally charged with a crime would be listed in the NCIC computer. In July of 1975, however, John Tunney, then chairman of the Senate Subcommittee on Constitutional Rights, announced the discovery that the bureau had violated its own regulations by using the NCIC "to keep track of individuals who might be of interest to the FBI for whatever purpose, including possible political reasons."

Three months later, the Justice Department confirmed that from 1971 to 1974 the FBI had instructed its NCIC's computers to sound an alarm any time a local law-enforcement agency sent a message to Washington indicating that any one of 4,700 individuals was arrested. When it is remembered what a large part of the population have arrest records and how many persons were being arrested during that particular period for taking part in civil rights and antiwar demonstrations, the automated flagging mechanism can be viewed as a potentially powerful surveillance device.

One indication of how embarrassed the Justice Department was about the FBI's secret operation of a surveillance system outside the limits set down in its own regulation was the way the project was abruptly halted on the precise day that the Senate subcommittee staff made its first inquiry. But seven years later, there are indications that the FBI and other law-enforcement agencies of the Reagan administration would like to resurrect the use of the NCIC computers to track persons who are not the subject of a formal arrest warrant.

The first hint of this possible shift in NCIC policy came at a meeting of the NCIC advisory board in June of 1981 in a talk by Kier T. Boyd, an FBI inspector and the deputy assistant director of that part of the bureau that controls the FBI's very large computerized telecommunication system. According to the minutes of the advisory board meeting, Mr. Boyd openly advocated the start-up of the same kind of surveillance that had been so suddenly halted in 1974.

The official began by acknowledging that the tracking of the early 1970s had run into a wave of adverse reaction because "of the political climate at that time" and that the policy under consideration in the spring of 1981 "smacks of the tracking system which in the past has not been very well received by certain quarters of Congress."

In an apparent reference to the growing power of conservatives in the Congress, however, Mr. Boyd said he now felt "that the climate is very definitely changing and now we have an opportunity to raise the system to a new level."

The FBI inspector told the policy board that if they examined "our past use of the system for tracking, that they would see these things were done pretty much unilaterally," without the approval of Congress. "I believe now is the time when things like this, which are controversial, if they are raised in the present climate and given a full airing, could have a good chance of succeeding and performing very material assistance to segments of the criminal justice community."

One of the major forces currently shaping the political climate of the United States is fear. People are afraid of communism. People are afraid of crime. People are afraid of terrorism. Whether these fears are entirely valid, whether these fears are greatly enhanced by television, whether other ages have had much more to fear are all irrelevant questions.

A powerful example of the violence many Americans believe has now become a world epidemic occurred on March 30, 1981, when a confused young man named John Hinckley tried to murder President Reagan. It is not entirely surprising, therefore, that the Secret Service, the agency responsible for protecting the president, has used the assassination attempt as an argument in favor of once again using the FBI computers to track individuals who have been determined "dangerous" but who are not subject to an arrest warrant. H. S. Knight, director of the Secret Service, made his argument in a letter to William Webster, the director of the FBI, on November 21, 1981.

The use of the NCIC computers to flag the names of persons of interest, Mr. Knight said, could be "a positive step in a more comprehensive coverage of individuals whom we have evaluated to be a continuing danger to the protectees of this service." It also could be used "as another resource to monitor or keep aware of the location of such individuals whose travels may not otherwise be known to us."

In the summer of 1982, the Justice Department approved the request of the Secret Service to use the FBI computer to keep track of persons it suspects may be a danger to officials. But Representative Edwards, the one-time FBI agent, asked the Justice Department not to implement the plan until a thorough public examination of the issues had been completed and possible legislation considered.

Without a law, Mr. Edwards said in a letter to Attorney General William French Smith, "what assurances do we have that this system will not evolve into the sort of system maintained by the Secret Service in the 1970's when 'dangerousness' and 'threat' were interpreted to include political dissent? In 1972, the Secret Service had nearly 50,000 individuals on its lists, including such 'threats' as Jane Fonda, Tom Hayden, Ralph Abernathy, Cesar Chavez, Benjamin Spock and Walter Fauntroy. Among the organizations listed were the NAACP, the Southern Christian Leadership Conference and the John Birch Society."

It is very hard to challenge a Secret Service request for a tool that it declares will provide improved protection for the president. But it is easy to understand that the principle of restricting the FBI's computerized telecommunications network only to tracking criminal suspects is an important one. It also is easy to understand that changes in a powerful instrument of federal surveillance should not be made without public discussion, congressional hearings and legislative authorization. Once an exception has been made for one category of persons, each succeeding category will be that much easier.

18. *The Right to Privacy*

Samuel D. Warren
and Louis D. Brandeis

"It could be done only on principles of private justice, moral fitness, and public convenience, which, when applied to a new subject, make common law without a precedent; much more when received and approved by usage."

Willes, J., in Millar *v.* Taylor, 4 Burr. 2303, 2312.

THAT THE INDIVIDUAL shall have full protection in person and in property is a principle as old as the common law; but it has been found necessary from time to time to define anew the exact nature and extent of such protection. Political, social, and economic changes entail the recognition of new rights, and the common law, in its eternal youth, grows to meet the demands of society. Thus, in very early times, the law gave a remedy only for physical interference with life and property, for trespasses *vi et armis*. Then the "right to life" served only to protect the subject from battery in its various forms: liberty meant freedom from

From *Harvard Law Review* 4, 5 (December 15, 1890), pp. 193–220. Notes deleted.

actual restraint; and the right to property secured to the individual his lands and his cattle. Later, there came a recognition of man's spiritual nature, of his feelings and his intellect. Gradually the scope of these legal rights broadened; and now the right to life has come to mean the right to enjoy life,—the right to be let alone; the right to liberty secures the exercise of extensive civil privileges; and the term "property" has grown to comprise every form of possession—intangible, as well as tangible.

Thus, with the recognition of the legal value of sensations, the protection against actual bodily injury was extended to prohibit mere attempts to do such injury; that is, the putting another in fear of such injury. From the action of battery grew that of assault. Much later there came a qualified protection of the individual against offensive noises and odors, against dust and smoke, and excessive vibration. The law of nuisance was developed. So regard for human emotions soon extended the scope of personal immunity beyond the body of the individual. His reputation, the standing among his fellow-men, was considered, and the law of slander and libel arose. Man's family relations became a part of the legal conception of his life, and the alienation of a wife's affection was held remediable. Occasionally the law halted,—as in its refusal to recognize the intrusion by seduction upon the honor of the family. But even here the demands of society were met. A mean fiction, the action *per quod servitium amisit,* was resorted to, and by allowing damages for injury to the parents' feelings, an adequate remedy was ordinarily afforded. Similar to the expansion of the right to life was the growth of the legal conception of property. From corporeal property arose the incorporeal rights issuing out of it; and then there opened the wide realm of intangible property, in the products and processes of the mind, as works of literature and art, goodwill, trade secrets, and trademarks.

This development of the law was inevitable. The intense intellectual and emotional life, and the heightening of sensations which came with the advance of civilization, made it clear to men that only a part of the pain, pleasure, and profit of life lay in physical things. Thoughts, emotions, and sensations demanded legal recognition, and the beautiful capacity for growth which characterizes the common law enabled the judges to afford the requisite protection, without the interposition of the legislature.

Recent inventions and business methods call attention to the next step which must be taken for the protection of the person, and for securing to the individual what Judge Cooley calls the right "to be let alone." Instantaneous photographs and newspaper enterprise have invaded the sacred precincts of private and domestic life; and numerous mechanical devices threaten to make good the prediction that "what is whispered in the closet shall be proclaimed from the house-tops." For years there has been a feeling that the law must afford some remedy for the unauthorized circulation of portraits of private persons; and the evil of the invasion of privacy by the newspapers, long keenly felt, has been but recently discussed by an able writer. The alleged facts of a somewhat notorious case brought before an inferior tribunal in New York a few months ago, directly involved the consideration of the right of circulating portraits; and the question whether our law will recognize and protect the right to privacy in this and in other respects must soon come before our courts for consideration.

Of the desirability—indeed of the necessity—of some such protection, there can, it is believed, be no doubt. The press is overstepping in every direction the obvious bounds of propriety and of decency. Gossip is no longer the resource of the idle and of the vicious, but has become a trade, which is pursued with industry as well as effrontery. To satisfy a prurient taste the details of sexual relations are spread broadcast in the columns of the daily papers. To occupy the indolent, column upon column is filled with idle gossip, which can only be procured by intrusion upon the domestic circle. The intensity and complexity of life, attendant upon advancing civilization, have rendered necessary some retreat from the world, and man, under the refining influence of culture, has become more sensitive to publicity, so that solitude and privacy have become more essential to the individual; but modern enterprise and invention have, through invasions upon his privacy, subjected him to mental pain and distress, far greater than could be inflicted by mere bodily injury. Nor is the harm wrought by such invasions confined to the suffering of those who may be made the subjects of journalistic or other enterprise. In this, as in other branches of commerce, the supply creates the demand. Each crop of unseemly gossip, thus harvested, becomes the seed of more, and, in direct proportion to its circulation, results in a lowering of social standards and of morality. Even gossip apparently harmless, when widely and persistently circulated, is potent for evil. It both belittles and perverts. It belittles by inverting the relative importance of things, thus dwarfing the thoughts and aspirations of a people. When personal gossip attains the dignity of print, and crowds the space available for matters of real interest to the community, what wonder that the ignorant and thoughtless mistake its relative importance. Easy of comprehension, appealing to that weak side of human nature which is never wholly cast down by the misfortunes and frailties of our neighbors, no one can be surprised that it usurps the place of interest in brains capable of other things. Triviality destroys at once robustness of thought and delicacy of feeling. No enthusiasm can flourish, no generous impulse can survive under its blighting influence.

It is our purpose to consider whether the existing law affords a principle which can properly be invoked to protect the privacy of the individual; and, if it does, what the nature and extent of such protection is.

Owing to the nature of the instruments by which privacy is invaded, the injury inflicted bears a superficial resemblance to the wrongs dealt with by the law of slander and of libel, while a legal remedy for such injury seems to involve the treatment of mere wounded feelings, as a substantive cause of action. The principle on which the law of defamation rests, covers, however, a radically different class of effects from those for which attention is now asked. It deals only with damage to reputation, with the injury done to the individual in his external relations to the community, by lowering him in the estimation of his fellows. The matter published of him, however widely circulated, and however unsuited to publicity, must, in order to be actionable, have a direct tendency to injure him in his intercourse with others, and even if in writing or in print, must subject him to the hatred, ridicule, or contempt of his fellowmen,—the effect of the publication upon his estimate of himself and upon his own feelings not forming an essential element in the cause of action. In short, the wrongs and correlative rights recognized by the law of slander and libel are in their nature material rather than spiritual. That branch of the law simply extends the protection surrounding physical property to certain of the conditions necessary or helpful to worldly prosperity. On the other hand, our law recognizes no principle upon which compensation can be granted for mere injury to the feelings. However painful the mental effects upon another of an act, though purely wanton or even malicious, yet if the act itself is otherwise lawful, the suffering inflicted is *damnum absque injuria*. Injury of feelings may indeed be taken account of in ascertaining the amount of damages when attending what is recognized as a legal injury; but our system, unlike the Roman law, does not afford a remedy even for mental suffering which results from mere contumely and insult, from an intentional and unwarranted violation of the "honor" of another.

It is not however necessary, in order to sustain the view that the common law recognizes and upholds a principle applicable to cases of invasion of privacy, to invoke the analogy, which is but superficial, to injuries sustained, either by an attack upon reputation or by what the civilians called a violation of honor; for the legal doctrines relating to infractions of what is ordinarily termed the common-law right to intellectual and artistic property are, it is believed, but instances and applications of a general right to privacy, which properly understood afford a remedy for the evils under consideration.

The common law secures to each individual the right of determining, ordinarily, to what extent his thoughts, sentiments, and emotions shall be communicated to others. Under our system of government, he can never be compelled to express them (except when upon the witness-stand); and even if he has chosen to give them expression, he generally retains the power to fix the limits of the publicity which shall be given them. The existence of this right does not depend upon the particular method of expression adopted. It is immaterial whether it be by word or by signs, in painting, by sculpture, or in music. Neither does the existence of the right depend upon the nature or value of the thought or emotion, nor upon the excellence of the means of expression. The same protection is accorded to a casual letter or an entry in a diary and to the most valuable poem or essay, to a botch or daub and to a masterpiece. In every such case the individual is entitled to decide whether that which is his shall be given to the public. No other has the right to publish his productions in any form, without his consent. This right is wholly independent of the material on which, or the means by which, the thought, sentiment, or emotion is expressed. It may exist independently of any corporeal being, as in words spoken, a song sung, a drama acted. Or if expressed on any material, as a poem in writing, the author may have parted with the paper, without forfeiting any proprietary right in the composition itself. The right is lost only when the author himself communicates his production to the public,—in other words, publishes it. It is entirely independent of the copyright laws, and their extension into the domain of art. The aim of those statutes is to secure to the author, composer, or artist the entire profits arising from publication; but the common-law protection enables him to control absolutely the act of publication, and in the exercise of his own discretion, to decide whether there shall be any publication at all. The statutory right is of no value, *unless* there is a publication; the common-law right is lost *as soon as* there is a publication.

What is the nature, the basis, of this right to prevent the publication of manuscripts or works of art? It is stated to be the enforcement of a right of property; and no difficulty arises in accepting this view, so long as we have only to deal with the reproduction of literary and artistic compositions. They certainly possess many of the attributes of ordinary property: they are transferable; they have a value; and publication or reproduction is a use by which that value is realized. But where the value of the production is found not in the right to take the profits arising from publication, but in the peace of mind or the relief afforded by the ability to prevent any publication at all, it is difficult to regard the right as one of property, in the common acceptation of that term. A man records in a letter to his son, or in his diary, that he did not dine with his wife on a certain day. No one into whose hands those papers fall could publish them to the world, even if possession of the documents had been obtained rightfully; and the prohibition would not be confined to the publication of a copy of the letter itself, or of the diary entry; the restraint extends also to a publication of the contents. What is the thing which is protected? Surely, not the intellectual act of recording the fact that the husband did not dine with his wife, but that fact itself. It is not the intellectual product, but the domestic occurrence. A man writes a dozen letters to different people. No person would be permitted to publish a list of the letters written. If the letters or the contents of the diary were protected as literary compositions, the scope of the protection afforded should be the same secured to a published writing under the copyright law. But the copyright law would not prevent an enumeration of the letters, or the publication of some of the facts contained therein. The copyright of a series of paintings or etchings would prevent a reproduction of the paintings as pictures; but it would not prevent a publication of a list or even a description of them. Yet in the famous case of Prince Albert *v*. Strange, the court held that the common-law rule prohibited not merely the reproduction of the etchings which the plaintiff and Queen Victoria had made for their own pleasure, but also "the publishing (at least by printing or writing), though not by copy or resemblance, a description of them, whether more or less limited or summary, whether in the form of a catalogue or otherwise." Likewise, an unpublished collection of news possessing no element of a literary nature is protected from piracy.

That this protection cannot rest upon the right to literary or artistic property in any exact sense, appears the more clearly when the subject-matter for which protection is invoked is not even in the form of intellectual property, but has the attributes of ordinary tangible property. Suppose a man has a collection of gems or curiosities which he keeps private: it would hardly be contended that any person could publish a catalogue of them, and yet the articles enumerated are certainly not intellectual property in the legal sense, any more than a collection of stoves or of chairs.

The belief that the idea of property in its narrow sense was the basis of the protection of unpublished manuscripts led an able court to refuse, in several cases, injunctions against the publication of private letters, on the ground that "letters not possessing the attributes of literary compositions are not property entitled to protection"; and that it was "evident the plaintiff could not have considered the letters as of any value whatever as literary productions, for a letter cannot be considered of value to the author which he never would consent to have published." But these decisions have not been followed, and it may now be considered settled that the protection afforded by the common law to the author of any writing is entirely independent of its pecuniary value, its intrinsic merits, or of any intention to publish the same, and, of course, also, wholly independent of the material, if any, upon which, or the mode in which, the thought or sentiment was expressed.

Although the courts have asserted that they rested their decisions on the narrow grounds of protection to property, yet there are recognitions of a more liberal doctrine. Thus in the case of *Prince Albert* v. *Strange,* already referred to, the opinions both of the Vice-Chancellor and of the Lord Chancellor, on appeal, show a more or less clearly defined perception of a principle broader than those which were mainly discussed, and on which they both placed their chief reliance. Vice-Chancellor Knight Bruce referred to publishing of a man that he had "written to particular persons or on particular subjects" as an instance of possibly injurious disclosures as to private matters, that the courts would in a proper case prevent; yet it is difficult to perceive how, in such a case, any right of property, in the narrow sense, would be drawn in question, or why, if such a publication would be restrained when it threatened to expose the victim not merely to sarcasm, but to ruin, it should not equally be enjoined, if it threatened to embitter his life. To deprive a man of the potential profits to be realized by publishing a catalogue of his gems cannot *per se* be a wrong to him. The possibility of future profits is not a right of property which the law ordinarily recognizes; it must, therefore, be an infraction of other rights which constitutes the wrongful act, and that infraction is equally wrongful, whether its results are to forestall the profits that the individual himself might secure by giving the matter a publicity obnoxious to him, or to gain an advantage at the expense of his mental pain and suffering. If the fiction of property in a narrow sense must be preserved, it is still true that the end accomplished by the gossip-monger is attained by the use of that which is another's, the facts relating to his private life, which he has seen fit to keep private. Lord Cottenham stated that a man "is entitled to be protected in the exclusive use and enjoyment of that which is exclusively his," and cited with approval the opinion of Lord Eldon, as reported in a manuscript note of the case of *Wyatt* v. *Wilson,* in 1820, respecting an engraving of George the Third during his illness, to the effect that "if one of the late king's physicians had kept a diary of what he heard and saw, the court would not, in the king's lifetime, have permitted him to print and publish it"; and Lord Cottenham declared, in respect to the acts of the defendants in the case before him, that "privacy is the right invaded." But if privacy is once recognized as a right entitled to legal protection, the interposition of the courts cannot depend on the particular nature of the injuries resulting.

These considerations lead to the conclusion that the protection afforded to thoughts, sentiments, and emotions, expressed through the medium of writing or of the arts, so far as it consists in preventing publication, is merely an instance of the enforcement of the more general right of the individual to be let alone. It is like the right not to be assaulted or beaten, the right not to be imprisoned, the right not to be maliciously prosecuted, the right not to be defamed. In each of these rights, as indeed in all other rights recognized by the law, there inheres the quality of being owned or possessed—and (as that is the distinguishing attribute of property) there may be some propriety in speaking of those rights as property. But, obviously, they bear little resemblance to what is ordinarily comprehended under that term. The principle which protects personal writings and all other personal productions, not against theft and physical appropriation, but against publication in any form, is in reality not the principle of private property, but that of an inviolate personality.

If we are correct in this conclusion, the existing law affords a principle which may be invoked to protect the privacy of the individual from invasion either by the too enterprising press, the photographer, or the possesser of any other modern device for recording or reproducing scenes or sounds. For the protection afforded is not confined by the authorities to those cases where any particular medium or form of expression has been adopted, nor to products of the intellect. The same protection is afforded to emotions and sensations expressed in a musical composition or other work of art as to a literary composition; and words spoken, a pantomime acted, a sonata performed, is no less entitled to protection than if each had been reduced to writing. The circumstance that a thought or emotion has been recorded in a permanent form renders its identification easier, and hence may be important from the point of view of evidence, but it has no significance as a matter of substantive right. If, then, the decisions indicate a general right to privacy for thoughts, emotions, and sensations, these should receive the same protection, whether expressed in writing, or in conduct, in conversation, in attitudes, or in facial expression.

It may be urged that a distinction should be taken between the deliberate expression of thoughts and emotions in literary or artistic compositions and the casual and often involuntary expression given to them in the ordinary conduct of life. In other words, it may be contended that the protection afforded is granted to the conscious products of labor, perhaps as an encouragement to effort. This contention, however plausible, has, in fact, little to recommend it. If the amount of labor involved be adopted as the test, we might well find that the effort to conduct one's self properly in business and in domestic relations had been far greater than that involved in painting a picture or writing a book; one would find that it was far easier to express lofty sentiments in a diary than in the conduct of a noble life. If the test of deliberateness of the act be adopted, much casual correspondence which is now accorded full protection would be excluded from the beneficent operation of existing rules. After the decisions denying the distinction attempted to be made between those literary productions which it was intended to publish and those which it was not, all considerations of the amount of labor involved, the degree of deliberation, the value of the product, and the intention of publishing must be abandoned, and no basis is discerned upon which the right to restrain publication and reproduction of such so-called literary and artistic works can be rested, except the right to privacy, as a part of the more general right to the immunity of the person,—the right to one's personality.

It should be stated that, in some instances where protection has been afforded against wrongful publication, the jurisdiction has been asserted, not on the ground of property, or at least not wholly on that ground, but upon the ground of an alleged breach of an implied contract or of a trust or confidence.

Thus, in *Abernathy* v. *Hutchinson,* 3 L. J. Ch. 209 (1825), where the plaintiff, a distinguished surgeon, sought to restrain the publication in the "Lancet" of unpublished lectures which he had delivered at St. Batholomew's Hospital in London, Lord Eldon doubted whether there could be property in lectures which had not been reduced to writing, but granted the injunction on the ground of breach of confidence, holding "that when persons were admitted as pupils or otherwise, to hear these lectures, although they were orally delivered, and although the parties might go to the extent, if they were able to do so, of putting down the whole by means of short-hand, yet they could do that only for the purposes of their own information, and could not publish, for profit, that which they had not obtained the right of selling."

In *Prince Albert* v. *Strange,* 1 McN. & G. 25 (1849), Lord Cottenham, on appeal, while recognizing a right of property in the etchings which of itself would justify the issuance of the injunction, stated, after discussing the evidence, that he was bound to assume that the possession of the etchings by the defendant had "its foundation in a breach of trust, confidence, or contract," and that upon such ground also the plaintiff's title to the injunction was fully sustained.

In *Tuck* v. *Priester,* 19 Q. B. D. 639 (1887), the plaintiffs were owners of a picture, and employed the defendant to make a certain number of copies. He did so, and made also a number of other copies for himself, and offered them for sale in England at a lower price. Subsequently, the plaintiffs registered their copyright in the picture, and then brought suit for an injunction and damages. The Lords Justices differed as to the application of the copyright acts to the case, but held unanimously that independently of those acts, the plaintiffs were entitled to an injunction and damages for breach of contract.

In *Pollard* v. *Photographic Co.,* 40 Ch. Div. 345 (1888), a photographer who had taken a lady's photograph under the ordinary circumstances was restrained from exhibiting it, and also from selling copies of it, on the ground that it was a breach of an implied term in the contract, and also that it was a breach of confidence. Mr. Justice North interjected in the argument of the plaintiff's counsel the inquiry: "Do you dispute that if the negative likeness were taken on the sly, the person who took it might exhibit copies?" and counsel for the plaintiff answered: "In that case there would be no trust or consideration to support a contract." Later, the defendant's counsel argued that "a person has no property in his own features; short of doing what is libellous or otherwise illegal, there is no restriction on the photographer's using his negative." But the court, while expressly finding a breach of contract and of trust sufficient to justify its interposition, still seems to have felt the necessity of resting the decision also upon a right of property, in order to bring it within the line of those cases which were relied upon as precedents.

This process of implying a term in a contract, or of implying a trust (particularly where the contract is written, and where there is no established usage or custom), is nothing more nor less than a judicial declaration that public morality, private justice, and general convenience demand the recognition of such a rule, and that the publication under similar circumstances would be considered an intolerable abuse. So long as these circumstances happen to present a contract upon which such a term can be engrafted by the judicial mind, or to supply relations upon which a trust or confidence can be erected, there may be no objection to working out the desired protection through the doctrines of contract or of trust. But the court can hardly stop there. The narrower doctrine may have satisfied the demands of society at a time when the abuse to be guarded against could rarely have arisen without violating a contract or a special confidence; but now that modern devices afford abundant opportunities for the perpetration of such wrongs without any participation by the injured party, the protection granted by the law must be placed upon a broader foundation. While, for instance, the state of the photographic art was such that one's picture could seldom be taken without his consciously "sitting" for the purpose, the law of contract or of trust might afford the prudent man sufficient safeguards against the improper circulation of his portrait; but since the latest advances in photographic art have rendered it possible to take pictures surreptitiously, the doctrines of contract and of trust are inadequate to support the required protection, and the law of tort must be resorted to. The right of property in its widest sense, including all possession, including all rights and privileges, and hence embracing the right to an inviolate personality, affords alone that broad basis upon which the protection which the individual demands can be rested.

Thus, the courts, in searching for some principle upon which the publication of private letters could be enjoined, naturally came upon the ideas of a breach of confidence, and of an implied contract; but it required little consideration to discern that this doctrine could not afford all the protection required, since it would not support the court in granting a remedy against a stranger; and so the theory of property in the contents of letters was adopted. Indeed, it is difficult to conceive on what theory of the law the casual recipient of a letter, who proceeds to publish it, is guilty of a breach of contract, express or implied, or of any breach of trust, in the ordinary acceptation of that term. Suppose a letter has been addressed to him without his solicitation. He opens it, and reads. Surely, he has not made any contract; he has not accepted any trust. He cannot, by opening and reading the letter, have come under any obligation save what the law declares; and, however expressed, that obligation is simply to observe the legal right of the sender, whatever it may be, and whether it be called his right of property in the contents of the letter, or his right to privacy.

A similar groping for the principle upon which a wrongful publication can be enjoined is found in the law of trade secrets. There, injunctions have generally been granted on the theory of a breach of contract, or of an abuse of confidence. It would, of course, rarely happen that anyone would be in the possession of a secret unless confidence had been reposed in him. But can it be supposed that the court would hesitate to grant relief against one who had obtained his knowledge by an ordinary trespass,—for instance, by wrongfully looking into a book in which the secret was recorded, or by eavesdropping? Indeed, in *Yovatt* v. *Winyard,* 1 J. & W. 394 (1820), where an injunction was granted against making any use of or communicating certain recipes for veterinary medicine, it appeared that the defendant, while in the plaintiff's employ, had surreptitiously got access to his book of recipes, and copied them. Lord Eldon "granted the injunction, upon the ground of there having been a breach of trust and confidence;" but it would seem to be difficult to draw any sound legal distinction between such a case and one where a mere stranger wrongfully obtained access to the book.

We must therefore conclude that the rights, so protected, whatever their exact nature, are not rights arising from contract or from special trust, but are rights as against the world; and, as above stated, the principle which has been applied to protect these rights is in reality not the principle of private property, unless that word be used in an extended and unusual sense. The principle which protects personal writings and any other productions of the intellect or of the emotions, is the right to privacy, and the law has no new principle to formulate when it extends this protection to the personal appearance, sayings, acts, and to personal relation, domestic or otherwise.

If the invasion of privacy constitutes a legal *injuria,* the elements for demanding redress exist, since already the value of mental suffering, caused by an act wrongful in itself, is recognized as a basis for compensation.

The right of one who has remained a private individual, to prevent his public portraiture, presents the simplest case for such extension; the right to protect one's self from pen portraiture, from a discussion by the press of one's private affairs, would be a more important and far-reaching one. If casual and unimportant statements in a letter, if handiwork, however inartistic and valueless, if possessions of all sorts are protected not only against reproduction, but against description and enumeration, how much more should the acts and sayings of a man in his social and domestic relations be guarded from ruthless publicity. If you may not reproduce a woman's face photographically without her consent, how much less should be tolerated the reproduction of her face, her form, and her actions, by graphic descriptions colored to suit a gross and depraved imagination.

The right to privacy, limited as such right must necessarily be, has already found expression in the law of France.

It remains to consider what are the limitations of this right to privacy, and what remedies may be granted for the enforcement of the right. To determine in advance of experience the exact line at which the dignity and convenience of the individual must yield to the demands of the public welfare or of private justice would be a difficult task; but the more general rules are furnished by the legal analogies already developed in the law of slander and libel, and in the law of literary and artistic property.

1. The right to privacy does not prohibit any publication of matter which is of public or general interest.

In determining the scope of this rule, aid would be afforded by the analogy, in the law of libel and slander, of cases which deal with the qualified privilege of comment and criticism on matters of public and general interest. There are of course difficulties in applying such a rule, but they are inherent in the subject-matter, and are certainly no greater than those which exist in many other branches of the law,—for instance, in that large class of cases in which the reasonableness or unreasonableness of an act is made the test of liability. The design of the law must be to protect those persons with whose affairs the community has no legitimate concern, from being dragged into an undesirable and un-desired publicity and to protect all persons, whatsoever; their position or station, from having matters which they may properly prefer to keep private, made public against their will. It is the unwarranted invasion of individual privacy which is reprehended, and to be, so far as possible, prevented. The distinction, however, noted in the above statement is obvious and fundamental. There are persons who may reasonably claim as a right, protection from the notoriety entailed by being made the victims of journalistic enterprise. There are others who, in varying degrees, have renounced the right to live their lives screened from public observation. Matters which men of the first class may justly contend, concern them-selves alone, may in those of the second be the subject of legitimate interest to their fellow-citizens. Peculiarities of manner and person, which in the ordinary individual should be free from comment, may acquire a public importance, if found in a candidate for political office. Some further discrimination is necessary, therefore, than to class facts or deeds as public or private according to a standard to be applied to the fact or deed *per se*. To publish of a modest and retiring individual that he suffers from an impediment in his speech or that he cannot spell correctly, is an unwarranted, if not an unexampled, infringement of his rights, while to state and comment on the same characteristics found in a would-be congressman could not be regarded as beyond the pale of propriety.

The general object in view is to protect the privacy of private life, and to whatever degree and in whatever connection a man's life has ceased to be private, before the pub-lication under consideration has been made, to that extent the protection is to be withdrawn. Since, then, the propriety of publishing the very same facts may depend wholly upon the person concerning whom they are published, no fixed formula can be used to prohibit obnoxious publications. Any rule of liability adopted must have in it an elasticity which shall take account of the varying circumstances of each case,—a necessity which unfortu-nately renders such a doctrine not only more difficult of application, but also to a certain extent uncertain in its operation and easily rendered abortive. Besides, it is only the more flagrant breaches of decency and propriety that could in practice be reached, and it is not perhaps desirable even to attempt to repress everything which the nicest taste and keenest sense of the respect due to private life would condemn.

In general, then, the matters of which the publication should be repressed may be described as those which concern the private life, habits, acts, and relations of an individual, and have no legitimate connection with his fitness for a public office which he seeks or for which he is suggested, or for any public or quasi public position which he seeks or for which he is suggested, and have no legitimate relation to or bearing upon any act done by him in a public or quasi public capacity. The foregoing is not designed as a wholly accurate or exhaustive definition, since that which must ultimately in a vast number of cases become a question of individual judgment and opinion is incapable of such definition; but it is an attempt to indicate broadly the class of matters referred to. Some things all men alike are entitled to keep from popular curiosity, whether in public life or not, while others are only private because the persons concerned have not assumed a position which makes their doings legitimate matters of public investigation.

2. The right to privacy does not prohibit the communication of any matter, though in its nature private, when the publication is made under circumstances which would render it a privileged communication according to the law of slander and libel.

Under this rule, the right to privacy is not invaded by any publication made in a court of justice, in legislative bodies, or the committees of those bodies; in municipal assemblies, or the committees of such assemblies, or practically by any communication made in any other public body, municipal or parochial, or in any body quasi public, like the large voluntary associations formed for almost every purpose of benevolence, business or other general interest; and (at least in many jurisdictions) reports of any such proceedings would in some measure be accorded a like privilege. Nor would the rule prohibit any publication made by one in the discharge of some public or private duty, whether legal or moral, or in conduct of one's own affairs, in matters where his own interest is concerned.

3. The law would probably not grant any redress for the invasion of privacy by oral publication in the absence of special damage.

The same reasons exist for distinguishing between oral and written publications of private matters, as is afforded in the law of defamation by the restricted liability for slander as compared with the liability for libel. The injury resulting from such oral communications would ordinarily be so trifling that the law might well, in the interest of free speech, disregard it altogether.

4. The right to privacy ceases upon the publication of the facts by the individual, or with his consent.

This is but another application of the rule which has become familiar in the law of literary and artistic property. The cases there decided establish also what should be deemed a publication,—the important principle in this connection being that a private communication of circulation for a restricted purpose is not a publication within the meaning of the law.

5. The truth of the matter published does not afford a defence.

Obviously this branch of the law should have no concern with the truth of falsehood of the matters published. It is not for injury to the individual's character that redress or prevention is sought, but for injury to the right of privacy. For the former, the law of slander and libel provides perhaps a sufficient safeguard. The latter implies the right not merely to prevent inaccurate portrayal of private life, but to prevent its being depicted at all.

6. The absence of "malice" in the publisher does not afford a defence.

Personal ill-will is not an ingredient of the offence, any more than in an ordinary case of trespass to person or to property. Such malice is never necessary to be shown in an action for libel or slander at common law, except in rebuttal of some defence, *e.g.,* that the occasion rendered the communication privileged, or, under the statutes in this State and elsewhere, that the statement complained of was true. The invasion of the privacy that is to be protected is equally complete and equally injurious, whether the motives by which the speaker or writer was actuated are, taken by themselves, culpable or not; just as the damage to character, and to some extent the tendency to provoke a breach of the peace, is equally the result of defamation without regard to the motives leading to its publication. Viewed as a wrong to the individual, this rule is the same pervading the whole law of torts, by which one is held responsible for his intentional acts, even though they are committed with no sinister intent; and viewed as a wrong to society, it is the same principle adopted in a large category of statutory offences.

The remedies for an invasion of the right of privacy are also suggested by those administered in the law of defamation, and in the law of literary and artistic property, namely:—

1. An action of tort for damages in all cases. Even in the absence of special damages, substantial compensation could be allowed for injury to feelings as in the action of slander and libel.
2. An injunction, in perhaps a very limited class of cases.

It would doubtless be desirable that the privacy of the individual should receive the added protection of the criminal law, but for this, legislation would be required. Perhaps it would be deemed proper to bring the criminal liability for such publication within narrower limits; but that the community has an interest in preventing such invasions of privacy, sufficiently strong to justify the introduction of such a remedy, cannot be doubted. Still, the protection of society must come mainly through a recognition of the rights of the individual. Each man is responsible for his own acts and omissions only. If he condones what he reprobates, with a weapon at hand equal to his defence, he is responsible for the results. If he resists, public opinion will rally to his support. Has he then such a weapon? It is believed that the common law provides him with one, forged in the slow fire of the centuries, and to-day fitly tempered to his hand. The common law has always recognized a man's house as his castle, impregnable, often, even to its own officers engaged in the execution of its commands. Shall the courts thus close the front entrance to constituted authority, and open wide the back door to idle or prurient curiosity?

19. Privacy in the Modern Democratic State

Alan Westin

Privacy and Political Systems

IT IS OBVIOUS that the political system in each society will be a fundamental force in shaping its balance of privacy, since certain patterns of privacy, disclosure, and surveillance are functional necessities for particular kinds of political regime. This is shown most vividly by contrasting privacy in the democratic and the totalitarian state.

The modern totalitarian state relies on secrecy for the regime, but high surveillance and disclosure for all other groups. With their demand for a complete commitment of loyalties to the regime, the literature of both fascism and communism traditionally attacks the idea of privacy as "immoral," "antisocial," and "part of the cult of individualism." This attitude is most strongly expressed in the consolidation phase of a new totalitarian regime. Autonomous units are denied privacy, traditional confidential relationships are destroyed, surveillance systems and informers are widely installed, and thorough dossiers are compiled on millions of citizens. Most important, the individual is not allowed to gain security by conforming without opposition and quietly doing his job. The regime demands active and positive loyalty. These policies, by creating fear and distrust, tend to foster a sense of loneliness and isolation in the citizen; for relief, he turns to identification with the state and its programs so that he may find the satisfactions of affiliation and achievement.

Once the regime has consolidated its power and a new generation has grown up under totalitarian rule, some of the anti-privacy measures are relaxed. A degree of privacy is allowed to families, church, science, and the arts, and police terror is reduced. However, the public has been well conditioned by the old methods, and occasional punishment of those who use their new privacy too aggressively is sufficient to restore the required amount of regime control. Furthermore, the primary surveillance systems of paid and volunteer spies, eavesdropping and watching devices, and strict records control are retained to keep the regime on its guard.

Just as a social balance favoring disclosure and surveillance over privacy is a functional necessity for totalitarian systems, so a balance that ensures strong citadels of individual and group privacy and limits both disclosure and surveillance is a prerequisite for liberal democratic societies. The democractic society relies on publicity as a control over government, and on privacy as a shield for group and individual life. The reasons for protecting privacy tend to be familiar to citizens of liberal democracies; thus the specific functions that privacy performs in their political systems are often left unexpressed. The discussion that follows will treat these functions briefly.

Excerpted from Alan F. Westin, *Privacy and Freedom* (New York: Atheneum, 1967), pp. 23–26, 32–42. Notes deleted. Copyright © 1967 The Association of the Bar of the City of New York. Reprinted by permission of Atheneum Publishers, Inc.

Liberal democratic theory assumes that a good life for the individual must have substantial areas of interest apart from political participation—time devoted to sports, arts, literature, and similar non-political pursuits. These areas of individual pursuit prevent the total politicizing of life and permit other models of success and happiness to serve as alternatives to the political career and the citizenship role. Personal retreats for securing perspective and critical judgment are also significant for democratic life. A liberal democratic system maintains a strong commitment to the family as a basic and autonomous unit responsible for important educational, religious, and moral roles, and therefore the family is allowed to assert claims to physical and legal privacy against both society and the state. As a result of religious diversity and ideas of toleration, most democratic systems make religious choice a "private" concern; both law and custom forbid government controls over the nature and legitimacy of religious affiliations and allow maximum privacy for religious observance and for religious examination of public policy issues.

Because of the central role played by groups in a democratic society—they provide opportunities for sociability, expression of independent ideas, resolution of community conflicts, criticism of government, and formation of a consensus on public policy—citizens are given wide freedom to join associations and participate in group affairs. To this end, privacy of membership and intra-group action are protected. Associations themselves are given substantial organizational privacy to achieve their objectives efficiently and responsibly. Liberal democracy recognizes the special needs of scholars and scientists to be free of constant community and government examination so that paths to truth and discovery can be pursued even in directions that offend dominant opinion. Liberal democratic systems ensure maximum freedom for political choice by providing a secret ballot to protect the voting process and by forbidding governmental inquiries into a citizen's past voting record. Through a network of constitutional, legal, and political restraints, democratic societies protect the individual's person and personality from improper police conduct such as physical brutality, compulsory self-incrimination, and unreasonable searches and seizures. Finally, liberal democratic societies set a balance between government's organizational needs for preparatory and institutional privacy and the need of the press, interest groups, and other governmental agencies for the knowledge of government operations required to keep government conduct responsible.

The functions of privacy in liberal systems do not require that it be an absolute right. The exercise of privacy creates dangers for a democracy that may call for social and legal responses. Private-life commitments can produce such indifference to political and governmental needs on the part of citizens that society must work to bring its members back to participating responsibility. In some situations claims to organizational privacy can give rise to anonymous influences over public life, can overweigh the organized sectors of the citizenry, and can foster the growth of conspiracies that will threaten the democracy's survival. Persons who venture into public debates or civic life sometimes claim an unjustified right to privacy from fair reply or fair criticism. Rules protecting the privacy of the person by forbidding new but not necessarily unreasonable law-enforcement methods can seriously impede protection of the public from crime and lessen the nation's internal security. Privacy may also frustrate the public's "need to know," important behavioral research, and effective administration of government and business. An overly strict cloak of privacy for governmental affairs can cover manipulation of the public, misuse of office, and aggrandizement of power by government agencies. Thus the constant search in democracies must be for the proper boundary line in each specific situation and for an over-all equilibrium that serves to strengthen democratic institutions and processes.

No one has written more sensitively on this problem than the political sociologist, Edward Shils:

> Democracy requires the occasional political participation of most of its citizenry some of the time, and a moderate and dim perceptiveness—as if from the corner of the eye—the rest of the time. It could not function if politics and the state of the social order were always on everyone's mind. If most men, most of the time, regarded themselves as their brother-citizens' keepers, freedom, which flourishes in the indifference of privacy, would be abolished.

Shils sees the "first principle of individualist democracy" to be "the partial autonomy of individuals and of corporate bodies or institutions."

> Autonomy involves the right to make decisions, to promulgate rules of action, to dispose over resources and to recruit associates in accordance with criteria which the individual or organization deems appropriate to its tasks. The principle of partial autonomy assumes that, by and large, an individual's or a corporate group's life is its own business, that only marginal circumstances justify intrusion by others, and that only more exceptional circumstances justify enforced and entire disclosure, to the eyes of the broader public, of the private affairs of the corporate body or individual.

Shils makes an important distinction between privacy and secrecy. In secrecy, he notes, law forbids the disclosure of information. In privacy, disclosure "is at the discretion of the possessor, and such sanctions as laws provide are directed only against coercive acquisition" by persons to whom the individual does not want to disclose.

In over-all terms, the goal of a liberal society is to achieve a state of political "civility," which Shils defines as a condition in which there is enough privacy to nourish individual creativity and group expression; enough publicity of government affairs to let the public know the facts necessary to form judgments in political matters; and a small area of secrecy for government to preserve the integrity of certain secret information and the privacy of internal policy-making processes. . . .

The Functions of Individual Privacy

This analysis of the various states of privacy is useful in discussing the basic question of the functions privacy performs for individuals in democratic societies. These can also be grouped conveniently under four headings—personal autonomy, emotional release, self-evaluation, and limited and protected communication. Since every human being is a whole organism, these four functions constantly flow into one another, but their separation for analytical purposes helps to clarify the important choices about individual privacy that American law may have to make in the coming decade.

Personal Autonomy

In democratic societies there is a fundamental belief in the uniqueness of the individual, in his basic dignity and worth as a creature of God and a human being, and in the need to maintain social processes that safeguard his sacred individuality. Psychologists and sociologists have linked the development and maintenance of this sense of individuality to the human need for autonomy—the desire to avoid being manipulated or dominated wholly by others.

One of the accepted ways of representing the individual's need for an ultimate core of autonomy, as expressed by such theorists as Simmel, R. E. Park, Kurt Lewin, and Erving Goffman, has been to describe the individual's relations with others in terms of a series of "zones" or "regions" of privacy leading to a "core self." This core self is pictured as an inner circle surrounded by a series of larger concentric circles. The inner circle shelters the individual's "ultimate secrets"—those hopes, fears, and prayers that are beyond sharing with anyone unless the individual comes under such stress that he must pour out these ultimate secrets to secure emotional relief. Under normal circumstances no one is admitted to this sanctuary of the personality. The next circle outward contains "intimate secrets," those that can be willingly shared with close relations, confessors, or strangers who pass by and cannot injure. The next circle is open to members of the individual's friendship group. The series continues until it reaches the outer circles of casual conversation and physical expression that are open to all observers.

The most serious threat to the individual's autonomy is the possibility that someone may penetrate the inner zone and learn his ultimate secrets, either by physical or psychological means. This deliberate penetration of the individual's protective shell, his psychological armor, would leave him naked to ridicule and shame and would put him under the control of those who knew his secrets. Autonomy is also threatened by those who penetrate the core self because they do not recognize the importance of ultimate privacy or think that the casual and uninvited help they may be rendering compensates for the violation.

Each person is aware of the gap between what he wants to be and what he actually is, between what the world sees of him and what he knows to be his much more complex reality. In addition, there are aspects of himself that the individual does not fully understand but is slowly exploring and shaping as he develops. Every individual lives behind a mask in this manner; indeed, the first etymological meaning of the word "person" was "mask," indicating both the conscious and expressive presentation of the self to a social audience. If this mask is torn off and the individual's real self bared to a world in which everyone else still wears his mask and believes in masked performances, the individual can be seared by the hot light of selective, forced exposure. The numerous instances of suicides and nervous breakdowns resulting from such exposures by government investigation, press stories, and even published research constantly remind a free society that only grave social need can ever justify destruction of the privacy which guards the individual's ultimate autonomy.

The autonomy that privacy protects is also vital to the development of individuality and consciousness of individual choice in life. Leontine Young has noted that "without privacy there is no individuality. There are only types. Who can know what he thinks and feels if he never has the opportunity to be alone with his thoughts and feelings?" This development of individuality is particularly important in democratic societies, since qualities of independent thought, diversity of views, and non-conformity are considered desirable traits for individuals. Such independence requires time for sheltered experimentation and testing of ideas, for preparation and practice in thought and conduct, without fear of ridicule or penalty, and for the opportunity to alter opinions before making them public. The individual's sense that it is he who decides when to "go public" is a crucial aspect of his feeling of autonomy. Without such time for incubation and growth, through privacy, many ideas and positions would be launched into the world with dangerous prematurity. As Robert MacIver has stated, "Everything that grows first of all does so in the darkness before it sends its shoots out into the light."

Summing up the importance of privacy for political liberty, Clinton Rossiter has also stressed the feature of autonomy:

> Privacy is a special kind of independence, which can be understood as an attempt to secure autonomy in at least a few personal and spiritual concerns, if necessary in defiance of all the pressures of modern society. . . . [I]t seeks to erect an unbreachable wall of dignity and reserve against the entire world. The free man is the private man, the man who still keeps some of his thoughts and judgments entirely to himself, who feels no over-riding compulsion to share everything of value with others, not even those he loves and trusts.

Emotional Release

Life in society generates such tensions for the individual that both physical and psychological health demand periods of privacy for various types of emotional release. At one level, such relaxation is required from the pressure of playing social roles. Social scientists agree that each person constantly plays a series of varied and multiple roles, depending on his audience and behavioral situation. On any given day a man may move through the roles of stern father, loving husband, car-pool comedian, skilled lathe operator, union steward, water-cooler flirt, and American Legion committee chairman—all psychologically different roles that he adopts as he moves from scene to scene on the social stage. Like actors on the dramatic stage, Goffman has noted, individuals can sustain roles only for reasonable periods of time, and no individual can play indefinitely, without relief, the variety of roles that life demands. There have to be moments "off stage" when the individual can be "himself": tender, angry, irritable, lustful, or dream-filled. Such moments may come in solitude; in the intimacy of family, peers, or woman-to-woman and man-to-man relaxation; in the anonymity of park or street; or in a state of reserve while in a group. Privacy in this aspect gives individuals, from factory workers to Presidents, a chance to lay their masks aside for rest. To be always "on" would destroy the human organism.

Closely related to this form of release is the need of individuals for respite from the emotional stimulation of daily life. For most persons the constant experiences and surprises of active life are what make it worth living; indeed, we all search for richer and more varied stimulation. But the whirlpool of active life must lead to some quiet waters, if only so that the appetite can be whetted for renewed social engagement. Privacy provides the change of pace that makes life worth savoring.

Another form of emotional release is provided by the protection privacy gives to minor non-compliance with social norms. Some norms are formally adopted—perhaps as law—which society really expects many persons to break. This ambivalence produces a situation in which almost everyone does break some social or institutional norms—for example, violating traffic laws, breaking sexual mores, cheating on expense accounts, overstating income-tax deductions, or smoking in rest rooms when this is prohibited. Although society will usually punish the most flagrant abuses, it tolerates the great bulk of the violations as "permissible" deviations. If there were no privacy to permit society to ignore these deviations—if all transgressions were known—most persons in society would be under organizational discipline or in jail, or could be manipulated by threats of such action. The firm expectation of having privacy for permissible deviations is a distinguishing characteristic of life in a free society. At a lesser but still important level, privacy also allows individuals to deviate temporarily from social etiquette when alone or among intimates, as by putting feet on desks, cursing, letting one's face go slack, or scratching wherever one itches.

Another aspect of release is the "safety-valve" function afforded by privacy. Most persons need to give vent to their anger at "the system," "city hall," "the boss," and various others who exercise authority over them, and to do this in the intimacy of family or friendship circles, or in private papers, without fear of being held responsible for such comments. This is very different from freedom of speech or press, which involves publicly voiced criticism without fear of interference by government and subject only to private suit. Rather, the aspect of release concerned here involves commentary that may be wholly unfair, frivolous, nasty, and libelous, but is never socially measured because it is uttered in privacy. Without the aid of such release in accommodating the daily abrasions with authorities, most people would experience serious emotional pressure. Even Presidents and other high public officials have been well known, under the strains of office, to lash out momentarily in angry commentary that they really do not mean. Their privacy in such moments is respected because society knows that these occasional outbursts make possible the measured and responsible speech that is produced for public presentation.

Still another aspect of release through privacy arises in the management of bodily and sexual functions. American society has strong codes requiring privacy for evacuation, dressing the body, and arranging the body while in public; and privacy for sexual relations is deeply rooted in our culture. Though poverty may produce crowded conditions which deny privacy for bodily and sexual functions, it is not accidental that surveillance of such functions by outsiders is practiced with social approval only in what sociologists call "total institutions"—such as jails, mental institutions, and monasteries—or on volunteers in medical or behavioral-science experiments. Even then, prisoners and patients usually complain about being watched and seek ways to escape the constant surveillance of guards.

Finally, emotional release through privacy plays an important part in individual life at times of loss, shock, or sorrow. In such moments society provides comfort both through communal support by gatherings of friends and through respect for the privacy of the individual and his intimates. A similar need is often felt by individuals in public life who have suffered defeats or loss of face and need to retire from public view to regroup their psychological forces. Reporters, legislative committees, and social scientists do not always respect the claim of restorative privacy by public figures in temporary distress, but it is striking how often the rules of "decency" do provide substantial privacy in these circumstances. Privacy also performs a protective function at moments of less intense stress, during the periods of anxiety and uncertainty which are part of daily life.

Self-Evaluation

Every individual needs to integrate his experiences into a meaningful pattern and to exert his individuality on events. To carry on such self-evaluation, privacy is essential.

At the intellectual level, individuals need to process the information that is constantly bombarding them, information that cannot be processed while they are still "on the go." Alan Bates has written that privacy in such circumstances enables a person to "assess the flood of information received, to consider alternatives and possible consequences so that he may then act as consistently and appropriately as possible."

Privacy serves not only a processing but a planning need, by providing a time "to anticipate, to recast, and to originate." This is particularly true of creative persons. Studies of creativity show that it is in reflective solitude and even "daydreaming" during moments of reserve that most creative "non-verbal" thought takes place. At such moments the individual runs ideas and impressions through his mind in a flow of associations; the active presence of others tends to inhibit this process. For example, the Yale studies of "brainstorming" found that group-think sessions produced fewer ideas quantitatively than periods of individual, private work by the same number of people. Many studies and autobiographies have described the "creative loneliness" needed by artists and writers to produce their works.

The evaluative function of privacy also has a major moral dimension—the exercise of conscience by which the individual "repossesses himself." While people often consider the moral consequences of their acts during the course of daily affairs, it is primarily in periods of privacy that they take a moral inventory of ongoing conduct and measure current performance against personal ideals. For many persons this process is a religious exercise. Religious contemplation, said Coe, was a time for "organizing the self," and William James called religion the experience of "individual men in their solitude." Thus, periods for rumination over past events and for communication with oneself have been said to be "institutionalized in all societies." The tradition of religious retreats is another means of providing a time and setting for moral inventory. Even for an individual who is not a religious believer, privacy serves to bring the conscience into play, for, when alone, he must find a way to continue living with himself.

A final contribution of privacy to evaluation is its role in the proper timing of the decision to move from private reflection or intimate conversation to a more general publication of acts and thoughts. This is the process by which one tests his own evaluations against the responses of his peers. Given the delicacy of a person's relations with intimates and associates, deciding when and to what extent to disclose facts about himself—and to put others in the position of receiving such confidences—is a matter of enormous concern in personal interaction, almost as important as whether to disclose at all.

Limited and Protected Communication

The greatest threat to civilized social life would be a situation in which each individual was utterly candid in his communications with others, saying exactly what he knew or felt at all times. The havoc done to interpersonal relations by children, saints, mental patients, and adult "innocents" is legendary.

In real life, among mature persons all communication is partial and limited, based on the complementary relation between reserve and discretion that has already been discussed. Limited communication is particularly vital in urban life, with its heightened stimulation, crowded environment, and continuous physical and psychological confrontations between individuals who do not know one another in the extended, softening fashion of small-town life. Reserved communication is the means of psychic self-preservation for men in the metropolis.

Privacy for limited and protected communication has two general aspects. First, it provides the individual with the opportunities he needs for sharing confidences and intimacies with those he trusts—spouse, "the family," personal friends, and close associates at work. The individual discloses because he knows that his confidences will be held, and because he knows that breach of confidence violates social norms in a civilized society. "A friend," said Emerson, "is someone before . . . [whom] I can think aloud." In addition, the individual often wants to secure counsel from persons with whom he does not have to live daily after disclosing his confidences. He seeks professionally objective advice from persons whose status in society promises that they will not later use his distress to take advantage of him. To protect freedom of limited communication, such relationships—with doctors, lawyers, ministers, psychiatrists, psychologists, and others—are given varying but important degrees of legal privilege against forced disclosure. The privacy given to the religious confessional in democratic societies is well known, but the need for confession is so general that those without religious commitment have institutionalized their substitute in psychiatric and counseling services. Confessional relief also comes through the stranger, to whom communication is limited because what he is told will not be repeated in the "home sphere" of the person who has confided in him. For this reason, certain places where the real world is seemingly held in suspension "outside"—such as trains, boats, and bars—lend themselves to free conversation.

In its second general aspect, privacy through limited communication serves to set necessary boundaries of mental distance in interpersonal situations ranging from the most intimate to the most formal and public. In marriage, for example, husbands and wives need to retain islands of privacy in the midst of their intimacy if they are to preserve a saving respect and mystery in the relation. These elements of reserved communication will range from small matters, involving management of money, personal habits, and outside activities, to the more serious levels of past experiences and inner secrets of personality. Successful marriages usually depend on the discovery of the ideal line between privacy and revelation and on the respect of both partners for that line. In work situations, mental distance is necessary so that the relations of superior and subordinate do not slip into an intimacy which would create a lack of respect and an impediment to directions and correction. Thus, physical arrangements shield superiors from constant observation by subordinates, and social etiquette forbids conversations or off-duty contacts that are "too close" for the work relationship. Similar distance is observed in relations between professor and student, parent and child, minister and communicant, and many others.

Psychological distance is also used in crowded settings to provide privacy for the participants of group and public encounters; a complex but well-understood etiquette of privacy is part of our social scenario. Bates remarked that "we request or recognize withdrawal into privacy in facial expressions, bodily gestures, conventions like changing the subject, and by exchanging meaning in ways which exclude others present, such as private words, jokes, winks, and grimaces." We learn to ignore people and to be ignored by them as a way of achieving privacy in subways, on streets, and in the "non-presence" of servants or children. There are also social conventions within various sub-groups in the population establishing fairly clearly the proper and improper matters for discussion among intimates, workmates, persons on a bus, and other groups. And, as James Thurber showed so engagingly, the individual can simply go off into mental privacy when he needs to, as the Walter Mittys of society work off their aggressions and dream their fantasies.

The Individual's Quest for Intra-Psychic Balance

So far, the discussion has stressed the individual's need for privacy and the functions privacy performs in his personal life. But privacy is neither a self-sufficient state nor an end in itself, even for the hermit and the recluse. It is basically an instrument for achieving individual goals of self-realization. As such, it is only part of the individual's complex and shifting system of social needs, part of the way he adjusts his emotional mechanism to the barrage of personal and social stimuli that he encounters in daily life. Individuals have needs for disclosure and companionship every bit as important as their needs for privacy. As ancient and modern philosophers agree, man is a social animal, a gregarious being whose need for affiliation marks his conduct in every society. Thus, at one hour a person may want lively companionship and group affiliation; at another moment, the intimacy of family or close friends; at another, the anonymity of the city street or the movie; and at still other times, to be totally alone and unobserved. To be left in privacy when one wants companionship is as uncomfortable as the inability to have privacy when one craves it.

This balance of privacy and disclosure will be powerfully influenced, of course, by both the society's cultural norms and the particular individual's status and life situation. In American society, for example, which prefers "activism" over contemplation, people tend to use their leisure time to "do things" rather than to rest, read, and think in privacy. And, in any society, differences in occupation, socio-economic level, and religious commitment are broad conditioning factors in the way each person allots his time and tunes his emotional wave length for privacy.

This fact raises an interesting question about "status tensions" and privacy in America. Many claims to privacy or expectations of receiving privacy arise out of certain statuses—rich man, university professor, corporation executive, lawyer, and the like. Privacy rights and roles grow out of the legitimacy and prestige of these statuses. Yet, as noted earlier, American society from its inception has had a commitment to egalitarianism and social democracy that presses against the kind of privacy rules that are so well defined and well observed in European systems, which developed out of feudal traditions and still have definite class lines. In the United States this situation means that both the individual who occupies a high-status position and the low-status persons who came in contact with him are not always sure of what privacy rules ought to apply, of where proper reserve and discretion begin. This egalitarian-democratic ethos accounts for the "openness" and disregard for privacy in so many areas of American interpersonal life, but it makes the individual's adjustment of his intra-psychic privacy balance a more experimental and fluid matter than in most other systems, including most European democracies.

In general, however, all individuals are constantly engaged in an attempt to find sufficient privacy to serve their general social roles as well as their individual needs of the moment. Either too much or too little privacy can create imbalances which seriously jeopardize the individual's well-being. Too much privacy can be a result of social or physical conditions that lie largely beyond the individual's power to control. Thus, it can come from forced physical separation from society, as in the experiences of children raised by animals away from human society or the reactions of volunteers in sensory-deprivation experiments. More relevant is the solitary confinement of the prisoner or the isolation of explorers and disaster victims; memoirs and scholarly studies document the depression, hallucinations, and even mental collapse that such isolation can create. Or it may be the effect of life in complex, impersonal, industrial societies; many studies testify to the sense of rootlessness, anomie, and psychological isolation that this evokes in segments of the citizenry. Although the individual has no control over the conditions creating too much privacy in these situations, whether or not he adapts successfully depends on his own emotional capacities.

Too much privacy can also result from the individual's failure to adjust his own life situation to achieve a healthy emotional state, even though he enjoys "normal" social conditions. Karen Horney has described the individual who invokes an unnatural degree of privacy because he cannot relate successfully to daily life as one of the three major types of neurotics in our society.

> [This type of neurotic] is like a person in a hotel room who rarely removes the "Do-Not-Disturb" sign from his door. Even books may be regarded as intruders, as something from outside. Any question put to him about his personal life may shock him; he tends to shroud himself in a veil of secrecy. A patient once told me that at the age of forty-five he still resented the idea of God's omniscience quite as much as when his mother told him that God could look through the shutters and see him biting his fingernails.

At its extreme, this state produces the total privacy of the mental patient, alone in a self-sealed world as only the mad can be totally alone in the midst of society.

The opposite pole of imbalance is too little privacy. Here, too, some factors beyond the individual's effective control limit his opportunities for a "normal" privacy balance. These may be environmental factors such as crowded and noisy living conditions; economic factors such as poverty that make privacy less important than the satisfaction of more basic family needs; political factors such as widespread government surveillance of speech and communications; business and social factors such as intrusions into the home by telephone solicitors, door-to-door salesmen, and opinion surveyors; or cultural pressures such as the ethic of activism and the pressure on middle-class persons to participate in group affairs. Such limits on privacy in democratic societies require the individual to adjust his psychological balances, to find sufficient privacy *despite* these limiting factors. Thus, people in crowded living quarters find privacy outdoors—in the streets of cities, in the corners of bars, in motion-picture houses, and in a host of "public" places where the necessary solitude, intimacy, anonymity, and reserve can be found. Individuals find ways to bypass governmental surveillance of their private messages. Householders slam doors on solicitors or put "No Trespassing" signs on their property. These attempts to secure privacy even under hostile social conditions illustrate the quest for intra-psychic balance at work.

Too little privacy can also be present as a result of the way individuals manage their own lives. Nervous breakdowns and physical collapses from overwork often have as one major ingredient the lack of that emotional relief from stimulation which is a function of privacy. This factor is often much more basic to the collapse than physical strain. Psychiatrists have described the mental conflicts created by individuals who deliberately avoid solitude because they do not want to confront themselves with the moral implications of their own conduct; constant activity is an attempt to silence conscience by those who are abnormally afraid of being alone. A similar phenomenon [happens] when people reject normal levels of intimacy with those close to them. In another type of neurotic conduct the individual, to avoid "threatening" normal intimacies, immerses himself in group activity; this is a retreat into public life.

The basic point is that each individual must, within the larger context of his culture, his status, and his personal situation, make a continuous adjustment between his needs for solitude and companionship; for intimacy and general social intercourse; for anonymity and responsible participation in society; for reserve and disclosure. A free society leaves this choice to the individual, for this is the core of the "right of individual privacy"—the right of the individual to decide for himself, with only extraordinary exceptions in the interests of society, when and on what terms his acts should be revealed to the general public. . . .

20. Why Privacy Is Important

James Rachels

ACCORDING TO THOMAS Scanlon, the first element of a theory of privacy should be "a characterization of the special interest we have in being able to be free from certain kinds of intrusions." Since I agree that is the right place to begin, I shall begin there. Then I shall comment briefly on Judith Jarvis Thomson's proposals.[1]

I

Why, exactly, is privacy important to us? There is no one simple answer to this question, since people have a number of interests that may be harmed by invasions of their privacy.

1. Privacy is sometimes necessary to protect people's interests in competitive situations. For example, it obviously would be a disadvantage to Bobby Fischer if he could not analyze

From *Philosophy & Public Affairs,* Vol. 4, No. 4 (Summer 1975), pp. 323–333. Copyright © 1975 by Princeton University Press. Reprinted by permission of Princeton University Press.

the adjourned position in a chess game in private, without his opponent learning his results.

2. In other cases someone may want to keep some aspect of his life or behavior private simply because it would be embarrassing for other people to know about it. There is a splendid example of this in John Barth's novel *End of the Road*. The narrator of the story, Jake Horner, is with Joe Morgan's wife, Rennie, and they are approaching the Morgan house where Joe is at home alone:

> "Want to eavesdrop?" I whispered impulsively to Rennie. "Come on, it's great! See the animals in their natural habitat."
>
> Rennie looked shocked. "What for?"
>
> "You mean you never spy on people when they're alone? It's wonderful! Come on, be a sneak! It's the most unfair thing you can do to a person."
>
> "You disgust me, Jake!" Rennie hissed. "He's just reading. You don't know Joe at all, do you?"
>
> "What does that mean?"
>
> "*Real* people aren't any different when they're alone. No masks. What you see of them is authentic."
>
> . . . Quite reluctantly, she came over to the window and peeped in beside me.
>
> It is indeed the grossest of injustices to observe a person who believes himself to be alone. Joe Morgan, back from his Boy Scout meeting, had evidently intended to do some reading, for there were books lying open on the writing table and on the floor beside the bookcase. But Joe wasn't reading. He was standing in the exact center of the bare room, fully dressed, smartly executing military commands. About *face*! Right *dress*! 'Ten-*shun*! Parade *rest*! He saluted briskly, his cheeks blown out and his tongue extended, and then proceeded to cavort about the room—spinning, pirouetting, bowing, leaping, kicking. I watched entranced by his performance, for I cannot say that in my strangest moments (and a bachelor has strange ones) I have surpassed him. Rennie trembled from head to foot.[2]

The scene continues even more embarrassingly.

3. There are several reasons why medical records should be kept private, having to do with the consequences to individuals of facts about them becoming public knowledge. "The average patient doesn't realize the importance of the confidentiality of medical records. Passing out information on venereal disease can wreck a marriage. Revealing a pattern of alcoholism or drug abuse can result in a man's losing his job or make it impossible for him to obtain insurance protection."[3]

4. When people apply for credit (or for large amounts of insurance or for jobs of certain types) they are often investigated, and the result is a fat file of information about them. Now there is something to be said in favor of such investigations, for business people surely do have the right to know whether credit-applicants are financially reliable. The trouble is that all sorts of other information goes into such files, for example, information about the applicant's sex-life, his political views, and so forth. Clearly it is unfair for one's application for credit to be influenced by such irrelevant matters.

These examples illustrate the variety of interests that may be protected by guaranteeing people's privacy, and it would be easy to give further examples of the same general sort. However, I do not think that examining such cases will provide a complete understanding of the importance of privacy, for two reasons.

First, these cases all involve relatively unusual sorts of situations, in which someone has something to hide or in which information about a person might provide someone with a reason for mistreating him in some way. Thus, reflection on these cases gives us little help in understanding the value which privacy has in *normal* or *ordinary* situations. By this I mean situations in which there is nothing embarrassing or shameful or unpopular in what we are doing, and nothing ominous or threatening connected with its possible disclosure. For example, even married couples whose sex-lives are normal (whatever that is), and so who have nothing to be ashamed of, by even the most conventional standards, and certainly nothing to be blackmailed about, do not want their bedrooms bugged. We need an account of the value which privacy has for us, not only in the few special cases but in the many common and unremarkable cases as well.

Second, even those invasions of privacy that *do* result in embarrassment or in some specific harm to our other interests are objectionable on other grounds. A woman may rightly be upset if her credit-rating is adversely affected by a report about her sexual behavior because the use of such information is unfair; however, she may also object to the report simply because she feels—as most of us do—that her sex-life is *nobody else's business*. This, I think, is an extremely important point. We have a "sense of privacy" which is violated in such affairs, and this sense of privacy cannot adequately be explained merely in terms of our fear of being embarrassed or disadvantaged in one of these obvious ways. An adequate account of privacy should help us to understand what makes something "someone's business" and why intrusions into things that are "none of your business" are, as such, offensive.

These considerations lead me to suspect that there is something important about privacy which we shall miss if we confine our attention to examples such as [1–4]. In what follows I will try to bring out what this something is.

II

I want now to give an account of the value of privacy based on the idea that there is a close connection between our ability to control who has access to us and to information about us, and our ability to create and maintain different sorts of social relationships with different people. According to this account, privacy is necessary if we are to maintain the variety of social relationships with other people that we want to have, and that is why it is important to us. By a "social relationship" I do not mean anything especially unusual or technical; I mean the sort of thing which we usually have in mind when we say of two people that they are friends or that they are husband and wife or that one is the other's employer.

The first point I want to make about these relationships is that, often, there are fairly definite patterns of behavior associated with them. Our relationships with other people determine, in large part, how we act toward them and how they behave toward us. Moreover, there are *different* patterns of behavior associated with different relationships. Thus a man may be playful and affectionate with his children (although sometimes firm), businesslike with his employees, and respectful and polite with his mother-in-law. And to his close friends he may show a side of his personality that others never see—perhaps he is secretly a poet, and rather shy about it, and shows his verse only to his best friends.

It is sometimes suggested that there is something deceitful or hypocritical about such differences in behavior. It is suggested that underneath all the role-playing there is the "real" person, and that the various "masks" that we wear in dealing with some people are some sort of phony disguise that we use to conceal our "true" selves from them. I take it that this is what is behind Rennie's remark, in the passage from Barth, that, "*Real* people aren't any different when they're alone. No masks. What you see of them is authentic." According to this way of looking at things, the fact that we observe different standards of conduct with different people is merely a sign of dishonesty. Thus the cold-hearted businessman who reads poetry to his friends is "really" a gentle poetic soul whose businesslike demeanor in front of his employees is only a false front; and the man who curses and swears when talking to his friends, but who would never use such language around his mother-in-law, is just putting on an act for her.

This, I think, is quite wrong. Of course the man who does not swear in front of his mother-in-law may be just putting on an act so that, for example, she will not disinherit him, when otherwise he would curse freely in front of her without caring what she thinks. But it may be that his conception of how he ought to behave with his mother-in-law is very different from his conception of how he may behave with his friends. Or it may not be appropriate for him to swear around *her* because "she is not that sort of person." Similarly, the businessman may be putting up a false front for his employees, perhaps because he dislikes his work and has to make a continual, disagreeable effort to maintain the role. But on the other hand he may be, quite comfortably and naturally, a businessman with a certain conception of how it is appropriate for a businessman to behave; and this conception is compatible with his also being a husband, a father, and a friend, with different conceptions of how it is appropriate to behave with his wife, his children, and his friends. There need be nothing dishonest or hypocritical in any of this, and neither side of his personality need be the "real" him, any more than any of the others.

It is not merely accidental that we vary our behavior with different people according to the different social relationships that we have with them. Rather, the different patterns of behavior are (partly) what define the different relationships; they are an important part of what makes the different relationships what they are. The relation of friendship, for example, involves bonds of affection and special obligations, such as the duty of loyalty, which friends owe to one another; but it is also an important part of what it means to have a friend that we welcome his company, that we confide in him, that we tell him things about ourselves, and that we show him sides of our personalities which we would not tell or show to just anyone.[4] Suppose I believe that someone is my close friend, and then I discover that he is worried about his job and is afraid of being fired. But, while he has discussed this situation with several other people, he has not mentioned it at all to me. And then I learn that he writes poetry, and that this is an important part of his life; but while he has shown his poems to many other people, he has not shown them to me. Moreover, I learn that he behaves with his other friends in a much more informal way than he behaves with me, that he makes a point of seeing them socially much more than he sees me, and so on. In the absence of some special explanation of his behavior, I would have to conclude that we are not as close as I had thought.

The same general point can be made about other sorts of human relationships: businessman to employee, minister to congregant, doctor to patient, husband to wife, parent to child, and so on. In each case, the sort of relationship that people have to one another involves a conception of how it is appropriate for them to behave with each other, and what is more, a conception of the kind and degree of knowledge concerning one another which it is appropriate for them to have. (I will say more about this later.) I do not mean to imply that such relationships are, or ought to be, structured in exactly the same way for everyone. Some parents are casual and easy-going with their children, while others are more formal and reserved. Some doctors want to be friends with at least some of their patients; others are businesslike with all. Moreover, the requirements of social roles may vary from community to community—for example, the role of wife may not require exactly the same sort of behavior in rural Alabama as it does in New York or New Guinea. And, the requirements of social roles may change: the women's liberation movement is making an attempt to redefine the husband-wife relationship. The examples that I have been giving are drawn, loosely speaking, from contemporary American society; but this is mainly a matter of convenience. The only point that I want to insist on is that *however* one conceives one's relations with other people, there is inseparable from that conception an idea of how it is appropriate to behave with and around them, and what information about oneself it is appropriate for them to have.

The point may be underscored by observing that new types of social institutions and practices sometimes make possible new sorts of human relationships, which in turn make it appropriate to behave around people, and to say things in their presence, that would have been inappropriate before. "Group therapy" is a case in point. Many psychological patients find the prospect of group therapy unsettling, because they will have to speak openly to the group about intimate matters. They sense that there is something inappropriate about this: one simply does not reveal one's deepest feelings to strangers. Our aspirations, our problems, our frustrations and disappointments are things that we may confide to our husbands and wives, our friends, and perhaps to some others—but it is out of the question to speak of such matters to people that we do not even know. Resistance to this aspect of group therapy is overcome when the patients begin to think of each other not as strangers but as *fellow members of the group*. The definition of a kind of relation between them makes possible frank and intimate conversation which would have been totally out of place when they were merely strangers.

All of this has to do with the way that a crucial part of our lives—our relations with other people—is organized, and as such its importance to us can hardly be exaggerated. Thus we have good reason to object to anything that interferes with these relationships and makes it difficult or impossible for us to maintain them in the way that we want to. Conversely, because our ability to control who has access to us, and who knows what about us, allows us to maintain the variety of relationships with other people that we want to have, it is, I think, one of the most important reasons why we value privacy.

First, consider what happens when two close friends are joined by a casual acquaintance. The character of the group changes; and one of the changes is that conversation about intimate matters is now out of order. Then suppose these friends could *never* be alone; suppose there were always third parties (let us say casual acquaintances or strangers) intruding. Then they could do either of two things. They could carry on as close friends do, sharing confidences, freely expressing their feelings about things, and so on. But this would mean violating their sense of how it is appropriate to behave around casual acquaintances or strangers. Or they could avoid doing or saying anything which they think inappropriate to do or say around a third party. But this would mean that they could no longer behave with one another in the way that friends do and further that, eventually, they would no longer *be* close friends.

Again, consider the differences between the way that a husband and wife behave when they are alone and the way they behave in the company of third parties. Alone, they may be affectionate, sexually intimate, have their fights and quarrels, and so on; but with others, a more "public" face is in order. If they could never be alone together, they would either have to abandon the relationship that they would otherwise have as husband and wife or else behave in front of others in ways they now deem inappropriate.[5]

These considerations suggest that we need to separate our associations, at least to some extent, if we are to maintain a system of different relationships with different people. Separation allows us to behave with certain people in the way that is appropriate to the sort of relationship we have with them, without at the same time violating our sense of how it is appropriate to behave with, and in the presence of, others with whom we have a different kind of relationship. Thus, if we are to be able to control the relationships that we have with other people, we must have control over who has access to us.

We now have an explanation of the value of privacy in ordinary situations in which we have nothing to hide. The explanation is that, even in the most common and unremarkable circumstances, we regulate our behavior according to the kinds of relationships we have with the people around us. If we cannot control who has access to us, sometimes including and sometimes excluding various people, then we cannot control the patterns of behavior we need to adopt (this is one reason why privacy is an aspect of liberty) or the kinds of relations with other people that we will have. But what about our feeling that certain facts about us are "simply nobody else's business"? Here, too, I think the answer requires reference to our relationships with people. If someone is our doctor, then it literally is his business to keep track of our health; if someone is our employer, then it literally is his business to know what salary we are paid; our financial dealings literally are the business of the people who extend us credit; and so on. In general, a fact about ourselves is someone's business if there is a specific social relationship between us which entitles them to know. We are often free to choose whether or not to enter into such relationships, and those who want to maintain as much privacy as possible will enter them only reluctantly. What we cannot do is accept such a social role with respect to another person and then expect to retain the same degree of privacy relative to him that we had before. Thus, if we are asked how much money we have in the bank, we cannot say, "It's none of your business," to our banker, to prospective creditors, or to our spouses, because their relationships with us do entitle them to know. But, at the risk of being boorish, we could say that to others with whom we have no such relationship.

III

Thomson suggests, "as a simplifying hypothesis, that the right to privacy is itself a cluster of rights, and that it is not a distinct cluster of rights but itself intersects with the cluster of rights which the right over the person consists of, and also with the cluster of rights which owning property consists of." This hypothesis is "simplifying" because it eliminates the right to privacy as anything distinctive.

"The right over the person" consists of such "un-grand" rights as the right not to have various parts of one's body looked at, the right not to have one's elbow painted green, and so on. Thomson understands these rights as analogous to property rights. The idea is that our bodies are *ours* and so we have the same rights with respect to them that we have with respect to our other possessions.

But now consider the right not to have various parts of one's body looked at. Insofar as this is a matter of *privacy,* it is not simply analogous to property rights; for the kind of interest we have in controlling who looks at what parts of our bodies is very different from the interest we have in our cars or fountain pens. For most of us, physical intimacy is a part of very special sorts of personal relationships. Exposing one's knee or one's face to someone may not count for us as physical intimacy, but exposing a breast, and allowing it to be seen and touched, does. Of course the details are to some extent a matter of social convention; that is why it is easy for us to imagine, say, a Victorian woman for whom an exposed knee would be a sign of intimacy. She would be right to be distressed at learning that she had absent-mindedly left a knee uncovered and that someone was looking at it— if the observer was not her spouse or her lover. By dissociating the body from ideas of physical intimacy, and the complex of personal relationships of which such intimacies are a part, we can make this "right over the body" seem to be nothing more than an un-grand kind of property right; but that dissociation separates this right from the matters that make *privacy* important.

Thomson asks whether it violates your right to privacy for acquaintances to indulge in "very personal gossip" about you, when they got the information without violating your rights, and they are not violating any confidences in telling what they tell. . . . She thinks they do not violate your right to privacy, but that if they do "there is trouble for the simplifying hypothesis."

This is, as she says, a debatable case, but if my account of why privacy is important is correct, we have at least some reason to think that your right to privacy can be violated in such a case. Let us fill in some details. Suppose you are recently divorced, and the reason your marriage failed is that you became impotent shortly after the wedding. You have shared your troubles with your closest friend, but this is not the sort of thing you want everyone to know. Not only would it be humiliating for everyone to know, it is none of their business. It is the sort of intimate fact about you that is not appropriate for strangers or casual acquaintances to know. But now the gossips have obtained the information (perhaps one of them innocently overheard your discussion with your friend; it was not his fault, so he did not violate your privacy in the hearing, but then you did not know he was within earshot) and now they are spreading it around to everyone who knows you and to some who do not. Are they violating your right to privacy? I think they are. If so, it is not surprising, for the interest involved in this case is just the sort of interest which the right to privacy typically protects. Since the right that is violated in this case is not also a property right, or a right over the person, the simplifying hypothesis fails. But this should not be surprising, either, for if the right to privacy has a different *point* than these other rights, we should not expect it always to overlap with them. And even if it did always overlap, we could still regard the right to privacy as a distinctive sort of right in virtue of the special kind of interest it protects.

Notes

1. Judith Jarvis Thomson, "The Right to Privacy," *Philosophy & Public Affairs,* 4, no. 4 (Summer 1975): 295–314.
2. John Barth, *End of the Road* (New York, 1960), pp. 57–58.

3. Dr. Malcolm Todd, President of the A.M.A., quoted in the *Miami Herald,* 26 October 1973, p. 18-A.

4. My view about friendship and its relation to privacy is similar to Charles Fried's view in his book *An Anatomy of Values* (Cambridge, Mass., 1970).

5. I found this in a television program-guide in the *Miami Herald,* 21 October 1973, p. 17:

> "I think it was one of the most awkward scenes I've ever done," said actress Brenda Benet after doing a romantic scene with her husband, Bill Bixby, in his new NBC-TV series, "The Magician."
>
> "It was even hard to kiss him," she continued. "It's the same old mouth, but it was terrible. I was so abnormally shy; I guess because I don't think it's anybody's business. The scene would have been easier had I done it with a total stranger because that would be real acting. With Bill, it was like being on exhibition."

I should stress that, on the view that I am defending, it is *not* "abnormal shyness" or shyness of any type that is behind such feelings. Rather, it is a sense of what is appropriate with and around people with whom one has various sorts of personal relationships. Kissing *another actor* in front of the camera crew, the director, and so on, is one thing; but kissing *one's husband* in front of all these people is quite another thing. What made Ms. Benet's position confusing was that her husband *was* another actor, and the behavior that was permitted by the one relationship was discouraged by the other.

21. Privacy, Morality, and the Law

W. A. Parent

I. The Definition of Privacy

DEFINING PRIVACY REQUIRES a familiarity with its ordinary usage, of course, but this is not enough since our common ways of talking and using language are riddled with inconsistencies, ambiguities, and paradoxes. What we need is a definition which is by and large consistent with ordinary language, so that capable speakers of English will not be genuinely surprised that the term "privacy" should be defined in this way, but which also enables us to talk consistently, clearly, and precisely about the family of concepts to which privacy belongs. Moreover the definition must not usurp or encroach upon the basic meanings and functions of the other concepts within this family. Drawing useful and legitimate distinctions

From *Philosophy & Public Affairs,* Vol. 12, No. 4 (Fall 1983), pp. 269–288. Copyright © 1983 by Princeton University Press. Reprinted by permission of Princeton University Press.

between different values is the best antidote to exploitation and evisceration of the concept of privacy.

Let me first state and then elaborate on my definition. Privacy is the condition of not having undocumented personal knowledge about one possessed by others. A person's privacy is diminished exactly to the degree that others possess this kind of knowledge about him. I want to stress that what I am defining is the condition of privacy, not the right to privacy. I will talk about the latter shortly. My definition is new, and I believe it to be superior to all of the other conceptions that have been proffered when measured against the desiderata of conceptual analysis above.

A full explication of the personal knowledge definition requires that we clarify the concept of personal information. My suggestion is that it be understood to consist of *facts* about a person[1] which most individuals in a given society at a given time do not want widely known about themselves. They may not be concerned that a few close friends, relatives, or professional associates know these facts, but they would be very much concerned if the information passed beyond this limited circle. In contemporary America facts about a person's sexual preferences, drinking or drug habits, income, the state of his or her marriage and health belong to the class of personal information. Ten years from now some of these facts may be a part of everyday conversation; if so their disclosure would not diminish individual privacy.

This account of personal information, which makes it a function of existing cultural norms and social practices, needs to be broadened a bit to accommodate a particular and unusual class of cases of the following sort. Most of us don't care if our height, say, is widely known. But there are a few persons who are extremely sensitive about their height (or weight or voice pitch).[2] They might take extreme measures to ensure that other people not find it out. For such individuals height is a very personal matter. Were someone to find it out by ingenious snooping we should not hesitate to talk about an invasion of privacy.

Let us, then, say that personal information consists of facts which most persons in a given society choose not to reveal about themselves (except to close friends, family, . . .) or of facts about which a particular individual is acutely sensitive and which he therefore does not choose to reveal about himself, even though most people don't care if these same facts are widely known about themselves.

Here we can question the status of information belonging to the public record, that is, information to be found in newspapers, court proceedings, and other official documents open to public inspection. (We might discover, for example, that Jones and Smith were arrested many years ago for engaging in homosexual activities.) Should such information be excluded from the category of personal information? The answer is that it should not. There is, after all, nothing extraordinary about public documents containing some very personal information. I will hereafter refer to personal facts belonging to the public record as documented.

My definition of privacy excludes knowledge of documented personal information. I do this for a simple reason. Suppose that A is browsing through some old newspapers and happens to see B's name in a story about child prodigies who unaccountably failed to succeed as adults. B had become as obsessive gambler and an alcoholic. Should we accuse A of invading B's privacy? No. An affirmative answer blurs the distinction between the public and the private. What belongs to the public domain cannot without glaring paradox be called private; consequently it should not be incorporated within our concept of privacy.

But, someone might object, *A* might decide to turn the information about *B*'s gambling and drinking problems over to a reporter who then publishes it in a popular news magazine. Isn't *B*'s privacy diminished by this occurrence?[3] No. I would certainly say that his reputation might well suffer from it. And I would also say that the publication is a form of gratuitous exploitation. But to challenge it as an invasion of privacy is not at all reasonable since the information revealed was publicly available and could have been found out by anyone, without resort to snooping or prying. In this crucial respect, the story about *B* no more diminished his privacy than would have disclosures about his property interests, say, or about any other facts concerning him that belonged to the public domain.

I hasten to add that a person does lose a measure of privacy at the time when personal information about him first becomes a part of the public record, since the information was until that time undocumented. It is also important not to confuse documented facts as I define them here with facts about individuals which are kept on file for special purposes but which are not available for public consumption, for example, health records. Publication of the latter does imperil privacy; for this reason special precautions are usually taken to ensure that the information does not become public property.

I believe the personal knowledge definition isolates the conceptual one of privacy, its distinctive and unique meaning. It does not appropriate ideas which properly belong to other concepts. Unfortunately the three most popular definitions do just this, confusing privacy with quite different values.

1. *Privacy consists of being let alone.* Warren and Brandeis were the first to advocate this broad definition.[4] Brandeis movingly appealed to it again in his celebrated dissent to the U.S. Supreme Court's majority ruling in *Olmstead* v. *U.S.*[5] Objecting to the Court's view that telephone wiretapping does not constitute a search and seizure, Brandeis delivered an impassioned defense of every citizen's right to be let alone, which he called our most cherished entitlement. Several other former U.S. Supreme Court Justices have endorsed this conception of privacy, among them Douglas, Fortas, and Steward.[6] And a number of distinguished law professors have done likewise.[7]

What proponents of the Brandeis definition fail to see is that there are innumerable ways of failing to let a person alone which have nothing to do with his privacy. Suppose, for instance, that *A* clubs *B* on the head or repeatedly insults him. We should describe and evaluate such actions by appeal to concepts like force, violence, and harassment. Nothing in the way of analytical clarity and justificatory power is lost if the concept of privacy is limited, as I have suggested that it be, to cases involving the acquisition of undocumented personal knowledge. Inflationary conceptions of privacy invite muddled reasoning.

2. *Privacy consists of a form of autonomy or control over significant personal matters.* "If the right to privacy means anything, it is the right of the individual, married or single, to be free from unwarranted government invasion into matters so fundamentally affecting a person as the decision whether to bear or beget a child."[8] With these words, from the Supreme Court case of *Eisenstadt* v. *Baird,* Mr. Justice Brennan expresses a second influential theory of privacy.

Indeed, definitions of privacy in terms of control dominate the literature. Perhaps the most favored among them equates privacy with the control over personal information about oneself. Fried, Wasserstrom, Gross, and Beardsley all adopt it or a close variation of it.[9] Other lawyers and philosophers, including Van Den Haag, Altman, and Parker,[10] identify privacy with control over access to oneself, or in Parker's words, "control over when and by whom the various parts of us can be sensed by others."

All of these definitions should be jettisoned. To see why, consider the example of a person who voluntarily divulges all sorts of intimate, personal, and undocumented information about herself to a friend. She is doubtless exercising control, in a paradigm sense of the term, over personal information about herself as well as over (cognitive) access to herself. But we would not and should not say that in doing so she is preserving or protecting her privacy. On the contrary, she is voluntarily relinquishing much of her privacy. People can and do choose to give up privacy for many reasons. An adequate conception of privacy must allow for this fact. Control definitions do not.[11]

I believe the voluntary disclosure counterexample is symptomatic of a deep confusion underlying the thesis that privacy is a form of control. It is a conceptual confusion, the mistaking of privacy for a part of liberty. The defining idea of liberty is the absence of external restraints or coercion. A person who is behind bars or locked in a room or physically pinned to the ground is unfree[12] to do many things. Similarly a person who is prohibited by law from making certain choices should be described as having been denied the liberty or freedom to make them. The loss of liberty in these cases takes the form of a deprivation of autonomy. Hence we can meaningfully say that the right to liberty embraces in part the right of persons to make fundamentally important choices about their lives and therewith to exercise significant control over different aspects of their behavior. It is clearly distinguishable from the right to privacy, which condemns the unwarranted acquisition of undocumented personal knowledge.[13]

3. *Privacy is the limitation on access to the self.* This definition, defended by Garrett and Gavison[14] among others, has the virtue of separating privacy from liberty. But it still is unsatisfactory. If we understand "access" to mean something like "physical proximity," then the difficulty becomes that there are other viable concepts which much more precisely describe what is at stake by limiting such access. Among these concepts I would include personal property, solitude, and peace. If, on the other hand, "access" is interpreted as referring to the acquisition of personal knowledge, we're still faced with a seemingly intractable counterexample. *A* taps *B*'s phone and overhears many of her conversations, including some of a very intimate nature. Official restraints have been imposed on *A*'s snooping, though. He must obtain permission from a judge before listening in on *B*. This case shows that limitation of cognitive access does not imply privacy.

A response sympathetic with the Garrett-Gavison conception to the above criticism might suggest that they really meant to identify privacy with certain kinds of limitations on access to the self. But why then didn't they say this, and why didn't they tell us what relevant limitations they had in mind?

Let us suppose that privacy is thought to consist of certain normal limitations on cognitive access to the self. Should we accept this conception? I think not, since it confuses privacy with the existential conditions that are necessary for its realization. To achieve happiness I must have some good luck, but this doesn't mean that happiness is good luck. Similarly, if I am to enjoy privacy there have to be limitations on cognitive access to me, but these limitations are not themselves privacy. Rather privacy is what they safeguard.

II. The Value of Privacy

Is privacy a basic human value? There are many unpersuasive arguments that it is. Consider one of the most well-known, that given by Fried: "to respect, love, trust, feel affection for others, and to regard ourselves as the objects of love, trust, and affection is at the heart of our notion of ourselves as persons among persons, and privacy is the necessary atmosphere for these attitudes and actions, as oxygen is for combustion."[15] Privacy is essential for intimate relationships because, in Fried's view, their defining mark is the sharing of information about oneself that is not shared with others, and without privacy this would be impossible.

The difficulty with Fried's argument is that it relies on a skewed conception of intimacy. Intimacy involves much more than the exclusive sharing of information. It also involves the sharing of one's total self—one's experiences, aspirations, weaknesses, and values. This kind of emotional commitment, and concomitant giving, is entirely overlooked by Fried. He furnishes no argument for the claim that it cannot survive the loss of privacy.

Several so-called functional arguments on behalf of privacy also fail. Thus it is sometimes said that privacy is needed for relaxation, emotional release, self-reflection, and self-analysis,[16] but this account confuses privacy with solitude, that is, the condition of being physically alone. Granted A might not be able to relax or think about her life unless she is left by herself, we are still not being told why *privacy* is important. Of course A might have to believe that her privacy is being respected if she is to relax and reflect successfully, but this still doesn't show that privacy itself (as opposed to the belief that we have it) is necessary to do these things.

Nor should we buy the thesis that privacy is necessary for individuality and freedom.[17] It is easy to imagine a person who has little or no privacy but who nonetheless possesses the determination and strength of will to think and act individually. Even those lacking in such determination might still be able to think and act for themselves so long as they believe (rightly or wrongly) that their privacy is intact. Similarly, persons without privacy might still enjoy considerable freedom. This will be true in cases where A is not aware of and has no reason for thinking that someone else is watching her every move and so is not deterred from pursuing various activities. It will also be true in cases where A simply doesn't care whether anyone else is watching her.

Lest you now begin to wonder whether privacy has any value at all, let me quickly point to several very good reasons why people in societies like ours desire privacy as I have defined it. First of all, if others manage to obtain sensitive personal knowledge about us they will by that very fact acquire power over us. Their power could then be used to our disadvantage. The possibilities for exploitation become very real. The definite connection between harm and the invasion of privacy explains why we place a value on not having undocumented personal information about ourselves widely known.

Second, as long as we live in a society where individuals are generally intolerant of life styles, habits, and ways of thinking that differ significantly from their own, and where human foibles tend to become the object of scorn and ridicule, our desire for privacy will continue unabated. No one wants to be laughed at and made to feel ashamed of himself. And we all have things about us which, if known, might very well trigger these kinds of unfeeling and wholly unwarranted responses.

Third, we desire privacy out of a sincere conviction that there are certain facts about us which other people, particularly strangers and casual acquaintances, are not entitled to know. This conviction is constitutive of "the liberal ethic," a conviction centering on the basic thesis that individuals are not to be treated as mere property of the state but instead are to be respected as autonomous, independent beings with unique aims to fulfill. These aims, in turn, will perforce lead people down life's separate paths. Those of us educated under this liberal ideology feel that our lives are our own business (hence the importance of personal liberty) and that personal facts about our lives are for the most part ours alone to know. The suggestion that all personal facts should be made available for public inspection is contrary to this view. Thus, our desire for privacy is to a large extent a matter of principle.[18]

For most people, this desire is perfectly innocent. We are not seeking to hurt or disadvantage anyone by exercising it. Unquestionably some people at times demand privacy for fraudulent purposes, for example, to hide discreditable facts about themselves from future employers who are entitled to this information. Posner emphasizes this motive for privacy.[19] But not everyone values privacy for this reason, and, even for those who do, misrepresentation is most often not the only or the overriding motive.

So there are several good reasons why we hold privacy to be an important value, one worth arguing for, and defending from unwarranted invasion. Now I want to suggest that anyone who deliberately and without justification frustrates or contravenes our desire for privacy violates the distinctively liberal, moral principle of respect for persons. Let us say that A frustrates B's desire for privacy if he invades B's privacy and B knows it. A acts in contravention of B's desire for privacy if he invades B's privacy without B's knowing it. Assuming that A has no justification for doing either, we can and should accuse him of acting in disregard of B's own desires and interests. A's action displays contempt for B in the sense that it is undertaken with no effort to identify with her life purposes or to appreciate what the fulfillment of these purposes might mean to her. Specifically by gratuitously or indiscriminately invading B's privacy (I will explain these terms shortly) A manifests disrespect for B in the sense that he ignores or counts as having no significance B's desire, spawned and nutured by the liberal values of her society, not to have personal facts about herself known by ingenious or persistent snooping.[20]

III.   The Moral Right to Privacy

The above argument establishes that privacy is indeed a moral value for persons who also prize freedom and individuality. That we should seek to protect it against unwarranted invasion should come, then, as no surprise. Advocating a moral right to privacy comprises an integral part of this effort. It expresses our conviction that privacy should only be infringed under exigent circumstances and for the most compelling reasons, for example, law enforcement and health care provision.

The moral right to privacy does not embody the rule "privacy may never be invaded." It is important to emphasize that there are such things as justifiable invasions of privacy. Our concern is not to condemn invasions but to declare our right not to become the victims of wrongful invasions (see Section IV). Discussion of a right to privacy presupposes that privacy is a good, vulnerable to loss by human contrivance. It does not presuppose that such loss is always bad.

Davis and Thomson[21] have recently tried to deflate the right to privacy. The latter's essay is the better known so I will now discuss it. Thomson wants us to believe that there is no one independently identifiable right to privacy. Instead there are a number of diverse rights under "privacy" each of which is a right of some other kind. Moreover, the right to privacy is derivative in the sense that we can explain why we possess each of the rights subsumable under privacy without ever mentioning the right of privacy itself. And we can also explain the wrongness of every violation of the right to privacy without once mentioning it. So according to Thomson we really don't need to talk about a distinct right to privacy at all. She supports her argument with the following analyses.

1. *A* owns a pornographic picture which he keeps locked up in a safe. *B* trains his special X-ray device on the safe and sees the picture. Thomson concedes that *B* has violated *A*'s right to privacy, but she thinks a more fundamental explanation of why *B* acted wrongly is in terms of *A*'s right that others not do certain things with what he owns. These include looking at them and selling them. These are property rights and it is by infringing one of them that *B* wrongs *A*.

2. *B* finds out by entirely legitimate means that *A* owns the pornographic picture. He proceeds to publish this fact in a newspaper. If anyone thinks that *B* has invaded *A*'s right to privacy, a very simple explanation is available: *A* has the right not to be caused mental distress, and it is this right that *B*'s action violates.

3. *A* doesn't want her face looked at and so keeps it covered. *B* uses his X-ray device to look at *A*'s face through the covering. In doing so *B* violates *A*'s right that her face not be looked at (how simple!). This is one of the rights over our person that we possess.

4. *A* is a great opera singer who no longer wants to be listened to. She only sings quietly behind closed doors and soundproof walls. *B* trains an amplifier on *A*'s home and listens to her sing. In so doing *B* transgresses *A*'s right not to be listened to, which according to Thomson is another one of those basic rights over the person we possess. Here, as in each of the preceding cases, we have no need to invoke the right to privacy.

Thomson's attempt to diminish the status of the right to privacy fails to persuade. It requires that we recognize a plethora of rights whose status is certainly more problematic than that of the right whose significance she wants to impugn. Do we really think of ourselves as possessing the rights not to be looked at and listened to? Must we talk about a right not to have our property looked at? Thomson's claim that we waive these rights all the time—a claim she has to make to avoid the absurd implication that our rights are violated thousands of times every day—flies in the face of common sense and common experience. Just ask whether you thought of yourself as having waived the right not to be listened to before speaking with people today. The idea seems preposterous. I certainly didn't conceive of myself as waiving a right not to be looked at before entering the classroom this morning. And I venture to add that it would bemuse my students to hear me speak of my right not to be looked at.

Thomson's simplifying strategy is unmistakably convoluted. It is possible to deal in a much less ad hoc and tortuous manner with her examples once we have settled on an adequate definition of privacy.

1. If *B*'s looking at *A*'s picture is unjustified, and if *A* is entitled to possess the pornographic picture, then by my account of the moral right to privacy *B* does violate this right in *A*.

We could also say that A has a concrete moral right that her picture not be looked at which can be deduced from the more fundamental right of privacy when applied to the particular circumstances of this case.

2. If B has no justification for publishing the fact that A possesses a pornographic picture, then he has violated A's right to privacy. And it is by virtue of violating this right that B causes A mental distress.

3. If A has no evil intention in covering her face and if B has no substantial reason for peeking at it, then B's intrusion violates A's right to privacy. We could express this point by saying that A's right to privacy when applied to the particular circumstances of this case yields her concrete right not to be looked at. (Remember that a person's physical appearance can constitute personal information.)

4. If B's snooping is without justification it should be condemned as a violation of A's right to privacy.

The basic failing of Thomson's essay is that she makes no attempt to define privacy. We have good reason to ask how she hopes to convince anyone that the right to privacy is derivative and quite dispensable without first telling us what the right means. My position is that once the meaning of privacy is clarified and its value articulated no one will have cause to question the legitimacy of our talk about a fundamental right of privacy.

IV. Criteria of Wrongful Invasion

Which invasions of privacy are justifiable and which are not? A complete conception of the right to privacy must address this question, providing general criteria of wrongful invasion, which will then have to be applied to specific cases. Whether the right to privacy has been violated in a specific case can often only be answered through a process of making difficult and controversial value judgments. No conception of the right to privacy, no matter how detailed and sophisticated will allow us to eliminate or bypass this process.

The following questions are central to assessing alleged violations of the right to privacy:

1. For what purpose(s) is the undocumented personal knowledge sought?
2. Is this purpose a legitimate and important one?
3. Is the knowledge sought through invasion of privacy relevant to its justifying purpose?
4. Is invasion of privacy the only or the least offensive means of obtaining the knowledge?
5. What restrictions or procedural restraints have been placed on the privacy-invading techniques?
6. What protection is to be afforded the personal knowledge once it has been acquired?

The first four questions all have to do with the rationale for invading privacy. We can say that the right to privacy is violated by *gratuitous* invasions and that these occur when: there is no purpose at all to them; when the purpose is less than compelling; when the personal facts sought have nothing to do with the justifying purposes; when the personal information could have been obtained by less intrusive measures. Among the legitimate purposes for acquiring undocumented personal information are efficient law enforcement, confirmation of eligibility criteria set forth in various government welfare programs, and the compilation of statistical data concerning important behavioral trends.

Question 5 pertains to the actual invasion of privacy itself. We can say that the right to privacy is violated by *indiscriminate* invasions and that these occur when insufficient procedural safeguards have been imposed on the techniques employed so that either: all sorts of personal information, some germane to the investigation but some totally irrelevant thereto, is obtained; or persons with no business knowing the personal facts acquired are allowed to gain cognitive access to them. One can argue against a proposed invasion of privacy on the grounds that it is too likely to be indiscriminate in either of these two senses.

Question 6 pertains to postinvasion safeguards. We can say that the right to privacy is violated when the undocumented personal information acquired is not adequately protected against unwarranted cognitive intrusion or unauthorized uses. It is also violated, of course, by actual instances of such intrusions and uses.

Let us look at a concrete example. Suppose a large city is faced with the growing problem of welfare fraud. It decides that to combat this problem an elaborate system of surveillance must be initiated. Personal information regarding welfare recipients' income, family status, sexual habits, and spending habits is to be obtained. Search warrants are obtained permitting unlimited surveillance and specifying the kind of information being sought. Once obtained the information is to be stored on magnetic tapes and kept in the welfare department.

Any person who takes the right to privacy seriously will raise the following questions and make the following observations about this city's (*C*'s) action:

i. *C* presents no arguments or evidence in support of its belief that the problem of welfare fraud can be solved by resorting to large-scale surveillance. We should demand that *C* do so.

ii. *C* presents no arguments or evidence showing that surveillance is the only way to acquire the relevant personal information. Did it first try to obtain knowledge of welfare recipients' life style by asking them about it or sending them questionnaires? Were there other, less intensive measures available for acquiring this knowledge?

iii. Search warrants permitting unlimited surveillance are insufficiently discriminating. So are warrants which do not particularly describe the places to be observed and the facts to be gathered. *C* should have insisted that the warrants place restrictions on the time periods of surveillance as well as on its scope.

iv. Why is it necessary to acquire information about welfare recipients' sexual habits? How is this knowledge relevant to the object of eradicating fraud?

v. What kind of security does *C* intend to provide for the magnetic tapes containing the acquired information? Who will enjoy access to these tapes? Will they eventually be erased or destroyed? *C* has the duty to guard against the potential abuse of the stored facts.

I hope this brief analysis is helpful in isolating some of the crucial issues and difficult questions that must be confronted when applying the right of privacy to particular cases. Often there will be strong disagreement over whether proposed programs of physical, psychological, and data surveillance are gratuitous or indiscriminate. This is to be expected. The results of these disputes will determine the contours of the privacy right.

V. *The Legal Right to Privacy*

One final inquiry remains regarding how the moral right to privacy has fared in the law. To what extent is it receiving legal protection, and should it be receiving more? The account that follows is largely descriptive. My purpose is to show how contemporary privacy jurisprudence could have benefited from the use of disciplined philosophical analysis.

We must begin with the well-known U.S. Supreme Court case of *Griswold* v. *Connecticut*,[22] for this decision more than any other is responsible for the jurisprudential notoriety that now attends the right to privacy. In *Griswold* the Court struck down a law that made it a criminal offense for married couples to use contraceptives. Writing the majority opinion, Justice Douglas argued that even though the Constitution does not explicitly mention a right to privacy, one can still justifiably infer its existence from examining the penumbras or emanations of various specific constitutional provisions. The contraceptive law under challenge, according to Douglas, violated this right.

Unfortunately Douglas never explained why it did. Of course there is an obvious reason why the law's enforcement would invade privacy, but the Court made only passing reference to this problem. What precisely did Douglas mean by the expression "right of privacy"? *Eisenstadt* v. *Baird* provided an answer. In that case, decided seven years after *Griswold,* a majority of the Court equated the right to privacy with the right to make fundamentally important choices free from unwarranted government intrusion.[23] They went on to find a Massachusetts law forbidding the use of contraceptives among unmarried persons in violation of this right.

Since *Eisenstadt* the Supreme Court has invoked the right to privacy, conceived of as a species of the right to choose, in voiding several state laws which prohibited women from choosing an abortion except when necessary to save their lives.[24] And several state supreme courts have embraced this conception of the right to privacy and have applied it to cases involving euthanasia,[25] the use of marijuana,[26] and the prescription of laetrile as a cancer cure.[27]

All of these cases conflate the right to privacy with the right to liberty. I won't repeat my critique of the *Eisenstadt* definition set out in Section I. Suffice it to say that laws preempting the choice of citizens are coercive in an obvious sense of the term. Consequently they involve a denial of liberty and must therefore be evaluated against the Fourteenth Amendment's guarantee that citizens shall not be deprived of liberty without due process of law.[28] For years the U.S. Supreme Court decided cases like *Griswold* by Fourteenth Amendment interpretation. Thus legislation interfering with prospective employees' choice of work,[29] with students' choice whether to study foreign languages in private or public elementary schools,[30] and with parents' choice whether to send their children to public or private schools[31] was properly seen as implicating liberty interests and was assessed accordingly. That some of these decisions (I am thinking particularly of *Lochner*) met with severe criticism from later scholars and were even repudiated by later courts does not justify judicial indulgence in conceptual legerdemain. Confusing liberty with privacy only serves to impugn the intellectual integrity of the judiciary.

Another class of spurious privacy cases needs to be exposed. Consider the question whether a "music as you ride" program on buses and streetcars violates passengers' right to privacy; or whether solicitors and peddlers who go on private property and disturb homeowners infringe the latters' right to privacy; or whether sound trucks that emit loud and raucous noises in residential neighborhoods violate homeowners' right to privacy. The U.S. Supreme Court has had to consider such questions, and it has treated them as raising bona fide privacy interests.[32] This was a mistake. Unwanted or excessive solicitation or noise imperil homeowners' peace and their right to property, understood in the broad but widely accepted sense of the right to enjoy what one owns. Being exposed to music on buses might rattle the nerves and thereby threaten our peace. It certainly preempts the choice whether to listen or not while riding. But that is all. The concept of privacy has no useful role to play in any of these cases. Indeed, its introduction only obscures the gravamen of petitioners' complaints.

Invasion of privacy must consist of truthful disclosures about a person. Occasionally aggrieved parties will forget or ignore this. The case of *Paul* v. *Davis* will illustrate: The police distributed a five-page flyer to some 800 store owners in the Louisville, Kentucky, area which contained the names and photographs of persons identified as "known shop-lifters." Davis's picture and name appeared there. He had been arrested for shoplifting but the charges against him were dropped shortly after the flyer's distribution. Davis brought an invasion of privacy suit against the police. He ought not to have done so, for the flyer did not reveal any personal facts about him. His only legitimate course would have been to bring a cause of action for defamation. Justice Rehnquist said precisely this in his majority opinion.[33]

The unfortunate view that cases like this can be argued in terms of privacy finds support in William Prosser's extraordinarily influential 1960 essay.[34] Prosser maintained that the law of privacy comprises four distinct torts, the third of which he identified with placing the plaintiff in a false light in the public eye. This false light categorization displays an egregious misunderstanding of privacy.

Are Prosser's remaining three torts similarly confused? The first form of privacy invasion he distinguishes is intrusion upon the plaintiff's seclusion or solitude, or into his private affairs. My personal knowledge definition shows that privacy is invaded by certain kinds of intrusions, namely those of a cognitive nature that result in the acquisition of undocumented personal facts. Other kinds of intrusion, for example, those involving causal access (see definition 3 discussed in Section I) and environmental disturbances, are more exactly and perspicuously described by concepts like trespass, nuisance, and peace.

Prosser's second privacy tort, the public disclosure of embarrassing private facts, is legitimate provided the facts are undocumented. The fourth tort, appropriation for the defendant's advantage of the plaintiff's name or likeness, should not be subsumed under privacy for the simple reason that such appropriation does not result in the obtaining of undocumented personal knowledge about the plaintiff. It does, however, preempt the choice whether or not to have one's name or likeness used (usually for advertising purposes) and could therefore be challenged on liberty grounds. It could also be challenged on property grounds, particularly in circumstances where the plaintiff is seeking financial remuneration for the use of his name or likeness.

Some First Amendment cases involving the disclosure of personal information implicate genuine privacy interests, others do not. Two well-known cases which ought not to have been decided in terms of privacy are *Cox Broadcasting Co.* v. *Cohn* and *Briscoe* v. *Reader's Digest.* In *Cohn* a newspaper published the name of a rape victim.[35] In *Briscoe,* the identity of a former truck hijacker was disclosed.[36] Because these facts belonged to the public record their disclosure cannot plausibly be condemned on privacy grounds.

However, the press sometimes does gratuitously invade privacy. One former case comes immediately to mind. William Sidis was a child prodigy (at the age of eleven he lectured to Harvard professors on the Fourth Dimension) who in his later years sought solitude and privacy. *The New Yorker* decided to do a story on him. The article focused on Sidis's life as a recluse. Sidis sued for invasion of privacy and lost.[37] In my judgment he should have won. Granted there is the First Amendment guarantee of a free press, but this has never been interpreted to mean that the press can publish anything it wants. There are limitations (for example, pornography, libel), and invasions of privacy which serve no useful purpose should be included among them. The public had no need to know about Sidis's later life.

Other First Amendment-privacy cases are more difficult to decide. Much depends on the particular facts of the situation and the plaintiff's status. Public officials are not entitled to the same degree of protection as are private citizens. Warren and Brandeis took note of this many years ago when they wrote: "to publish of a modest and retiring individual that he suffers from an impediment of his speech or that he cannot spell correctly is an unwarranted, if not unexampled, infringement upon his privacy, while to state and comment on the same characteristic found in a would-be congressman would not be regarded as beyond the pale of propriety."[38]

Thus far our conclusion must be that privacy is not receiving significant legal protection. It is only when we look at Fourth Amendment cases that privacy enthusiasts can begin to take heart. In having to formulate criteria for unreasonable searches and seizures the Supreme Court has been slowly evolving a conception of the right to privacy.[39] In many of these cases the Court has provided substantial protection to privacy interests.[40]

Moreover, the Court may be sympathetic to privacy grievances not related to searches and seizures. Consider the recent and important case of *Whalen* v. *Roe*.[41] The State of New York required that the names and addresses of all persons obtaining schedule II drugs— opium, cocaine, amphetamines, and other drugs for which there is both a lawful and an unlawful use—be kept on record in a centralized computer file. This information was put on magnetic tapes which were then stored in a vault. After five years the tapes would be destroyed. A locked fence and alarm system provided security for the information-processing system. Public disclosure of the patient's identity was prohibited.

The Court unanimously agreed that this legislation did not infringe the patient's right to privacy. But in reaching this (reasonable, I believe) conclusion, the judges exhibited a genuine sensitivity to the privacy interests at stake. Thus Justice Stevens wrote:

> We are not aware of the threat to privacy implied in the accumulation of vast amounts of personal information in computerized data banks or other massive government files. The collecting of taxes, the distribution of welfare and society security benefits, the supervision of public health, the direction of our armed forces, and the enforcement of the criminal laws all require the orderly preservation of great quantities of information, much of which is personal in nature and potentially embarrassing or harmful if disclosed. The right to collect and use such data for public purposes is typically accompanied by a concomitant statutory or regulatory duty to avoid unwarranted disclosures.[42]

So the *Whalen* decision should not be a source of despair for privacy advocates. Privacy might yet come to occupy a significant place in American jurisprudence.

Notes

1. The spreading of falsehoods or purely subjective opinions about a person does not constitute an invasion of his privacy. It is condemnable in the language of libel or slander.
2. I know a recently divorced man who doesn't want anyone to know the fact. He and his former wife still live together, so it is possible for him to conceal their marital status from most everyone.
3. I owe this example, as well as other useful comments and suggestions, to an Editor of *Philosophy & Public Affairs.*
4. Samuel Warren and Louis Brandeis, "The Right to Privacy," *The Harvard Law Review,* 4 (1890): 205–07.
5. *Olmstead v. U.S.* 277 U.S. 438 (1928): 475–76.
6. See William Douglas, *The Rights of the People* (Westport, CT: Greenwood Press, 1958). See Fortas's decision in *Time v. Hill,* 385 U.S. 374 (1967): 412; and in *Gertz v. Robert Welch, Inc.,* 418 U.S. 323 (1974): 412–13. See Stewart's decision in *Katz v. U.S.,* 389 U.S. 347 (1967): 350; and in *Whalen v. Roe,* 429 U.S. 589 (1977): 608.
7. For example, Edward Bloustein, in "Group Privacy: The Right to Huddle," from his *Individual and Group Privacy* (New Brunswick, NJ: Transaction Books, 1978), pp. 123–86; Paul Freund, in "Privacy: One Concept or Many?" ed. J. Pennock and J. Chapman, *Nomos XIII: Privacy* (New York: Atherton Press, 1971), pp. 182–98; Henry Paul Monagham, "Of 'Liberty' and 'Property,'" *Cornell Law Review* 62 (1977): pp. 405–14; and Richard Posner, *The Economics of Justice* (Cambridge, MA: Harvard University Press, 1981), p. 123.
8. *Eisenstadt v. Baird,* 405 U.S. 438 (1972): 453.
9. Charles Fried, *An Anatomy of Values* (Cambridge, MA: Harvard University Press, 1970), chap. 9, p. 141; Richard Wasserstom, "Privacy: Some Assumptions and Arguments," in *Philosophical Law,* ed. Richard Bronaugh (Westport, CT: Greenwood Press, 1979), pp. 148–67; Hyman Gross, "Privacy and Autonomy," *Nomos XIII,* p. 170; Elizabeth Beardsley, "Privacy, Autonomy, and Selective Disclosure," *Nomos XIII,* p. 65.
10. Ernest Van Den Haag, "On Privacy," *Nomos XIII,* p. 147ff.; Irwin Altman, "Privacy—A Conceptual Analysis," *Environment and Behavior* 8 (1976): 8; and "Privacy Regulation: Culturally Universal or Culturally Specific?" *The Journal of Social Issues* 33 (1977): 67; Richard Parker, "A Definition of Privacy," *Rutgers Law Review* 27 (1974): 280.
11. Proponents of a control definition might respond by saying that they are really interested in identifying *the right to privacy* with the right to control personal information about or access to ourselves. But then they should have said so explicitly instead of formulating their contention in terms of privacy alone. And even if they had done so their position would still be confused, since the right to choose is an integral aspect of the right to liberty, not the right to privacy.
12. Here I use "unfree" to mean "lacking liberty." My concern is not with the metaphysical notion of free will.
13. I do not mean to ascribe to proponents of control definitions the view that every interference with liberty is by that very fact an infringement to privacy. I do mean to criticize them for failing to recognize that interferences with personal choice or control, taken by themselves and with no consideration given to undocumented personal knowledge that might be acquired from them, are not appropriately described or persuasively condemned in the language of privacy.
14. Roland Garrett, "The Nature of Privacy," *Philosophy Today* 18 (1974): 264; and Ruth Gavison, "Privacy and the Limits of the Law," *Yale Law Journal* 89 (1980): 428.
15. Charles Fried, "Privacy," *Yale Law Journal* 77 (1968): 477.

16. Westin, Bazelon, and Weinstein are among those who advance the relaxation argument. See, respectively: Alan Westin's *Privacy and Freedom* (New York: Atheneum Press, 1967), p. 34; David Bazelon, "Probing Privacy," *Georgia Law Review* 12 (1977): 588ff.; and Michael Weinstein, "The Uses of Privacy in the Good Life," *Nomos XIII,* p. 99. Westin (p. 36), Weinstein (p. 104), and Gavison (p. 449) are among those who defend the argument from query.

17. Westin (p. 33) and Bloustein, particularly in his essay, "Privacy as an Aspect of Human Dignity: An Answer to Dean Prosser," *The New York University Law Review* 39 (1964): 970, are among those who defend the argument from individuality.

18. This argument from liberalism invites rebuttal from socialists and communists, of course, who want to maintain that the "ideal" of privacy does nothing but encourage unnecessary (and unnatural) conflict among human beings.

19. Richard Posner, "The Right to Privacy," *The Georgia Law Review* 12 (1978): 491–522.

20. I don't mean to identify the liberal principle of respect for persons with Kant's conception of respect for humanity. Kant does not formulate his conception in terms of what persons desire. Instead he focuses on the property of rationality that all persons possess and that, in his view, confers intrinsic worth upon them.

21. Frederick Davis, "What Do We Mean by 'Right to Privacy'?" *The San Diego Law Review* 4 (1959): 1–23; Judith J. Thomson, "The Right to Privacy," *Philosophy & Public Affairs* 4 (1975): 295–315.

22. *Griswold v. Connecticut,* 381 U.S. 479 (1965).

23. *Eisenstadt v. Baird,* 405 U.S. 438 (1972): 453.

24. See, for example, *Roe v. Wade,* 410 U.S. 113 (1973).

25. *In the matter of Quinlan,* 355 A.2d 647 (1976). Here the New Jersey Supreme Court ruled that the right to privacy is broad enough to encompass a patient's decision to decline life-sustaining medical treatment under certain circumstances.

26. *Ravin v. State,* 537 P.2d 494 (1975). Here Alaska's Supreme Court ruled that a law forbidding the possession of marijuana by adults for their personal use in their homes violated the right to privacy.

27. *People v. Privitera,* 74 C.A. 3d (1977), and *People v. Privitera,* 23 Cal. 3d 687 (1979). The California Court of Appeal ruled that the right to privacy protects the choice of cancer patients to use laetrile as a treatment. The California Supreme Court disagreed. It accepted the privacy conceptualization of the issue but contended that the right is not broad enough to legitimate the choice of laetrile.

28. The Fourteenth Amendment provides in part that no state shall "deprive any person of life, liberty, or property, without due process of law. . . ." The Fifth Amendment protects liberty against arbitrary infringement by the Federal Government.

29. *Lochner v. N.Y.,* 198 U.S. 45 (1905). In this controversial case the Court ruled that legislation forbidding employees from contracting to work more than sixty hours a week or ten hours a day in bakeries gratuitously infringed the right to liberty.

30. *Meyer v. Nebraska,* 262 U.S. 390 (1923). Here the Court invalidated a law that barred the teaching of foreign languages in private and public elementary schools on the grounds that it constituted an arbitrary infringement on the right to liberty.

31. *Pierce v. Society of Sisters,* 268 U.S. 510 (1925). In this case the Court invalidated a law that compelled children aged eight to sixteen to attend public schools on the ground that it unjustifiably abridged the right to liberty.

32. The cases are: *Public Utilities Commission v. Pollack,* 345 U.S. 451 (1952); *Breard v. Alexandria,* 341 U.S. 622 (1951); and *Kovacs v. Cooper* 336 U.S. 77 (1949).

33. *Paul v. Davis,* 424 U.S. 693 (1978).

34. William Prosser, "Privacy," *California Law Review* 48 (1960): 383–423.

35. *Cox Broadcasting Co. v. Cohn,* 420 U.S. 469 (1975). The U.S. Supreme Court correctly ruled that Cohn had no bona fide privacy complaint.

36. *Briscoe v. Reader's Digest,* 93 Cal. Rptr. 866 (1971). Briscoe won this case principally because so long a time had passed between his offense and the publication. The California Court should have realized, however, that personal information contained in official records which have not been destroyed is undeniably public.

37. *Sidis v. F-R Publishing Corp.,* 34 F. Supp. 19 (1938).

38. Warren and Brandeis, "The Right to Privacy," p. 205.

39. The Fourth Amendment reads: "The right of the people to secure in their persons, house, papers, effects, against unreasonable searches and seizures shall not be violated, and no warrants shall issue, but upon probable cause, supported by oath or affirmation, and particularly describing the place to be searched and the persons or things to be seized." One can plausibly argue that this Amendment presupposes a right to privacy.

40. I have the following cases in mind: *Katz v. U.S.* 389 U.S. 347 (1967), where the Court ruled that the police may not attach electronic listening devices to the outside of a telephone booth in order to record the conversations on bets and wagers without first obtaining a search warrant; *Berger v. New York,* 388 U.S. 41 (1967), where the Court invalidated a permissive eavesdropping statute authorizing the indiscriminate use of electronic surveillance devices; *Stanley v. Georgia,* 394 U.S. 447 (1969), in which the Court ruled that allegedly pornographic movies seized without a search warrant from the defendant's home could not be used as evidence in his trial; *Lo-ji Sales, Inc. v. N.Y.,* 442 U.S. 319 (1979) in which the Court declared that a search of an adult bookstore resulting in the seizure of several films and magazines violated petitioner's Fourth Amendment rights because the warrant issued failed to particularly describe the things to be seized; and *Steagold v. U.S.,* 101 S. Ct. 1642 (1981), where the Court ruled that the police may not search for the subject of an arrest warrant in the home of a third party without first obtaining a search warrant.

41. *Whalen v. Roe,* 429 U.S. 589 (1976).

42. Ibid., p. 605.

22. Introduction to Personal Privacy in an Information Society
Privacy Protection Study Commission

THIS REPORT IS about records and people. It looks toward a national policy to guide the way public and private organizations treat the records they keep about individuals. Its findings reflect the fact that in American society today records mediate relationships between in-

From *Personal Privacy in an Information Society* (Washington, D.C.: U.S. Government Printing Office, July 1977), pp. 3–29.

dividuals and organizations and thus affect an individual more easily, more broadly, and often more unfairly than was possible in the past. This is true in spite of almost a decade of effort to frame the objectives of a national policy to protect personal privacy in an information-dependent society. It will remain true unless steps are taken soon to strike a proper balance between the individual's personal privacy interests and society's information needs. In this report, the Privacy Protection Study Commission identifies the steps necessary to strike that balance and presents the Commission's specific recommendations for achieving it. This introductory chapter briefly describes the problem and focuses and defines the objectives of a national policy. It also weighs major competing values and interests and explains how the Commission believes its policy recommendations should be implemented.

Record Keeping and Personal Privacy

One need only glance at the dramatic changes in our country during the last hundred years to understand why the relationship between organizational record keeping and personal privacy has become an issue in almost all modern societies. The records of a hundred years ago tell little about the average American, except when he died, perhaps when and where he was born, and if he owned land, how he got his title to it. Three quarters of the adult population worked for themselves on farms or in small towns. Attendance at the village schoolhouse was not compulsory and only a tiny fraction pursued formal education beyond it. No national military service was required, and few programs brought individuals into contact with the Federal government. Local governments to be sure made decisions about individuals, but these mainly had to do with taxation, business promotion and regulation, prevention and prosecution of crime, and in some instances, public relief for the poor or the insane.

Record keeping about individuals was correspondingly limited and local in nature. The most complete record was probably kept by churches, who recorded births, baptisms, marriages, and deaths. Town officials and county courts kept records of similar activities. Merchants and bankers maintained financial accounts for their customers, and when they extended credit, it was on the basis of personal knowledge of the borrower's circumstances, Few individuals had insurance of any kind, and a patient's medical record very likely existed only in the doctor's memory. Records about individuals rarely circulated beyond the place they were made.

The past hundred years, and particularly the last three decades, have changed all that. Three out of four Americans now live in cities or their surrounding suburbs, only one in ten of the individuals in the workforce today is self-employed, and education is compulsory for every child. The yeoman farmer and small-town merchant have given way to the skilled workers and white-collar employees who manage and staff the organizations, both public and private, that keep society functioning.

In addition, most Americans now do at least some of their buying on credit, and most have some form of life, health, property, or liability insurance. Institutionalized medical care is almost universally available. Government social services programs now reach deep into the population along with government licensing of occupations and professions, Federal taxation of individuals, and government regulation of business and labor union affairs. Today, government regulates and supports large areas of economic and social life through some of the nation's largest bureaucratic organizations, many of which deal directly with individuals. In fact, many of the private-sector record-keeping relationships discussed in this report are to varying degrees replicated in programs administered or funded by Federal agencies.

A significant consequence of this marked change in the variety and concentration of institutional relationships with individuals is that record keeping about individuals now covers almost everyone and influences everyone's life, from the business executive applying for a personal loan to the school teacher applying for a national credit card, from the riveter seeking check-guarantee privileges from the local bank to the young married couple trying to finance furniture for its first home. All will have their creditworthiness evaluated on the basis of recorded information in the files of one or more organizations. So also with insurance, medical care, employment, education, and social services. Each of those relationships requires the individual to divulge information about himself, and usually leads to some evaluation of him based on information about him that some other record keeper has compiled.

The substitution of records for face-to-face contact in these relationships is what makes the situation today dramatically different from the way it was even as recently as 30 years ago. It is now commonplace for an individual to be asked to divulge information about himself for use by unseen strangers who make decisions about him that directly affect his everyday life. Furthermore, because so many of the services offered by organizations are, or have come to be considered, necessities, an individual has little choice but to submit to whatever demands for information about him an organization may make. Organizations must have some substitute for personal evaluation in order to distinguish between one individual and the next in the endless stream of otherwise anonymous individuals they deal with, and most organizations have come to rely on records as that substitute.

It is important to note, moreover, that organizations increasingly desire information that will facilitate fine-grained decisions about individuals. A credit-card issuer wants to avoid people who do not pay their bills, but it also strives to identify slow payers and well intentioned people who could easily get into debt beyond their ability to repay. Insurance companies seek to avoid people whose reputation or life style suggest that they may have more than the average number of accidents or other types of losses. Employers look for job applicants who give promise of being healthy, productive members of a work force. Social services agencies must sort individuals according to legally established eligibility criteria, but also try to see that people in need take advantage of all the services available to them. Schools try to take "the whole child" into account in making decisions about his progress, and government authorities make increasingly detailed evaluations of an individual's tax liability.

Each individual plays a dual role in this connection—as an object of information gathering and as a consumer of the benefits and services that depend on it. Public opinion data suggest that most Americans treasure their personal privacy, both in the abstract and in their own daily lives, but individuals are clearly also willing to give information about themselves, or allow others to do so, when they can see a concrete benefit to be gained by it. Most of us are pleased to have the conveniences that fine-grained, record-based decisions about us make possible. It is the rare individual who will forego having a credit card because he knows that if he has one, details about his use of it will accumulate in the card issuer's files.

Often one also hears people assert that nobody minds organizational record-keeping practices "if you have nothing to hide," and many apparently like to think of themselves as having nothing to hide, not realizing that whether an individual does or not can be a matter of opinion. We live, inescapably, in an "information society," and few of us have the option of avoiding relationships with record-keeping organizations. To do so is to forego not only credit but also insurance, employment, medical care, education, and all forms of government services to individuals. This being so, each individual has, or should have, a concern that the records organizations make and keep about him do not lead to unfair decisions about him.

In a larger context, Americans must also be concerned about the long-term effect record-keeping practices can have not only on relationships between individuals and organizations, but also on the balance of power between government and the rest of society. Accumulations of information about individuals tend to enhance authority by making it easier for authority to reach individuals directly. Thus, growth in society's record-keeping capability poses the risk that existing power balances will be upset. Recent events illustrate how easily this can happen, and also how difficult it can be to preserve such balances once they are seriously threatened.

This report concentrates on the delicate balance between various types of organizations' need for information about individuals and each individual's desire to be secure and fairly treated. It also recognizes, however, that government's expanding role as regulator and distributor of largess gives it new ways to intrude, creating new privacy protection problems. By opening more avenues for collecting information and more decision-making forums in which it can employ that information, government has enormously broadened its opportunities both to help and to embarrass, harass, and injure the individual. These new avenues and needs for collecting information, particularly when coupled with modern information technology, multiply the dangers of official abuse against which the Constitution seeks to protect. Recent history reminds us that these are real, not mythical, dangers and that while our efforts to protect ourselves against them must ultimately be fashioned into law, the choices they require are not mere legal choices; they are social and political value choices of the most basic kind.

The Framework for a National Policy

The imbalance in the relationship between individuals and record-keeping institutions today is pointedly illustrated by the experiences of Catherine Tarver, a "welfare mother" from the State of Washington, and Mitchell Miller, a businessman from Kathleen, Georgia.

In the late 1960's Mrs. Tarver became ill and was hospitalized. The Juvenile Court, after reviewing a report by her caseworker which contained "assertedly derogatory contents," including an allegation of child neglect, placed her children temporarily in the custody of the Department of Public Assistance. A few months later, the Juvenile Court, after another hearing, exonerated Mrs. Tarver and returned her children to her, but the caseworker's report remained in her file at the Department of Public Assistance.

Although Mrs. Tarver had her children back and was no longer on the welfare rolls, she still wanted to have the caseworker's report removed from her file on the grounds that it was false, misleading, and prejudicial and would be available to other State social services agencies with whom she might subsequently have contact. When she asked for a fair hearing[1] to challenge the report, the Public Assistance Department rejected her request because the grievance was not directly related to eligibility for public assistance. She sued in a State court but lost, the court agreeing with the welfare agency that the fair hearing procedure was not meant to deal with collateral problems. The U.S. Supreme Court refused to review her case and the caseworker's report remained in her file.

Mitchell Miller's difficulties began on December 18, 1972, when a deputy sheriff from Houston County, Georgia, stopped a Pepsico truck purportedly owned by Miller and found it was transporting 150 five-gallon plastic jugs, two 100-pound bags of wheat shorts, cylinders of bottled gas, and a shotgun condenser. Less than a month later, while fighting a warehouse fire, the sheriff and fire department officials found a 7,500 gallon distillery and 175 gallons of untaxed whiskey. An agent from the U.S. Treasury Department's Bureau of Alcohol, Tobacco and Firearms suspected Miller of direct involvement in both events and two weeks later presented grand jury subpoenas to the two banks where Miller maintained accounts. Without notifying Miller, copies of his checks and bank statements were either shown or given to the Treasury agents as soon as they presented the subpoenas. The subpoenas did not require immediate disclosure, but the bank officers nonetheless responded at once.

After he had been indicted, Miller attempted to persuade the court that the grand jury subpoenas used by the Treasury Department were invalid and, thus, the evidence obtained with them could not be used against him. He pointed out that the subpoenas had not been issued by the grand jury itself, and further, that they were returnable on a day when the grand jury was not in session. Finally, Miller argued that the Bank Secrecy Act's requirement that banks maintain microfilm copies of checks for two years[2] was an unconstitutional invasion of his Fourth Amendment rights. The trial court rejected Miller's arguments and he appealed.

The Fifth Circuit Court of Appeals also rejected Miller's claim that the Bank Secrecy Act was unconstitutional, an issue that had already been resolved by the U.S. Supreme Court in 1974.[3] The Court of Appeals agreed, however, that Miller's rights, as well as the bank's, were threatened and that he should be accorded the right to legal process to challenge the validity of the grand jury subpoenas. The Court of Appeals saw Miller's interest in the bank's records as deriving from the Fourth Amendment protection against unreasonble searches and seizures which protected him against "compulsory production of a man's private papers to establish a criminal charge against him."

On April 21, 1976, a fateful day for personal privacy, the U.S. Supreme Court decided that Mitchell Miller had no legitimate "expectation of privacy" in his bank records and thus no protectible interest for the Court to consider. The Court reasoned that because checks are an independent record of an individual's participation in the flow of commerce, they cannot be considered confidential communications. The account record, moreover, is the property of the bank, not of the individual account holder. Thus, according to the Court, Miller's expectation of privacy was neither legitimate, warranted, nor enforceable.

The *Tarver* and *Miller* decisions[4] are the law of the land, and the Commission takes no issue with their legal correctness. Viewed from one perspective, these cases are very narrow and affect only a minute percentage of the population. *Tarver* might be seen as simply refusing an additional request from a welfare mother who had received the benefits she was entitled to under a program; *Miller* as a decision affecting only the technical procedural rights of a criminal defendant. Perhaps these two cases are not very compelling, but the Commission singles them out because each starkly underscores an individual's present defenselessness with respect to records maintained about him. Who is there to raise such issues if not people in trouble? They are the ones who reach for and test the limits of existing legal protections, and if the protections are not there for them, they will not be there for anyone.

In both cases, institutional policies and the legal system failed individuals in their efforts to limit the impact of records on their lives. The *Tarver* case warns that one may be able to do nothing about a damaging record, not even if it is false, until some adverse action is taken on the basis of it; that one has no way to prevent the damage such an action can do. The *Miller* decision goes even further, making records the property solely of the record keeper, so that the individual cannot assert any interest in them, although his interest would be assertible if he himself held the same records. Even worse, it warns that not only a "revenuer" but anyone, public or private, can gain access to an individual's bank records if the bank agrees to disclose them.

Each case illustrates systematic flaws in the existing means available to any individual who tries to protect himself against the untoward consequences of organizational record keeping. Together they strongly suggest that if Americans still value personal privacy, they must make certain changes in the way records about individuals are made, used, and disclosed.

Since so much of an individual's life is now shaped by his relationships with organizations, his interest in the records organizations keep about him is obvious and compelling. The above cases and the rest of this report show how poorly that interest is protected. If it is to be protected, public policy must focus on five systemic features of personal-data record keeping in America today.

> *First,* while an organization makes and keeps records about individuals to facilitate relationships with them, it also makes and keeps records about individuals for other purposes, such as documenting the record-keeping organization's own actions and making it possible for other organizations—government agencies, for example—to monitor the actions of individuals.
>
> *Second,* there is an accelerating trend, most obvious in the credit and financial areas, toward the accumulation in records of more and more personal details about an individual.
>
> *Third,* more and more records about an individual are collected, maintained, and disclosed by organizations with which the individual has no direct relationship but whose records help to shape his life.
>
> *Fourth,* most record-keeping organizations consult the records of other organizations to verify the information they obtain from an individual and thus pay as much or more attention to what other organizations report about him than they pay to what he reports about himself; and
>
> *Fifth,* neither law nor technology now gives an individual the tools he needs to protect his legitimate interests in the records organizations keep about him.

The topical chapters that follow document the importance of these five systemic characteristics of personal-data record keeping in America today and present the Commission's recommended approach to solving the problems they create. The Commission believes that by focusing on these five characteristics constructive solutions to most of the record-related privacy protection problems that confront American society today and in the foreseeable future can be found.

The first characteristic—the fact that an organization may use its records about individuals in accounting for its operations to other centers of power and authority in society—has important implications for any policy of record-keeping regulation. It prompts caution in considering prohibitions on the collection of items of information from or about individuals, but at the same time draws attention to the need for special safeguards when requiring an organization to record any information about an individual that it does not need to facilitate its own relationship with him.

The second systemic characteristic—the accumulation in records of more and more personal details—is clearly visible in some of an individual's credit and financial relationships. It will become even more apparent as electronic funds transfer systems mature. This accumulation, moreover, is not the result of more and more people being asked more and more questions, but rather reflects the need and capacity of a particular type of record-keeping organization to monitor and control transactions with its individual customers. As the Commission points out . . . , it is now perilously easy for such a build-up, however innocently practical the purpose, to crystallize into a personal profile of an individual. The possession of such profiles invites the use of them for marketing, research, and law enforcement, and, in an electronic funds transfer environment, could provide a way of tracking an individual's current movements. The dramatic shift in the balance of power between government and the rest of society that such a development could portend has persuaded the Commission of the compelling need to single it out for special public-policy attention and action.

The third systemic characteristic—the attenuation of an individual's relationships with record-keeping organizations when information generated in a direct relationship is recorded in the files of other organizations that have no direct relationship with him—lies at the core of the recommendations in this report. The Commission finds that most organizations that keep records about individuals fall into one of three categories: (1) the primary record keeper (such as a credit grantor, insurer, or social services agency) that has a direct relationship with the individual; (2) support organizations whose sole sources of information are the primary record keepers they serve; and (3) support organizations (usually of an investigative character) that have independent sources of information. While this typology does not fit all cases—credit bureaus, for example, supplement the information they receive from credit grantors with information they search out from public records—it can serve as a guide in apportioning responsibilities among record-keeping institutions.

The fourth characteristic—that a primary record keeper normally verifies the information about himself that an individual provides, and tends to lean as much or more on the verification information it gets from other organizations than on what the individual divulges about himself—gives rise to some of the most difficult privacy protection issues. As records progressively displace face-to-face acquaintance, individuals are more and more driven to permit information in records about them to be disclosed as a condition of receiving services and benefits. For example, an individual who wants a credit card usually cannot have one unless he is willing to permit information about his credit usage to be disclosed regularly to credit bureaus, and through them to other credit grantors. An individual who applies for life insurance must agree to allow medical information about him to be disclosed to the Medical Information Bureau, and through the Bureau to later inquiring life and health insurers. An individual must now allow information to be disclosed from his medical records for a growing number of purposes even though the medical-care relationship requires him to divulge the most intimate details of his life and undergo the most intimate observation.

The sharing of information among record-keeping organizations also transmits the stigma that goes with some kinds of information. One's own physician, for example, may heartily approve of taking a minor or temporary problem to a psychiatrist, but the potential consequences of disclosing the mere fact that one has had psychiatric treatment are too well known to need description. Equally serious for some individuals are the consequences of disclosing arrest records, military discharge codes, and previous adverse insurance decisions, and the simple fact that a number of credit grantors asked for credit reports on a particular individual during a short span of time can adversely affect an evaluation of his credit worthiness. Such problems stem in part from the tendency of organizations to accept at face value information they get about individuals from other organizations. Questions are seldom asked about the social or bureaucratic processes by which the information came to be in the other organization's records, so that unwarranted assumptions can easily be made about its value. For the individual, of course, such an unwarranted assumption can start a progression of fortuitous events that may permanently deprive him of opportunities he deserves, or make it impossible for him to escape a particular line of inquiry whenever he seeks to establish a relationship with another organization.

The fifth and last characteristic—that neither law nor technology gives an individual the tools he needs to protect himself from the undeserved difficulties a record can create for him—may also leave him helpless to stop damage once it has started. Current law is neither strong enough nor specific enough to solve the problems that now exist. In some cases, changes in record-keeping practice have already made even recent legal protections obsolete. As record-keeping systems come to be used to preclude action by the individual, a recent trend in the credit and financial areas, it is important that the individual also be given preventive protections to supplement the after-the-fact protections he sometimes has today. The fact that Fair Credit Reporting Act procedures will enable him to get errors in the record corrected can be small and bitter comfort to a traveler stranded in a strange city late at night because information about his credit-card account status was inaccurately reported to an independent authorization service. He would undoubtedly prefer a procedure that would enable him to get an error corrected *before* it entered into an adverse decision about him, and so would most everyone if he stopped and thought about it.

The Commission also found numerous examples of situations in which decisions or judgments made on the basis of a record about an individual can matter to the individual very much but in which he has no substantive or procedural protection at all. The law as it now stands simply ignores the strong interest many people have in records about them— applicants to graduate and professional schools, people being considered for jobs or promotions for which they have not formally applied, patients whose records are subpoenaed as evidence in court cases that do not involve them directly, proprietors of small businesses who are the subjects of commercial-credit investigations, and individuals who are the subjects of Federal agency records the agency retrieves and uses by reference to some characteristic of the individual other than his name or an assigned identifying particular.

Paralleling the categories of *individuals* without protection under current law, there are categories of *records* that are subject to existing legal requirements if they are created by one particular type of organization, but not if they are created by any other type of organization, although the record and its purpose may be the same in all cases. For example, an investigative report is subject to restrictions if it was prepared by an investigative agency, but not if it was prepared by an insurance company or employer.

The Commission also found that whether a record is subject to existing law can depend on the *technique* by which it is generated or retrieved. For example, how does the Equal Credit Opportunity Act, a law drawn on the assumption that credit decisions turn on one or two particular items of information about the applicant, apply when a credit grantor uses "point scoring," a new method of evaluating credit applicants which submerges all the particular items of information about the applicant into one overall score?

The prescreening of mailing lists[5] is another record-keeping technique that muddies the assumptions underlying existing legal protections. If a mailing list is to be used by a credit grantor to solicit new customers but is first run through an automated credit bureau where an individual's name is deleted from the list because his credit bureau records are in error as to the promptness with which he pays his bills, has he been subjected to an adverse credit decision? The law is currently unclear.

The role that technique can play in determining whether a particular type of record or record-keeping operation is or is not within the scope of existing legal protections is comparatively new. It arises in the main from automation, which multiplies the uses that can be made of a record about an individual, and will grow in importance as new record-keeping applications of computer and telecommunications technology are developed. Computers and telecommunications serve the interests of institutions and can be best appreciated as extensions of those interests, as subsequent chapters suggest. The failure to recognize that relationship has deflected attention from the essential policy choices the new technologies offer. Nonetheless, without the new technologies, certain record-keeping practices and the organizational activities they support would not be possible.

The board availability and low cost of computer and telecommunications technologies provides both the *impetus* and the *means* to perform new record-keeping functions. These functions can bring the individual substantial benefits, but there are also disadvantages for the individual. On one hand, they can give him easier access to services that make his life more comfortable or convenient. On the other, they also tempt others to demand, and make it easier for them to get access to, information about him for purposes he does not expect and would not agree to if he were asked.

It is also quite evident that record-keeping organizations exploiting these new technologies to facilitate their own operations now pay little heed to the ways they could use the same technologies to facilitate exercise of the individual's rights and prerogatives in records used to make important decisions about him. It is ironic but true that in a society as dependent as ours on computer and telecommunications technology, an individual may still have to make a personal visit to a credit bureau if he wants access to the information the bureau maintains about him, or to get an erroneous record corrected. Although an error in a record can now be propagated all over the country at the speed of light, many organizations have made no provision to propagate corrections through the same channels, and existing law seldom requires them to do so. As a general proposition, system designers by and large have not fully used their knowledge and capabilities to make record-keeping systems serve individual as well as organizational needs and interests.

This is not to lay the blame on system designers, who are people doing what they are asked to do by the record-keeping organizations that support or pay for their services. The fault lies in the lack of strong incentives for the organization to ask them to do what they know how to do in the individual's interest. One reason for the way sytems are designed and have been operated in the past has been their high cost. Instead of costing more, however, increased technological capability is now costing less and less, making it easier than ever for record-keeping organizations to take account of the individual's interests as well as their own, if they have incentives to do so.

One of the most striking of the Commission's several findings with respect to the current state of record-keeping law and practice is how difficult it can be for an individual even to find out how records about him are developed and used. What makes the difficulty the more serious is that the limited rights he now has depend in the main on his taking the initiative to exercise them. The list of records kept about an individual of which he is not likely to be aware seems endless. Even when he knows a record is being compiled, he often does not know what his rights with respect to it are, much less how to exercise them effectively, nor is he likely to be aware at the time he enters a record-keeping relationship of the importance of finding out.

In most cases, the individual can only guess at what types of information or records will be marshaled by those making any particular decision about him; furthermore, the specific sources are likely to be concealed from him. The situation makes it all but impossible for him to identify errors, or if he does, to trace them to their source. It also makes it impossible for him to know whether organizations with which he believes he has a confidential relationship have disclosed records about him to others without his knowledge or consent.

The Objectives of a National Policy

Every member of a modern society acts out the major events and transitions of his life with organizations as attentive partners. Each of his countless transactions with them leaves its mark in the records they maintain about him. The uniqueness of this record-generating pressure cannot be overemphasized. Never before the Twentieth Century have organizations tried or been expected to deal with individuals in such an exacting fashion on such a scale. Never before have so many organizations had the facilities for keeping available the information that makes it possible for them to complete daily a multitude of transactions with a multitude of individuals, and to have the relevant facts on each individual available as a basis for making subsequent decisions about him. Obviously the advent of computing technology has greatly contributed to these changes, but automated record-keeping has grown in concert with many other changes in administrative techniques, and in public attitudes and expectations.

The Commission finds that as records continue to supplant face-to-face encounters in our society, there has been no compensating tendency to give the individual the kind of control over the collection, use, and disclosure of information about him that his face-to-face encounters normally entail.

What two people divulge about themselves when they meet for the first time depends on how much personal revelation they believe the situation warrants and how much confidence each has that the other will not misinterpret or misuse what is said. If they meet again, and particularly if they develop a relationship, their self-revelation may expand both in scope and detail. All the while, however, each is in a position to correct any misperception that may develop, and to judge whether the other is likely to misuse the personal revelations, or pass them on to others without asking permission. Should either suspect that the other has violated the trust on which the candor of their communication depends, he can sever the relationship altogether, or alter its terms, perhaps by refusing thereafter to discuss certain topics or to reveal certain details about himself. Face-to-face encounters of this type, and the human relationships that result from them, are the threads from which the fabric of society is woven. The situations in which they arise are inherently social, not private, in that the disclosure of information about oneself is expected.

An individual's relationship with a record-keeping organization has some of the features of his face-to-face relationships with other individuals. It, too, arises in an inherently social context, depends on the individual's willingness to divulge information about himself or to allow others to do so, and often carries some expectation as to its practical consequences. Beyond that, however, the resemblance quickly fades.

By and large it is the organization's sole prerogative to decide what information the individual shall divulge for its records or allow others to divulge about him, and the pace at which he must divulge it. If the record-keeping organization is a private-sector one, the individual theoretically can take his business elsewhere if he objects to the divulgences required of him. Yet in a society in which time is often at a premium, in which organizations performing similar functions tend to ask similar questions, and in which organizational record-keeping practices and the differences among them are poorly perceived or understood, the individual often has little real opportunity to pick and choose. Moreover, if the record-keeping organization is a public-sector one, the individual may have no alternative but to yield whatever information is demanded of him.

Once an individual establishes a relationship with a record-keeping organization, he has even less practical control over what actually gets into a record about him, and almost none over how the record is subsequently used. In contrast to his face-to-face relationships with other individuals, he can seldom check on the accuracy of the information the organization develops about him, or discover and correct errors and misperceptions, or even find out how the information is used, much less participate in deciding to whom it may be disclosed. Nor, as a practical matter, can he sever or alter the terms of the relationship if he finds its informational demands unacceptable.

A society that increasingly relies on records to mediate relationships between individuals and organizations, and in which an individual's survival increasingly depends on his ability to maintain a variety of such relationships, must concern itself with such a situation. Ours has begun to do so, and the Commission's inquiry showed that the individual's ability to protect himself from obvious record-keeping abuses has improved somewhat in recent years. Nevertheless, most record-keeping relationships are still dangerously one-sided and likely to become even more so unless public policy makers create incentives for organizations to modify their record-keeping practices for the individual's protection, and give individuals rights to participate in record-keeping relationships commensurate with their interest in the records organizations create and keep about them.

Accordingly, the Commission has concluded that an effective privacy protection policy must have three concurrent objectives:

> to create a proper balance between what an individual is expected to divulge to a record-keeping organization and what he seeks in return (*to minimize intrusiveness*)
>
> to open up record-keeping operations in ways that will minimize the extent to which recorded information about an individual is itself a source of unfairness in any decision about him made on the basis of it (*to maximize fairness*), and
>
> to create and define obligations with respect to the uses and disclosures that will be made of recorded information about an individual (*to create legitimate, enforceable expectations of confidentiality*).

These three objectives both subsume and conceptually augment the principles of the Privacy Act of 1974[6] and the five fair information practice principles set forth in the 1973 report of the Department of Health, Education, and Welfare's Secretary's Advisory Committee on Automated Personal Data Systems.[7] The second objective, to maximize fairness, in a sense subsumes all of them, and many of the Commission's specific recommendations articulate them in detail. The Commission has gone about protecting personal privacy largely by giving an individual access to records that pertain to him. Taken together, however, the three proposed objectives go beyond the openness and fairness concerns by specifically recognizing the occasional need for *a priori* determinations prohibiting the use, or collection and use, of certain types of information, and by calling for legal definitions of the individual's interest in controlling the disclosure of certain types of records about him.

Minimizing Intrusiveness

The Commission believes that society may have to cope more adequately in the future with objections to the collection of information about an individual on the grounds that it is "nobody's business but his own." There are only a few instances where the collection, or collection and use, of a particular type of information has been proscribed on grounds of impropriety, i.e., unwarranted intrusiveness. There are a number of examples of the proscription of certain *uses* of particular types of information, such as race, sex and marital status, but the character of these fairness-based proscriptions is not the same as when unwarranted intrusiveness is the rationale. When fairness is the overriding concern, organizations must often continue to collect the information in question in order to demonstrate compliance. For example, how can an employer or credit grantor show that it is not systematically using sex and race to discriminate among applicants unless it records the sex and race of all applicants? When impropriety is the main concern, however, the mere asking of the question must be proscribed. The proscription may also apply to use, but only to make sure that if the proscribed information is already on record, it will not enter into the decision-making process.

The intrusiveness issue is perhaps the most difficult one the Commission addresses.

Whether or not the questions an organization asks individuals constitute intrusions on personal privacy is a problem that begins with the lines of inquiry society accepts as proper for an organization to pursue in making decisions about individuals. Thus, so long as society countenances a particular line of inquiry, questions as to how far it may properly go seem largely aesthetic. Indeed, if an individual's only concern is to be fairly treated, he should logically prefer to have recorded as much information as possible about himself as protection against inaccurate evaluation. For the individual there is clearly a trade-off. Does he always want to be evaluated on the basis of information that is, from an objective standpoint, strictly relevant, or does he prefer to be evaluated on the basis of a thoroughgoing inquiry that may give context to his particular situation and allow extenuating but not patently relevant circumstances to be taken into account? Such questions are extremely difficult if not impossible to answer. The Commission, in the chapters that follow, recommends four ways of addressing them.

First, the Commission recommends that individuals be informed more fully than they now are of the information needs and collection practices of a record-keeping organization in advance of committing themselves to a relationship with it. If the individual is to serve as a check on unreasonable demands for information or objectionable methods of acquiring it, he must know what to expect so that he will have a proper basis for deciding whether the trade-off is worthwhile for him.

Second, the Commission also recommends that a few specific types of information not be collected at all. For example, in the employment and personnel area, the Commission will recommend that arrest information not be collected by employers for use in hiring and promotion decisions unless its use for such purposes is required by law.

Third, the Commission proposes certain limitations on the information collection methods used by record-keeping organizations. In general, the Commission believes that if an organization, public or private, has declared at the start its intent to make certain inquires of third parties, and to use certain sources and techniques in doing so, it should be constrained only from exceeding the scope of its declaration. The Commission also recommends that private-sector record keepers be required to exercise reasonable care in selecting and retaining other organizations to collect information about individuals on their behalf. These "reasonable care" recommendations and the ones that would bar pretext interviews and make acquiring confidential information under false pretenses punishable as a criminal offense, are the Commission's response to testimony showing that some organizations make a business of acquiring confidential records about individuals without their authorization for use by lawyers and insurance claim adjusters.

Finally, in some areas, the Commission supports the idea of having governmental mechanisms both to receive complaints about the property of inquiries made of individuals and to bring them to the attention of bodies responsible for establishing public policy. The Commission believes, however, that such complaints require the most delicate public-policy response. Our society is wary of government interference in information flows, and rightly so, even when personal privacy is at stake. It may be warranted in some cases, but only as a last resort. Thus, the Commission prefers to see such concerns addressed to the greatest possible extent by enabling the individual to balance what are essentially competing interests within his own scheme of values.

227

Maximizing Fairness

A principal objective of the Privacy Act of 1974 is to assure that the records a Federal agency maintains about an individual are as accurate, timely, complete, and relevant as is necessary to assure that they are not the cause of unfairness in any decision about the individual made on the basis of them. Proper management of records about individuals is the key to this objective, and the Privacy Act seeks to enlist the individual's help in achieving it by giving him a right to see, copy, and correct or amend records about himself. The Fair Credit Reporting Act (FCRA) and the Fair Credit Billing Act (FCBA) also focus on fairness in record keeping, though their scope of application and their specific requirements differ from those of the Privacy Act. FCRA requirements apply primarily to the support organizations which verify and supplement the information a credit, insurance, or employment applicant divulges to the primary record keepers in those three areas, but which do not themselves participate in decisions about applicants. The FCBA, however, applies to primary record keepers but only to a particular type—grantors of credit that involves regular billing—and only to a particular aspect of their operations—the settlement of billing disputes.

Other recent legislation centering on fairness in record keeping includes the Family Educational Rights and Privacy Act of 1974 and the several State fair-information-practice statutes. Their scope and specific requirements approximate those of the Privacy Act more closely than do those of any of the fairness-centered statutes that currently apply to the private sector.

All of these efforts to establish fairness protections for records about individuals have been resisted. The arguments against them have ranged from the alleged need to keep secret the identity of third-party sources, even institutional sources, to fear that organizations would be inundated with requests to see, copy, and correct records. These arguments are still heard, despite the fact that wherever such protections have been established, most of the anticipated difficulties have failed to materialize.

The vast majority of the Commission's recommendations relate directly or indirectly to fairness in record keeping. For the individual, necessary fairness protections include a right of access to records about himself for the purpose of reviewing, copying, and correcting or amending them as necessary plus some control over the collection and disclosure of information about him. For organizations, fairness protection includes the responsibility to apprise individuals that records have or will be created about them, and to have reasonable procedures for assuring the necessary accuracy, timeliness, completeness, and relevance of the information in the records they maintain about individuals, including a responsibility to forward corrections to other organizations under specific circumstances. The Commission believes, however, that *achieving the fairness objective will depend on varying the combination of rights for individuals and responsibilities for organizations according to the particular circumstances of each type of record-keeping relationship.*

For example, the Commission will recommend that applicants in several areas of record keeping be apprised of the scope, sources, and methods of inquiry the organization intends to use in verifying application information, but the recommended requirement is not precisely the same in each case. Similarly, the Commission will also recommend a general right of access for individuals to the records about them maintained by insurance institutions and medical-care providers. But because credit and depository institutions typically have procedures for keeping an individual apprised of the content of the records they maintain about him, the Commission there will recommend a more limited right of access for individuals to be triggered by an adverse decision. So also the Commission concluded that the individual's right of access to records about him maintained for research and statistical purposes can safely be limited to situations in which such a record may be used in making a decision about him.

The right to correct or amend a record is essential to fairness in many areas. To be effective, it must usually be coupled with an obligation of the record-keeping organization to forward the correction or amendment to past recipients of inaccurate or incomplete information. The Commission has recommended modifying this blanket obligation some-what to require that record keepers need forward corrections and amendments only to past recipients designated by the individual and those to which the record-keeping organization regularly discloses the kind of information in question. The Commission believes that this modification has the desirable effect of relieving record-keeping organizations of the obligation to keep an accounting of every disclosure of every record about an individual without materially weakening the individual's protection. Amendments would, of course, still have to be forwarded to *future* recipients and the insurance and employment rec-ommendations call, in addition, for automatic propagation of corrections and amendments to investigative support organizations that were sources of corrected or amended infor-mation. All of the correction and amendment recommendations also make provision for disagreements between the individual and a record-keeping organization about the accuracy, timeliness, or completeness of a record.

In regard to fairness in disclosure, the Commission recommends requiring the indi-vidual's authorization where it finds that a necessary protection, and specifies what it believes the authorization statement should contain if it is to serve both the information needs of, for example, insurers and employers and the individual's interest in controlling the divul-gence of information about himself by record keepers with which he has a confidential relationship. The Commission's recommendations in this regard recognize the *gatekeeping* role that certain types of records play—that is, the role they play in decisions as to whether an individual will be allowed to enter into particular social, economic, or political rela-tionships, and if so, under what circumstances. Where records play such a role, the individual usually has no choice but to allow them to be used in making decisions about him. Since informed consent is valid only if wholly voluntary, it means little in this context. Hence, the Commission finds *authorization* the appropriate pre-condition of disclosure, rather than *informed consent,* and couples it with a *principle of limited disclosure.* This principle is a key concept because it asserts that a disclosure should include no more of the recorded information than the authorized request for disclosure specifies. The Commission recog-nizes, and indeed emphasizes, that the holder of a record cannot and should not bear the burden of deciding what information to disclose when presented with a valid authorization statement of the type the Commission recommends. The main problem is that some keepers of records that contain intimate personal details routinely disclose much more information about individuals than they are asked for, simply as a matter of convenience and economy. The Commission, therefore, has established the principle of limited disclosure as a general tenet of fair record-keeping practice.

The Commission's fairness recommendations generally call for reasonable procedures to assure accuracy, timeliness, and completeness in records of information about individuals. For example, in the public sector, the Commission recommends that reasonable procedures be an affirmative management obligation, while in the private sector, it relies on the rights it recommends for individuals to assure that organizations adopt reasonable procedures.

The Commission believes that by opening up record-keeping practices and by giving an individual opportunities to interact easily with a record keeper, particularly at crucial points in a record-keeping relationship, both individuals and organizations will benefit. The quality of the information in records will be improved while at the same time the individual and the organization will both be protected from errors or other deficiencies that can have untoward consequences for both.

Legitimizing Expectations of Confidentiality

The third public-policy objective, protecting confidentiality, pertains to the disclosure of information about an individual without his consent. Confidential treatment of recorded information is necessary for the maintenance of many kinds of relationships between individuals and organizations. The medical-care relationship, for example, often demands uninhibited candor from the individual about the most intimate details of his private life. There are also relationships between individuals and organizations that depend on the accumulation of extremely detailed records about the individual's activities, such as those compiled by a bank or by an independent credit-card issuer. The records of these relationships provide a revealing, if often incomplete, portrait of the individual, often touching on his beliefs and interests as well as his actions. While in theory these relationships are voluntary, in reality an individual today has little choice but to establish them as he would be severely, and perhaps insurmountably, disadvantaged if he did not.

There is also the fact that many of the records about individuals which these record keepers now maintain are the kinds of records the individual formerly would have kept in his exclusive possession. The transactional record a checking account creates, for example, would have existed a century ago in the form of receipts or, at most, ledger entries kept by the individual himself at home.

As long as records remained in his possession, both law and societal values recognized his right to control their use and disclosure. Government in particular was restricted in its ability to gain access to them, even to facilitate a criminal prosecution. When organizations began to maintain such records, however, the individual began to lose control over who might see and use them. The balance society had deemed crucial was disrupted.

Although individuals have tended to retain the old value system, expecting certain records to be held in confidence by the organizations that now maintain them, the law has not taken account of that fact. The protections that exist still apply in almost all instances only to records in the individual's exclusive possession. The lack of a legal interest for the individual in the records organizations maintain about him has put him in an extremely vulnerable position. The scale and impersonality of organizational record keeping today allows him little opportunity to influence an organization's own use and disclosure practices, and as the *Miller* case showed, he has no interest whatsoever to assert when government demands access to the records an organization maintains about him. The *Miller* case said, in effect, that government no longer has to operate within the strictures of the Fourth and

Fifth Amendments when it wants to acquire financial records pertaining to an individual; that what were once his private papers are now open to government scrutiny. What amounts to mere curiosity will suffice as justification if government agents want to see them.

To help redress the imbalances between individuals and organizations on one hand, and individuals, organizations and government on the other, the Commission recommends in this report that a legally enforceable "expectation of confidentiality" be created in several areas. The concept of a legally enforceable expectation of confidentiality has two distinct, though complementary, elements. The first is an enforceable duty of the record keeper which preserves the record keeper's ability to protect itself from improper actions by the individual, but otherwise restricts its discretion to disclose a record about him voluntarily. The second is a legal interest in the record for the individual which he can assert to protect himself against improper or unreasonable demands for disclosure by government or anyone else. The Commission has concluded that without this combination of duty and assertible interest, the law as it stands now will continue to deprive the individual of any opportunity to participate in decisions of organizations to disclose records kept about him, whether the disclosure is voluntary or in response to an authoritative demand.

The Commission specifies what it considers to be the proper terms of the individual's enforceable expectation in relationships with credit grantors, depository institutions, insurers, medical-care providers, the Internal Revenue Service, and providers of long-distance telephone service. Once again the recommendations are tailored to the particulars of each kind of record-keeping relationship. In each case, the Commission recommends that a protectible legal interest for the individual be created by statute; specifies the voluntary disclosures it believes should be permissible without the individual's consent and the procedures for establishing them; and sets forth the rules for initiating and complying with government demands for access to records. In no instance, however, does the Commission advocate complete, unilateral control by the individual. In every case it has respected the record-keeping organization's legitimate interests when threatened by actions of the individual. In essence, the Commission has said that the individual's interest must be recognized; that there must be procedures to force conflicting claims into the open; and that within this framework established by public policy, value conflicts should be resolved on a case-by-case basis.

Competing Public-Policy Interests

A major theme of this report is that privacy, both as a societal value and as an individual interest, does not and cannot exist in a vacuum. Indeed, "privacy" is a poor label for many of the issues the Commission addresses because to many people the concept connotes isolation and secrecy, whereas the relationships the Commission is concerned with are inherently social. Because they are, moreover, the privacy protections afforded them must be balanced against other significant societal values and interests. The Commission has identified five such competing societal values that must be taken into account in formulating public policy to protect personal privacy: (1) First Amendment interests; (2) freedom of information interests; (3) the societal interest in law enforcement; (4) cost; and (5) Federal-State relations.

The First Amendment and Privacy

The legitimate expectation of confidentiality is a concept the Commission endorses for several of the record-keeping relationships examined in this report. The policy objective is that when the relationship is one involving confidentiality of records, the record keeper shall be constrained from disclosing information about an individual without his authorization, either voluntarily or in response to a demand for it. The Commission recognizes that recommending any restriction on the free flow of truthful information raises serious questions in a democratic society, and sought ways to avoid conflict with both the goals of the First Amendment to the Constitution, and with the policy of broad access to public information articulated in statutes like the Freedom of Information Act.

When the Commission recommends rules to govern a record keeper's voluntary disclosure of a record about an individual, it does not attempt to specify, nor does it assign to either government or the individual the responsibility of determining which information in the record may or may not be disclosed. Neither does the Commission recommend any liability for third parties who merely receive information or records generated by a confidential relationship. The Commission's recommendations simply specify *to whom* information may be disclosed without the individual's consent. The role of government in the enforcement of a recommended expectation of confidentiality would be simply to act, through the courts, as referee in disputes between a record keeper and an individual about whether an expectation is legitimate and whether it has been violated. Government would have no independent interest to enforce, and would take no enforcement initiative, except where deception or misrepresentation is used to acquire medical records without the patient's consent. Only the individual would have an enforceable interest.

The Commission takes great care to avoid recommendations that would amount to regulating the content of records collected, maintained, or disclosed by private-sector organizations because of two related considerations, one abstract, the other concrete. The first consideration is that a democratic society must keep governmental intrusion into the flow of information to a minimum; the second is that the First Amendment sharply limits such government intrusion. Of importance here are the recent decisions of the U.S. Supreme Court that have found private commercial information flows as deserving of First Amendment protections as the personal exercise of the right of free speech.

In simplified terms, the First Amendment prohibits the Federal government (and through the Fourteenth Amendment, the States) from enacting any law which would abridge the right to communicate information to others or to receive information from others.[8] Broad as it is, this interpretation of the right to free speech does not mean the right is unlimited. It allows for such familiar strictures on the content of information exchanges as prohibiting slanderous or libelous communications, and, more pertinent to the question here, it allows for certain regulation of the *process* of communication when it occurs in a public forum. In other words, government may properly regulate the flow of information to the extent its regulations apply only to the process of communication in public places.

In addition, the Supreme Court has been willing to accept some government actions which require private organizations to comply with the decision *an individual* has made regarding the communications he does not want to receive. In *Lamont v. Postmaster General,*[9] for example, the issue was the constitutionality of a Federal statute requiring the

Postal Service to prevent firms from mailing material to individuals who have indicated that they do not want it because they consider it obscene. Because the statute leaves all determinations about content to the individual and requires the Postal Service only to see that the individual's wishes are respected, the Supreme Court held the statute constitutional. In other words, it is not unconstitutional to give an individual standing to assert his own interest in the flow of communication between private parties.

Individuals and organizations that do not engage in commercial activities have traditionally enjoyed the full range of constitutional free speech protections. For commercial entities, however, First Amendment protections have been virtually nonexistent[10] until a few years ago when the U.S. Supreme Court, in *Virginia State Board of Pharmacy v. Virginia Citizens Consumer Council,*[11] declared that the doctrine denying First Amendment protection to commercial speech had been swept away. In sweeping it away, the Court did, however, indicate that some restrictions on commercial communications are legitimate, though it left the standards for such restriction unclear.

The Court in the Virginia case stressed that the decision did not mean that a regulation prohibiting the advertising of an illegal activity would be unconstitutional. In 1974, in *Pittsburgh Press v. Human Relations Commission,*[12] there was a challenge to a municipal ordinance prohibiting the publication of lists of job openings by sex unless the designations were based on *bona fide* occupational considerations. The Court rejected the First Amendment challenge and sustained the ordinance. The majority opinion described the advertisements as "classic examples of commercial speech" and went on to note that commercial advertising ordinarily enjoys some First Amendment protection. What made this particular advertising susceptible to regulation was the illegitimacy of the activity advertised. In effect, the Court argued that if a commercial activity is illegal, then speech which promotes or assists in effecting such activity may be prohibited.

Such a rationale is not entirely satisfactory. Is the decision of the legislature that a certain commercial activity is illegal enough to deny communication concerning that activity free speech and free press protections? If the illegal activity is in part a result of the mere communication of information or ideas, should First Amendment analyses apply? Or should some other standard be employed to test the propriety of the legislative determination restricting communication? In any case, since the illegal-activity standard of *Pittsburgh Press* applies only to commercial communication, this test appears to establish that commercial speech remains doctrinally outside the mainstream of the First Amendment in some ways.

The Commission believes that the extension of First Amendment protections to commercial communication as defined in these recent Supreme Court cases, which almost exclusively concern advertising, does not pose any obstacle to the establishment of legitimate expectations of confidentiality for individuals in the private sector. The Commission is in no instance recommending an absolute restriction on the communication of information; rather, it recommends that an individual be informed at the beginning of a relationship what information may be disclosed from records about him and for what purposes. Following *Lamont,* it also recommends that an individual be given an opportunity to participate in any change that would materially affect his legitimate expectation.

Protection of privacy against *government* intrusions is a complementary limitation to protection of communications from government interference. Therefore, the Commission further recommends that if the requestor of records is a government agency, such agency bear the burden of notifying the individual, and that laws be enacted to allow the individual standing to assert his interest as defined in the recommended measures. This clearly raises no First Amendment issues.

Freedom of Information and Privacy

The second competing societal value the Commission identified is freedom of information. In enacting the Freedom of Information Act (FOIA) in 1966,[13] and strengthening it eight years later, the Congress gave expression to society's strong interest in opening the records of Federal government agencies to public inspection. The FOIA, to be sure, allows for exceptions from the general openness rule which an agency may invoke for certain information pertaining to national defense and foreign policy, law enforcement, individuals, internal agency deliberations, trade secrets, and information specifically declared confidential by other statutes. The withholding of exempt records, however, is subject to administrative and judicial review. Most of the States have enacted their own FOIA statutes in one form or another. Other statutes, both Federal and State, open meetings of certain governmental bodies to the public. The legal actions brought to test these statutes have shown the courts to be generally sympathetic to broadening public access to government records and deliberations, and, of course, journalists are natural advocates to full access and disclosure. Altogether, the presumption against secrecy in decision making and record keeping by government agencies is now firmly established.

The Commission has recommended the continuation of restrictions on the disclosure of specific records about individuals maintained by government agencies. While this recommendation may seem to conflict with the principle of freedom of information and openness, the Commission firmly believes that it is compatible with those principles and, indeed, that they are complementary aspects of a coherent public policy concerning public records.

In the Federal government, adjustments between freedom of information policy and confidentiality policy are made at two levels. At the first of these levels, the Federal FOIA makes adjustments by incorporating several statutes which, with particularity, direct that specific records be withheld from the public. The Federal FOIA does not require the disclosure of matters that are:

> specifically exempted from disclosure by statute (other than section 552b of this title), provided that such statute (A) requires that the matter be withheld from the public in such a manner as to leave no discretion on the issue, or (B) establishes particular criteria for withholding or refers to particular types of matters to be withheld. *[5 U.S.C. 552(b)(3)(1976)]*

Tax returns and the responses of individual households to Census Bureau inquiries fall into this category. The Commission believes that it is preferable for the Congress to create this sort of explicit confidentiality policy than for government administrators to decide when such records should or should not be disclosed.

The second level at which freedom of information and privacy interests relate becomes apparent when a Federal agency receives a legitimate Freedom of Information Act request for access to a record about an individual and finds that the record is subject to the Privacy Act of 1974. When the two Acts are read together any disclosure of a record about an individual in a system of records as defined by the Privacy Act to any member of the public other than the individual to whom the record pertains is forbidden if the disclosure would constitute a "clearly unwarranted invasion of personal privacy." The reverse obligation also holds: even though a record is about an individual, it cannot be withheld from any member of the public who requests it if the disclosure would *not* constitute a clearly unwarranted invasion of personal privacy. The courts are the final arbiters of which disclosures do or do not meet the unwarranted-invasion test and over the years they have established certain types of recorded information which *must* be disclosed without question. Two examples are Civil Service grades of Federal employees, and the names of persons who have participated in elections supervised by the National Labor Relations Board.

For government, the Commission believes that the policy of combining explicit legislation for particular types of records with a general standard to be applied in all other cases is an appropriate way to balance the freedom of information interests and confidentiality interests. . . . the combination does not lead to resolution of difficult cases overnight, but it does create a framework within which the conflicts between the two competing though compatible interests can be resolved.

The general concept of freedom of information has no currency in the private sector. Issuers of regulated securities must publicly disclose particular items of information about the individuals who control or manage companies, but organizations in the private sector by and large have no affirmative obligation to disclose their records about individuals to the public. They may be required to disclose such records to government agencies for a variety of reasons, . . . but in many cases government is prohibited from subsequently disclosing that information to the public. Thus, in the private sector there is no freedom of information policy to conflict with a confidentiality of records policy.

Indeed, the Commission believes that in most instances the persuasive power of an active press can be relied on to work out a proper adjustment between the right to privacy and the freedom of information principle as it applies to public disclosure of information in records about individuals maintained by private-sector organizations. However, the Commission also believes that the individual needs some limited control over the public disclosure of particular types of information about him. An individual should be able to limit the public disclosure of credit, insurance, medical, employment, and education record information about himself. In these areas, the Commission has recommended for the individual an assertible interest so that he can have a role in determining whether information about him should be publicly released. In fact, as to certain identifying information referred to as *directory information,* the Commission's recommendations recognize the general practice of public disclosure in such areas as employment, medical care, and education. Thus, reporters should be able to continue to find out who is in what hospital, who is employed by what firm, and who is enrolled in what school.

The Commission's recommendations, with one exception, do not limit or affect the ability of the press to request or obtain information. The area of medical records is the one area where the Commission not only recommends a duty on the record keeper to respect an individual's expectation of confidentiality but also suggests that it be made a crime to seek such information through misrepresentation or deception. Specific abuses by persons seeking medical-record information for use in adversary situations have led the Commission to conclude that such a recommendation is necessary. In all other cases, the

Commission's recommendations do not limit or affect the ability of the press to request or obtain information. These balances are difficult to strike and the Commission has attempted to establish mechanisms for doing so rather than recommend specific disclosure prohibitions.

Law Enforcement and Privacy

The third competing interest the Commission identified is the interest in preventing and prosecuting crime. Organizations do and should have the means of protecting themselves from suspected fraud in insurance claims, fraudulent use of credit cards, multiple welfare applications, and the like. Organizations, both private and public, exchange information among themselves and with law enforcement authorities to protect against such losses and to assist in the prosecution of crime. The Commission has not suggested that this organizational interest be curtailed. Rather, it recommends that individuals be apprised, at the time they establish a relationship involving confidential records that information about them may be disclosed for investigative or enforcement purposes if the record keeper develops evidence that points to criminal behavior on their part.

Government requests or demands for recorded information about individuals for law enforcement purposes pose a special problem. As a result of the *Miller* decision discussed earlier, an individual has no constitutional protections against government demands for access to records third parties maintain about him. There are some statutory protections, such as those for census records, Federal income-tax returns, and records developed in connection with federally funded drug abuse research and treatment programs. The Commission believes, however, that the individual should have an assertible interest in other types of records about him, such as those maintained by financial institutions, insurance companies, medical-care providers, and providers of long-distance telephone service, as a matter of general policy.

Government agencies have testified that to enforce the law, they need full and complete access to records kept about individuals by third parties. They argue that to restrict their access, or more specifically to subject it to the assertion of an individual's interest, would unduly handicap their legitimate law enforcement activities. The Commission seriously considered these arguments and has developed a set of recommendations that allow for continued law enforcement access, but under stricter rules. These rules are in two parts. First, they require law enforcement agencies to use legal process of some form whenever they seek information about an individual from a third-party record keeper. Second, when they seek access to records in which the individual has legitimate expectation of confidentiality, the Commission recommends that the individual involved be given notice and the legal capacity to contest the action. The Commission has not recommended prohibiting government access, but rather giving the individual an assertible interest in the process of government information gathering about him. The requirement for legal process in all instances has the further advantage that it creates the basis for meaningful accountability mechanisms.

The Cost of Privacy

The fourth competing interest the Commission identified is cost. In maximizing fairness, this is the most compelling competing interest. Whether an organization is public or private, to make changes in record-keeping practices can increase its cost of operation and thus make the product or service it provides either more expensive or less accessible, or both. When this happens, both the record-keeping organization and some if not all of its customers or clients suffer. Adoption of the Commission's recommendations means that a great many organizations will have to make some changes in their record keeping. The costs of compliance will be higher or lower depending on how well an organization's current practices reflect the recommended balance between organizational interests and the individual's interest. The Commission has tried to keep compliance costs to a minimum by not recommending that organizations be required to report periodically to Federal or State government agencies, and also by not recommending inflexible procedural requirements.

The Commission's recommendations are aimed at getting results. Thus, they try to take advantage of the shared interest of individuals and organizations in keeping records accurate, timely, and complete. As previously noted, one reason for giving an individual a right of access to records about him is that doing so affords an organization the free help of an expert—the individual himself—on the accuracy of the information the organization uses to make decisions about him. Organizations, however, need some assurance before they are willing to enlist such help that it will not turn out to be unduly or undeservedly expensive.

To open an insurance company's underwriting files to inspection by applicants and policyholders, for example, gives the company a powerful motive to record only accurate, pertinent information about them and to keep its records as timely and complete as necessary. To encourage applicants and policyholders to look for information in underwriting files that could serve as the basis for defamation actions and windfall recoveries, however, would be contrary to the Commission's cost-minimizing objective and also an impediment to systemic reform. *The Commission wants organizations to invest in improving their record-keeping practices; not to spend their money in costly litigation over past practices and honest mistakes.* Hence the Commission's recommendation is to limit the liability of a record keeper that responds to an individual's request for access to a record it maintains about him.

Organizations in the private sector have a strong interest in keeping their decisions about customers, clients, applicants, or employees free of unreasonable government interference. The Commission's recommendations recognize this interest by concentrating on the quality of the information an organization uses as the basis for making a decision about an individual, rather than on the decision itself. For private-sector organizations the adverse-decision requirements the Commission recommends will expose the records used in arriving at a decision to reject an applicant, but the Commission relies on the incentives of the marketplace to prompt reconsideration of a rejection if it turns out to have been made on the basis of inaccurate or otherwise defective information.

For public-sector organizations, the Commission recommends no affirmative requirement that they reverse an adverse decision made on the basis of faulty information. For educational institutions, where the procedures for correcting or amending records are likely to be divorced from decision-making procedures, and where the individual has no easily invokable due process protections, the Commission proposes an affirmative requirement to *reconsider* but not a requirement to *reverse*. The Commission strongly believes that to mix concern about the outcome of individual decisions with concern about the quality of the information used in arriving at them not only risks undesirable interference with organizational prerogatives but also invites confusion as to the nature and extent of the individual's privacy interest, possibly to its detriment in the long run.

Federal-State Relations and Privacy

A major interest that must be weighed in the balance of organizations' needs for information against the individual's interest in having his personal privacy protected is society's interest in maintaining the integrity of the Federal system. The division of responsibility and authority between the Federal government and States is a cornerstone of the American political system and the Commission has been particularly attentive to it in both the methods it recommends for establishing legal requirements and the regulatory mechanisms and sanctions for enforcing such requirements.

In areas of record keeping where the States are prominent record keepers, or where records are generated in carrying out State programs, the Commission pays particular attention to the reserved-powers principle enunciated in the Tenth Amendment to the Constitution, emulating the Supreme Court's care[14] not to interfere with the conduct of essential State government functions. Thus, where Federal regulation seems necessary, the Commission recommends making the requirements a condition of Federal benefits, which leaves the States some degree of choice. The Commission recommends tempering such exercise of Federal spending power by leaving considerable latitude in how the States implement the policies, and by urging them to make the minimum Federal requirements part of their own State legislation and to assume most of the responsibility for enforcing them.

In the areas of private-sector record keeping where the States share regulatory power with the Federal government, the Commission recommends maintaining the current balance. For example, in financial areas where the Federal government now does most of the regulating, the Commission relies heavily on current Federal mechanisms in the implementation of the measures it recommends, with the State playing a supplemental role. In the insurance area, where the States now do most of the regulating, the Commission recognizes a need for some limited Federal intervention in order to provide the necessary uniformity, but relies on the State enforcement mechanisms that now have primary responsibility.

Each of the implementation measures the Commission recommends is designed to avoid disturbance of the current Federal-State political balance of power. Indeed, the structure of the Commission's recommendations as a whole should strengthen the Federal-State partnership and increase the State's role in protecting the interests of the individual. . . .

Notes

1. For a discussion of the fair hearing procedures, see Chapter 11.
2. *Bank Secrecy Act,* 12 U.S.C. 1829b, 1953; 12 C.F.R. §103.36.
3. *California Bankers Association v. Schultz,* 416 U.S. 21 (1975).
4. *State ex rel. Tarver v. Smith* 78 Wash. 2d 152, 470 P.2d 172, *cert. denied,* 402 U.S. 1001 (1971); *United States v. Miller,* 425 U.S. 435 (1976).
5. See Chapter 4.

6. For an analysis of the Privacy Act principles, see Chapter 13.
7. U.S. Department of Health, Education and Welfare, Secretary's Advisory Committee on Automated Personal Data Systems, *Records, Computers, and the Rights of Citizens* (Washington, D.C.: 1973), p. 41. The five fair information principles were: (1) there must be no personal-data record-keeping systems whose very existence is secret; (2) there must be a way for an individual to find out what information about him is in a record and how it is used; (3) there must be a way for an individual to prevent information about him obtained for one purpose from being used or made available for other purposes, without his consent; (4) there must be a way for an individual to correct or amend a record of identifiable information about him; and (5) any organization creating, maintaining, using, or disseminating records of identifiable personal data must assure the reliability of the data for their intended use and must take reasonable precautions to prevent misuse of the data.
8. See, e.g., *Stanley v. Georgia,* 394 U.S. 557 (1969); *Kliendist v. Mandel,* 408 U.S. 753 (1972); *Cox Broadcasting Corp. v. Cohn,* 420 U.S. 469 (1975).
9. 391 U.S. 301 (1965).
10. Thomas I. Emerson, *The System of Freedom of Expression* (New York: Vintage, 1970), p. 414.
11. 425 U.S. 748 (1976).
12. 413 U.S. 376 (1973).
13. 5 U.S.C. 552.
14. *National League of Cities v. Usery,* 426 U.S. 833 (1976).

Computers and Power

I N THE INTRODUCTION to Part 3, we suggested that the privacy issue may at base be a power issue—that is, an issue having to do with computers enhancing the power of large bureaucratic organizations in their dealings with individuals. In Part 4 we turn to a set of questions that explicitly concern how computers affect the distribution of power. For the most part, the issues here are not concerned simply with the record-keeping capability of computers, but rather with other uses such as communications, budget and planning, and statistical analysis. In the late 1960s and early 1970s, when a good deal of public concern was being expressed about computers and privacy, this concern was often expressed as a fear of increasing power for government and, hence, increasing centralization. Concern centered on the suggestion that computers tend to facilitate, support, or even promote centralization of power. Later, in reaction and perhaps as the technology itself changed, arguments were presented which suggested that computers could be an enormous tool for decentralization of power.

To introduce this issue we have chosen an excerpt from Joseph Weizenbaum's *Computer Power and Human Reason,* which was one of the first works to express concern about the impact of computers on our society. At first reading this excerpt may seem to support the claim that computers favor centralization of power. Certainly, Weizenbaum's examples of the military bureaucracy, the welfare system, and the stock and commodities exchange suggest that we might have been forced to decentralize those institutions if the computer had not come along when it did. However, a second reading of Weizenbaum may suggest more subtle and in some ways more troubling concerns. Weizenbaum seems concerned that computers tend to reinforce the status quo. They resist change. He makes us wonder whether computers have caused a so-called "revolution" or whether in fact they have slowed fundamental changes in the structure of our society and our way of life.

Next we have included a short selection from Abbe Mowshowitz's *Conquest of the Will*. This provides an example of some typical arguments for centralization and decentralization. The reading by Herbert Simon provides a more concrete discussion of centralization and decentralization by clarifying the meaning of centralization and decentralization, by providing a number of useful examples, and by arguing that whether computers tend toward one or the other depends on what we mean by centralization or decentralization of power.

Rob Kling takes us in a somewhat different direction, for he is concerned not so much with centralization-decentralization of power as with the fact that a computerized system will affect power relationships and will favor or incorporate some values over others. Whose values are built into the system, of course, has everything to do with the hierarchical structure of the organization. When we design computer systems we should be aware of the subtle ways the system may favor some values over others and may affect relationships in an organization.

In a quite different vein, building on the idea of computers as a powerful tool that may affect one's competitive advantage, we have included a rather alarming piece from *Time*. Whatever else we say about computers and power, it would seem true that as the use of computers increases, having skill at using computers may be very important for getting a job. As our society becomes even more computerized than it is now, having access to a computer and knowing how to use a computer may become critical for having power, even over one's own life. Thus, the question of which children we educate about computers and how we do so may become a matter of justice. If we aren't careful, computers will further widen the gap between haves and have nots in our society. Finally, Herbert Schiller suggests that the gap between rich developed nations and poor developing nations may, also, be widened in incredible proportion by increasing dependence on computer technology.

---

23. *Excerpt from* Computer Power and Human Reason

Joseph Weizenbaum

"EVERY THINKER," JOHN Dewey wrote, "puts some portion of an apparently stable world in peril and no one can predict what will emerge in its place." So too does everyone who invents a new tool or, what amounts to the same thing, finds a new use for an old one.

From *Computer Power and Human Reason: From Judgement to Calculation* (San Francisco: W. H. Freeman, 1976), pp. 26–38. Notes deleted. Copyright © 1976. Reprinted by permission of W. H. Freeman and Company.

The long historical perspective which aids our understanding of Classical antiquity, of the Middle Ages, and of the beginnings of the Modern Age also helps us to formulate plausible hypotheses to account for the new realities which emerged in those times to replace older ones imperiled by the introduction of new tools. But as we approach the task of understanding the warp and woof of the stories that tell, on the one hand, of the changing consciousness of modern man, and, on the other, of the development of contemporary tools and particularly of the computer, our perspective necessarily flattens out. We have little choice but to project the lessons yielded by our understanding of the past, our plausible hypotheses, onto the present and the future. And the difficulty of that task is vastly increased by the fact that modern tools impact on society far more critically in a much shorter time than earlier ones did.

The impulse the clock contributed toward the alienation of man from nature required centuries to penetrate and decisively affect mankind as a whole. And even then, it had to synergistically combine with many other emerging factors to exercise its influence. The steam engine arrived when, in the common-sense view, time and space were already quantified. An eternal nature governed by immutable laws of periodicity implied a mandate, one made explicit in holy books and exercised by institutional vicars of the eternal order. That quasi-constitutional, hence constrained, authority had long since been displaced by, for example, the relatively unconstrained authority of money, i.e., of value quantified, and especially the value of a man's labor quantified. These and many other circumstances combined to make it possible for the steam engine to eventually transform society radically. Later tools, e.g., the telephone, the automobile, radio, impinged on a culture already enthralled by what economists call the pig principle: if something is good, more is better. The hunger for more communication capacity and more speed, often stimulated by the new devices themselves, as well by new marketing techniques associated with them, enabled their rapid spread throughout society and society's increasingly rapid transformation under their influence.

When the first telegraph line connecting Texas with New York was laid, doubts were expressed as to whether the people in those places would have anything to say to one another. But by the time the digital computer emerged from university laboratories and entered the American business, military, and industrial establishments, there were no doubts about its potential utility. To the contrary, American managers and technicians agreed that the computer had come along just in time to avert catastrophic crises: were it not for the timely introduction of computers, it was argued, not enough people could have been found to staff the banks, the ever increasingly complex communication and logistic problems of American armed forces spread all over the world could not have been met, and trading on the stock and commodity exchanges could not have been maintained. The American corporation was faced with a "command and control" problem similar to that confronting its military counterpart. And like the Pentagon, it too was increasingly diversified and internationalized. Unprecedentedly large and complex computational tasks awaited American society at the end of the Second World War, and the computer, almost miraculously it would seem, arrived just in time to handle them.

In fact, huge managerial, technological, and scientific problems had been solved without the aid of electronic computers in the decades preceding the Second World War and especially during the war itself. A dominant fraction of the industrial plant of the United

States was coordinated to provide the tools of war—foodstuffs, clothing, etc.—and to supply the required transport to vast armies spread all over the globe. The Manhattan Project produced the atomic bomb without using electronic computers; yet the scientific and engineering problems solved under its auspices required probably more computations than had been needed for all astronomical calculations performed up to that time. The magnitude of its managerial task surely rivaled that of the Apollo Project of the sixties. Most people today probably believe that the Apollo Project could not have been managed without computers. The history of the Manhattan Project seems to contradict that belief. There are corresponding beliefs about the need for computers in the management of large corporations and of the military, about the indispensability of computers in modern scientific computations, and, indeed, about the impossibility of pursuing modern science and modern commerce at all without the aid of computers.[1]

The belief in the indispensability of the computer is not entirely mistaken. The computer becomes an indispensable component of any structure once it is so thoroughly integrated with the structure, so enmeshed in various vital substructures, that it can no longer be factored out without fatally impairing the whole structure. That is virtually a tautology. The utililty of this tautology is that it can reawaken us to the possibility that some human actions, e.g., the introduction of computers into some complex human activities, may constitute an irreversible commitment. It is not true that the American banking system or the stock and commodity markets or the great manufacturing enterprises would have collapsed had the computer not come along "just in time." It is true that the specific way in which these systems actually developed in the past two decades, and are still developing, would have been impossible without the computer. It is true that, were all computers to suddenly disappear, much of the modern industrialized and militarized world would be thrown into great confusion and possibly utter chaos. The computer was not a prerequisite to the survival of modern society in the postwar period and beyond: its enthusiastic, uncritical embrace by the most "progressive" elements of American government, business, and industry quickly made it a resource essential to society's survival *in the form* that the computer itself had been instrumental in shaping.

In 1947 J. W. Forrester wrote a memorandum to the U.S. Navy "On the Use of Electronic Digital Computers as Automatic Combat Information Centers." Commenting on subsequent developments in 1961, he wrote,

> one could probably not have found [in 1947] five military officers who would have acknowledged the possibility of a machine's being able to analyze the available information sources, the proper assignment of weapons, the generation of command instructions, and the coordination of adjacent areas of military operations. . . . During the following decade the speed of military operations increased until it became clear that, regardless of the assumed advantages of human judgment decisions, the internal communication speed of the human organization simply was not able to cope with the pace of modern air warfare. This inability to act provided the incentive.

The decade of which Forrester speaks was filled with such incentives, with discoveries that existing human organizations were approaching certain limits to their ability to cope with the ever faster pace of modern life. The image Forrester invokes is of small teams of men hurrying to keep up with events but falling ever further behind because things are happening too fast and there is too much to do. They have reached the limit of the team's "internal speed." Perhaps this same imagery may serve as a provocative characterization also for teams of bank clerks frantically sorting and posting checks in the middle of the night, attacking ever larger mountains of checks that must, according to law, be cleared by a fixed deadline. Perhaps all, or at least many, of the limits of other kinds that were being approached during that decade may usefully be so characterized. After all, it is ultimately the "internal speed" of some human organization that will prove the limiting factor when, say, an automobile firm attempts to run a production line capable of producing an astronomical variety of cars at a high and constant rate, or when, say, some central government agency takes the responsibility for guarding millions of welfare clients against the temptation to cheat by closely monitoring both their welfare payments and whatever other income they may, possibly illicitly, receive.

The "inability to act" which, as Forrester points out, "provided the incentive" to augment or replace the low-internal-speed human organizations with computers, might in some other historical situation have been an incentive for modifying the task to be accomplished, perhaps doing away with it altogether, or for restructuring the human organizations whose inherent limitations were, after all, seen as the root of the trouble. It may be that the incentive provided by the military's inability to cope with the increasing complexity of air warfare in the 1950's could have been translated into a concern, not for mustering techniques to enable the military to keep up with their traditional missions, but for inventing new human organizations with new missions, missions relevant to more fundamental questions about how peoples of diverse interests are to live with one another. But the computer was used to build, in the words of one air force colonel, "a servomechanism spread out over an area comparable to the whole American continent," that is, the SAGE air-defense system. Of course, once "we" had such a system, we had to assume "they" had one too. We therefore had to apply our technology to designing offensive weapons and strategies that could overpower "our" defenses, i.e., "their" presumed defenses. We then had to assume that "they" had similar weapons and strategies and therefore . . . , and so on to today's MIRVs and MARVs and ABMs.

It may be that the people's cultivated and finally addictive hunger for private automobiles could have been satiated by giving them a choice among, say, a hundred vehicles that actually differ substantially from one another, instead of a choice among the astronomical number of basically identical "models" that differ only trivially from one another. Indeed, perhaps the private automobile could have been downgraded as a means of personal transportation in favor of mass transit in, and the passenger rail between, the cities. But the computer was used to automate the flow of parts to automobile production lines so that people could choose from among millions of trivial options on their new cars.

It may be that social services such as welfare could have been administered by humans exercising human judgment if the dispensing of such services were organized around decentralized, indigenous population groupings, such as neighborhoods and natural regions. But the computer was used to automate the administration of social services and to centralize it along established political lines. If the computer had not facilitated the perpetuation and "improvement" of existing welfare distribution systems—hence of their philosophical rationales—perhaps someone might have thought of eliminating much of the need for welfare by, for example, introducing negative income tax. The very erection of an enormously large and complex computer based welfare administration apparatus, however, created an interest in its maintenance and therefore in the perpetuation of the welfare system itself. And such interests soon become substantial barriers to innovation even if good reasons to innovate later accumulate. In other words, many of the problems of growth and complexity that pressed insistently and irresistibly for response during the postwar decades could have served as incentives for social and political innovation. An enormous acceleration of social invention, had it begun then, would now seem to us as natural a consequence of man's predicament in that time as does the flood of technological invention and innovation that was actually stimulated.

Yes, the computer did arrive "just in time." But in time for what? In time to save— and save very nearly intact, indeed, to entrench and stabilize—social and political structures that otherwise might have been either radically renovated or allowed to totter under the demands that were sure to be made on them. The computer, then, was used to conserve America's social and political institutions. It buttressed them and immunized them, at least temporarily, against enormous pressures for change. Its influence has been substantially the same in other societies that have allowed the computer to make substantial inroads upon their institutions: Japan and Germany immediately come to mind.

The invention of the computer put a portion of an apparently stable world in peril, as it is the function of almost every one of man's creative acts to do. And, true to Dewey's dictum, no one could have predicted what would emerge in its place. But of the many paths to social innovation it opened to man, the most fateful was to make it possible for him to eschew all deliberate thought of substantive change. That was the option man chose to exercise. The arrival of the Computer Revolution and the founding of the Computer Age have been announced many times. But if the triumph of a revolution is to be measured in terms of the profundity of the social revisions it entrained, then there has been no computer revolution. And however the present age is to be characterized, the computer is not eponymic of it.

To say that the computer was initially used mainly to do things pretty much as they had always been done, except to do them more rapidly or, by some criteria, more efficiently, is not to distinguish it from other tools. Only rarely, if indeed ever, are a tool and an altogether original job it is to do, invested together. Tools as symbols, however, invite their imaginative displacements into other than their original contexts. In their new frames of reference, that is, as new symbols in an already established imaginative calculus, they may themselves be transformed, and may even transform the originally prescriptive calculus. These transformations may, in turn, create entirely new problems which then engender the invention of hitherto literally unimaginable tools. In 1804, a hundred years after the first stationary steam engines of Newcomen and Savery had found common use in England to, for example, pump water out of mines, Trevithik put a steam engine on a carriage and the carriage on the tracks of a horse-tramway in Wales. This ripping out of context of the stationary steam engine and its displacement into an entirely new context transformed the engine into a locomotive, and began the transformation of the horse-tramway into the modern railroad. And incidentally, since it soon became necessary to guard against collisions of trains traveling on the same track, a whole new signaling technology was stimulated. New problems had been created and, in response to them, new tools invented.

It is noteworthy that Thomas Savery, the builder of the first steam engine that was applied practically in industry (circa 1700), was also the first to use the term "horsepower" in approximately its modern sense. Perhaps the term arose only because there were so many horses when the steam engine replaced them, not only in its first incarnation as a stationary power source, but also in its reincarnation as a locomotive. Still, the term "horsepower," so very pointed in its suggestiveness, might well have provoked Trevithik's imagination to probe in the direction it finally moved, to make the creative leap that combined the steam engine and the horse-tramway in a single unified frame of reference. Invention involves the imaginative projection of symbols from one existing, and generally well-developed, frame of reference to another. It is to be expected that some potent symbols will survive the passage nearly intact, and will exert their influence on even the new framework.

Computers had horses of another color to replace. Before the first modern electronic digital computers became available for what we now call business data processing—that is, before the acquisition of UNIVAC I by the U.S. Bureau of the Census in 1951—many American businesses operated large so-called "tab rooms." These rooms housed machines that could punch the same kind of cards (now commonly, if often mistakenly, called IBM cards) that are still in use today, sort these cards according to arbitrary criteria, and "tabulate" decks of such cards, i.e., list the information they contained in long printed tables. Tab rooms produced mountains of management reports for American government and industry, using acres of huge clanking mechanical monsters. These machines could perform only one operation on a deck of cards at a time. They could, for example, sort the deck on a specific sorting key. If the sorted deck had to be further sorted according to yet another criterion, the new criterion had to be manually set into the machine and the deck fed through the machine once more. Tab rooms were the horse-tramways of business data processing, tab machines the horses.

In principle, even the earliest commercially available electronic computers, the UNIVAC I's, made entirely new and much more efficient data-processing techniques possible, just as, in principle, the earliest steam engines could already have been mounted on carriages and the carriages on tracks. Indeed, during and just after the Second World War, the arts of operation research and systems analysis, on which the sophisticated use of computers in business was ultimately grounded, were developed to very nearly their full maturity. Still, business used the early computers to simply "automate" its tab rooms, i.e., to perform exactly the earlier operations, only now automatically and, presumably, more efficiently. The crucial transition, from the business computer as a mere substitute for work-horse tab machines to its present status as a versatile information engine, began when the power of the computer was projected onto the framework already established by operations research and systems analysis.

It must be added here that although the railroad in England became important in its own right—it employed many workers, for example—it also enormously increased the importance of many other forms of transportation. Similarly, the synergistic combination of computers and systems analysis played a crucial role in the creation and growth of the computer industry. It also breathed a new vitality into systems analysis as such. During the first decade of the computer's serious invasion of business, when managers often decided their businesses needed computers even though they had only the flimsiest bases for such decisions, they also often undertook fairly penetrating systems analyses of their operations in order to determine what their new computers were to do. In a great many cases such studies revealed opportunities to improve operations, sometimes radically, without introducing computers at all. Nor were computers used in the studies themselves. Often, of course, computers were installed anyway for reasons of, say, fashion or prestige.

A side effect of this oft-repeated experience was to firmly establish systems analysis, and to a lesser extent operations research, as a methodology for making business decisions. As the prestige of systems analysis was fortified by its successes and as, simultaneously, the computer grew in power, the problems tackled by systems analysts became more and more complex, and the computer appeared an ever more suitable instrument to handle great complexity. Normally systems analysis appears, to the casual observer at least, to have been swallowed up by the computer. This appearance is misleading but not without significance. Systems analysis has survived and prospered as a discipline in its own right. The computer has put muscles on its techniques. It has so greatly strengthened them as to make them qualitatively different from their early manual counterparts. The latter, consequently, have largely disappeared. And the computer can no longer be factored out of the former.

The interaction of the computer with systems analysis is instructive from another point of view as well. It is important to understand very clearly that strengthening a particular technique—putting muscles on it—contributes nothing to its validity. For example, there are computer programs that carry out with great precision all the calculations required to cast the horoscope of an individual whose time and place of birth are known. Because the computer does all the tedious symbol manipulations, they can be done much more quickly and in much more detail than is normally possible for a human astrologer. But such an improvement in the technique of horoscope casting is irrelevant to the validity of astrological forecasting. If astrology is nonsense, then computerized astrology is just as surely nonsense. Now, sometimes certain simple techniques are invalid for the domains to which they are applied merely because of their very simplicity, whereas much more complicated techniques of the *same* kind are valid in those domains. That is not true for astrology, but may well be true of, say, numerical weather forecasting. For the latter, the number of data that must be taken into account, and the amount of computation that must be done on them in order to produce an accurate weather forecast, may well be so large that no team of humans, however large, could complete the computations in any reasonable time whatever. And any simplification of the technique sufficient to reduce the computational task to proportions manageable by humans would invalidate the technique itself. In such cases the computer may contribute to making a hitherto impractical technique practical. But what has to be remembered is that the validity of a technique is a question that involves the technique and its subject matter. If a bad idea is to be converted into a good one, the *source* of its weakness must be discovered and repaired. A person falling into a manhole is rarely helped by making it possible for him to fall faster or more efficiently.

It may seem odd, even paradoxical, that the enhancement of a technique may expose its weaknesses and limitations, but it should not surprise us. The capacity of the human mind for sloppy thinking and for rationalizing, for explaining away the consequences of its sloppy thinking, is very large. If a particular technique requires an enormous amount of computation and if only a limited computational effort can be devoted to it, then a failure of the technique can easily be explained away on the ground that, because of computational limitations, it was never really tested. The technique itself is immunized against critical examination by such evasions. Indeed, it may well be fortified, for the belief that an otherwise faultless and probably enormously powerful technique is cramped by some single limitation tends to lead the devotee to put effort into removing that limitation. When this limitation seems to him to be entirely computational, and when a computer is offered to help remove it, he may well launch a program of intensive, time-consuming "research" aimed simply at "computerizing" his technique. Such programs usually generate subproblems of a strictly computational nature that tend, by virtue of their very magnitude, to increasingly dominate the task and, unless great care is taken to avoid it, to eventually become the center of attention. As ever more investment is made in attacking these initially ancillary subproblems, and as progress is made in cracking them, an illusion tends to grow that real work is being done on the main problem. The poverty of the technique, if it is indeed impotent to deal with its presumed subject matter, is thus hidden behind a mountain of effort, much of which may well be successful in its own terms. But these are terms in a constructed context that has no substantive overlap with, or even relationship to, the context determined by the problem to which the original technique is to be applied. The collection of subproblems together with the lore, jargon, and subtechniques which crystalized around them, becomes reified. The larger this collection is, and the more human energy has been invested in its creation, the more real it seems. And the harder the subproblems were to solve and the more technical success was gained in solving them, the more is the original technique fortified.

I have discussed the role that tools play in man's imaginative reconstruction of his world and in the sharpening of his techniques. However, tools play another related role as well: they constitute a kind of language for the society that employs them, a language of social action. Later on I will say more about language. Let it suffice for now to characterize language somewhat incompletely as consisting of a vocabulary—the words of the language—and a set of rules that determine how individual vocabulary items may be concatenated to form meaningful sentences. I leave to one side for the moment the innumerable mysteries that surround the concept of meaning. I restrict myself to its narrowest conception, namely, that of the action which a particular "sentence" in the language of tools initiates and accomplishes.

Ordinary language gains its expressive power in part from the fact that each of its words has a restricted domain of meaning. It would be impossible to say anything in a language that consisted entirely of pronouns, for example. A tool too gains its power from the fact that it permits certain actions and not others. For example, a hammer has to be rigid. It can therefore not be used as a rope. There can be no such things as general-purpose tools, just as there can be no general-purpose words. We know that the use of specific words in vastly general ways, for example, such words as "like" and "y'know," impoverishes rather than enriches current American English.

Perhaps it is as difficult to invent truly new tools as it is to invent truly new words. But the twentieth century has witnessed the invention of at least a modest number of tools that do actually extend the range of action of which the society is capable. The automobile and the highway, radio and television, and modern drugs and surgical procedures immediately come to mind. These things have enabled society to articulate patterns of action that were never before possible. What is less often said, however, is that the society's newly created ways to act often eliminate the very possibility of acting in older ways. An analogous thing happens in ordinary language. For example, now that the word "inoperative" has been used by high government officials as a euphemism for the word "lie," it can no longer be used to communicate its earlier meaning. Terms like "free" (as in "the free world"), "final solution," "defense," and "aggression" have been so thoroughly debased by corrupt usage that they have become essentially useless for ordinary discourse. Similarly, a highway permits people to travel between the geographical centers it connects, but, because of the side effects that it and other factors synergistically engender, it imprisons poor people in inner cities as effectively as if the cities were walled in. The mass-communication media are sometimes said to have reduced the earth to a global village and to have enabled national and even global town meetings. But, in contrast to the traditional New England town meeting which was—and remains so in my home town—an exercise in *participatory* politics, the mass media permit essentially no talking back. Like highways and automobiles, they enable the society to articulate entirely new forms of social action, but at the same time they irreversibly disable formerly available modes of social behavior.

The computer is, in a sense, a tool of this kind. It helped pry open the door to outer space, and it saved certain societal institutions that were threatened with collapse under the weight of a rapidly growing population. But its impact has also closed certain doors that were once open . . . whether irreversibly or not, we cannot say with certainty. There is a myth that computers are today making important decisions of the kind that were earlier made by people. Perhaps there are isolated examples of that here and there in our society. But the widely believed picture of managers typing questions of the form "What shall we do now?" into their computers and then waiting for their computers to "decide" is largely wrong. What is happening instead is that people have turned the processing of information on which decisions must be based over to enormously complex computer systems. They have, with few exceptions, reserved for themselves the right to make decisions based on the outcome of such computing processes. People are thus able to maintain the illusion, and it is often just that, that they are after all the decisionmakers. But, as we shall argue, a computing system that permits the asking of only certain kinds of questions, that accepts only certain kinds of "data," and that cannot even in principle be understood by those who rely on it, such a computing system has effectively closed many doors that were open before it was installed. . . .

Note

1. I am sure that, had computers attained their present sophistication by 1940, technicians participating in the Manhattan Project would have sworn that it too would have been impossible without computers. And we would have had similarly fervent testimony from the designers of Second World War aircraft, and from the managers of logistics of that war. If Germany had had computers from the outset of Hitler's dictatorship, common sense would today hold that only with the aid of computers could the Nazis have controlled the German people and implemented the systematic transportation of millions of people to death camps and their subsequent murder. But the Second World War was fought, and the millions did die, when there were still no computers.

24. *Excerpts from* Conquest of the Will: Information Processing in Human Affairs

Abbe Mowshowitz

Centralization of Control

THE EFFECTS OF computer applications on the structure of control in the modern corporation is perhaps the most significant social issue associated with management information systems. Although the evidence is not completely unambiguous, there is substantial support for the conclusion that computers do contribute to centralized decision-making, at least in the short-run. Much of the disagreement over this issue stems from the difficulty of assessing the phenomenon in precise terms. The measures developed thus far tend to be crude, and do not adequately discriminate between the effects of computers and other characteristics of organizational change. This is especially problematic since the introduction of computer systems often affords an opportunity to reorganize departments or otherwise modify corporate structure in ways which are not always strictly essential to the operation of those systems. On the other hand, the changes accompanying computerized management systems may be regarded as part of the corporate response to a new way of thinking associated with computer utilization. We will adopt this broader view in the following discussion.

Before examining some of the evidence pertaining to centralization of control, let us consider the significance of the issue. It is difficult to overestimate the power of large corporations in contemporary society. "[T]he fact is that today the great American Corporations seem more like states within states than simply private businesses" (Mills, 1956, p. 124). Through the resources it controls, Big Business plays a dominant role in shaping public policy and in determining the character of everyday life. Corporate policies affect everything from the work people do to the products and services they believe are indispensable for the "good life." More generally, economic issues form the basis of political decisions, thus placing corporate interests in the position of power broker. In view of the influence exerted by corporations on society, it is clear, as asserted earlier, that the forms of decision-making are of vital social concern.

Concentration of decision-making in the upper echelons of management may possibly promote increased efficiency of production, but at the same time it poses a threat to democratic institutions. There is little difference between consolidation of power by a small group of political managers, and centralization of control in the large corporations which dominate our economic life. In either case, the average individual with limited resources has virtually no voice in shaping the course of events. One might argue, however, that the form of corporate decision-making does not materially affect the basis for corporate power.

From *Conquest of the Will: Information Processing in Human Affairs* (Reading, MA: Addison-Wesley, 1976), pp. 81–84, 202–206. © 1976 Addison-Wesley. Reprinted by permission of Addison-Wesley.

In some sense this is true, but the potential abuse of that power is inversely proportional to the number of individuals sharing it.

Centralization of control has the effect of isolating decision-makers from the lower levels of management and from the rank and file. As in the military, information flow is formalized, and responsibilities are rigidly defined. The will of authority is more easily exercised, but innovative thinking is discouraged. Distortions which inevitably occur in reporting are amplified, errors are more likely to have disastrous effects, and the organization is potentially more vulnerable as a result (DeCarlo, 1967). Examples of natural systems exhibiting hierarchical structure with central control are inappropriate models for social organizations. An individual in a corporation is not comparable to a liver cell. The latter is incapable of informing the brain of its views on the desirability of some action which does not have a direct effect on the liver. It is a mistake to suppose that specialization in social organizations extends to the point of requiring expert credentials for judging the desirability of organizational goals. Such judgments involve human values and call for wisdom in addition to expert testimony. The establishment of goals without the active participation of a large number of individuals works to the detriment of society as a whole.

The historical trend toward the centralization of power in society has been aided in no small measure by modern technology. The question now is whether or not the computer is helping to accelerate the process. Whisler (1967) distinguishes between two forms of control in organizations. Systems control refers to the direct influence of an individual on organizational achievement and is reflected in his share of compensation paid. Interpersonal control, on the other hand, involves the authority exercised by some individuals over others, and may be measured by the span of influence of superiors over subordinates. In a variety of examples of the development of computer systems, both types of control were found to increase for top management at the expense of the lower levels. The introduction of information systems results in fewer managers being paid more, and some levels in the decision hierarchy being eliminated, thus facilitating increased scope of control at the top. The expected concomitants of centralized control are also observed. There is tighter discipline in the utilization of time, and a noticeable routinization of activities at the lower levels in the hierarchy.

Whisler (1970) argues that computers can be expected to increase centralization of systems control for the following reasons.

> Computers tie together and integrate areas of decision-making and control that formerly were relatively independent of one another. . . . Given the typical pyramidal structure of business organizations, this integration results in shifting system control . . . up higher in the organization than where it formerly was located. (Whisler, 1970, pp. 98–99)

The empirical evidence in the case of the insurance industry strongly corroborates this view. Respondents agreed almost unanimously that centralization of control accompanied computer use. The only difference of opinion on this issue was the degree of change brought about by computers.

The current trend is unmistakable, but it may not be an inevitable consequence of computer applications. Forrester (1967) views present organizational changes as characteristic of a transitional stage in the development of computer-based systems. The computer is seen as an instrument which can be used "to create either more confinement or more freedom." In principle, management information systems could be designed to inhibit excessive centralization of authority and promote individual autonomy. Whisler (1967) reasons that although the observed centralizing effects of computers will proceed for a time, there are limiting factors. Natural boundaries between independent corporate divisions act to limit extensions of central authority, and the high educational levels of professionalized managerial personnel militate against restrictive conditions.

Based on his analysis of hierarchical structure, Simon (1965) resolves the question of centralization of control into two distinct issues. The relative sizes of the building blocks in the organizational hierarchy determine the degree of centralization. Authority structure is seen as a separate matter governed by the relations between the building blocks. Exactly how an array of building blocks of various sizes can exhibit the property of centralization apart from the relations defining their interaction is not explained. This putative framework is interesting, however, as an example of an attempt to turn the issue of centralization into a purely technical problem, thereby rendering it socially innocuous. As noted in the previous section, hierarchical structure evolves in response to the needs of efficient production, and unity of command or centralized control is an inescapable feature of hierarchy.

The possibility that computer use in large organizations may ultimately lead to greater autonomy and personal satisfaction raises basic questions about hierarchical structure. One of the rallying cries of modern technology is the elimination of drudgery in work. The belief in the long-term contribution of management information systems to personal autonomy derives from a similar expectation, namely, that computers will free managers for creative tasks. However, just as the elaboration of machinery for factory production succeeded in alienating the craftsman from his work, there is no reason to believe that computers will not have a comparable effect on management in the context of hierarchically structured organizations.

The apparent limitations on centralization are not nearly so effective as the pressures for reductions in operating costs. Forrester (1967) may be justified in supposing that authoritarian direction of large organizations will prove to be inherently unstable in the long-run. But this supposition is rooted in a philosophical position which rejects social absolutism. It is just possible that the organizational changes taking place now in response to computer applications will alter this position before we have a chance to restructure the organizations. . . .

Computers and Political Power

In the context of the . . . issue of the effects of databanks on democratic institutions, the central problem can . . . be posed in terms of achieving a balance: between the individual's "right to participate" and government's "need for autonomy" in decision-making. Shifts in power along the lines indicated for urban governments lead to greater centralization of decision-making and a consequent decline in participation by the average citizen in the political process.

Michael (1968) points to the increasing dependence of those with political power on esoteric knowledge, and the decreasing ability of the concerned citizen to get the knowledge he needs to participate. Weizenbaum (1969) confirms this development in his analysis of the "two cultures" surrounding the use of computers. Exclusive social groupings based on privileged information have a long history in our culture. The underlying rationale for the Pythagorean mystery cult may be different from that of the Communist party of the U.S.S.R., but both organizations share the tendency to promote a power elite based to some extent on access to secrets or privileged information. The comparison may appear ludicrous, but perhaps the only real difference lies in the nature of the secrets. Just imagine the change in the course of history if the alchemists had succeeded in their efforts to transmute base metals into gold.

The association of power with esoteric knowledge has many facets. Power has a built-in tendency to preserve itself, so that control of information may very well provide a basis for "adjusting" the external world to suit a particular government agency. This sort of thing is already a common occurrence as governments struggle to survive under conditions of eonomic instability. Although not unique to the contemporary world of computer-based information systems, the problems are made more acute, since access to databanks is restricted and information is often unavailable for challenge. Another aspect of the same underlying issue, is the possibility of partisan use of incomplete or selectively emphasized technological knowledge.

For the concerned citizen, decision-making based on information in restricted data-banks, poses some very difficult problems. How is the ordinary citizen to judge whether he knows enough about a policy? How will he know what data were used in arriving at a particular policy choice? Michael's solution [is to allow] maximum access to procedures of social planning and evaluation. The citizen ought to be able to look over the shoulder of the planner and decision-maker. A computer utility could provide the technical means for this capability.

Perhaps the most interesting claim for this approach is that it might lead to more openness on the part of government and greater citizen involvement in decision-making. Moreover, it is claimed that unfettered development of information systems with relatively open databanks will allow for the possibility of social experimentation.

The theme of social experimentation is explored in depth by Sackman (1968). Out of the mists of computer-based military command and control systems comes the real-time information system which monitors events in a specified environment, and controls the outcome of such events in a desired direction. Such systems give rise to the possibility of a new class of social institutions—one which is able to meet and deal with problems at the time they occur and in time to modify their outcome. Real-time systems involve a fusion of information and action and thus raise critical questions concerning the social control of "information power."

According to Sackman, social change via real-time information systems is self-change, since information power in a democracy resides in the public; that is to say, the public ideally authorizes and warrants social change. A new level of participant democracy is required. Here Sackman recommends the usual package of educational changes and *ad hoc* legal and regulatory devices to prevent concentration of information power. But the central part of his new philosophy is social experimentation—the possibility of which he attributes to computers and the development of real-time information systems.

Social experimentation is linked to the philosophical tradition of American pragmatism as exemplified in the works of Charles Peirce, William James and John Dewey. Dewey's work is particularly important in this regard. He proposed operational measures of effectiveness of human organizational and social performance, a position which places a high value on freedom of social inquiry. As noted before, Sackman conjectures that the public information utility may be the instrumentality through which Dewey's dream could be realized. A public information utility could in principle provide for citizen participation in social experimentation through the agency of real-time information systems.

The possibilities of incorporating information technology into the political life of our society seem unlimited. If every home were equipped with a communications terminal connected to a nationwide computer network, and if the network's (presumably rich) information resources were accessible to all users, the ordinary citizen would have the means for making intelligent decisions and communicating opinions to others. This vision of the future underlies speculation on citizen participation in politics and government administration. There are, of course, many different forms of participation. The range of alternatives runs from opinion polling and electronic voting to direct participatory democracy. Opinion polling by means of an information utility would be a reasonably straightforward extension of existing practices designed to provide legislators and government officials with information on public attitudes. Extending a partial legislative authority to the whole citizenry would require considerably more adjustment.

The most far reaching alternative is direct participatory democracy. What this might mean is not entirely clear, but it would entail the evolution of political structures to facilitate public discussion and decision-making. It is not likely that society would be willing to dispense with executives or managers, so that the emphasis would be on policy formation, planning, and legislation. Developments in this direction are made possible by the accessibility of information and expert knowledge, and the ability to share experience among the members of the community. Whether or not people would take advantage of the opportunities is another matter.

Umpleby (1972) examines the various arguments against the use of a mass information utility as the vehicle for direct democracy. The "establishment social scientist" views increased citizen participation as a threat to civil liberties and democratic procedures. Liberal traditions are believed to be more secure in a political system dominated by a wealthy, educated minority than in one ruled by the capricious and highly impressionable masses. Technologically oriented observers fear that there would be a decline in the information and technical knowledge brought to bear on public decision-making, which would ultimately result in the dissolution of effective government. Although the "technologists" and "pluralists" differ in the value accorded to different forms of knowledge and the motives for using such knowledge in decision-making, they both accept the principle of elitist rule. Radical elements are also opposed to citizen participation, but for entirely different reasons. They argue that the new media will inevitably come to be owned and operated by powerful vested interests who will exploit it for their own partisan objectives. Instead of contributing to genuine power sharing, the technology would then serve as a vehicle for preserving existing privilege by enabling elite groups to exercise inordinate influence on public discussion.

Predicting the consequences of unknown forms of citizen participation in public decision-making is hazardous at best. Perhaps the greatest source of uncertainty derives from possible changes in public attitudes. Conceivably, political scientists will be astounded to discover that people actually become more involved when given the opportunity for genuine participation. On the other hand, we may witness the emergence of powerful forms of political control disguised as interactive systems; there is the distinct possibility of continued citizen acquiescence in "rule by experts." The destruction of democratic institutions need not result from conscious acts, nor from the sinister designs of power hungry men. Coercion can become institutionalized without anyone being particularly aware of it.

References

DeCarlo, Charles R. (1967). "Changes in management environment and their effect on human values," in *The Impact of Computers on Management,* edited by Charles A. Myers (1967).

Forrester, Jay W. (1967). "Comments on the conference discussion," in *The Impact of Computers on Management,* edited by Charles A. Myers (1967).

Michael, Donald N. (1968). "On coping with complexity: planning and politics," *Daedalus* 97 (Fall), pp. 1179–1193.

Mills, C. Wright. (1956). *The Power Elite.* London: Oxford University Press.

Myers, Charles A., ed. (1967). *The Impact of Computers on Management.* Cambridge, Mass.: MIT Press.

Sackman, Harold. (1968). "A public philosophy for real time information systems," in *Proc. of the 1968 Fall Joint Computer Conference.* Montvale, N.J.: AFIPS Press, 1968.

Simon, Herbert A. (1965). *The Shape of Automation for Man and Management.* New York: Harper and Row.

Umpleby, Stuart A. (1972). "Is greater citizen participation in planning possible and desirable?" *Technological Forecasting and Social Change* 4, pp. 61–76.

Weizenbaum, Joseph. (1969). "The two cultures of the computer age," *Technology Review* 71, pp. 54–57.

Whisler, Thomas L. (1967). "The impact of information technology on organizational control," in *The Impact of Computers on Management* edited by Charles A. Myers (1967).

Whisler, Thomas L. (1970). *The Impact of Computers on Organizations.* New York: Praeger.

25. The Consequences of Computers for Centralization and Decentralization

Herbert A. Simon

TODAY, THE TERMS *centralization* and *decentralization* are heavily laden with value. In general, decentralization is the good thing and centralization the bad thing. Decentralization is commonly equated with autonomy, self-determination, or even self-actualization. Centralization is equated with bureaucracy (in the pejorative sense of that term) or with authoritarianism and is often named as a prime force in the dehumanization of organizations and the alienation of their members. If the reader shares these common attitudes toward centralization and decentralization, I shall ask him to hold them in suspension until I have inquired more closely into their meanings.

The Nature of Centralization and Decentralization

Picture a typical organization in hierarchical form with various decision-making functions being carried out at the nodes. Centralization is any transfer of such functions from a lower node to a higher one, decentralization any transfer from a higher node to a lower one. Centralization is always a relative matter, for decision making is never fully concentrated at the very top or at the very bottom of an organization. When we ask what effect computers will have on the centralization and decentralization of the institutions and organizations of our society, we are asking in what direction they will move the balance. It is perfectly possible, of course, for both movements to go on concurrently in an organization, some functions being passed upward at the same time that others are passed downward. Thus, in the 1950s, many production and marketing decisions in large American corporations were being decentralized to product divisions at the same time that labor relations decisions were being centralized.

Functions of Centralization

There are three main motives for centralizing decision functions: to gain economies of scale, to coordinate interdependent activities, and to control lower-level activities in the interest of higher-level goals.

1. In decision making, economy of scale means mainly creating central units for handling certain classes of decisions expertly, where it would be too costly to distribute experts more widely through the organization—a classic application of Adam Smith's principle of the division of labor, although in this case the labor is mental, not physical.

From Michael L. Dertouzos and Joel Moses (eds.), *The Computer Age: A Twenty-Year View* (Cambridge, MA: MIT Press, 1979), pp. 212–228. Reprinted by permission of MIT Press.

2. The interdependencies that make coordination desirable are those that the economist calls externalities; that is, actions whose consequences fall on a part of the organization other than the one taking the decision. These external consequences may be undervalued or ignored if decisions are not centralized. It may be possible, however, so to design the reward system that a decentralized decision-making unit will be charged fully with the indirect consequences of its actions, in which case interdependence ceases to be a reason for centralization. Pricing mechanisms provide an important means for reconciling decentralization with interdependence whenever appropriate prices can be assigned to all of the relevant consequences of an action. On the other hand, prices that do not reflect important externalities can be a cause for divergence between decentralized decisions and higher-level goals, and hence a motive for centralization.

3. Even without interdependencies among units, some measure of centralization may be thought necessary in order to guarantee that the actions of individual organization units will reflect the goals of the whole organization. Successful decentralization assumes that lower-level administrators can be motivated to make their decisions in terms of higher-level goals.

Decision Premises

Making a decision involves weaving together many diverse premises—goal premises, constraints, side conditions, and factual assumptions based on data and theory—and deriving from them the choice of a course of action. Centralization need not involve transporting the whole decision process from one node in an organization to a higher one but may consist in establishing and communicating from the higher node one or more decision premises, with the injunction that they be employed in making the decision. One organization unit may provide another with objectives, with rules and constraints, or with facts. A single decision, then, may be manufactured out of a diversity of component materials that were themselves fabricated elsewhere in the organization.

It is important to view decision making as more than just the final signing on the dotted line. The decision-making process in an organization encompasses (1) determining what items will be on the agenda and receive attention; (2) inventing and designing alternative plans of action; (3) evaluating alternatives and making the choice; and (4) postauditing decisions and their consequences. If we take a longer view, we also have to include in the decision process all the varieties of investigation and research that build the organization's understanding of its environment and of the laws by which it operates. It is from this understanding that the invention of plans of action proceeds, as well as the estimation of decision consequences.

Decision making begins, then, with activities directed toward understanding the environment, proceeds through attending to selected aspects of the environment and the problems it presents, to devising courses of action, choosing among them, and reevaluating them by hindsight. For example, the energy shortage and rising energy prices may cause a company management to attend to the reliability of its energy supply and the efficiency of its use of energy. Means may be sought, discovered, and adopted for insulating buildings, reducing the energy requirements of manufacturing processes, or remodeling power plants to enable them to use alternative fuels. This whole stream of activities constitutes the decision-making process.

Decision premises do not only flow downward through the organization's channels of formal authority; they also flow upward and sideward. If the higher organizational levels provide authoritative instruction and information for decision making at the lower levels, the lower levels also provide much of the information that goes into higher-level decisions. In the unhappy history of the Vietnam War, no small part was played by the "body counts" and other local assessments of the battle situation that flowed upward to the top command in Saigon and thence to Washington. Whether this information was believed, or only partly believed, it provided a substantial part of the "facts" on which the decisions of war or peace were based. The information received by the top organizational levels is not always as bad, fortunately, as it was in this instance. In any event, it is typical of organizations that a large proportion of the facts for decision making at all levels originate either near the bottom or in specialized units outside the chain of command that perform one or another kind of expert or intelligence function (e.g., economic forecasters, market analysts, research and development departments).

Where decisions involve resource allocation, as they commonly do, much of the needed information can be encapsulated in the form of prices of inputs and outputs to each particular organization unit. Clearly the dissemination of this kind of information is not limited to any particular communication channels. Hence, where prices can be used to represent interactions, the decision-making process can be carried out in close proximity to the points where the decisions will be executed. Whether an increased communication flow to a decision center means more or less centralization of decision making depends, therefore, on whether the flow is from a lower level in order to inform decisions at a higher level, from a higher level to control decisions at a lower level, or from some expert source to a collateral point of decision making. Reduced autonomy for a high-level decision maker may imply a greater degree of decentralization (i.e., increased reliance on decentralized information sources) rather than centralization.

Perception of Autonomy

The premises of any particular decision may have their origins far back in time and may be stored in a variety of repositories—human memories, organization records, or books—before they are brought to bear on that decision. How centralized or decentralized we regard the decision as being will depend on whether we trace back these premises or consider only where they were stored at the time the decision was made. Herbert Kaufman, in his classic work, *The Forest Ranger,* describes a highly decentralized decision-making system in which the district ranger in the Forest Service exhibits great autonomy within his district. But Kaufman also shows how the forest ranger's training and indoctrination have instilled in his memory the decision premises—both goals and techniques—that give the organization confidence that he will work toward its objectives and will do so expertly and predictably. Thus, in this case and many others, autonomy in decision making goes hand in hand with the internalization of goals and the knowledge that make decentralization safe from the viewpoint of the higher levels of the organization.

From the standpoint of the autonomous decision maker's attitudes and motivation, it makes a great difference whether the premises on which he is acting have been received in the form of directives from other parts of the organization or whether they have come from his own memory, where they have long resided and become part of himself. But suppose one of his decisional premises comes neither from a directive nor from his memory, but from a reference book? Does he then view himself as acting autonomously, or under direction? Suppose it resides in a computer memory that he interrogates from a terminal? Is he acting autonomously, or is he being controlled by the computer?

His perception of his autonomy in these circumstances may depend on what motivated him to consult the book or computer memory in the first place. Was he instructed to do so by an organizational directive? Did his professional training teach him to turn to this source? What confidence does he have in the validity of the information? Clearly, autonomy resides in the mind of the decider and in his identification or nonidentification with the various parts of his informational environment. Any conclusions we draw about the implications of computers for centralization, and particularly its psychological consequences, must be carefully weighed in terms of the decision maker's attitudes toward the sources of information on which he draws and the extent to which he has internalized his recourse to those sources.

Feasibility of Centralization

Finally, the degree to which decisions are centralized or decentralized in an organization depends not only on the desirability of one or the other mode of operation but also on its feasibility. Any change in technology that makes it cheaper and easier either to centralize or to decentralize decisions will tip balance in that direction.

Computers and Communication

An analysis of the consequences of computers for centralization and decentralization must take account of the electronic communications systems in which computers are embedded. It may even be that the communications systems, with or without computers, are of more import than the computers themselves.

Effects of Modern Communications Technology

Modern communications technology was introduced long before the computer. First the telegraph and cable, then the wireless, and then the telephone revolutionized communication at long distance. Already in the nineteenth century, the autonomy of ambassadors was greatly curtailed by the possibility of communicating almost instantaneously with the foreign ministry in the home capital. The same is true of overseas executives of corporations. On the other hand—and there almost always is another hand—the speeding up and cheapening of international communication and transportation greatly increased the volume of international transactions.

As a consequence of these countervailing trends, it is not obvious that the foreign representative of a governmental or business organization perceives himself as having less decision-making responsibility than his ancestors had. On the one hand, it is easier to instruct him. On the other hand, there is much more to instruct him about. Moreover, these communication links are two-way links; they enable the foreign representative to inform and advise the home office as readily as they enable the home office to inform and instruct him. As the costs of long-distance communication go down and the volume of information that can be transmitted increases, the opportunities for low-level inputs to high-level decisions are greatly enhanced. As I have already shown, this is a force toward greater decentralization.

These comments apply, of course, not only to international communications but also to communications within a single country, a single city, or even a single office building. Large volumes of information can flow electronically between any two points in an organization where it pays to install a broadband communication link, and the cost of such a link decreases each year.

The fact that information can be transmitted to a decision point does not mean that it can and will be used there. The world of modern communications is an information-rich world, in which the problem of absorbing information is generally perceived as more acute than the problem of generating or transmitting it. A decade ago, the U.S. State Department "modernized" its communications system by installing fast line printers to handle the traffic of messages from foreign embassies. Nothing was said about how the department staff would deal with the inundation of messages. Today, improvements in the efficiency of such a system would certainly encompass information filtering and information compression, as well as transmission.

Characteristics of the Computer

What can be done faster and better with a computer than without it? A computer can analyze the behavior of systems with many interacting variables—systems much too large to analyze without its help. It can store sizable bodies of information, indexed so as to meet a great variety of information needs. It can copy, input, and output information with great speed. And it can do all of these things not only with numerical data but with information in various forms, including natural-language texts and other nonnumerical information. Moreover, next year its descendants will be able to handle more information faster and cheaper than it can.

Modeling and Analyzing Interdependent Systems

The ability of the computer to model systems with many interdependent variables was exploited in one of its early management applications: making ordering, inventory, production, and shipping decisions for large, geographically dispersed manufacturing operations. These were decisions that had previously been made by factory and warehouse inventory managers and schedulers; hence the introduction of the computer has brought about a substantial centralization of these activities in many companies, where it has produced large reductions in average inventory holdings. It is undoubtedly the most striking example of computer-produced centralization, but it is perhaps not typical of the ways in which computers have been used.

A different use of computers to analyze complex systems of interdependent variables are the models of energy systems or combined energy and environmental systems that have been constructed in the past several years to help guide the formation of public policy. Here is another case where the power of the computer is needed to assemble a previously fragmented structure of numerous interacting mechanisms. But in instances like this it would be misleading to say that the computer brings about centralization. It would be more accurate to say that it allows a systematic, analytic approach to problems that previously were addressed in an unsystematic, almost chaotic way. It is not that energy policy was previously arrived at in a decentralized way; it is that there was no energy policy. The cause of centralization, if there has been any, is not the computer but the need to address the whole problem rather than isolated fragments of it. The computer enhances our ability to do this; it does not create the necessity for it.

Similarly, building a model of the economic and market environment of a corporation does not centralize management decision making so much as it allows top management to adopt an orderly, analytic approach to decisions it had already been making—but by seat-of-the-pants methods. Taking account of relevant variables that had previously been ignored is not to be confused with centralizing the locus of the decision process.

Two related fields of research, operations research and artificial intelligence, have built tools to enlarge the capabilities of computers for modeling complex systems and have devised more and more powerful analytic techniques for this purpose during the past thirty years. Of course these tools are applicable to a particular set of phenomena only to the extent that the phenomena themselves are understood. But the combination of research on systems analysis techniques with basic scientific research is permitting us each year to approach complex decision problems in business organizations and in the public domain with greater sophistication.

Information Storage and Retrieval

One form of centralization, although not necessarily of decision making, is the gathering of large bodies of information into central computer memories as the basis for information retrieval systems of one kind or another. An airlines reservations system is an interesting application of this sort, particularly because it involves remote access to the central memory over long distances. It can be seen that in this instance hardware centralization does not bring about any centralization of decision making. On the contrary, it allows each of the decentralized decision points to take actions independently, confident that automatic updating by the central memory will take care of all interactions among decisions.

An example of a different sort is the computerized systems for medical diagnosis that are just on the verge of moving from research and development into practical application. Let us suppose that a perfected version of such a system existed in some central location where it could be accessed from remote terminals. By an interactive procedure, information about the patient would be entered, say, from the local hospital. The system could request additional information or ask that additional tests be performed on the patient before arriving at a diagnosis. By any reasonable definition, such a system would represent a centralization of the decision-making process, even if its diagnoses were only advisory. But the important question is the psychological one: would the physician perceive the system as replacing him in his diagnostic function, or would he perceive it as a tool—like penicillin or an X-ray machine—to help him carry out his task? The answer to this question probably depends on the way the system is introduced and the institutional framework within which it is used. Physicians, after all, do not usually regard reference books as threatening automation of their functions, however good the answers or advice they may obtain by consulting them. The automated diagnostic system can simply be regarded as a more powerful and more easily consulted reference book—or it can be regarded as a "robot doctor." What it "really" is lies mainly in the mind of the physician.

Trends in Computer Technology

During the first twenty or so years that computers were on the scene, they had two characteristics that suggested their widespread use would inevitably move decision making toward centralization. The first was that the efficiency of computers increased rapidly with their size: a single large computer was substantially cheaper (perhaps by a factor of three) than ten small computers of the same aggregate computing power. The economics of scale seemed to argue for one or a few centrally located computers rather than many computers distributed through an organization. The second characteristic of early computer systems was that they could only be used by someone in physical proximity to them. Therefore, if the computers were geographically centralized, so would be their use.

In the past decade advances in technology have made drastic changes in these two characteristics, and the shift is still continuing. Minicomputers have been developed that for many purposes compete very well in efficiency with the largest computers. Economies of scale no longer provide a conclusive argument for centralization. Second, and perhaps even more important, with time sharing and remote access, many users in different locations can share the same central computer. (As the examples of the plane reservation system and the medical diagnosis system show, not only can processing capacity be shared, but also access to a memory bank.)

With the new and emerging computer technology of minicomputers, time sharing, and remote access, the decisions about where to locate components of the decision-making process can be pretty completely detached from decisions about the hardware configuration. Of course, long-line access to computers is not without cost, but the costs are relatively low today and still dropping, so that it is not at all unreasonable to look toward the development of nationwide networks. In fact, several experimental networks of this kind (in addition to special-purpose networks like the reservations systems) already exist.

The Impact of Computers on Organizations

Although the computer revolution is far from having run its course, it has been under way for thirty years, and by now we have accumulated a considerable body of experience that should help us predict its direction. Its most visible consequence to date has been the automation of many clerical information-processing functions in accounting departments, insurance companies, and banks. This development, however important it may be from other standpoints, has no particular implications for centralization or decentralization.

Operations Research

Another consequence of the computer revolution is the centralization of middle-management decisions relating to inventory, production scheduling, and the like. At the same time, there has been a great expansion in the use of formal operations research models for making many kinds of middle-management decisions. At the outset, the introduction of such models probably caused some centralization of decision making in special operations research departments, but this was a transitory phase of a kind that often occurs when a new technology requiring specialized knowledge is introduced into an organization. As soon as knowledge of operations research techniques was diffused widely enough to become a part of the standard equipment of industrial engineers and other managers at middle levels, the decision-making responsibilities tended to return to their previous locations in the factory and departmental organizations. Middle managers now make some different kinds of decisions than they did traditionally, and use management-science tools in making many of them, but the management-science tools have become *their* tools and are not generally viewed as removing them from the decision process.

Strategic Planning

The spread in the use of complex models as an aid to decision making has not been limited to middle-management decisions. I have already mentioned the governmental use of models to aid in making decisions about energy and environmental policy. Increasingly, corporate planning at top management levels is being informed and assisted by a variety of computerized analytic techniques (systems analysis), including modeling of the firm itself and its economic environment.

The growing use of modeling as a component of strategy formulation and strategic planning has led to some expansion of corporate planning staffs and their counterparts in government agencies to carry out this function, producing new flows of information and advice from these staffs to top management. Again, it is difficult to interpret this development as an increase in centralization. What it principally means is that a considerable amount of managerial and technical effort all up and down the line, which previously was devoted to day-to-day decision making, is now devoted to the design of the decision process itself and to developing and maintaining the basic models and data bases required for strategic analysis. The change in managerial role is analogous to the change in supervisory role with the introduction of automated control into processing plants, where the main task of foremen and supervisors shifts from making operating decisions to maintaining and monitoring the performance of the automated decision system.

I should insert parenthetically, because there has been some confusion on this point, that the development of strategic planning systems and techniques has had relatively little to do with the development of so-called "management information systems" (MIS). Most of the MIS work has been aimed at computerizing existing internal accounting and production records systems and incorporating in them procedures (usually elaborate) for producing reports addressed to management at various levels. Experience with management information systems has generally been disappointing, mainly because insufficient thought was given to the nature of the management decisions they were to inform and because it was not realized that the important function of computers in organizations is not to multiply information but to analyze it so that it can be filtered, compressed, and diffused selectively. The systems that have been designed under the strategic planning label are generally more relevant for these purposes than are typical MIS systems.

The Qualitative Change in Decision Making

In summary, the very large impact that computers are having on business and governmental organizations cannot be described in terms of centralization and decentralization. What is occurring is a profound qualitative change in the decision-making process, which is being formalized, made explicit, and subjected to deliberate planning.

As decision processes become more explicit, and as their components are more and more embedded in computer programs, decisions and their underlying analyses become more and more transportable. If the method of analysis is explicit and the informational and other premises that enter into it can be specified, then it does not matter very much at what organizational locations the analysis is carried out. As a matter of fact, it becomes increasingly feasible to carry out alternative analyses, using different assumptions and even different decision frameworks and analytic techniques, and employ them all as inputs to the final decision process. With all sorts of organizational and extraorganizational sources providing inputs, the locus of decision making becomes even more diffuse than it has been in the past. The organizational hierarchy remains as a critical mechanism for monitoring the process, but an increasing part of the flow of decisional premises overlaps the boundaries of the formal hierarchy.

Implications for the Political System

Decentralization has entered the political rhetoric of our time in the discussion of two related questions about the organization of our governmental system. The first of these is the question of the relations among the different levels of government, national, state, and local. The second is the question of the participation of citizens in the governmental process. Although often discussed together, these really are separate issues which should be looked at individually.

Federal, State, and Local Relations

There is a long-standing myth abroad in America that local government is "closer to the grass roots" than state government and state government closer than the federal government. In the purely numerical sense that each person represents a larger fraction of the electorate of his city than of his state, and of his state than of the nation, the claim is undeniably true. But it does not follow from this arithmetic that each person has a greater influence on local decisions than on state decisions, or on state decisions than on national ones. It could be argued, in fact, that because it is easier to focus public attention on major national issues than on state or local ones, there is greater popular influence on national decisions than on the others—the Vietnam War and the impeachment of Nixon being cases in point. The principal mass media in this country, and particularly TV and the news magazines, attend largely to national affairs, attracting public attention to them to the relative neglect of what is going on at the state and local levels. While political participation is highly selective at all levels of government, it is probably most selective at the state and local levels.

As a matter of fact, the transfer of power from national to local government, a policy that has had wide popularity during the past few years and especially during the Nixon administration, is not motivated primarily by the desire for greater public participation in government decisions. Part of the support for the movement does come from advocates of participatory democracy, but a much larger part has had two other motives: (1) equalization of the disparate financial capacities of the states and cities to provide governmental services; and (2) the desire of a conservative administration faced by a liberal Congress to put power back in the hands of state and local governments believed to be more congenial than Congress to the administration's point of view.

That government in the United States has tended to become more centralized over the years cannot be doubted. It has become more centralized as activities throughout the nation, and particularly economic activities, have become more interdependent. A highly integrated economy with a highly mobile population cannot behave as though it were fifty independent states or three thousand independent counties. Any important trend toward decentralized decision making is unlikely to occur unless technical means can be found to deal with the real interdependencies that exist.

All of this is preliminary to putting two questions about computer technology: (1) Has the computer contributed, or is it contributing, to the movement toward centralization in American government? (2) Does the computer provide means for checking or reversing that movement? From what has just been said, it is reasonably clear that the answer to the first question must be no. The trend toward centralization long predated the computer, and is adequately explained by other causes. Nothing I have said about computer technology suggests a positive answer to the second question, either. However, there have been some claims, and even some experiments to verify them, alleging that the computer could become an important means for enabling citizens to participate more fully in public decisions. I should like to examine those claims next.

Participatory Democracy

A few years ago, a well-known physicist proposed putting a simple electronic voting device in all homes, so that a referendum could be held almost instantaneously on any issue. The same suggestion has been made by others, and an experiment along these lines appears to be under way at the present time in a West Coast community. Such a device would certainly go a long way toward solving one problem—that of ascertaining the state of opinion of any citizen on any issue at any time. (I hope provision would be made for a "no opinion" response!) The question is whether this is the problem that needs to be solved in order to enhance anything that could justifiably be called citizen participation.

The genius of democratic government is not arithmetic; it is informed consensus. Most questions of public policy do not begin life as dichotomies that can be decided by yes or no. Yet courses of action must be framed and decisions about them reached. Democratic institutions define a process for getting issues on the agenda, generating proposed courses of action, and modifying and amending those proposals until some measure achieves enough support to be enacted, but only in the most spacious sense can we say that the chosen course represents the will of the majority. There is almost never a single action that is preferred by a majority over all alternative actions. There may, of course, be a majority preference for that action among all politically feasible actions—where "politically feasible" is defined by the decision process itself.

Different democratic systems define differently the processes for forming majorities. In many European democracies, the legislative body consists of members of numerous political parties, each having a more or less definable ideology and none commanding a majority. In such systems, the formation of coalitions among parties, a process in which each of them relinquishes some of its ideological purity, plays a central role in the formation of majorities. In the American system, with two amorphous political parties with almost unidentifiable ideologies, one of which is usually able to form a legislative majority, the formation of majorities is accomplished primarily through the process that creates and maintains the parties themselves.

This is not the place to enter into a lengthy discourse on political institutions, beyond demonstrating that they are not merely or mostly mechanisms for counting noses. To be sure, elections play a major role in our system and referenda a significant role in some states. But the question to be asked about elections and referenda is not whether the alternative finally chosen obtained a majority or plurality vote, but whether the process by which the decision was reached commanded consensus, whether the decision bore some reasonable relation to informed preferences, and whether—a point I wish to elaborate— the process was spacious enough to accommodate fact and reason along with all the other factors that enter into the formation of public opinion.

The political process, then, is not simply a mechanism for recording a majority of opinions already formed. It is a process for reaching decisions, often about complex matters of policy, in the light not only of already existing goals but also of the probable conse- quences of alternative courses of action. When we have legislative and public debate about measures to be taken to protect the environment, it is not that there are some people who are "for" the environment and others who are "against" it. There are deep disagreements, some about values, but most about the magnitude and seriousness of the consequences that would follow protection or failure to protect. Is the benefit to public health that will be gained by reducing the NOx emission standard for automobiles to 0.4 grams per mile substantial enough to justify the expenditure of several billions of dollars to achieve it? On many, if not most, questions of this kind, disagreement stems much less from conflicts of interest than from uncertainties about outcomes. Even where both are involved, we probably would regard it as an improvement in the democratic process if its participants could make more accurate estimates of where their interests lay.

Informing Public Opinion

If the computer has any implications for the effectiveness of democratic institutions, they have to do with the processes for forming and informing opinion rather than the processes for recording it. The computer enters as a tool that permits policy alternatives to be ex- amined with a sophistication and explicitness that would otherwise be impossible.

Already one can begin to point to examples where the computer, used in conjunction with the tools of systems analysis, is beginning to play such a role. The debate on federal financing for the SST is one such example, the debate on the antiballistic missile is another. In both these cases, intelligent public debate was facilitated by analyses, some of them aided by computer, of what might result from choosing one alternative over another. With such analyses available, their assumptions explicit and open to examination and question, a layman could acquire not merely an opinion on the policy issue but an informed opinion.

Over the next decade, I think it is predictable that the computer is going to play an even more important role in helping us to understand the choices with which we are faced in matters relating to energy and the environment. The complexities here are an order of magnitude greater than in the SST or ABM decisions, and there is probably greater consensus about the values to be served by the decisions. But the computer is simply a tool in the process that enables us to calculate interactions better than we could without it. It will help us only to the extent that we have valid scientific theories of the systems whose behavior we are trying to model and predict. (It will help us too, of course, in developing and testing those theories.)

The effectiveness of democratic institutions, as well as people's confidence in them, depends in part on the soundness of the decision-making processes they use. Democracy does not require a town meeting in which every member of the public can participate directly in every decision. But it is enhanced by an open and explicit decision process that enables members of the public to judge on what premises the decisions rest and whether the decisions are informed by the best available facts and theories. In fact, such a decision process is a precondition to intelligent public participation of any kind. To the extent that computers can contribute to its growth, they can strengthen democratic institutions and help combat public feelings of helplessness and alienation.

Conclusion

I began by arguing that there are three main motives for centralizing the decision-making process: to gain economies of scale (expertness), to coordinate interdependent activities, and to control lower-level activities in the interest of higher-level goals. I went on to examine the implications of computer technology for centralization and decentralization in both management decision making and the formation of public policy. What remains is to show how the introduction of the computer affects the motives favoring centralization, hence tipping the balance in one direction or another.

The computer is making major contributions to raising the level of expertness in decision making on complex matters. It is doing this, however, not by concentrating the decision process at higher levels of management but by either (1) facilitating the construction and use of systems models that can incorporate expert knowledge about system structure and system behavior or (2) permitting the assembly of expert knowledge in large data banks that can be consulted readily from any organizational location provided with a terminal. It is a psychological question whether these sophisticated aids to decision making will be perceived as reducing the autonomy of executives or as enlarging and extending their capabilities. If care is taken in the ways in which computerized decisions aids are introduced into organizations and employed in them, there is no reason why they should either be or appear to be centralizing mechanisms.

There probably exists a continuing long-term trend toward the centralization of decision making in both business and government as the matters about which decisions have to be made become more and more interdependent. It has perhaps been slowed but certainly not halted by the use of price and market mechanisms to reconcile interdependence with decentralization. It does not appear that computers have contributed to this trend. What they have contributed, through the modeling capabilities already mentioned, are powerful new means for decision makers to deal with problems involving large numbers of interacting variables. Decisions will not be more centralized as a result of the introduction of computers, but centralized decisions will be made in a far more sophisticated way, taking a fuller account of the real-world complications of the situation, than was possible before.

The use of computers in decision making has important implications for control over the goals to which administrative action and policy are directed, but these implications can as easily support broader as narrower participation in goal setting. What computers do in this respect is mainly to open the decision process to inspection. They objectify the process and make fully explicit the premises of fact and value that enter into it. As a result, the use of the computer will facilitate top management's control over decisions made elsewhere in the organization—in this way reconciling the notion of central control over goals with the notion of decentralization of the actual decision process.

More generally, the use of computers will permit multiple inputs into the decision process from a variety of sources, along with mutually independent alternate analyses of problems. In this way, computers will facilitate—and already have facilitated—a more extensive participation of both experts and laymen in debates on public policy, not by providing means for expressing uninformed opinions but in enabling opinions to be better informed.

Modern communications and computers have moved us from a world in which information was a scarce, valuable commodity, to be cherished and preserved, to a world so full of information that what is scarce is the capacity to attend to it. The computer has often been used incorrectly, as in many MIS systems, as a producer of information. Increasingly, we are learning to use it as a compactor of information, reducing the amount of data managers and policymakers must absorb and shouldering an important part of the burden of analysis that transforms a multitude of premises and predicted consequences into a decision to embark on a course of action.

Whether we employ computers to centralize decision making or to decentralize it is not determined by any inherent characteristics of the new technology. It is a choice for us to make whenever we design or modify our organizations. The technology does offer us a wide range of alternatives for fitting our decision-making systems to our requirements, whatever they may be.

References

Kaufman, Herbert. *The Forest Ranger: A Study in Administrative Behavior*. Baltimore: Johns Hopkins Press, 1960.

Sackman, Harold, ed. *Computers and the Problems of Society*. Montvale, N.J.: AFIPS Press, 1972.

Sackman, Harold, and Barry W. Boehm, eds. *Planning Community Information Utilities*. Montvale, N.J.: AFIPS Press, 1972.

Simon, Herbert A. *The New Science of Management Decision*. 3d ed. Englewood Cliffs, N.J.: Prentice-Hall, 1977.

———— *Administrative Behavior*. 3d ed. New York: Free Press, 1976. Chaps. 13 and 14.

Whisler, Thomas L. *The Impact of Computers on Organizations*. New York: Praeger, 1970.

26. Computers and Social Power
Rob Kling

WHAT KINDS OF impacts do computer based information systems have upon public agencies and the polity? It is widely believed that automating routine high volume transactions usually produces increased operating efficiencies. Well constructed models cannot help but improve the quality of decision-making in organizations (Simon, 1973). In short, people view computing as a tool to cut costs, help coordinate organizationally distinct but substantively related activities, and help rationalize organizational decision-making.[1]

Automated information systems appear to effect the balance of power between the organizational users and the other actors in their environment(s). Consequently a particular group (organized community group, department, agency or organization) opposes the automation of some process and/or refuses to share its data as a participant in the venture. The way in which power flows with information is common to many information technologies, not just computing. However, power shifts like privacy/confidentiality can become salient issues in the design of automated information systems (AIS).

The Relevance of Power

In this brief essay, I'd like to situate the design and use of AIS in the context of organizational and political power. While concerns of power are central for political scientists and important for many students of organizational behavior (Zald, 1970), they are usually outside the intellectual focus of AIS designers and computer scientists who tend to emphasize the (rational) flow of information and the possible impacts of various kinds of information on "decision-making" (Simon, 1973). In effect, computer scientists study the nervous system of organizations abstracted from the muscular and skeletal systems.

Concepts of "power" permeate discussions of public policy, legislation, and the behavior of various political groups. We attend to power within organizations when we seek resources to implement a new AIS and to restructure the data flows to feed it. The power we prefer to ignore is that which flows along with the data. When we restrict our attention to information flows and decision-making, we affirm our belief in rationality and as a byproduct help various groups become more efficient and effective. The concept of "power," however, indicates taking sides and possibly acting nonrationally as well. As professionals or scientists we'd prefer not to let values get in the way of work.

I believe that the balances of power and influence in an organization change when information is channeled through automated systems. The balances tend inescapably to shift

---

From *Computers & Society* 5, 3 (Fall 1974), pp. 6–11. Reprinted by permission of the Association for Computing Machinery and Rob Kling.

in favor of those who receive information. When police agencies share files on suspects, stolen properties and warrants through a metropolitan region, police in one locality can more easily apprehend people suspected of crimes in an adjacent locality. The relative effectiveness of police in catching criminals is enhanced.[2] However, gains in power are modulated by the scope of power and authority of the information receivers relative to the actions they would prefer to take. While an employer may fire an employee who is stealing on the job, he may not be able to fire one who is stealing elsewhere. Similarly, a regional planning agency may forecast a water shortage during the next decade, but have little ability to either reduce the population growth of an area or to commit new sources of water. "Knowledge is power" is simply too glib a slogan to carry us very far in analyzing the power impacts of AIS.

In the following sections flows of power and influence are analyzed by examining specific AIS which include: (1) evaluation and reporting systems; (2) police patrol deployment systems; (3) electronic funds transfer system (EFTS) or electronic money; and (4) land use data banks. This exposition differs from the few previous works that relate AIS and social power (Boguslaw, 1965; Downs, 1967; Wilensky, 1967) by grounding the analysis in the functioning of particular AIS. In addition, I suggest how the typical working conditions of computing professionals and AIS designers influence their designs.

Power, Influence, Authority and Organizations

Students of power have articulated a family of subtle variations on a common theme (Aiken & Mott, 1970). Power is viewed as a *relationship* between two or more parties in which one of the parties can get the other(s) to do something s/he otherwise wouldn't do. This concept of power can be sharpened in the following way:

"A power relationship exists when: (a) there is a conflict of values or course of action between (two parties) A and B; (b) B complies with A's wishes; and (c) B does so because s/he is fearful that A will deprive him of a value or values which B regards more highly than those which would have been achieved by non-compliance" (Bachrach and Baratz, 1970). Power is not a commodity like land, money or information which may be hoarded. Yet A has increased power over B. A may do this by: (a) increasing access to sanctions B cares about; or (b) increasing the range of B's values and actions A can effect (scope). A can also make power over B more effective by learning the degree to which B acts in accordance with A's desires. This is one link between information and social control.

Analysts distinguish between "power" and "influence" by noting that A influences B by causing him or her to change a course of action without resorting to overt or covert threats of sanction. Authority is similar to these since it too indicates a relationship between two parties. However, in contrast with power which emphasizes the sanctions available to the party making a demand, "authority" focuses upon the beliefs of the compliant party. Party A does not possess authority over party B. Rather, B regards A's demands as authoritative. B could, if necessary, construct a rationale for complying with A in terms of B's values rather than in terms of some threat posed by A. B simply considers A's demands as legitimate (Bachrach and Baratz, 1970).

None of these relationships need be unilateral. Two parties can have different kinds of power over each other. In fact, workers in subordinate authority and power relationships can maintain considerable control over "excesses" by their supervisors. They may reduce their output (slowdowns) or reveal common "illegitimate" practices which could embarrass the supervisors (Rubinstein, 1973). While these distinctions are analytically clear, in practice they may, at times, blur when *B* has confused or multiple motives for complying with *A*.

Organizations may be viewed as social systems that attempt to achieve a set of goals, such as producing various goods and services, maximizing growth or profits, etc. Some organizations are more effective than others in tapping the energies of their members, coordinating them, and focusing them on various specific activities. Some members of an organization have greater access to these pooled energies through the control of resources such as budgets, special skills and the commitments of other members (Mott, 1970).

Such control may follow patterns of authority, but it may find other bases as well. For example, a person's charisma or technical expertise may give one greater opportunity to influence one's colleagues than one's formal authority alone would warrant. This portrait of an organization as a system of pooled energy neglects the "structures" of position, and the members' expectations of each other. For a real organization, to channel its energies effectively, each member must have a relatively stable expectation of the scope of authority and powers that accrue to various organizationally defined positions such as prisoner, guard and warden, student, professor, dean and chancellor, or salesman, sales manager and chief accountant. Different members may have different expectations and none need actually conform to the "formal lines of authority" as defined by an organizational chart. I refer the interested reader to the more detailed and sophisticated elaboration of these concepts in the references cited above.

Routine AIS in Organizations

In the preceding discussion, I have left the identities of resource controllers undefined and their relationship to organizational goals problematic. In *practice* most AIS are designed for complex organizations differentiated into clusters of specialized activities which are coordinated through a hierarchy of positions of increasing scope of authority available to the position holder. Controllers of resources such as budgets and organizational sanctions such as salary, hiring and firing tend to be up the hierarchy of positions. Since AIS are usually costly to design, implement and maintain, key managers in the hierarchy are usually the clients of AIS designers although they need not be the direct users. I will return to this point when I discuss "vertical" flows of information in the next section.

It is not surprising that the first organizations to employ AIS on a large scale were large corporate and government bureaucracies who had already developed a number of large formal systems for routinely reporting cash flows, employee activities, and the production of goods and services. The resulting information flowed up the organization[3] to various managers and officials charged with controlling the resources and coordinating various tasks. Patterns of authority and standard operating procedures were long established around these systems and the earliest AIS designers tended to automate what was there. Early data processing systems simply rendered these routine record keeping systems more efficient and cheaper to operate. Since these record keeping systems were designed to serve higher level officials, the earliest automation simply acted in their service.

New Reporting Systems

By the early 60's, most AIS designers believed that their mission lay in helping redesign the flow of information in organizations. While many of the housekeeping activities such as payroll and billing were adequately organized in their manual forms, other less-routine information which would help top managers and officials control and coordinate their departments was either not being collected or not flowing up adequately.

The literature of this period is loaded with proposals for various information and planning systems that would help the "men at the top." One gets the impression that the only really *meaningful* computer aids were those that would most appeal to these higher level managers like budgeting and long-range planning models.

At this point, I want to introduce one additional concept which may help explain our professional commitment to top level managers: the "hierarchy of credibility" (Becker, 1967).

> In any system of ranked groups, participants take it as given that members of the highest group have the right to define the way things really are. In any organization, no matter what the rest of the organization chart shows, the arrows indicating the flow of information point up, thus demonstrating (at least formally) that those at the top have access to a more complete picture of what is going on than anyone else. Members of lower groups will have incomplete information, and their view of reality will be partial and distorted in consequence. Therefore, from the point of view of a well socialized participant in the system, any tale told by those at the top intrinsically deserves to be regarded as the most credible account obtainable of the organizations' workings. And since, . . . matters of rank and status are contained in the mores, this belief has a moral quality. We are, if we are proper members of this group, morally bound to accept the definition imposed on reality by a superordinate group in preference to the definitions espoused by subordinates. (By analogy, the same argument holds for the social classes of a community.) Thus, credibility and the right to be heard are differentially distributed through the ranks of the system.

The concept of a "hierarchy of credibility" may help predict whose world view of institutional goals and procedures an outsider or layman would accept. For example, many would accept the goals of schooling articulated by a principal rather than those espoused by a teacher's aide or a student. In a prison, one is more likely to attend to the views of a warden over those of a guard, or a guard than a prisoner.

AIS implicitly embody a set of values of "what an organization is about." For example, a police-car scheduling system that was used by several big city police departments was designed to minimize mean response time to a call (Larson, 1974). Such a criteria embodies a particular philosophy of how police should spend their time. First they should be patrolling. Secondly they should answer any calls as fast as possible. While this approach is congruent with TV police dramas (and can be supported by some extraordinary episodes in police work) it is not the only valid approach to law enforcement and crime prevention (Weis and Milakovich, 1974). An alternative approach which tries to keep patrolmen at the scene of one call to gather evidence and console victims is not very congruent with deployments that minimize mean response time. However, if a city police department uses an AIS to assist the deployments of patrolmen, one would expect it to be congruent with the theory of policing held by the police chief, rather than the alternative views of precinct captains, some patrolmen, or members of community-relations teams.

This example drawn from police work illustrates a common feature of many AIS designs. Two factors support this pattern. First, a naive acceptance of the "hierarchy of credibility" leads one to pay special attention to the professional philosophies of top managers. After all, the computer scientist is an expert in AIS design, not in policing, finance, marketing, public works, etc. In practice, we tend to accept the professional ideology of our high level contacts in the client or employing organization.

Secondly, AIS are often expensive to build and may redirect the traditional flow of data. It's easier (or necessary) to get approval from the top to design and implement an AIS rather than attempting to buck or change the values of top officials. On this point Shepard (Shepard, 1967) observes:

> An organization is itself an innovation, but most organizations of the past have been designed to be innovation resisting. Like fully automated factories, organizations that contain people have customarily been designed to do a narrowly prescribed assortment of things and to do them reliably. To insure reliable repetition of prescribed operations, the organization requires strong defenses against innovation. Efforts to innovate must be relegated to the categories of error, irresponsibility, and insubordination, and appropriate corrective action taken to bring the would-be innovators "back in line." Any change is likely to run counter to certain territorial rights. Sentiments of vested interest and territorial rights are sanctified as delegations of legitimate authority in traditional organizations, thus guaranteeing quick and effective counteraction against disturbances. In theory, the innovation-resisting organization is not resistant to innovations issuing from the top of its authority structure. In the Preface to one of the first Operations Research books, its authors stressed the importance of having the Operations Research team report directly to the chief executive, recognizing that the military organization can learn only at the top; changes in operations at lower levels occur by instruction from higher levels. But even the power of command is not always equal to the power of resistance, especially as society puts ever greater limitations on the power of command in civilian life.

Shepard would argue that major, highly visible technical innovations, such as a new AIS, need the support of top officials in order to get off the drawing boards. Of course this does not guarantee acceptance or success. In a recent study of advanced AIS in police, health and welfare agencies Kenneth Laudon found that the major AIS supported the agency roles as perceived by the topmost officials. These AIS emphasize crook catching (rather than crime prevention) for police and check processing (rather than relieving social deprivations) in welfare (Laudon, 1974). Similarly, the workload inventory systems installed in some welfare agencies (Quinn; Weiss, 1972) are used to impose an approach to casework which is at variance with that valued by the professional social workers. We shall return to these findings later on.

These examples illustrate how certain AIS help top officials to control staffs by implementing more comprehensive and timely reporting systems which more thoroughly penetrate the organization to its lowest levels. Traditionally, each effort of top-officials to control their staffs leads to internal countermeasures by employees. Shepard observes:

> Almost all policing systems have loopholes. Perhaps the commonest example of concealment is the machine operator who develops a device to simplify his work but does not use it when industrial engineers are setting standards for his job. Similarly, salesmen often use methods that increase their effectiveness but are unknown to their superiors

and even explicitly contrary to company rules. Most organizations possess an under-world of technique and technology, some of which is simply used to gain freedom from the impositions of higher levels of authority and some of which contributes to the achievement of corporate goals. (Shepard, 1967)

At this time we have little systematic evidence of the extent to which AIS of the sort described above are less vulnerable to subterfuge than the traditional supervisory media. But we suspect they are. If so, one impact of these AIS is to enhance the degree to which higher level staff can exercise their authority at the expense of lower level staff.

This shift of locus of control is at times intended. Simon has claimed that while an AIS enables decision-makers (e.g., top officials) to allocate resources (e.g., money, staff time) more rationally (through enhanced monitoring), it will also enhance the effectiveness of the computing using organizations (Simon, 1973). I believe that this assumption may be unfounded. It may be especially wrong when there is tremendous dissension about what goals an organization should pursue and how it may best follow them. For example, at the time Laudon investigated the use of AIS by police, health and welfare departments during 1968–72, there was tremendous public controversy about the goals and appropriate means to be employed by the agencies. Administrative reformers, who were concerned with pro-viding a limited set of services (crook catching, welfare check dispersing) more efficiently, employed AIS to support the strategies of centralization and elimination of duplication. At the same time, groups of political reformers, working through grassroots organizations or federal agencies (HUD and HEW) and supported by some federal legislation were attempting to increase the scope of local agencies and render them more responsive to clients and local control. In this agenda, police were to prevent crime rather than simply catch crooks. Health and welfare agencies were to help diminish social deprivation through job training, family planning, and related activities rather than simply passing out checks. Laudon found that the AIS he investigated enabled local agencies to pursue their narrow goals more efficiently, but rendered them less responsive to the kinds of changes advocated by the political reformers.

Consider the patrol scheduling program mentioned above. Some criminologists argue that crook-catching is expedited by getting to the scene of an incident as rapidly as possible. Thus, a system which deploys patrolmen so that they can respond to calls most rapidly will enhance the effectiveness of police as crook catchers (Larson, 1974). Critics of this approach argue that while patrolmen do regularly respond to emergencies (accidents, crimes in progress), this is not the *bulk* of their work. Patrol cars spend a good deal of time on surveillance. Most burglaries are reported hours or days after the theft. Police are called to break up family squabbles more often than they are to stop a bank robbery. These critics argue that police should spend more time in contact with citizens and less time responding around to random calls. One city police department, which shifted to this latter approach, had to dismantle its automated patrol allocation model because the optimization criteria used by the model were incompatible with a broader conception of effective police work. This example does not rule out a possible contribution of AIS to the broader and more effective functioning of public agencies. However, it does question tacitly acceptance of the professional values and agendas of top agency officials.

One example of an AIS which allegedly supports broader agency goals is a case management system used by 170 social service agencies in Chattanooga, Tennessee, and 13 nearby counties.

Traditionally, a client would apply separately to the relevant agency for welfare checks, day care assistance, medical care, family planning, dental care, etc. The Chattanooga integrated service system enables a person to make one application at any of several intake centers and then be referred to all the relevant agencies to provide the services s/he needs. Appointments are scheduled at each relevant agency, the client is sent a computer generated reminder, and the case is kept active until all the services have been provided. However, this system may also be "the exception which proves the rule." It was initially advocated by the Mayor of Chattanooga, and it provides caseload information which may also be used to keep closer track of the individual case workers activities. Nevertheless, it contrasts strongly with workload inventory systems which provide information only for administrative control.

Shifts of Power and Influence
Across Organizational Boundaries

Veblen coined the term "professional psychosis" to describe the systematic distortions of reality that accrue to various professionals. For example, accountants, as a group, are preoccupied with costs and tangible benefits. Their professional training emphasizes various explicit techniques of costing and assessing dollar benefits. Thus, when computer scientists advocate time-sharing systems, graphics terminals, fancy debugging systems, or modelling systems which will pay off in terms of enhanced uses of computing, speed of programming, and ease of implementing large and complex systems, auditors may be remarkably unwilling to accept such an assessment. Every profession has such blind spots or aspects of the world in which its practitioners are *trained not to see.* I believe that computing and IS designed professionals are systematically blind to the way in which power relations shape and are shaped by AIS. Earlier, I focused on the flows of information, and power up an organization, and the flow of policies down. I'd now like to focus on the role of AIS in supporting shifts of power and influence across organizational boundaries.

In the last few years, the Federal Reserve Board has been increasing pressure to create a nationwide electronic money system. This electronic funds transfer system (EFTS) is designed: 1) to automate the flow of money in *individual accounts* between participating banks; and 2) to tie point-of-sale terminals and individual check processing into the interbank transfers. Such an integrated system would rapidly transfer cash from a consumer's account for items purchased through a point of sale terminal or for checks processed at his or her creditor's bank. In effect, cash flows would be expedited nationwide, merchants would receive a large volume of small accounts payable more rapidly, and consumers might find their decrease in check writing more convenient. The cost of check processing would diminish, and the banks in the Federal Reserve System would gain more precise and timely information on daily cash flows throughout the country. EFTS seems to provide overwhelming technical and economic benefits to all major parties.

Articles that describe EFTS in the computing literature emphasize convenience benefits and focus on several narrow technical concerns:

security: how to reduce the likelihood of electronic money theft

reliability: how to insure that EFTS will not crash and prevent a large number of clients from transacting business through their on-line accounts

hardware integration: how to link the various hardware configurations used by various automated money clearing houses, banks and businesses.

While all these issues are both valid and relevant, EFTS also raises a set of power issues that are neither mentioned nor analyzed in the computing literature.

The banking industry is composed of several classes of banks (Federal Reserve Banks; independent banks; and savings and loan institutions) each of which compete for business in the money markets. In 1947, 52 per cent of the nation's banks belonged to the Federal Reserve System and held 86 per cent of the total deposits. However, by 1973, only 41 per cent of banks were Fed members and their share of total deposits dropped to 78 per cent. Each year banks leave the Fed system through either charter conversion or through merger with non-member banks (Boehne, 1974).[4] If the Fed is able to successfully develop and implement an EFTS, it would be more attractive for banks to join. Only banks can issue checking accounts, but recently, several savings and loan institutions have initiated a surrogate check system by providing a voucher to their clients. Because EFTS would make checking more convenient it would undercut the surrogate check business of the savings and loan institutions. In both cases, the Fed would regain (or increase) its relative influence among banking institutions. These are the primary concerns that motivate the Fed to strongly advocate EFTS. They are the concerns Fed officials stress when they testify before congressional committees. Payoffs of economy, data collection, increased efficiency and convenience are secondary. Anyone who helps develop or design components for EFTS is an actor in this power play between the banking institutions. One can choose whether or not to pay attention to these conflicts, but one must recognize such a role.

In the last decade, several urban information system designers have advocated integrated urban information systems to aid local officials in coordinating local government activities (Kraemer, 1969). Such systems would insure that much of the operating data collected by various departments would be stored in compatible formats and be easily linked. For example, local tax assessors maintain accurate and up-to-date housing and business inventories, and public works departments maintain descriptions of roads and sewerage pipes. Urban planners could typically use that data, along with other demographic and land use information, to assist in creating land use plans and in assessing requests for zoning variances. However, such sharing of routine operating data between various local government agencies is problematic. In particular, tax assessors tend to keep tight hold of building inventories. I suspect that fear of losing power or influence inhibits these officials from sharing data.

Urban Alliance, a biracial, interfaith, non-partisan voter information and candidate rating organization in Detroit conducts an annual analysis of voting trends in the city primary elections. The voting returns and a special survey are blended with socio-economic data by census-tract in order to provide a portrait of the way people in various socio-economic groups or neighborhoods assess various issues. Although most of the information used in the analysis is public information, the Urban Alliance makes its analyses freely available only to those candidates they endorse who can then select issues and campaign media that seem effective for special subgroups of voters. When and if the candidates supported by Urban Alliance win an election, influence with a majority of voters would be parlayed into an increase in power. Both the elected officials and Urban Alliance would gain power through such electoral success. The officials gain power through the prerogatives of office and Urban Alliance gains power vis-a-vis other political groups since its endorsement would guarantee a candidate community intelligence which could lead to a more effective campaign.

These three examples—EFTS, integrated urban data bases, and Urban Alliance's voting analysis, illustrate the way in which issues of power and influence can be especially salient features of AIS.

Alternative Clients

One gains another quite constructive way of viewing the flow of influence and power with AIS design by considering AIS created for atypical clients. Many people have trouble finding good professionals (doctors, plumbers, mechanics, carpenters, lawyers) except through word of mouth and trial and error search. A professional information system maintained for the public (by a local Chamber of Commerce?) which included descriptions of various professionals, their skills, fees, lauds and complaints, might enable one to find better professionals. Issues of data confidentiality, access and power that are common to many other data banks and evaluation systems are raised here as well. However, the traditional roles of evaluator and evaluated are reversed.

Most AIS that support computer assisted instruction [CAI] provide a sequenced set of prescribed activities for the students whose performance is monitored, aggregated and passed on to the teachers. It may be great for teachers and not so much fun for the kids. CAI designers who've designed especially for the kids tend to provide them with a rich, unsequenced set of computational aids. Such an environment is fun to explore, but tough to monitor and evaluate by traditional means (Pappert and Solomon, 1971).

Because welfare workers have tremendous discretion about informing their clients of aid programs for which they are eligible (Handler, 1973; Handler and Hollingsworth, 1971), case workers have tremendous coercive power over their clients. If clients dare to complain about the quality of service they receive, they may be given only minimal assistance in the future. However, if welfare clients were taken on as AIS users by IS designers, one might see some quite different systems. In contrast to work load inventory systems which evaluate some gross aspects of casework to welfare administrators (Weiss, 1972), and client dossier systems which provide data for caseworkers and administrators, AIS could index various programs by their services and requirements for eligibility. Such files could be publicly accessible in the waiting rooms of welfare offices, libraries and other appropriate public places.

Only one of these three families (CAI for kids) of systems has been designed and implemented for the typical client. However, these examples illustrate the way the structure, content, and provisions for access of AIS would change if the typically disenfranchised were taken on as clients by AIS designers.

Conclusions

The design of AIS may change the balance of power and influence between system users and other groups in social and organizational space. Often advocates promote AIS, such as performance and evaluation systems or EFTS, precisely because they expect such power impacts. The most elaborate AIS, developed for the larger corporations and government agencies, are often designed to enhance the power and influence of special subgroups within these organizations.

Computer professionals and AIS designers tend to ignore these power issues. We gravitate toward the organizational advocates of AIS, perceive resistance in terms of personality conflicts rather than loss of power, and tend to shroud our own advocacy in the limited rhetoric of rational decision making and organizational effectiveness (Simon, 1973). Some AIS designers believe that "we ought to be above these conflicts." I believe that is impossible. The examples I've elaborated illustrate AIS which may have substantial impacts on the relative power and influence of their users *regardless of how they are designed*. But the actual balance of power and influence that result could be effected in most of the examples by including different groups as system users and providing them different kinds of access to the AIS, *by a change in design*. Several years ago, I mentioned to an AIS developer the value of designing AIS of the sort suggested in the section "Alternate Clients." His jaw dropped, and with utter incredulity, he asked, "Whose side are you on?"

Shifts of power and influence are not the major impacts of all AIS. Substantial power impacts are not evident in the use of automated payroll, inventory control, or airline reservation systems. Like issues of data security, confidentiality and privacy, the locus of power, is a central issue for only some AIS. However, it is interesting to note that the vast majority of AIS for which influence and power impacts are most salient, are designed for and used by groups which already hold substantial power.

AIS designers typically act like hired guns who are merely servants of groups with established power. Most of us are simply employees with little professional or moral independence, and as a profession, we do not have role models like Ralph Nader (law) or Albert Schweitzer (medicine) who, through their work, articulate more humane alternatives. We naively laud almost any AIS built for a hospital or public agency as "for the public good" (ACM, 1973). Yet it's really an open issue whether one can actually design AIS to promote policies for public agencies which increase their responsiveness to the citizen publics, increase social equity and render the bureaucracies more transparent.

Notes

1. Sometimes these include whole classes of systems such as long-range planning models and large-scale social data banks.
2. Again, there is not "iron law" here. After all, the criminals may start working another area which is less effectively policed.
3. Even "personnel information systems" contain information about the staff of an organization for use by selected functionaries. They are not, in general, openly accessible to all the staff for *their* use.
4. Fed members gain rapid access to certain economic and cash flow indicators. How-

ever, they must maintain larger cash reserves than do non-Fed banks. Those bankers who leave the Fed believe their loss of leverage is not worth the information they got.

References

ACM, *Proceedings 1973 ACM National Conference*. Atlanta, Georgia (August, 1973).

Aiken, Michael, and Paul Mott, eds. *The Structure of Community Power*. Random House, New York, 1970.

Allison, Graham, "Conceptual Models and the Cuban Missile Crisis," *The American Political Science Review* 63 (Sept., 1969): 689–718.

Bachrach, Peter, and Morton S. Baratz, "Decisions and Non-Decisions: An Analytical Framework" reprinted in *The Structure of Community Power,* Aiken and Mott, eds., Random House, New York, 1970.

Becker, Howard S., "Whose Side Are We On?" *Social Problems* 14:239–47 (1967).

Boehne, E., "The Fed's Job is Getting Harder." Financial Section, *New York Times,* July 21, 1974.

Boguslaw, Robert, *The New Utopians*. Prentice-Hall, Englewood Cliffs, N.J., 1965 (esp. pp. 181–204).

Downs, Anthony, "A Realistic Look at the Final Payoffs from Urban Data Systems," *Public Administration Review* 27 (Sept., 1967): 204–209.

Handler, Joel, *The Coercive Social Worker*. Academic Press, New York, 1973.

Handler, Joel F., and Ellen Hollingsworth, *The "Deserving Poor."* Academic Press, New York, 1971.

Kraemer, Kenneth L. "A Model for Urban Information Systems," *Public Administration Review* 29 (July–August 1969): 389–402.

Larson, Richard, "Resource Planning for Urban Public Safety Systems," *Technology Review* vol. 76, no. 7 (June, 1974): 20–29.

Laudon, Kenneth, *Computers and Bureaucratic Reform*. Wiley Press, New York, 1974.

Mott, Paul, "Power, Influence and Authority" in *The Structure of Community Power*. Random House, New York, 1970.

Pappert, Seymour, and Cynthia Solomon, "Twenty Things to Do With a Computer" MIT Artificial Intelligence Memo #248 (June, 1971).

Quinn, Robert, "Individual and Organizational Impacts of a Human Service Information System" (unpublished manuscript) (n.d.)

Rubinstein, Jonathan, *City Police*. Random House, New York, 1973.

Shepard, Herbert, "Innovation-Resisting and Innovation Producing Organizations," *Journal of Business* 40, no. 4 (October, 1967): 470–477.

Simon, Herbert A. "Applying Information Technology to Organizational Design," *Public Administration Review* 33 (May/June 1973): 268–278.

Weis, Kurt, and Michael Milakovich, "Political Misuses of Crime Rates," *Society,* vol. 11, no. 5 (July/August, 1974): 27–33.

Weiss, Bernard, "Social Services and Systems Technology," *Proc. 3rd Milwaukee Institute on Social Welfare Issues of the Day*—School of Social Welfare, University of Wisconsin; Milwaukee, Oct., 1972.

Westin, Alan, ed., *Information Technology in a Democracy*. Harvard University Press, Cambridge, 1971.

Wilensky, Harold, *Organizational Intelligence*. Basic Books, New York, 1967. (especially pp. 182–191).

Zald, Meyer, "Political Economy: A Framework for Comparative Analysis" in *Power in Organizations,* ed. by Meyer Zald, Vanderbilt University Press, Nashville, Tenn., 1970.

27. Peering into the Poverty Gap

Philip Faflick

STUDENTS IN DIRT-POOR Hancock County, Ga., have always had to make do with less. They have no art teachers, no speech therapists and no full-time physical education program in the elementary schools. One thing they do have is computers. A pair of Apple II Plus micros was delivered to the high school two years ago, gifts of the Southeastern Consortium for Minorities in Engineering, a group of 22 colleges and universities that helps predominantly black high schools. This fall, impressed with what the new machines were doing for their students, county officials sprang for six more. "If we hadn't gotten the first two for free," says Superintendent M.E. Lewis, "we wouldn't have any at all."

Hancock County, deep in the cotton belt, is a lucky exception to a disturbing modernization of an old saw: the rich are getting a richer dose of the new technology, while the poor get left further behind. Computers are starting to appear in schools in large numbers. The total, which more than doubled in the past year, is approaching 130,000, or an average of 1.6 classroom computers for each of the nation's 82,000 public schools. But the number of machines available to each school varies widely. A survey of Market Data Retrieval Inc. found that 80% of the country's 2,000 largest and richest public high schools now have at least one micro, while 60% of the 2,000 poorest schools have none. Says Market Data President Herbert Lobsenz: "If computers are the wave of the future, a lot of America is being washed out."

In Menominee (pop. 10,000), a manufacturing town on Michigan's Upper Peninsula, 2,400 high school students must share just three Apple computers. Downstate in Ovid, teachers at the town's elementary school had to hook their only computer to a television set because they could not afford the standard video monitor. "We have a sense of panic," says Principal Tom Van Deventer. "A year ago, a computer was a luxury. Now it is a necessity." But there are competing necessities. In New Orleans, where fewer than 7% of the schools have computer classes, one school district administrator contends, "Kids here need a lot of other things. They need counselors, basic textbooks, a bathroom that works."

Even when poor rural and inner-city schools elect to spend their limited funds on computers, the teachers are often inadequately prepared. Pressured to improve basic skills quickly, they take the most direct route, using computers as electronic flash cards for simple drill and practice. By contrast, specially trained teachers at more sophisticated schools are introducing ever younger children to the art of programming. In Georgia's affluent De Kalb County, 445 teachers a year take four-hour instruction sessions one night a week. Says Frank Barber, the training coordinator: "We believe the nicest thing that can happen to a child is to have a teacher who really understands what computers can do."

Not surprisingly, rich private schools such as Dalton in New York City, Lamplighter in

Dallas and the Harvard School near Beverly Hills have enough machines to give every student access. And in areas where parents know and care about computers, like California's Silicon Valley or Boston's ring of electronics-oriented suburbs, public schools are using computers in most of the regular curriculum. Ann Arbor, Mich., which has been wired up for more than a decade, has 200 micros in its 26 elementary schools, 50 in its five intermediate schools, and 52 in the three senior high schools. Further, as more and more couples acquire low-priced home computers, often with the express purpose of giving Johnny a head start, they begin lobbying school boards to get the funds for classroom machines.

Even among educators who worry about too much tilt to technology, there is growing agreement that a computer is a powerful motivator of a schoolage child. Students with access to a micro spend more time studying and solving problems. Those who write at their keyboards compose more freely and revise their work more thoroughly. "It's not just a matter of number crunching," argues Arden Bement, a vice president of TRW. "It's a new way of thinking. The kids who don't get indoctrinated to computers by seventh grade are not going to develop the same proficiency." Says Andrew Molnar, computer education specialist at the National Science Foundation: "Power is not distributed evenly now, and computers will broaden that gap."

Other observers disagree, seeing instead a potential educational leveling device. "In the long run, all God's children will have computers," says Computer Consultant Charles Lecht. "Students who used to fail because they could not master geometry the first time around will be able to turn to the computer for relief. The machines will emerge as great equalizers." But the majority in the field worry about the near-term specter of the rich taking control of the technology while the poor play video games.

In an era of tight money and taxpayer rebellions, government is not likely to redress the disparity. In fact, the Reagan Administration is urging a one-third cut in the funding for the federal program under which most of the few computers in inner-city schools were purchased. Another much ballyhooed prospect for help is also in trouble. Steven Jobs, the 27-year-old chairman of Apple Computer, had proposed donating a free computer to every school in the country, provided Congress grant manufacturers the same tax break that would be available if they gave the equipment to a university. The companies that took advantage of the law would then have been able to do a public service, while also building future markets.

But Jobs is now backing off, unhappy with various limitations in the version of the tax break that has passed the House and is awaiting Senate action. If he were to get the bill he wants, the delivery of thousands of free machines would help to even out the inequities. "Computers will be taught in most schools eventually," says Jobs. "But that's five to ten years from now. The question is, why wait?"

28. Computer Systems: Power for Whom and for What?

Herbert I. Schiller

Is What's Good for IBM Good for the World? The Answer May Depend on the Kind of World That's Envisaged.

A VERY LARGE amount of data about all sorts of matters—individual and national, social, commercial, economic, and military—are now being processed and transmitted between international super-corporations, national governmental bureaucracies, and scientific and academic institutions. Already, institutional patterns have developed to facilitate these activities. An examination of the structures and relationships now in place may help to create a realistic assessment of the present world information order. Unless the social forces underlying and determining current computer communications[1] are revealed and understood, ground gained in overcoming information dependency in traditional areas may be retaken by those who dominate the new terrain (see [18]).

In attempting such an examination, it must be admitted at the outset that the complexity of the new information technology is beyond simple exposition. The developments are difficult to ascertain because of the private nature of most of the arrangements and the technical sheath that conceals many of the socioeconomic factors. Additionally, the field is new, changing rapidly, and has not yet congealed into hard and fast relationships. For these reasons, what follows must be regarded as far from comprehensive and is intended to be exploratory, suggestive, and only tentative. One central issue is addressed: how is information dependency of people and nations likely to be affected with the advent of the new instrumentation and its control mechanisms?

The Singular Institutional Attribute of the New Communication Technology is that Almost all the Hardware is Produced by a Very Small Number of Private Companies.

In the United States, the telephone industry is largely the domain of one corporation, American Telephone and Telegraph (A.T.&T.), and its production subsidiary, Western Electric Company. In the computer industry, International Business Machines Corporation (IBM) stands far ahead of its few competitors. In the manufacture of communication satellites, a couple of firms dominate the market. Because it is a more recent development, the electronics industry—which supplies the inner components for much of the equipment—is a little less concentrated.

A related structural factor is that the international market has crucial significance for the well-being of large-scale American enterprises. As older U.S. industries—textiles, footwear, even steel—have lost ground steadily in overseas markets, the new communication

From *Journal of Communication* 28, 4 (Autumn 1978), pp. 184–193. ©1978 by Herbert I. Schiller. Reprinted by permission of Herbert I. Schiller.

technology industry (as well as other high research and development industries) has been assigned a priority role in maintaining American world economic hegemony. Heavy sales of sophisticated equipment may compensate, at least in part, for declining exports and influence in other sectors. Therefore, the communication industry, which includes data generation and transmission, assumes enormous importance well beyond its substantial financial contribution.

In the business of communication technology, there is also one corporation which dominates domestically and internationally.[2] One account describes this condition:

> Watching the movements made by companies and governments in the industry world-wide is like watching 15 chess matches going on at the same time. Every match has one thing in common, though. IBM seems to control both queens on every board [11, p. 56].

Or, as the *un*authorized biographer of IBM writes, "IBM is not just a major international company in the area of computing, it is the international environment" [9, p. x]. Currently, IBM has 130,000 workers abroad in 21 plants and 10 laboratories. In 1975, it received more than half of its revenues from business outside the United States. In most of the major, developed countries in the world, its share of the communication market starts at 50 percent [11, p. 59].

The size of the market for computers already is impressive. Its near term potential, projecting current installation trends, suggest that computers will constitute one of the world's largest industries. The power these developments confer on a corporation that now dominates the field, therefore, hardly can be overestimated. The current situation and the short term trends are shown in Table 1.

In 1975, IBM had 52.6 percent of Western Europe's market for general purpose computers. Its share in 1980 is estimated to hold at 51.0 percent (*Datamation,* September 1976, p. 63). In Japan, which is making a determined effort to achieve independence in the

TABLE 1: *Worldwide computer industry: installed bases[a] in $ millions at sales value*

Country	as of 12/31/75 (in millions $)	as of 12/31/80 (in millions $)
United States	39,750	62,700
Western Europe	22,050	38,800
Other countries (including Japan)	11,600	23,050
	73,400	124,550

Source: Sperry Rand (*Datamation,* September 1976, p. 57).
[a]Installed base is the value of the equipment in place.

computer business, IBM's share of that market in 1975 was 26 percent (*Datamation,* September 1976, p. 93).

Because computer communication is seen as crucial for profit, facilitating industrial development, and, no less, securing cultural/informational influence, nowhere are commercial rivalries more evident than in this field. But the field of rivals is limited by the economic marketplace that prevents poorer nations from influencing the design and production of the hardware of the new information age. And cultural/informational dependency for the underdeveloped world almost seems built into the present kind of information instrumentation.

Less Observable, Though No Less Important, Are the Instructions for Organizing, Processing, and Transmitting the Data As Well As the Data Themselves—the Software.

One of the most important categories of software is the data base. Data bases are constructed for many purposes, the most familiar of which is the academic-technical-scientific base. This is a set of data in a specific category or area—chemistry, physics, medicine, education, sociology—which has been stored in some suitably accessible form. The size of a base varies but it may contain as many as millions of records.

Other data bases are organized for the production and marketing needs of large, private corporations (for payrolls, raw material flows, property accounting, customers) and for governmental and private administrative units (social security rolls, credit ratings, police records, health statistics and information). This type of data base presently accounts for the preponderant utilization of computer communications. However, most of these are unavailable for systematic analysis and review because they are regarded as proprietary. Information searches by computer, already widespread, are likely to become standard tools in much of the scientific community's future research activity, to say nothing of their application to everyday business and government operations. Meaningful information autonomy may then also require participation in the creation of the software. This means the fullest opportunity for the user to know what is and what is not in the data base, the criteria for data selection and classification, and how changes may be introduced.

Yet, paralleling developments in the production and marketing of hardware, the software industry too (apart from the totally proprietary intra-company computer systems) is being integrated rapidly into socioeconomic control structures. This follows from the considerable costs of assembling information. "Putting [a data base] into operation requires the equivalent of 30 man years of work, an initial cash outlay of $.08 to $1 million and an annual operating expenditure of between $120,000 and $200,000" [8]. In a market economy, the questions of costs and prices inevitably play the most important, if not determining, roles in what kind of base will be constructed and the category of user the base is intended to serve (and be paid for). The selection of material that goes into a data base is closely linked to the need for and the marketability of the information service. If corporate and government bureaucracies are the intended users—which happens most often because of their need and ability to pay—their informational requirements will strongly influence the items put into the base, as well as the classifications adopted for easy retrieval of the information.

An inventory of the data bases in operation worldwide can only be provisional at this time, as new bases are being created continually, both nationally and internationally. In

TABLE 2: Data bases in operation in 1975 in United States and Europe
(exclusive of private, intra-corporate bases)

Area	No. of bases	% of bases	No. of records held	% of records held
U.S.	160	58	46,300,000	89
Non-U.S.	117	42	5,700,000	11
	277	100	52,000,000	100

Source: [20, p. 20].

addition, corporate data banks, which comprise the bulk of data bases now in use, must be excluded from this analysis as they are not accessible to the public. Table 2 presents information on 277 data bases (exclusive of corporate bases) in operation in Europe and in the United States at the end of 1975. Two hundred small bases which had little effect on the general picture were not included.

With respect to *organized* data—the essential prerequisite for utilization in an information-based economy—the United States in 1975 was far ahead of other industrialized nations; almost nine-tenths of the records held in organized data banks were located in U.S. data bases. Of these, the U.S. Government accounted for 25 percent and the private sector for 75 percent. Of that 75 percent, for-profit organizations have 35 percent and the not-for-profit organizations 40 percent. (Actually, the not-for-profit component in the private sector may be misleading. Increasingly, the designation "not-for-profit" is a convenient organizational means to avoid certain obligations while providing *de facto* commercial opportunities and benefits to its administrators.)

One other characteristic of these existing data bases in the United States and Europe is worth mentioning. This is the distribution of the bases by category of information held. As shown in Table 3, it is striking that the non-scientific and technical category of information in all the reported data bases totalled only 8 percent of all non-corporate records held, whereas science-technology and science and technology-related records accounted for 79 percent of the data held. One European study suggests that this reflects the

> development of publicly available computer-based information services which has been a spin-off from the massive U.S. Government investment in Defense and Aerospace. These Government Agencies developed a methodology and technique of information handling to satisfy their own information needs. This methodology, updated to capitalize on advances in computer technology, is used by all the major international information services such as System Development Corporation (SDC) and Lockheed and also the major European operations, the Space Documentation Service of the European Space Agency [13, p. 1].

Moreover, much of the assembled data originated in the U.S. military and military-related research and development after World War II. The enormous R & D budgets of the Pentagon,

TABLE 3: Distribution of data bases in U.S. and Europe in 1975 by category of information held (exclusive of private, intra-corporate bases)

Information category	No. of bases	% of bases	No. of records	% of records
Science and technology	161	58	25,600,000	49
Medicine and life sciences	28	10	6,600,000	13
Non-science-technology	42	15	4,300,000	8
Science-technology related	46	17	15,500,000	30
	277	100	52,000,000	100

Source: [20, p. 21].

over three decades, have generated a good share of the information that currently resides in the data bases now functioning.

Although the Rapid Evolution of Computer Technology and Control Prevents Rigid Predictions, the Uninterrupted Assemblage of Bases into Ever Larger Aggregations of Available Data in the U.S. Cannot Be Ignored.

Already, a few corporations or corporate subsidiaries have emerged as significant data base organizers and data suppliers. Lockheed, for example, with its DIALOG information retrieval system, contends that it is "the largest and most extensive collection of on-line [interactive] data bases in the world" [2, p. 7]. At the end of 1975, it was estimated that there were 2000 organizational users of on-line search services worldwide of which 32 percent were commercial, 31 percent educational, 21 percent government agencies, 10 percent non-profit, and 6 percent other. Of the overall total of users, Lockheed claimed that its customers exceeded 1000, or more than half of the worldwide use at that time [1, p. 2]. In addition to Lockheed, other U.S. firms—System Development Corporation, Bibliographic Retrieval Services, Inc., Mead, and Informatics—actively promote these services. But it must be remembered that these data base search services, however concentrated, handle only a tiny fraction of the current data storage, processing, and transmission, the bulk of which are serving the needs of the multinational businesses—especially those involved in banking, air travel, and manufacturing.

Data Base Networks, Which May Become Rivals of the U.S. Networks, Also Are Being Organized in Europe.

The nine West European market economies which comprise the Common Market have set up EURONET. This network, scheduled for operation in 1978, will have access to a number of European-organized scientific, industrial, and agricultural data bases, as well as the main U.S. bases. It is, as one researcher notes, "an ambitious program with an excellent group of information specialists who see their major tasks at present as including, finding and selecting appropriate data bases, selecting hardware, selecting and expanding software, developing pricing policies, developing improved data bases and working toward filling of gaps, developing multilingual techniques, and developing standards" [19, p. 118]. These mostly technical tasks incident to creating a comprehensive informational network are secondary, however, to the political and economic aims of EURONET, which is seen "as a method of ensuring a system that has European control and is not in the hands of commercial [i.e., U.S.] distributors" [19, p. 118].

This is no trivial concern. According to U.S. Department of Commerce data for 1975, in the 24 OECD European countries, U.S. data processing and information-handling commercial interests showed earnings of "nearly $1 billion, growing at 15–25 percent yearly" [17]. This sum did *not* include the revenues of general industry (airlines, banks, hotels, U.S. trade associations, and automobile manufacturers) also heavily engaged in informational activities. Europeans, understandably, are considering ways and means of recapturing this business for their own companies. In accord with this objective, OECD called a meeting in Vienna in September 1977 to examine the implications of trans-border data flows and to consider whether an international regulatory agreement was necessary.

The United States dispatched a strong contingent to the meeting to represent its interest—"a platoon of nearly 50 Americans," according to *Computerworld*'s account. The newspaper further reported that the U.S. "won" at the data flow parley [5]. The victory consisted in the decision of the conference not to endorse any international agreement calling for restriction of data transmission across national boundaries.

Although U.S. interests were successful in this instance in holding open European data-handling markets, their future prospects remain uncertain. One responsible government official told Congress that "unquestioning acceptance of electronic data processing is ending . . . the possibility of development of non-tariff barriers that might effectively exclude or hinder our firms in the European markets [is real]" [17]. More emotionally still, an American businessman in the industry told a congressional committee examining these issues: "We alone are not fully aware that we are at economic war with the rest of the world. We will do our nation a disservice if we don't elevate this discussion" [7, p. 2].

The Transmission Structures That Are Being Established Nationally and Internationally Provide Additional Evidence of the Character of the Systems Emerging in the Information Age.

The utilization of data bases, data base networks, and private and governmental computerized information systems is dependent ultimately on some form of transmission—telephone, cable, microwave, or communications satellites. Communications satellites, which now offer thousands of circuits for telephone and TV and data transmission, are the properties of the same U.S. communications corporations that dominate the computer and telecommunications industries.

A few American companies, such as Hughes Aircraft Company, RCA Corporation's Astroelectronics Division, and General Electric's Space Division, have a hold on the building of communication satellites. A new combinatory enterprise, Satellite Business Systems, "a joint venture of subsidiaries of the International Business Machines Corporation (IBM), the Comsat General Corporation and the Aetna Life and Casualty Company," is contracting for the construction of data-transmission satellites through which it hopes to manage much of the rapidly-expanding data transmission requirements of corporate business [10].

Internationally, INTELSAT, the world-wide satellite communications system, remains an instrumentality under comparable U.S. corporate direction, with a few qualifying limitations imposed by the 95 member nations. Both nationally and internationally, the administrative, organizational, and technical features of communication satellite transmission tend to strengthen the world business system, while the pricing patterns, market efficiency, equipment monopoly, and the technical determinants of the system are important factors in consolidating old market patterns in a new sector [14].

To date, when the far-ranging implications of satellite communication systems have been noticed at all, public discussion has focused mostly on technical questions of access, comprehensiveness, language translation, and costs. It seems, however, that an overriding issue remains unaddressed—do these instantaneous and world-girdling information networks and systems now being installed have either the design, the capability, or, with respect to their administrators, the intention of assisting people and nations to overcome cultural and economic impoverishment? This matter requires and deserves full and open discussion and the most careful consideration by the community at large, not "technical experts" alone. If the capabilities that now are being developed are used for purposes and in ways no different from the communication facilities that preceded them, an enormous opportunity to redress some of the global informational and societal imbalances will be missed.

To be sure, optimistic appraisals of the new computer communication abound. "The advantages to mankind of progress in international communication" are extensively detailed. It will, it is contended: (a) increase the economy in world resource utilization; (b) accelerate technical progress overall; (c) meet the special information needs of the less developed countries; (d) facilitate and expand world trade; and (e) facilitate the diversification of world culture [12]. These attractive prospects are contingent, however, on conditions and assumptions that make it much more likely that the benefits of the new technology will continue to be unequally distributed and the dependency of countries and classes within countries will be extended, not diminished.

Evaluations of the oncoming Information Age that dwell on the splendors of the technological features while remaining silent about the socio-structural components *already manifest* in equipment manufacture and supply, data base construction and availability, transmission systems created, at best can be regarded with skepticism. These evaluations are inclined to place emphasis and trust on system-determined technology that is not neutral, to overcome socioeconomic deprivation which is also systemically created. The dangers are well assessed by Canada's Minister of State for Science and Technology, J. Hugh Faulkner, who observes that the problem of transnational data flow has "created the potential of growing dependence, rather than interdependence," and with it "the danger of loss of legitimate access to vital information and the danger that industrial and social development will largely be governed by the decisions of interest groups residing in another country" [4, p. 10]. An example of this type of information flow was noted in a recent annual report of the Harvard Program on Information Resources Policy:

> Internationally, political borders are as fuzzy as the computer/communications borders. Balkan Bulgarian Airlines, Malev Hungarian Airlines, and LOT Polish Airlines, among others, book *local* flights through a computer in Atlanta. Canadian plant payrolls are made up in St. Louis. An American-built satellite is broadcasting directly to villages in India. Whose information resources are these? Who controls them? With what means? In whose national interests? ([6], p. 8, emphasis added).

These are pertinent questions.

For the present at least, the United States lead in the communications technology is substantial. Recognizing this advantage, American policy-makers and economic leaders have pressed for the introduction and utilization of the new technology believing, reasonably enough, that its adoption would be in their benefit. "Operationalism"—the policy of installing and operating the equipment first and considering its regulation and social impact later—has been the American approach in forums concerned with economic development and international communications [15]. In promoting "operationalism," the U.S. representatives argue that "premature" regulation of direct satellite broadcasting, for example, might hamper its development and delay technical progress. Similarly with computer communications and transnational border data flows, the U.S. position is that "any international accord calling for restriction of data transmission across national boundaries, whether for reasons of protecting individual privacy or otherwise, [is] either unnecessary or premature" [4, p. 10].

Powerful Forces of Economics, Finance, and Technology Notwithstanding, the Future of the Information Age Cannot, at This Time, Be Regarded As Predetermined and Settled.

For one thing, most of the relationships detailed above, however monopolistic and market-oriented, are still in their early growth stage. The rate of technical change remains rapid and, although this is by no means a guarantee of satisfactory outcomes, it does prevent patterns of control from being frozen. Each generation of technical equipment, for example, far exceeds the capability of its predecessor. New models make existing facilities and processes obsolete. In such a period, stability and control are difficult to achieve, much less maintain.

There is increasing restiveness and growing awareness of people and leaders in many of the underdeveloped nations about the conditions of their economic and cultural dependency. Where do computer communications fit into this picture? Even at this relatively early stage of utilization of computer communication globally, some disturbing tendencies are observable. Elite classes in the less developed countries are being tied more closely to their decision-making counterparts in the industrialized states. The new communication technology rather than diminishing, seems to be widening the communications gaps *inside* the poorer nations and accentuating economic disparities between classes.

With a few notable exceptions, the evidence is slight that much re-thinking about what constitutes "development" has occurred in the underdeveloped world, or anywhere else, for that matter. Yet the expectations of repeating Western developmental experiences and achieving Western levels of "mass affluence" in Asia, Africa, the Middle East, and Latin America, are chimerical. Already, advanced, industrialized market economies are coming to recognize that the present levels of resource utilization are not maintainable.

Yet the most casual examination of computer communications reveals that its origins, development, and utilization have been tied directly to the structure, character, and functioning of a market-organized socioeconomic system. The director of the Science Information Division of the National Science Foundation explains it this way: ". . . the driving forces that are shaping the U.S. information economy . . . are derived from the dynamics of the major elements comprising the U.S. information economy. Information processing requirements of business, banking and other commercial enterprises are immense. So are those of the military and civilian side of the federal government" [3].

The necessity for the vast data processing grew and grows out of the kind of production and service activities that are undertaken. It regularizes the division of labor into technicians and workers in accordance with the control design of the system. It routinizes the organized (state) systems required to maintain social order, domestically and internationally.

Thus, it is reasonable to conclude that a considerable portion of systems and human accounting, individual and corporate, *in the present kind of economy,* can be facilitated enormously with the computer communications now available. But it is no less reasonable to believe that a very significant part of what is now regarded as vital record-keeping, requiring vast amounts of information processing, could be dispensed with entirely in a community with different social objectives and different underlying social structures and practices.

One may agree that computer communications are of potential benefit in *any* social system. The assumption that they are necessary and urgent as they are currently functioning is another matter entirely. To believe they are is to accept a developmental pattern that already has demonstrated that it is humanly dysfunctional.

Notes

1. As defined by Pool, computer communication is "any communication in which, at at least one point, the message is stored in computer memory and then processed or transmitted under computer control. This definition includes computer-to-computer communication, as in computer networks, man-to-computer or computer-to-man (as when a person works on a computer from a remote terminal) communication, and man-to-man communication if computers that store, address, and forward the message are placed between the men, as in message-switched communication systems" (see [12], p. 33).
2. It is a mark of IBM's standing in the national economy that the first cabinet of the Carter Administration contained three directors of IBM's board. Additionally, a vice-president of the corporation serves as chairman of the President's Science Coordinating Committee (see [16]).

References

1. *Advanced Technology/Libraries* 5(7), July 1976.
2. *Advanced Technology/Libraries* 6(1), January 1977.
3. Burchinal, Lee G. Paper presented to the Pittsburgh Conference on "The On-Line Revolution in Libraries," Pittsburgh, Pa., November 14–16, 1977.
4. French, Nancy. "Transnational Processing Cited as Canadian Bane." *Computerworld,* August 15, 1977.
5. French, Nancy. "U.S. 'Wins' at Data Flow Parley." *Computerworld,* October 3, 1977.

6. Harvard University, Program on Information and Resources. "Information Resources Policy." Annual Report 1975–76, Volume 2, Cambridge, Mass.
7. Holmes, Edith. "Transborder Data Taking Back Seat." *Computerworld,* October 24, 1977.
8. *Information Hot-Line* 8(9), October 1976.
9. Malik, Rex. *And Tomorrow the World?* London: Millington, 1975.
10. McElheny, Victor. "Technology." *New York Times,* August 17, 1977.
11. Pantages, Angeline. "The International Computer Industry." *Datamation,* September 1976.
12. Pool, Ithiel de Sola. "International Aspects of Computer Communications." *Telecommunications Policy,* December 1976, pp. 33–51.
13. Pratt, Gordon (Ed). *Information Economics.* London: Association of Special Libraries and Information Bureaus (ASLIB), and European Association of Scientific Information Dissemination Centres (EUSIDIC), 1976.
14. Schiller, Herbert I. Review of *Intelsat* by J. N. Pelton. *Journal of Communication* 25(1), Winter 1975, pp. 213–216.
15. Signitzer, Benno. *Regulation of Direct Broadcasting from Satellites: The UN Involvement.* New York: Praeger, 1976.
16. Smith, William D. "Three Nominated by Carter for Posts in Cabinet are I.B.M. Directors." *New York Times,* December 22, 1976.
17. U.S. Congress, House. Subcommittee on Communications. Statement to the Committee, June 21, 1977.
18. U.S. Congress, Senate. Committee on Foreign Relations, Subcommittee on International Operations. Statement to the Committee, June 8, 1977. Mimeo transcript.
19. Voigt, Melvin J. "Euronet." *Library Journal* 101(10), May 15, 1976.
20. Williams, Martha and Ted Brandhorst. "Data About Data Bases." *Bulletin of the American Society for Information Science* 3(2), December 1976.

Software As Property

T HE FOLLOWING CASE illustrates a common problem for computer personnel worried about claims of ownership to the products they create.

John has completed a lengthy program on which he has spent considerable effort and into which he has incorporated some new and ingenious programming techniques. Since it represents his own work, he has sought proprietary protection for it through a formal copyright. This lets him say who may make copies of the program. Mary, working on a related problem, reads John's program, seeking ideas on how to approach her own work. Assuming she does this without making any unauthorized copies, she does not infringe on John's ownership claim. Mary, however, goes further. She discovers in John's work an elegant new sorting procedure that resolves one of her problems in a dozen lines of code. She decides to use John's approach. Since John's dozen lines are really the most obvious and simple way to encode the algorithm, she ends up incorporating that bit of John's program into her own work. She is now worried about whether she has stolen something that belongs to John.

Mary's problem is both common and difficult to resolve. John's ownership claim is based on copyright, which was developed to protect creative writing such as essays and poems and may not adequately protect programs. It protects the manner in which ideas are expressed while leaving the ideas themselves open to anyone who may wish to use them. On those grounds, Mary is certainly free to use the ideas expressed in the program. Since this would be meaningless if she had no way to express the ideas, it follows that she may also use John's code if there is no reasonable alternate way to write up the algorithm. On legal grounds, she has acted properly. On the other hand, it is "John's algorithm" and not something likely to have occurred to her independently. As such we may feel that John should have an exclusive right to its use. We are here confronted with a complex of problems centering on new uses for old legal definitions, basic human freedoms, intuitions

293

on inventor's rights, and doubts about the notion of personal property. There are no simple solutions.

Researchers and sponsors of research on new computer software would like to keep economic control over their discoveries and developments. Recognizing the justice of their requests, it seems reasonable to grant to individuals or institutions the legal right to determine who may use innovative software techniques. If we do that, then we treat software as *property*.

Our notion of what counts as personal property is created by legal rules defining and governing such matters as theft, inheritance, transfer, trespass, and personal use. Many variations on these rules are possible. For instance, we could grant to individuals the right to prevent others from trespassing on "their" land, without permitting a transfer of this right through lease, gift, sale, or inheritance. Then we would have a different sense of ownership and a different kind of property than we now have. Since computer software is not the same sort of thing as a plot of land that can be occupied or a car that can only be used by one person at a time, what we mean by "ownership" of software will be very different from ownership of an estate and cars. Just because we know what it is like to own real estate and cars, it does not follow that we have any clear sense of what it means to "own" a computer program. Some very difficult decisions on how we ought to grant rights over software will have to be made, and these decisions will define the kind of property that software is. The laws will have to take into account a number of factors, including what we understand software to be, how we want research on and development of new software to proceed, what is "fair" protection for both innovators and users of new innovations.

Software ownership, if we are to make sense of the notion, resembles the ownership that inventors claim over their innovative machines and authors claim over their creative writing. Lawyers often call items of this sort "intellectual property" to distinguish it from "tangible property." Items of tangible property can be touched, seen, and occupied. Items of intellectual property are understood (as in the case of a poem or the design of a machine) or applied (as in the case of a new process for synthesizing rubber). Remember that the inventor of a machine generally seeks control over who may construct or use a machine based on his design and may give up the ownership of individual, tangible machines through sale without losing property rights over the design. Similarly, a writer may still claim that a series of lines is "my poem," even though the tangible page on which the poem is printed is owned by the buyer of the book. Computer software, if it is to be owned, will be a sort of intellectual property. Ownership will probably consist of control over who may copy the software and who may run programs based on the processes laid down in the software. It seems natural to provide that control through the use of the traditional forms of legal protection that grant similar proprietary control to inventors and creative writers. But software is also very different from traditional inventions, and the traditional protections do not easily adapt to it. Software is a new sort of entity and we must make new decisions on how we should protect it and how we should define ownership.

There are several forms of legal protection presently available for intellectual property. In the United States, these may be roughly divided into two groups: (1) protections granted by the federal government through statutory law and (2) protections acquired through other means.

Protections granted by the federal government include (a) patents that grant ownership over machines and processes, (b) copyrights that grant ownership over what is written down, and (c) trademarks that grant ownership over names. The government has the power to grant these sorts of property protections under section 1, article 8 of the Constitution.

> The Congress shall have the power to . . . promote the progress of science and useful arts securing for limited times to authors and inventors the exclusive rights to their respective writings and discoveries.

The precise forms of these property rights are spelled out in laws passed by Congress and interpreted by the federal courts.

The second group of protections includes those rights created by contracts and acquired as trade secrets. Trade secrets are particularly important in the protection of software as property. In fact, it is at present the preferred form of protection for much creative work in computer technology. Here, however, there is no clear written legal document that states the proper form of trade-secret protection. Instead there are traditions of business practice that without ever being codified in written law have been over the years recognized by the courts as binding on businesses. That is, there is a "common law" basis for trade-secret protections. In the extreme, for instance, it would be considered improper for a businessman to bribe a confidential secretary to reveal the direction of new research, even if there were no written laws explicitly outlawing the practice. The law of trade secret is largely defined in a document called the *Restatement of Torts*. This volume of legal definitions was written as a sort of dictionary for lawyers; and, although it has no formal legal status, it is widely referred to by judges and lawyers when they argue cases that are not covered by formal laws. Also, several states have enacted laws that define trade-secret violations, within those states, although it is often unclear how such laws apply to violations that, as is common in the computer industry, take place across state lines.

The papers in Part 5 discuss different aspects of the problem of software protection. Morris Cohen provides a philosophical background for the study of property. Justice Rehnquist and Justice Stevens in *Diamond* v. *Diehr* look at software patents. Judge Sloviter in *Apple* v. *Franklin* looks at software copyrights. Joseph Scafetta looks at software trade secrets. And Michael Gemignani attempts an overview of the legal situation with a sense of how computer property differs from traditional forms of property.

Cohen's paper "Property and Sovereignty" surveys several philosophical justifications of the legal institution of property. Cohen argues that ownership should not be viewed merely as control of the items that are owned, but also as control over those people who may want access to those items. Within this framework, he tests traditional theories of property to see if they can justify the influence an owner has over other members of society. The "labor theory" for instance might suggest that a programmer should own his programs simply because he worked hard on their creation. The significant question, however, in Cohen's view is whether that work justifies the influence the programmer may gain over other computer users.

In *Diamond* v. *Diehr,* Supreme Court judges discuss the use of patent protection for computer programs. Patents are in many respects the obvious form of protection to seek for computer programs because they give the patent holder a monopoly on the use of his inventions. Patents are used to protect such things as chemical processes for the synthesis of new chemicals. Since a computer program processes data, it is reasonable to treat it like other sorts of commercially valuable processes and grant patents on it. But there are also good reasons to deny patents on programs. Intrinsic to the notion of a patent are safeguards against the possibility that an inventor may grab too many controls over a discovery. The court, for instance, refused Samuel Morse a patent on all uses of electromagnetism to send messages (which would have been much too much), but granted one on the particular apparatus that is used in the telegraph. The court also has generally refused to grant patents on either mathematical formulas or natural laws. The stricture against patents on formulas turns out to be critical to the question of whether or not software qualifies for patent protection since executable programs can almost always be viewed as complex formulas for solving arithmetic problems.

The rationale for denying patents on mathematical formulas is not entirely clear. It may be that mathematical formulas are independently existing facts that are discovered rather than created and are therefore not inventions. It may be that mathematics is important to ongoing research and that rights over a formula would permit the patent holder to prevent other researchers from doing their work. For the most part, however, the patent office has said that programs are formulas and thus "unpatentable subject matter." In *Diamond* v. *Diehr,* Justice Rehnquist decided that a process for curing rubber developed by Diehr was patentable, even though the process included a computer program as a crucial component. Justice Stevens argued to the contrary that the only novel aspect of Diehr's process is the program that automates the machinery. So Stevens argued that Diehr really sought a patent on a program (which is unpatentable) while Rehnquist argued that Diehr sought a patent on a process for curing rubber (which is patentable). Rehnquist's position was the majority position (five to four) and Diehr now has the patent.

The underlying ethical issue here is whether, how, and when patent protections may be used to create intellectual property in software. We must ask ourselves whether the safeguard in the patent law that excludes patents on mathematical formulas is justified. We must ask what is guarded by this exclusion. And we must ask whether that safeguard should be used to exclude any or all software patents. And, if we are to grant patents on some software, we must ask ourselves how this is to be done while guarding against whatever the courts have meant to exclude by denying patents on software.

Since software can be written out in a manuscript form, it resembles the sort of thing that is generally copyrighted. But just as the patent law has safeguards against overly broad control of new technology, the copyright law has safeguards against the overly broad control of written ideas. And, as with patents, we find that those safeguards can have the consequence that copyrights are unsuitable for computer software. These issues are discussed in *Apple* v. *Franklin.* Apple Computer claims that Franklin Computer has reproduced copyrighted programs without permission. The decision presented here involves a "preliminary injunction" that would prevent Franklin from using the programs until the issues are resolved in court. A district court had denied the injunction because, in part, there are so many controversial issues surrounding the notion of a software copyright. In the decision presented here, Judge Sloviter reverses that prior decision and grants the preliminary injunction, dismissing some of the lower court's worries as unfounded. Judge Sloviter does note the significance of some of Franklin's challenges, but leaves them to be resolved later when the case itself is decided. Unfortunately, these issues will not now be discussed further in court. Franklin settled out of court, perhaps because Franklin believes that Judge Sloviter's decision reflects a widely held opposition to their arguments.

We obviously would not want a copyright to grant to a writer total control over who may discuss the theories presented in a copyrighted work. Albert Einstein, for instance, may have a copyright on his famous paper presenting relativity theory. But it would be wrong to therefore give him sole control over who may discuss relativity theory. In order to prevent this, copyright control is limited to the way in which a theory is worded, not over the ideas. Intrinsic to copyright law is a distinction between the *ideas* expressed in a manuscript (not protected) and the way in which those ideas are *expressed* (protected). This means that someone who has a copyright cannot prevent others from writing down the same ideas in their own words. Just as traditional essays express ideas, computer programs express methods for using computers. And as copyrights are invalid if they would limit consideration of ideas, they are also invalid if they would limit use of computing methods. (It is, of course, a difficult matter of judgment whether any particular manuscript is a copy that infringes or a restatement in other words of an original.)

The issue in *Apple* v. *Franklin* is whether Apple properly seeks protection only on a manner of expression, or whether its copyright would invalidly extend to control over a machine described in a program and the processes performed by the program. Franklin argues that any "system program" compatible with the Apple II computer must be so similar to the programs which Apple wishes to copyright, that a copyright would in fact give Apple control over their computer configurations. Although the circuit court accepts this argument in theory, it decides against Franklin because it sees no evidence that Franklin's claim is correct.

The treatment of software as property under trade secret protections is discussed by Joseph Scafetta in "Computer Software and Unfair Methods of Competition." Under the common law of trade secrets, software is sometimes viewed as property even though it cannot be protected by other forms of intellectual-property law. Whether we should permit common law to step around the safeguards in property law that preclude other protections for software is an ethical issue. If the arguments used in *Diamond* v. *Diehr* and *Apple* v. *Franklin* establish that we ought not treat software in certain ways, then we must decide whether its treatment as a trade secret is sufficiently different to be permissible. Certainly trade-secret protection creates software property and has done so without the challenges that software property has met in the statutory law. As Scafetta points out, one reason that computer companies seek trade-secret protections rather than other forms of proprietary control, is that they can then avoid discussion of the basic issues. In theory, common law is preempted by statutory law. So we should expect the courts to say that trade-secret property was eliminated when Congress passed laws creating other sorts of property protections for intellectual property. But that did not happen. The result is conflicting notions of intellectual property that now exist side by side. (With some possible odd exceptions, it is still the case that an item can no longer be considered a trade secret after a patent or copyright has been sought for it.) Scafetta shows how the failure of copyright and patent law has forced innovators to turn to trade-secret protections.

We are left with the task of evaluating the various forms of property protections available and deciding under what circumstances they apply. We should be aware that trade-secret protections are only available to research done under extreme security conditions. If we are to use trade secrets as a means to protect new software, then the publication of new technical results is restricted and employees find that they cannot change jobs with ease or freely discuss their work with other researchers. This observation could be the basis of a new sort of ethical evaluation of the need for patent or copyright protections. We may, for instance, ethically justify a stronger patent law as a means to avoid an environment of secrecy in technology. We should ask whether the safeguards against too much control by innovators over their discoveries are improperly ignored by trade-secret protections.

29. Property and Sovereignty

Morris Raphael Cohen

I. Property As Power

ANY ONE WHO frees himself from the crudest materialism readily recognizes that as a legal term "property" denotes not material things but certain rights. In the world of nature apart from more or less organized society, there are things but clearly no property rights.

Further reflection shows that a property right is not to be identified with the fact of physical possession. Whatever technical definition of property we may prefer, we must recognize that a property right is a relation not between an owner and a thing, but between the owner and other individuals in reference to things. A right is always against one or more individuals. This becomes unmistakably clear if we take specifically modern forms of property such as franchises, patents, goodwill, etc., which constitute such a large part of the capitalized assets of our industrial and commercial enterprises.

The classical view of property as a right over things resolves it into component rights such as the *jus utendi, jus disponendi,* etc. But the essence of private property is always the right to exclude others. The law does not guarantee me the physical or social ability of actually using what it calls mine. By public regulations it may indirectly aid me by removing certain general hindrances to the enjoyment of property. But the law of property helps me directly only to exclude others from using the things that it assigns to me. If, then, somebody else wants to use the food, the house, the land, or the plough that the law calls mine, he has to get my consent. To the extent that these things are necessary to the life of my neighbor, the law thus confers on me a power, limited but real, to make him do what I want. If Laban has the sole disposal of his daughters and his cattle, Jacob must

From *Cornell Law Quarterly* 13 (1927): 8–30 at 11–21. Reprinted by permission of the *Cornell Law Review* and Fred B. Rothman & Co.

serve him if he desires to possess them. In a regime where land is the principal source of obtaining a livelihood, he who has the legal right over the land receives homage and service from those who wish to live on it.

The character of property as sovereign power compelling service and obedience may be obscured for us in a commercial economy by the fiction of the so-called labor contract as a free bargain and by the frequency with which service is rendered indirectly through a money payment. But not only is there actually little freedom to bargain on the part of the steel-worker or miner who needs a job, but in some cases the medieval subject had as much power to bargain when he accepted the sovereignty of his lord. Today I do not directly serve my landlord if I wish to live in the city with a roof over my head, but I must work for others to pay him rent with which he obtains the personal services of others. The money needed for purchasing things must for the vast majority be acquired by hard labor and disagreeable service to those to whom the law has accorded dominion over the things necessary for subsistence.

To a philosopher this is of course not at all an argument against private property. It may well be that compulsion in the economic as well as the political realm is necessary for civilized life. But we must not overlook the actual fact that dominion over things is also *imperium* over our fellow human beings.

The extent of the power over the life of others which the legal order confers on those called owners is not fully appreciated by those who think of the law as merely protecting men in their possession. Property law does more. It determines what men shall acquire. Thus, protecting the property rights of a landlord means giving him the right to collect rent; protecting the property of a railroad or a public-service corporation means giving it the right to make certain charges. Hence the ownership of land and machinery, with the rights of drawing rent, interest, etc., determines the future distribution of the goods that will come into being—determines what share of such goods various individuals shall acquire. The average life of goods that are either consumable or used for production of other goods is very short. Hence a law that merely protected men in their possession and did not also regulate the acquisition of new goods would be of little use.

From this point of view it can readily be seen that when a court rules that a gas company is entitled to a return of 6 per cent on its investment, it is not merely protecting property already possessed, it is also determining that a portion of the future social produce shall under certain conditions go to that company. Thus not only medieval landlords but the owners of all revenue-producing property are in fact granted by the law certain powers to tax the future social product. When to this power of taxation there is added the power to command the services of large numbers who are not economically independent, we have the essence of what historically has constituted political sovereignty.

Though the sovereign power possessed by the modern large property owners assumes a somewhat different form from that formerly possessed by the lord of the land, they are not less real and no less extensive. Thus the ancient lord had a limited power to control the modes of expenditure of his subjects by direct sumptuary legislation. The modern captain of industry and of finance has no such direct power himself, though his direct or indirect influence with the legislation may in that respect be considerable. But those who have the power to standardize and advertise certain products do determine what we may buy and use. We cannot well wear clothes except within lines decreed by their manufacturers, and our food is becoming more and more restricted to the kinds that are branded and standardized.

This power of the modern owner of capital to make us feel the necessity of buying more and more of his material goods (that may be more profitable to produce than economical to use) is a phenomenon of the utmost significance to the moral philosopher. The moral philosopher must also note that the modern captain of industry of finance exercises great influence in setting the fashion of expenditure by his personal example. Between a landed aristocracy and the tenantry, the difference is sharp and fixed, so that imitation of the former's mode of life by the latter is regarded as absurd and even immoral. In a money or commercial economy differences of income and mode of life are more gradual and readily hidden, so that there is great pressure to engage in lavish expenditure in order to appear in a higher class than one's income really allows. Such expenditure may even advance one's business credit. This puts pressure not merely on ever greater expenditure but more specifically on expenditure for ostentation rather than for comfort. Though a landed aristocracy may be wasteful in keeping large tracts of land for hunting purposes, the need for discipline to keep in power compels the cultivation of a certain hardihood that the modern wealthy man can ignore. An aristocracy assured of its recognized superiority need not engage in the race of lavish expenditure regardless of enjoyment.

In addition to these indirect ways in which the wealthy few determine the mode of life of the many, there is the somewhat more direct mode that bankers and financiers exercise when they determine the flow of investment, e.g., when they influence building operations by the amount that they will lend on mortgages. This power becomes explicit and obvious when a needy country has to borrow foreign capital to develop its resources.

I have already mentioned that the recognition of private property as a form of sovereignty is not itself an argument against it. Some form of government we must always have. For the most part men prefer to obey and let others take the trouble to think out rules, regulations, and orders. That is why we are always setting up authorities; and when we cannot find any we write to the newspaper as the final arbiter. But although government is a necessity, not all forms of it are of equal value. At any rate it is necessary to apply to the law of property all those considerations of social ethics and enlightened public policy which ought to be brought to the discussion of any just form of government.

To do this, let us begin with a consideration of the usual justifications of private property.

II. The Justification of Property

1. The Occupation Theory

The oldest and until recently the most influential defense of private property was based on the assumed right of the original discoverer and occupant to dispose of that which thus became his. This view dominated the thought of Roman jurists and of modern philosophers—from Grotius to Kant—so much so that the right of the laborer to the produce of his work was sometimes defended on the ground that the laborer "occupied" the material that he fashioned into the finished product.

It is rather easy to find fatal flaws in this view. Few accumulations of great wealth were ever simply found. Rather were they acquired by the labor of many, by conquest, by business manipulation, and by other means. It is obvious that today at any rate few economic goods can be acquired by discovery and first occupancy. Even in the few cases when they are, as in fishing and trapping, we are apt rather to think of the labor involved as the proper basis of the property acquired. Indeed, there seems nothing ethically self-evident in the motto "Findings is keepings." There seems nothing wrong in a law that a treasure trove shall belong to the king or the state rather than to the finder. Shall the finder of a river be entitled to all the water in it?

Moreover, even if we were to grant that the original finder or occupier should have possession as against any one else, it by no means follows that he may use it arbitrarily or that his rule shall prevail indefinitely after his death. The right of others to acquire the property from him, by bargain, by inheritance, or by testamentary disposition, is not determined by the principle of occupation.

Despite all these objections, however, there is a kernel of positive value in this principle. Protecting the discoverer or first occupant is really part of the more general principle that possession as such should be protected. There is real human economy in doing so until somebody shows a better claim than the possessor. It makes for certainty and security of transaction as well as for public peace—provided the law is ready to set aside possession acquired in ways that are inimical to public order. Various principles of justice may determine the distribution of goods and the retribution to be made for acts of injustice. But the law must not ignore the principle of inertia in human affairs. Continued possession creates expectations in the possessor and in others, and only a very poor morality would ignore the hardship of frustrating these expectations and rendering human relations insecure, even to correct some old flaws in the original acquisition. Suppose some remote ancestor of yours did acquire your property by fraud, robbery, or conquest, e.g., in the days of William of Normandy. Would it be just to take it away from you and your dependents who have held it in good faith? Reflection on the general insecurity that would result from such procedure leads us to see that as habit is the basis of individual life, continued practice must be the basis of social procedure. Any form of property that exists has therefore a claim to continue until it can be shown that the effort to change it is worth while. Continual changes in property laws would certainly discourage enterprise.

Nevertheless, it would be as absurd to argue that the distribution of property must never be modified by law as it would be to argue that the distribution of political power must never be changed. No less a philosopher than Aristotle argued against changing even bad laws, lest the habit of obedience be thereby impaired. There is something to be said for this, but only so long as we are in the realm of merely mechanical obedience. When we introduce the notion of free or rational obedience, Aristotle's argument loses its force in the political realm; and similar considerations apply to any property system that can claim the respect of rational beings.

2. The Labor Theory

That every one is entitled to the full produce of his labor is assumed as self-evident both by socialists and by conservatives who believe that capital is the result of the savings of labor. However, as economic goods are never the result of any one man's unaided labor, our maxim is altogether inapplicable. How shall we determine what part of the value of a table should belong to the carpenter, to the lumberman, to the transport worker, to the policeman who guarded the peace while the work was being done, and to the indefinitely large numbers of others whose cooperation was necessary? Moreover, even if we could tell what any one individual has produced—let us imagine a Robinson Crusoe growing up all alone on an island and in no way indebted to any community—it would still be highly questionable whether he has a right to keep the full produce of his labor when some shipwrecked mariner needs his surplus food to keep from starving.

In actual society no one ever thinks it unjust that a wealthy old bachelor should have part of his presumably just earnings taken away in the form of a tax for the benefit of other people's children, or that one immune to certain diseases should be taxed to support hospitals, etc. We do not think there is any injustice involved in such cases because social interdependence is so intimate that no man can justly say: "This wealth is entirely and absolutely mine as the result of my own unaided effort."

The degree of social solidarity varies, of course; and it is easy to conceive of a sparsely settled community, such as Missouri at the beginning of the nineteenth century, where a family of hunters or isolated cultivators of the soil might regard everything that it acquired as the product of its own labor. Generally, however, human beings start with a stock of tools or information acquired from others and they are more or less dependent upon some government for protection against foreign aggression, etc.

Yet despite these and other criticisms, the labor theory contains too much substantial truth to be brushed aside. The essential truth is that labor has to be encouraged and that property must be distributed in such a way as to encourage even greater efforts at productivity.

As not all things produced are ultimately good, as even good things may be produced at an unjustified expense in human life and worth, it is obvious that other principles besides that of labor or productivity are needed for an adequate basis or justification of any system of property law. We can only say dialectically that all other things being equal, property should be distributed with due regard to the productive needs of the community. We must, however, recognize that a good deal of property accrues to those who are not productive, and a good deal of productivity does not and perhaps should not receive its reward in property. Nor should we leave this theme without recalling the Hebrew-Christian view— and for that matter, the specifically religious view—that the first claim on property is by the man who needs it rather than the man who has created it. Indeed, the only way of justifying the principle of distribution of property according to labor is to show that it serves the larger social need.

The occupation theory has shown us the necessity for security of possession, and the labor theory the need for encouraging enterprise. These two needs are mutually dependent. Anything that discourages enterprise makes our possessions less valuable, and it is obvious that it is not worth while engaging in economic enterprise if there is no prospect of securely possessing the fruit of it. Yet there is also a conflict between these two needs. The owners of land, wishing to secure the continued possession by the family, oppose laws that make it subject to free financial transactions or make it possible that land should be taken away from one's heirs by a judgment creditor for personal debts. In an agricultural economy security of possession demands that the owner of a horse should be able to reclaim it no matter into whose hands it has fallen. But in order that markets should be possible, it becomes necessary that the innocent purchaser should have a good title. This conflict between static and dynamic security has been treated most suggestively by Demogue.

3. Property and Personality

Hegels, Ahrens, Lorimer, and other idealists have tried to deduce the right of property from the individual's right to act as a free personality. To be free one must have a sphere of self-assertion in the external world. One's private property provides such an opportunity.

Waiving all traditional difficulties in applying the metaphysical idea of freedom to empirical legal acts, we may still object that the notion of personality is too vague to enable us to deduce definite legal consequences by means of it. How, for example, can the principle of personality help us to decide to what extent there shall be private rather than public property in railroads, mines, gas-works, and other public necessities?

Not the extremest communist would deny that in the interest of privacy certain personal belongings such as are typified by the toothbrush must be under the dominion of the individual owner, to the absolute exclusion of every one else. This, however, will not carry us far if we recall that the major effect of property in land, in the machinery of production, in capital goods, etc., is to enable the owner to exclude others from *their necessities,* and thus to compel them to serve him. Ahrens, one of the chief expounders of the personality theory, argues: "It is undoubtedly contrary to the right of personality to have persons dependent on others on account of material goods." But if this is so, the primary effect of property on a large scale is to limit freedom, since the one thing that private property law does not do is to guarantee a minimum of subsistence or the necessary tools of freedom to every one. So far as a regime of private property fails to do the latter it rather compels people to part with their freedom.

It may well be argued in reply that just as restraining traffic rules in the end give us greater freedom of motion, so, by giving control over things to individual property owners, greater economic freedom is in the end assured to all. This is a strong argument, as can be seen by comparing the different degrees of economic freedom that prevail in lawless and in law-abiding communities. It is, however, an argument for legal order rather than for any particular form of government or private property. It argues for a regime where every one has a definite sphere of rights and duties, but it does not tell us where these lines should be drawn. The principle of freedom of personality certainly cannot justify a legal order wherein a few can, by virtue of their legal monopoly over necessities, compel others to work under degrading and brutalizing conditions. A government that limits the right of large landholders limits the rights of property, and yet may promote real freedom. Property owners, like other individuals, are members of a community and must subordinate their ambition to the larger whole of which they are a part. They may find their compensation in spiritually identifying their good with that of the larger life.

4. The Economic Theory

The economic justification of private property is that by means of it a maximum of productivity is promoted. The classical economic argument may be put thus: The successful business man, the one who makes the greatest profit, is the one who has the greatest power to foresee effective demand. If he has not that power his enterprise fails. He is therefore, in fact, the best director of economic activities.

There can be little doubt that if we take the whole history of agriculture and industry, or compare the economic output in Russia under the *mir* system with that in the United States, there is a strong *prima facie* case for the contention that more intensive cultivation of the soil and greater productiveness of industry prevail under individual ownership. Many *a priori* psychologic and economic reasons can also be brought to explain why this must be so, why the individual cultivator will take greater care not to exhaust the soil, etc. All this, however, is so familiar that we may take it for granted and look at the other side of the case, at the considerations which show that there is a difference between socially desirable productivity and the desire for individual profits.

In the first place, let us note that of many things the supply is not increased by making them private property. This is obviously true of land in cities and of other monopoly or limited goods. Private ownership of land does not increase the amount of rainfall, and irrigation works to make the land more fruitful have been carried through by governments more than by private initiative. Nor was the productivity of French or Irish lands reduced when the property of their landlords in rent charges and other incidents of seigniorage was reduced or even abolished. In our own days, we frequently see tobacco, cotton, or wheat farmers in distress because they have succeeded in raising too plentiful crops; and manufacturers who are well informed know when greater profit is to be made by a decreased output. Patents for processes that would cheapen the product are often bought up by manufacturers and never used. Durable goods that are more economic to the consumer are very frequently crowded out of the market by shoddier goods which are more profitable to produce because of the larger turnover. Advertising campaigns often persuade people to buy the less economical goods and to pay the cost of the uneconomic advice.

In the second place, there are inherent sources of waste in a regime of private enterprise and free competition. If the biologic analogy of the struggle for existence were taken seriously, we should see that the natural survival of the economically fittest is attended, as in the biologic field, with frightful wastefulness. The elimination of the unsuccessful competitor may be a gain to the survivor, but all business failures are losses to the community.

Finally, a regime of private ownership in industry is too apt to sacrifice social interests to immediate monetary profits. This shows itself in speeding up industry to such a pitch that men are exhausted in a relatively few years, whereas a slower expenditure of their energy would prolong their useful years. It shows itself in the way in which private enterprise has wasted a good deal of the natural resources of the United States to obtain immediate profits. Even when the directors of a modern industrial enterprise see the uneconomic consequences of immediate profits, the demand of shareholders for immediate dividends, and the ease with which men can desert a business and leave it to others to stand the coming losses, tend to encourage ultimately wasteful and uneconomic activity. Possibly the best illustration of this is child labor, which by lowering wages increases immediate profits, but in the end is really wasteful of the most precious wealth of the country, its future manhood and womanhood.

Surveying our arguments thus far: We have seen the roots of property in custom, in the need for economic productivity, and in individual needs of privacy. But we have also noted that property, being only one among other human interests, cannot be pursued absolutely without detriment to human life. Hence we can no longer maintain Montesquieu's view that private property is sacrosanct and that the general government must in no way interfere with or retrench its domain. The issue before thoughtful people is therefore not the maintenance or abolition of private property, but the determination of the precise lines along which private enterprise must be given free scope and where it must be restricted in the interests of the common good.

30. Legal Protection for Computer Software: The View from '79

Michael C. Gemignani

Patents and copyrights approach, nearer than any other class of cases belonging to forensic discussions, to what may be called the metaphysics of the law, where the distinctions are, or at least may be, very subtile [sic] and refined, and, sometimes, almost evanescent. *Folsom v. Marsh,* 9 F. Cas. 342, 344 (C.C.D. Mass. 1841).

The more things change, the more they stay the same.—Old French Proverb

I. Introduction

THE YEARS 1966 TO 1970 saw a flurry of articles and notes concerning legal protection of computer software. The 1970's have seen important developments which influence the protection that might be accorded software. These developments include three major Supreme Court decisions, a number of decisions of the Court of Customs and Patent Appeals, major revisions of the Patent Act, the implementation of a new Copyright Act, the publication of the CONTU Report, and impressive advances in the technology of computers.

This note looks out upon the landscape of software protection as it has been reshaped by these events. In this tour of the changed landscape, certain questions will be addressed. Have the issues that were raised in the late 1960's been resolved? Were the forecasts of the earlier writers accurate? Are there now new questions to be answered? What answers seem best to questions old and new? A brief discussion of basic computer concepts is necessary to begin this analysis.

From *Rutgers Journal of Computers, Technology, and the Law* 7 (1980): 269–312. Notes deleted. Reprinted by permission of Michael C. Gemignani.

A. The Computer

The first general purpose, all-electronic digital computer, called ENIAC, was built in 1946. Despite the speed with which ENIAC could solve complex problems, this machine was extremely cumbersome by modern standards. One of its principal drawbacks was that it was externally programmed; that is, each time it was used, much of its circuitry had to be manually rewired to prepare it for the task at hand. Just one year after ENIAC was built, John von Neumann, a mathematician at Princeton University, devised a method by which the tedious hand wiring could be circumvented. Von Neumann suggested that the instructions for the machine be stored inside the machine in the same way that the data involved in the computations were stored. Both the programs for processing data and the data itself could be entered into the machine in the same manner; thus, the process of readying the machine to perform a given task was immensely simplified. ENIAC was replaced by EDVAC, the first stored-program digital computer. This same type of computer, with a vastly improved technology, is still in general use today.

The function of a computer is not unlike that of the human brain. A computer receives, transmits and stores vast quantities of information. It acts upon the information it receives to obtain new information or transforms the information to a more useful form. Yet the computer is still a machine, a huge array of switches which are either on or off. Some of these switches are set according to instructions given by the computer's manufacturer. This initial setting of switches "brings the machine up" and prepares it to accept further instructions and data from a user. The user then sets switches to prepare the computer to perform a particular task.

The process of setting the switches is called "programming." Of course, the modern computer user does not set the switches by hand. He is not confronted with the major engineering task of the ENIAC user who had to personally arrange the switches, plugboards and wires of that early computer. Now the machine is "brought up" by means of an operating systems program; the user generally introduces his own instructions by means of a source program. Both types of programs will be discussed at greater length below.

A computer without programming of any kind is simply an inert array of switches, a lifeless form incapable of any task. Once infused with life by means of its operating systems program, the computer becomes a general purpose machine, capable of receiving and carrying out special instructions from each individual user. After a user has further programmed the computer, the computer becomes a special purpose machine dedicated to carrying out the particular instructions that user has given it.

B. The Computer Program

In essence, a program is a set of instructions which tell the computer how to do its work. A program may be distinguished from the data which constitutes the raw material upon which the computer operates in accordance with the instructions contained in the program. Programs may be broadly grouped into operating systems programs and applications programs. Operating systems programs involve the general operation of the computer as outlined in the paragraph above. An applications program is what a user employs to get the computer (machine plus operating systems program) to do his particular job.

Programs are responses to problems to be solved. First, the problem in issue must be clearly formulated. Then a solution must be outlined. To be amenable to implementation on a computer, the solution must be expressible in a precise way as a series of steps to be carried out, each step being itself clearly defined. This expression of the solution is known as an algorithm. The algorithm is usually set forth as a flow chart, a stylized diagram showing the steps of the algorithm and their relationship to one another. Once a flow chart has been constructed, it is used as a guide for expressing the algorithm in a "language" that the computer can "understand." This "coding" of the program is almost certain to employ a "high level" computer language, such as BASIC or FORTRAN. When the algorithm is "coded" in a high level computer language, it is called a source program. A source program may bear a striking resemblance to a set of instructions expressed in literary form. The source program is fed into the computer by means of an input device, such as a terminal or card reader. The source program is "translated" by the compiler, a part of the operating systems program, into machine language, a language not at all similar to ordinary speech. The program expressed in machine language is called an object program. It is the object program which actuates the setting of switches which enables the computer to perform the underlying algorithm and solve the problem.

The program undergoes a striking metamorphosis as it progresses from a statement of the problem to be solved to a pattern of switch settings inside the computer. Both the languages and the symbols used to express the program are markedly different at different stages of the program's evolution. What is *the* program? If the process were stopped at any one stage, would the program as it existed at that point be entitled to legal protection? This question, as the extensive literature proves, is a profound and troubling one, embracing not merely science and law, but philosophy as well. What protection may be accorded a program is integrally bound up with what a program really is, and that is a matter of intense debate.

C. The Computer Industry

The computer industry includes a variety of interest groups. First, there are the manufacturers of hardware. Hardware is the underlying machinery of computing: the impressive cabinets, whirring disks and flashing lights that the public has come to associate with computers, and, of course, the box of switches that constitutes the core of any computer. Because the hardware is useless without programs, a segment of the computer industry devotes its time to the manufacture of software, that is, the programs that make the substantial outlay for the hardware a good investment. Because the hardware is absolutely useless without at least its operating systems programs, and the hardware manufacturer is in the best position to develop and maintain the operating systems programs for its own product, it has been traditional for the hardware manufacturer to supply such programs as an integral part of the package that it markets. Because hardware manufacturers are intimately involved in software manufacture as well, their economic power as a group is staggering. The combined revenues of the 42 members of the Computer and Business Equipment Manufacturers' Association (CBEMA) amounted to $32.7 billion in 1976; these same firms were also expected to produce $17 billion worth of software in the following three years.

The demand for programs and other computer support services had led to the development of software houses and service bureaus. The independent software products presently account for about 17% of the total data processing expenditures in the United States. Although this area of the computer industry appears to be growing more rapidly than the hardware segment, the software houses are vastly different from the hardware manufacturers. They are typically small; 80% have annual sales of less than $15 million. Hardware manufacturers devote about 39% of their gross revenues to manufacturing and maintenance of their product. They also spend 20% for marketing as opposed to only 7% for product development. On the other hand, software houses spend 50% for marketing a product that they used only 10% of their revenues to develop. Because most software is custom-produced in-house by its user, software houses must spend a good deal of money convincing potential customers of the need for their services.

The growth of the computer industry has rivaled that of the computers themselves. In 1950, the federal government had only two computers; in 1955, it had 45; in 1960, 531; in 1965, about 2,500; and in 1977, at least 10,000. But mere numbers tell only a small part of the story. The economic growth of this industry is surpassed by its technological development which has seen a roomful of vacuum tubes replaced by a "chip" smaller than a fingernail. The minicomputers of today can store more information than the largest computers of earlier years. As a computer's memory increased in size, the computer accommodated longer programs, more data, and more users. Increased efficiency of operation enables computers to carry out an unimaginably large number of operations in an unbelievably short time. The industry stands on the threshold of new and even more exotic advances, the only limitation being the speed of light.

This all too brief overview of computers, programs and the computer industry provides the background for the principal study of this note: the protection of computer software.

II. What Is a Program?

What a program is, or is not, determines the kind and extent of legal protection that will be accorded it. If a program is merely an idea, or a scientific principle, then it may not be the proper subject of either copyright or patent. If a program may be patented, then, of course, it is entitled to far broader protection than if it is merely copyrightable.

As noted previously, a program begins as a problem to be solved and ends as a pattern of switch settings inside a computer. To pinpoint more precisely the subject of this section, "program" will be taken to refer to the source program only. If program in some other sense is intended, that intention will be explicitly stated.

A program can contain thousands of instructions and cost hundreds of thousands of dollars to develop. But whatever their value or complexity, programs are generated for the purpose of solving problems or performing tasks. The program is created by translating the flow chart, which expresses the precise manner of solving the problem or doing the task, into a language compatible with a computer. The flow chart is a graphic way of portraying the algorithm; the program may, therefore, be viewed as merely a specially formulated expression of the flow chart (directly) or the algorithm itself (indirectly).

A perusal of articles which touch upon the subject yields a variety of definitions for program. Many of these definitions involve the phrase "set" or "series of instructions." Because a program is, in the technical sense at least, precisely a set of instructions, this notion bears further examination.

Those who understand the computer language in which a program is written can, at least theoretically, manually carry out the procedure the program embodies. A program might thus be viewed as a type of instruction manual. This view, however, is not technically correct. Although the process leading up to actually writing the program may be excellent training in dealing with a particular problem, the program itself is not designed as an instruction manual and no one, to this writer's knowledge, has ever used one for this purpose. In addition, many programs require "documentation" to explain how to use the program properly. Thus, there would be an instruction manual for an instruction manual.

But if a program is a set of instructions, and these instructions are not really intended for human beings, what or whom does the program instruct? One view is that the program instructs the computer. The ability to learn, to be instructed, is an attribute normally reserved to human beings or higher forms of life. Is a computer really learning as it is programmed? This issue is complicated by the fact that the program often looks much the same as instructions humans are accustomed to giving and receiving. But the computer does not, indeed cannot, see what the human being sees. Although the word ADD appearing in a program seems to the human reader to be a clear instruction to compute a sum, relative to the computer, it is "perceived" only as a series of switch settings. In other words, the program is merely a means to manipulate various components of the machine. The program may thus be viewed as a process or means of bringing about a desired result within the computer.

The function of a program is sometimes defined in terms of "control" rather than "instruct." If a program controls a computer in the same way that a distributor controls the sequence of firing the sparkplugs in an internal combustion engine, then the program can be viewed as an integral part of the computer itself. This view is strengthened by the fact that a computer will not, and cannot, carry out its appointed task until it has been properly programmed. The programming sets the switches, in effect redesigning the internal structure of the machine and becoming an inseparable part of the machine. The program may thus be viewed as a machine part or as the completion of a previously incomplete machine.

A reasonable objection to this argument is that the source program remains at all times outside the machine and separate from it; therefore, though it may result in the creation of a machine part, it itself is not a machine part. Just as a person who understands the language could use a program to reconstruct its algorithm, a person who has an adequate background in electrical engineering could use the program to build an electronic circuit which would carry out the program in conjunction with input and output devices. The program, to a suitably trained engineer, could be used as a circuit diagram or the blueprint for building special purpose hardware. Even if it is not part of a machine, the program could be used to construct a machine of a specific design, that design being contained implicitly in the program itself. The program thus stands midway between the abstract solution to a problem and a machine which actually carries out that solution.

There are other ways to describe a program. The Association for Computing Machinery defines a program as "an ordered set of data that are coded instructions or statements that when executed by a computer cause the computer to process data." This considers a program as a special kind of data compilation. Because the program is stored in a computer as data, the object program, when written out, appears as just a string of 0's and 1's. If "code" is taken in its cryptological sense, the ACM definition might inspire a view of a program as a coded message, an encrypted writing.

A program may also be thought of as bearing the same relationship to a computer as a phonograph record does to a record player. Nevertheless, there are highly significant differences between a record and record player on the one hand and a program committed to tape and a computer on the other. First, a record is specifically intended to communicate with human beings; the program is intended to communicate with a machine. Second, "[t]he record player has as its sole purpose the performance of the writing of an author in its audible form." The computer, on the other hand, uses the program to process data. The data processed by the computer acting in accordance with the instructions contained in the program is more analogous to a phonograph record. The purpose of the computer, however, is generally not to play back the data, but to transform it. People rate a record player according to the quality at which it reproduces the sound of the recording. But a computer which merely plays back the data fed into it is of little use to anyone. Third, the record does not determine what the phonograph can do; the phonograph has the ability to play the record even before it actually does so. But a computer has the ability to do very little until the program infuses it with a purpose and the means to carry it out. The record does not control the phonograph as a program does the computer.

Finally, a program may be described as a pattern of symbols, a nonsense writing so to speak. This view avoids any disturbing technical and philosophical questions which may force human beings to meditate on their uneasy relationship with machines that seem to mirror or even surpass the workings of the brain.

A computer program, therefore, may be viewed as any one or more of the following: a particular form of expression of a flowchart or algorithm, an instruction manual for human beings, a process for controlling or bringing about a desired result inside a computer, a machine part or completion of an incomplete machine, a circuit diagram or blueprint for a circuit board, a data compilation, a coded writing, a "phonograph record" or "sheet music," or a mere pattern of symbols or nonsense writing. What a program is determines how the law can and will protect it.

III. Programs and Copyright

In the 1960's commentators discussed the issue of whether programs were proper subject matter for copyright. The weight of authority now is that programs may be copyrighted as "literary works" under the new Copyright Law. However, at least one expert has challenged the view that Congress intended programs to fall within the scope of the new law, and CONTU has proposed an amendment that unambiguously declares programs subject to copyright.

There are three additional points which merit consideration, even if the clear language of the statute and the intent of Congress support the conclusion that copyright protection extends to computer programs. First, Article One of the Constitution may bar program copyrights regardless of the intent of Congress. Section 102(b) of the Copyright Law restates the Supreme Court's interpretation of the constitutional principle as follows:

> In no case does copyright protection . . . extend to any idea, procedure, process, system, method of operation, concept, principle, or discovery, regardless of the form in which it is described, explained, illustrated, or embodied in such work.

If the Supreme Court finds that a program is merely a process or method of operation, it will not be copyrightable. Second, even if an individual program copyright passes constitutional muster, it must still be an original work of authorship fixed in a tangible medium from which it can "be perceived, reproduced, or otherwise communicated, either directly or with the aid of a machine or device." The "author" of a program is simply the one who originates it. Origination implies some degree of originality, but the degree of originality required to obtain a copyright is minimal.

> All that is needed to satisfy both the Constitution and the statute is that the "author" contributed something more than a "merely trivial" variation, something recognizably "his own." Originality in this context "means little more than a prohibition of actual copying."

If the program is recorded on paper, tape, cards, etc., in a manner that permits it to be perceived directly or by means of a computer print-out, then it would seem to satisfy the requisite degree of "tangibility" or fixation required by the statute.

The third point is that even if a program is copyrighted, it is not at all clear what that protection includes. The Register of Copyrights has, in fact, accepted programs for registration since 1964. As of January 1, 1977, only 1,205 programs had been registered; 971 of these came from two large hardware manufacturers, IBM and Burroughs. It is estimated that some 1,000,000 programs are developed each year. These statistics tend to indicate that there is very little interest in copyright of programs. Moreover, there has not been a single suit filed either challenging the validity of a program copyright or charging infringement of such a copyright. The closest any court has come to ruling on the protection accorded programs by copyright is an opinion in which a data input format was held to be an idea expressed and not the expression of an idea. Therefore, the format was not entitled to copyright protection. Computer programs and formats are worthless, however, without an adequate instruction manual. The court was able to protect the developer of the special format by finding an infringement of the copyrighted instruction manual.

If a court is willing to uphold a program's copyright, what aspects of the program is it likely to find protected? Underlying any computer program is an algorithm or method of solving a problem. The algorithm, even if highly unique and of great commercial value, will not be protected. But the algorithm is often the most important aspect of the program and that which its creator most wants to protect. While translating a flow chart into a source language is only a straightforward, though tedious, task, considerable ingenuity and insight may be required to develop the algorithm itself. If, by examining a program, a competitor could gain knowledge of the underlying method, he could then design his own flow chart and write his own program, just as someone who learned to play bridge by reading a book by Charles Goren is free to write his own book on the subject.

How a court views a program will, of course, affect what protection it will consider appropriate. If the court believes that the program is an instruction manual, then it may find no infringement if an unauthorized individual follows those instructions by running the program on a computer. If the court views the program as a blueprint for a circuit board or a wiring diagram, then it may find that someone who actually builds the circuit in question or wires the computer according to the program also is not infringing. If the program is a data compilation, then a competitor is free to acquire a similar compilation of his own, provided he contributes some independent work to the project. Authorities disagree, however, whether the competitor may use the original compilation after verifying its statements, or whether he may use the original for verification only after he has completed his independent compilation.

But before any court will grant a plaintiff any remedy for an alleged infringement of his copyright, before it will protect any aspect of the work the plaintiff alleges was infringed upon, the court must find an infringement actually took place. Proving an infringement of a copyright of a computer program is a formidable task indeed, even without the added burden of sustaining the constitutionality of the copyright in the face of a possibly hostile court.

The plaintiff in a copyright infringement suit must prove that the defendant has copied the protected work *and* that the copying was of such a nature as to constitute an improper appropriation. Copying is an essential element of the plaintiff's case. Since it is virtually impossible for two programs of any length to be identical without copying, a court faced with identical programs could find the presence of "striking similarities." Striking similarities, that is, those which can only be explained by copying, have been held to establish copying. Plaintiff must also prove access. This may be done by showing that the defendant had a reasonable opportunity to see the plaintiff's program. Even if the defendant's computer program is identical to the plaintiff's, there is no infringement if the defendant establishes that he independently produced his program without having access to plaintiff's program.

After proving that copying has occurred, the plaintiff must still establish that the copying constituted an improper appropriation. In deciding this issue, the court must first ascertain what part of the plaintiff's work is entitled to protection. Then the court must determine if the appropriation of that protected part is improper. In *New York Times Co. v. Roxbury Data Interface, Inc.,* the district court noted that the taking of as few as three lines of text had been found to infringe, even though in other instances no infringement had been found in the taking of an entire work.

The line between improper appropriation and fair use is not easily drawn. A court will consider such factors as the extent to which the defendant relied on the plaintiff's work, and the quantity and quality of the defendant's own independent contribution to his "copy" in determining if there has been an infringement. Some courts have protected the labor expended by plaintiff by finding against a defendant who indulges in "lazy" copying even though there is little in the plaintiff's work, other than the effort expended to bring it about, that is entitled to protection. Infringement may be found even though there is no identity of language between the original and the copy.

Expert testimony can be introduced with regard to whether or not copying has occurred. The test, however, for improper appropriation, and hence for the ultimate claim of infringement where copying has been established, is the "response of the ordinary lay person." Both copying and infringement are questions of fact to be determined by the trier of facts.

Special problems are encountered in a suit alleging infringement of a program copyright. First, showing access may prove troublesome. The mere fact that a competitor has a program that is similar to the plaintiff's program is insufficient to establish infringement. If the competitor developed the program independently, there is no infringement. If the competitor's access to information stored inside computers goes undetected, plaintiff may be unable to prove the infringement. The contents of a computer's memory can be stolen over telephone lines from great distances, often without leaving a trace of the theft. Computers are electrical devices that emit electromagnetic signals while they operate. It is at least theoretically possible for someone to steal the contents of a computer by monitoring this radiation. Of course, in some instances proof of access may be easy: the presence of a common employee, a trial use by the accused of the program in issue, etc. But a computer specialist bent on misappropriating the work of another may use techniques that will make proof of access difficult, if not impossible.

It is also difficult to prove that there are striking similarities. Most courts do not possess sufficient technical background to determine whether striking similarities exist between seemingly dissimilar works. Therefore, expert witnesses are generally permitted to testify concerning the degree of similarity, or lack thereof, between the programs. Even experts, however, find it extremely difficult to determine if one computer program has been copied from another. If the plaintiff could find one expert who was willing to testify to striking similarities, the defendant could, no doubt, get two to swear to the contrary. The same computer process can appear in a bewildering array of forms including the flow chart, source program and object program. Both the source and the object programs can appear on a variety of media including magnetic tape, cards, and disk. The source program can be written in an ever increasing number of high level languages, e.g., FORTRAN, BASIC, ALGOL, COBOL, etc. There are even "dialects" of the source languages which vary with the computer operation. Even two source programs written in the same language and which do precisely the same job can be markedly different. They can differ in all of the following respects: the order and manner in which data is to be entered, the variable names, the order of instructions, the statement numbers, the way in which the same instruction can validly be expressed, the number and formulation of comment statements, and the format of the output. They could have different underlying algorithms (in which case copying is highly unlikely), and each could require the use of different input or output devices. All of these differences must be explained to, considered, and weighed by a trier of fact who has at best a minimal understanding of the source language and the technical terminology.

Most of the problems encountered when trying to prove striking similarity are also encountered when trying to prove substantial similarity, or improper appropriation. The algorithm underlying a program cannot be copyrighted; "protection is given only to the expression of the idea—not the idea itself." Given an uncopyrightable algorithm, a court may find that the range of ways in which the algorithm could be expressed as a program is so narrow, despite the differences that programs can display, that few programs can be copyrighted. The number of ways that an individual instruction can be expressed in a given source language is limited. Furthermore, many computing routines have a standard expression. The use of such expressions could not be found to have the element of originality needed for protection against use by the general public. Alternatively, the court might hold that copyrighted programs are entitled to protection only if there has been verbatim copying.

The broad wealth of common knowledge in the computer industry and the mobility of programmers presents additional problems. If Joe Programmer writes a program for Company A, leaves to work for Company B at a higher salary, and Company B then asks him to write that same program for them, there might be no infringement of Company A's copyright if he did so relying only on his memory and professional skill. The question is a close one, and the answer may have sweeping repercussions in the software industry since programmers often are hired away to do much the same work that they did for their previous employers. In any event, this represents but another issue that must be faced and argued by Company B either as plaintiff or as defendant.

Even this brief discussion should convince the reader of the formidable obstacles confronting the plaintiff in a program infringement suit. The trier of fact is uneducated in the terms and practices of the computer world; the law is unsettled, and, because of the paucity of cases in this area, argument must almost always be by analogy. At least one basic issue, the nature of a program, borders on the metaphysical.

The problems of the plaintiff begin even before any complaint is filed. Because a program can be copied from a great distance and without leaving a trace, and because someone who misappropriates a program will usually only use it inside his own computer operation rather than distributing it, the detection of any infringement may be extraordinarily difficult. A program is not performed publicly like a musical composition, nor does it necessarily depend on wide distribution to be of great commercial value to its owner. Moreover, a program can be read from one computer into another at almost the speed of light, even when the program being "copied" is actually being used. Simply transmitting the pattern of switch settings from one computer to another may not even be copying in the eyes of the law.

If an infringement is detected, the copyright owner must determine if the economics of the situation justify the risk and expense of a suit. If he wins, he may recoup both damages and attorney's fees. If he loses, he may not only be forced to pay the defendant's attorney's fees, but also may lose his copyright if the court declares it invalid. Furthermore, the owner may update and modify his program, and redesign it to meet the needs of individual licensees. Unless he has copyrighted every version of the program, he is faced with the question of what his copyright actually covers. A book which has entered the stream of commerce is not revised by its author; this is not the case with computer programs which are subject to constant revision.

The new copyright law, however, protects any program having the requisite degree of originality as soon as it becomes "fixed in any tangible medium of expression . . . from which [it] can be perceived, reproduced, or otherwise communicated," directly or with the aid of a computer. Because a limited distribution of such a program under a contract not to disclose would not be publication, the program owner does not have to put a copyright notice on his program to maintain this protection if the contract is the sole means by which his program is made available. He does not even have to register his program with the Copyright Office.

Nevertheless, given whatever protection copyright will afford, and the ease of registration, the software industry generally has not found copyright protection to be adequate. An infinitesimal fraction of existing programs have been registered, and no case involving direct infringement of any computer program has yet been reported. The reason for this apathy toward copyright is not hard to understand. It is not clear what copyright protects in programs, or even if it protects anything at all. The risk and expense of litigation is high, and the case would be argued before a court having no expertise in this difficult area. Finally, as will be seen, the software industry, while lobbying ineffectively for patent protection, has developed other means of protection which adequately serve its needs: contract and the law of trade secrets.

IV. Programs and Patent Law

If the state of program copyrights is confused, the state of program patents is utterly chaotic. The plot has all of the elements of a comic opera with four principal characters: the Patent Office, which steadfastly turns down every application for a patent on a computer program; the Court of Customs and Patent Appeals, which has fought for program patents in the face of increasing opposition from the Supreme Court; the Supreme Court, itself confused and trying to apply "nineteenth century legal notions to computer technology without understanding the technology," which keeps reversing the Court of Customs and Patent Appeals without directly confronting the issue of program patentability; and Congress, which, despite anxious pleas from the Supreme Court to resolve the issue by statute, does nothing.

Software manufacturers seem to be genuinely interested in patents, in contrast to their indifference toward copyright. This is because the protection provided by a patent is greater than the protection conferred by a copyright.

> A patent is a grant of the right to exclude others from making, using or selling one's invention, and includes the right to license others to make, use or sell it. It is a legitimate monopoly. . . .

Because a patent grants a monopoly, someone who develops a program substantially the same as a patented program, but without any knowledge whatsoever of the existence of the protected program, still infringes.

Broad patent protection is accorded only upon rigid terms. Instead of the minimal originality that suffices to support a copyright, utility, novelty, and unobviousness must all concur to support a patent. Utility is a condition most programs easily satisfy: the program must be able to perform at least one of the beneficial functions its inventor claims that it can. Novelty is a more difficult attribute to satisfy. A patent lacks novelty if all of the elements of the patent, or their equivalents, are found in a single prior art structure or device where they do substantially the same work in substantially the same way. Obviousness is the attribute that is likely to give applicants for program patents the most difficulty. The test for obviousness was set forth in *Graham v. John Deere Co.*:

> [T]he scope and content of the prior art are to be determined; differences between the prior art and the claims at issue are to be ascertained; and the level of ordinary skill in the pertinent art resolved. Against this background, the obviousness or non-obviousness of the subject matter is determined.

Novelty and obviousness are related. An invention that lacks novelty is likely to be obvious as well. However, an invention which is novel may still be obvious. The mere fact that no one has previously built a certain machine, or written a certain program, is sufficient to confer novelty, but not unobviousness. What the prior art is and what the claimed invention

315

is are both questions of fact. The test of obviousness is to be applied as one of the time of the invention, not at the time of a suit.

The process of obtaining a patent is far more tedious and expensive than the relatively simple and inexpensive procedure for registering a copyright. Although an author can register virtually any "writing" which he has independently created, an inventory seeking a patent is "chargeable with full knowledge of all prior art, although in fact he may be utterly ignorant of it." And although the Register of Copyrights makes no check of prior copyrights before issuing a certificate of registration, the Patent Office requires a search of all prior patents to determine if an invention submitted to it is truly novel enough to warrant a patent. As Mr. Justice Clark stated: "He who seeks to build a better mousetrap today has a long path to tread before reaching the Patent Office."

Despite the strict scrutiny given patent applications and the length and expense of the procedure for obtaining a patent, nothing discussed thus far precludes program patentability; indeed, software manufacturers say they are willing to expend the time, effort, and treasure to gain patent protection. There are things, however, which cannot be patented. Included among these are ideas, scientific principles, mathematical algorithms, a phenomenon of nature, and a mental process. These restrictions prevent the pre-emption of entire fields of science and the establishment of a monopoly on human thought. Even though an abstract idea or principle is not patentable, a device or process which utilizes it may be patentable. If a court determines that a program is identical to the algorithm it expresses, then the court will find the program unpatentable. But if the program is merely a useful process which utilizes the algorithm without pre-empting it, and the program clears the hurdles of novelty and unobviousness as well, the court will find patentability.

Patents and copyrights are divided into different categories. The classification (nature) of a copyrighted work determines the degree of protection of the copyright owner. In patent law, however, classification determines whether there will be any patent protection at all. A patent sought under the wrong classification may be held invalid, even though the invention is fully patentable if it had been classified correctly.

Claims for program patentability by their nature are concerned with either machines or processes. Machine patents cover devices which must be used in connection with an actual mechanism. On the other hand, a process is described as:

> [A] mode of treatment of certain materials to produce a given result. It is an act, or series of acts, performed upon the subject matter to be transformed and reduced to a different state or thing.

A process patent does not require that the machine used in carrying out the process be new or patentable.

This brief look at the principles of patent law paves the way for a summary of the strange history of program patents in the courts. In 1964, the Patent Office itself did not believe programs to be patentable because they were "creations in the area of thought," even though the Board of Patent Appeals had not yet ruled on the patentability of programs. In 1965, the President's Commission on the Patent System was established to suggest revisions of the Patent Act. The Commission released its report at the end of 1966. With regard to computer programs, the Commission made this recommendation:

> A series of instructions which control or condition the operation of a data processing machine, generally referred to as a "program," shall not be considered patentable regardless of whether the program is claimed as: (a) an article, (b) a process described in terms of the operations performed by a machine pursuant to the program, or (c) one or more machine configurations established by a program.

Legislation to implement this recommendation was introduced in both houses of Congress, but did not pass.

In 1968, the Patent Office officially declared that "computer programming per se [sic] . . . shall not be patentable." In 1969 the Court of Customs and Patent Appeals, in *In re Prater,* rejected this guideline. The court explicitly declared that it saw no grounds based on the Constitution, statute, or case law, for denying program patentability under either machine or process claims. The Patent Office contended that Prater's process, which could be carried out with pencil and paper alone, was an idea or mental process and therefore not patentable, even though Prater had produced a machine to carry out the steps for him. The Office rejected the machine claim because the novelty was in the process.

The Court of Customs and Patent Appeals rejected the "mental steps" doctrine in *In re Musgrave.* The Court indicated that the doctrine might have validity only when some step in a process was "purely mental" and incapable of being performed by a machine. In *In re Bernhart,* decided in 1969, the Court declared that a computer which is programmed in a new and unobvious way is physically different from the computer without that program. Even if programming did not produce a new machine, it was a "new and useful improvement" and therefore statutory subject matter for a patent. Bernhart's invention was a method of illustrating a three-dimensional object by means of an already existing computer and plotter. There was little question that the real novelty of Bernhart's invention was a set of mathematical equations which the computer was programmed to solve. In *In re McIlroy,* the Court of Customs and Patent Appeals reaffirmed what it had held in *In re Benson:* "A process having no practical value other than enhancing the internal operation . . ." of a computer is proper subject matter for a patent under 35 U.S.C. § 101. In 1972, the Supreme Court decided its first case dealing with program patentability.

Gary Benson and Arthur Talbott had developed a method of programming a computer to automatically convert the binary coded decimal notation for a number into the pure binary notation for the same number. The Supreme Court held that the process claimed by Benson was an algorithm, and, as such, was not patentable. The Court considered programs as "specific applications" of an algorithm which, in turn, was a "procedure for solving a given type of mathematical problem." Benson's claim was so broad that it included not just one application, but all possible applications and, hence, gave Benson a monopoly on the algorithm itself. The principal concern of the Court was that the patent would give Benson a monopoly on a general method of solving a mathematical problem as well as all such uses to which the method of solution could be put. While the Court noted that the entire process could be carried out with existing computers, or even without the use of a computer, it failed to pursue this theme, and did not rule on the "mental steps" doctrine. The Court also specifically indicated that the decision did not hold that programs are not patentable. The Court requested that Congress act in this area.

In the intervening years, the Court of Customs and Patent Appeals had continued the policy of finding statutory subject matter in inventions which included programs, provided that the claims combined apparatus and process.

The next Supreme Court decision regarding program patentability was *Dann v. Johnston* in 1976. Thomas Johnston had developed a "record-keeping machine system for financial accounts." The Board of Patent Appeals rejected Johnston's application in part because it felt that granting the patent would give him a monopoly on a method of banking. The Court of Customs and Patent Appeals reversed the Board of Patent Appeals, pointing out that Johnston's claims were in the form of an apparatus; hence a bank could conduct its business any way it wanted, provided that it did not use Johnston's particular apparatus. Judge Markey dissented on the grounds that the apparatus in question was obvious to those skilled in the art of record-keeping machine systems. Judge Rich dissented because he felt that the court could no longer, in the face of *Benson,* maintain the fiction that a program changes a computer into a new machine. Although critical of the Supreme Court's position and unhappy with the confusion *Benson* had created, he could not distinguish between Johnston's claim and Benson's. The Supreme Court, in striking down the Johnston decision of the Court of Customs and Patent Appeals, did not resolve the problems that troubled Judge Rich. The Court decided that Johnston's application failed because it was obvious.

As in *Benson,* the Court indicated that the decision did not hold that programs were not patentable. Perhaps the Supreme Court's purpose was to delay in order to allow Congress time to act. If so, the Court has been frustrated because Congress has consistently failed to provide guidance.

Chastened, but undaunted, the Court of Customs and Patent Appeals continued to reverse the Board of Patent Appeals, which likewise continued to reject applications involving computer programs. The Court of Customs and Patent Appeals upheld the Board whenever an applicant relied too heavily on merely using a computer to solve mathematical equations. It also reversed the Board and found the following patentable: a process using a computer to control and optimize the operation of a system of multi-plant units; a system for typesetting, using a computer-based control system in conjunction with a conventional typesetter; and a method of using a computer to carry out translations from one language into another.

The Court of Customs and Patent Appeals suggested a two-step analysis of program claims. It must be determined if a claim recites an algorithm in the *Benson* sense. If no algorithm is found, then there is no algorithm to pre-empt. If an algorithm is found, then the patent claim must be analyzed to determine whether it pre-empts the algorithm. The court found no mathematical equations or algorithms present in *In re Toma* and *In re Freeman.* In considering the multi-plant control process in *In re Deutsch,* the court conceded that there were algorithms in Deutsch's specifications, but held that there was no preemption since "these would be freely available to all and could be used for any purpose other than the operation of a system of plants." The presence of "post-solution" activity, that is, what the solution of the mathematical equations is used for, once found, was not the determinative factor.

The *Freeman* court also criticized the Supreme Court's definition of algorithm. The court pointed out that using the dictionary's definition of algorithm leads to the conclusion that most processes are actually algorithms. If the court had pursued this reasoning further, it could have also pointed out that virtually all inventions rely on algorithms and mathematical equations since all inventions depend on the laws of nature to make them work.

The Court of Customs and Patent Appeals stated that even if the only novel aspect of an invention is an algorithm, the invention may still be statutory subject matter. In *Parker v. Flook,* the Supreme Court disagreed. Flook had developed a method for update parameters, called "alarm limits," which were used to detect the presence of abnormal conditions in catalytic conversion. The method consisted of three steps: the measurement of the present value of the process variables used to compute the alarm limit, the calculation of an updated alarm limit value using a *Benson*-type algorithm, and the replacement of the previous alarm limit by the newly computed value. The only novelty in the process rested in the second step algorithm. The Court stated that the presence of the algorithm was not itself fatal to Flook's case, but that his invention was unpatentable "because once that algorithm is assumed to be within prior art, the application, considered as a whole, contains no patentable invention."

The Court's rule that the algorithm should be considered as within prior art stemmed from the Court's belief that an algorithm "reveals a relationship that has always existed." The philosophical perspective that a "law of nature" or a mathematical algorithm has some real existence outside of the human mind that first conceived it is not shared by everyone. While the Court admitted that natural phenomena could be processes, it denied that they were the kind of processes that the law was intended to protect. In essence, the Court said that those inventions which have universal impact or are of sufficient importance to our society ought not to be patentable. The *Benson* Court said: "Phenomena of nature, . . . mental processes, and abstract intellectual concepts are not patentable, as they are the *basic tools* of scientific and technological work." It is likely, however, that the safety pin and the bottle cap, both patentable, have been tools of greater significance than Benson's algorithm.

Flook did not pre-empt a single algorithm. His use of the algorithm in his process was narrowly related to catalytic conversions. The whole world could have used it in any way it wanted with the sole exception of computing alarm limits in the catalytic process. The Court held that a claim for "an improved method of calculation, even when tied to a specific end use, is unpatentable," under 35 U.S.C. § 101. Henceforth, a process may still be judged as a whole, but any algorithm it contains must be treated as prior art. Once again in *Flook,* the Court affirmed that computer programs may yet be patentable. Once again, the Court appealed to Congress to settle the difficult questions of policy.

What is the current status of the law on program patents? Does anyone dare say? The decision in *Flook* would appear to conflict with a number of previous decisions of the Court of Customs and Patent Appeals. Yet some program patents still stand, and the Supreme Court reiterates that under the proper circumstances a program may be patented.

Despite the fact that there are more cases dealing with program patents than with program copyrights, the state of the law in both areas is essentially the same: uncertain. This uncertainty is a serious impediment to those who have programs for which they would like patent protection. It is, however, far from the only problem with program patents. On balance, a patent may afford no better protection for the software developer than a copyright. Even assuming that no additional legal or administrative problems existed for the software developer than exist for any other inventor seeking a patent, the software developer would find that patents are not a suitable protective device for his work product.

Programs can be hideously long and complex. Drafting the claims for such programs would be an expensive, meticulous, and time-consuming task. Once the application is properly completed, it must be submitted to the Patent Office where it faces a delay of two to three years before the application is approved, assuming it is approved at all. If the patent is granted, its validity may be challenged as a defense by an alleged infringer. The odds are high that it would be found invalid at the appellate level, even without the special stigma attaching to program patents. Because of the rapidity of change within the computer industry, the applicant for a program patent may find that his product has no value before the Patent Office has considered the application and its validity is tested in the courts.

Patent protection and secrecy are incompatible. Once the patent has been obtained, the program is available for public inspection at the Patent Office, and anyone may obtain a copy of it. Detection of infringement would be difficult because many users would run the program only on their own machines and could destroy their legally obtained photocopies once they had loaded the program on tape or other media in which it could not be seen.

Once the patent holder has sufficient evidence to file suit for infringement, he faces difficulties as great, or greater than, those confronted in a suit for copyright infringement. First, there will undoubtedly be challenges to the validity of the patent itself. Such a challenge might assert that the program lacked novelty. The defendant could show the court many programs that look remarkably similar to the plaintiff's program. The court, lacking expertise in computer science, will be hard put to make an intelligent finding of fact.

The challenge may also attempt to establish the program's obviousness. The mere fact that a program is long, complicated, or commercially valuable, does not mean that a patent can be granted; indeed, if other programmers could have written the same program with the then existing state of the art, such program cannot be patented. With many programmers involved in intricate and often similar projects, it would be easy to build a strong case that a programmer of ordinary skill, particularly one working in the same specialty as the plaintiff, could easily have written the plaintiff's program using then-existing art. Once again, the technology will create confusion in the mind of the court and will work in the defendant's favor.

Although the protection accorded by a patent is broader than that accorded by a copyright, it is not limitless. A patent holder, for example, who relies on the law of gravity to make his machine work, does not acquire a monopoly on the law of gravity. What then constitutes an infringement of a patent? Generally, the allegedly infringing invention must have substantial identity of function, means, and results. Therefore, with regard to machines, an infringing device must perform substantially the same function by substantially the same means, and the principle or mode of operation must be the same as that of the machine infringed upon. An infringing process must operate in substantially the same manner and under the same physical laws as the infringed process to produce the same result. It is not at all clear what these tests imply with respect to computer programs.

Underlying any program is an algorithm. It could reasonably be argued that a court should never consider that two programs use the same "principle of operation" or operate "under the same physical laws" unless they use essentially the same algorithm. The Supreme Court has made it clear, however, that it will not tolerate any patent which attempts to preempt an algorithm, that is, to gain a monopoly on all uses to which an algorithm might be put. The claims for a program patent will, therefore, have to spell out precisely a particular result the patent holder is using the program to obtain, and his patent will extend only to that result. Would the fact that the challenged program had used the same algorithm to achieve the same result as stated in the patent holder's claim suffice to establish an infringement? Perhaps, but such a straightforward situation would be rare. It is more likely that the alleged infringing program would: use only a portion of the plaintiff's algorithm; combine that algorithm; produce in hardware form what the plaintiff has expressed in software; or obtain a result which is arguably different from that claimed by the plaintiff. Many of these possibilities involve difficult technical questions. Can any court reasonably be expected to cope with an "invention" two miles long? Even if the plaintiff ultimately prevails, his suit is likely to be lengthy and expensive.

Perhaps it would be different if the patentability of programs was firmly established; however, software developers are not beating a path to the Patent Office door. If the figure cited by the Supreme Court in 1965 is still valid today, some 100,000 patent applications are filed each year but only approximately 450 of these are for programs. The reality seems to be that software developers are less interested in patent protection than copyright protection.

V. Other Means of Protection

The principal method the computer industry uses to protect its software is trade secrecy. Even if copyright protection were available, testimony before CONTU indicated that the industry would not give up trade-secrecy protection. In addition to trade secrecy, the industry relies on criminal law and contract law. Criminal law may permit prosecution under state or federal larceny statutes if valuable property in the form of a program is stolen. Contract law can bind a party to an agreement not to make unauthorized copies of, or reveal to others, any program being used under license from a software developer, or which the party helped write. In some rare instances the doctrine of unfair competition may also be invoked. This section will briefly touch upon the law of trade secrets and its relation to program protection.

The threshold question is whether trade secret law has been pre-empted by the new Copyright Law. The Copyright Act of 1976 incorporates a provision indicating that Congress did not intend to pre-empt the state law in this area. Moreover, since the Supreme Court decision in *Kewanee Oil Co. v. Bicron,* it also seems well-settled that federal law generally does not pre-empt state trade secret law.

Trade secret law can, of course, vary significantly from jurisdiction to jurisdiction. In some states, theft of a trade secret is a tort, whereas in others it is a criminal act. The mere fact that a program is secret does not mean that it is a trade secret. David Bender, in his 1970 comprehensive review of trade secrets and programs, points out that a program must be in "continuous use in the operation of a business" before most jurisdictions accord it trade secret protection. Mr. Bender divides potentially protected material into three classes: (1) inventions reduced to practice, together with the "know-how" associated with them; (2) abstract or general ideas of a commercial or industrial nature; and (3) other information, involving no element of novelty, but of value to its owner. Authorities differ concerning which classes are entitled to protection as well as the scope of protection. There will, of course, also be disputes as to which class any given program falls into.

Secrecy is obviously essential to trade secrets. Secrecy is maintained as long as those to whom the secret is revealed are bound not to reveal the secret. Even if a competitor discovers the same secret and uses it, it remains a secret as long as the competitor also maintains secrecy. Methods of maintaining secrecy include non-disclosure clauses in contracts of employment and of license to use the secret, and allowing use of the secret without supplying enough documentation to enable the user to duplicate it. At times a court will be willing to find an implied contractual condition of non-disclosure.

If a trade secret does not have some novel aspect, it is unlikely that it gives its possessor a valuable competitive edge. Most courts, therefore, require some degree of novelty before they will find a true trade secret or award damages if the item is misappropriated. The purported trade secret is usually required to represent a real economic investment for its owner, or the effort in its development must be more than trivial.

There are several problems with trade secret protection from the software developer's point of view. First, the law is not uniform throughout the United States; this is a distinct disadvantage to any company which does business in many jurisdictions. Second, the law never fully addressed the novel questions raised by computer technology and therefore has uncertainties similar to patent and copyright law. Third, the developer must adequately protect the secrecy of his program, even if it is for his use alone. Failure to properly protect a trade secret is fatal in a suit for damages. Fourth, once secrecy is lost, there is no protection for the program. Even the limited protection afforded by copyright is unavailable. Furthermore, because programmers are so mobile and the developer cannot prevent his former employees from using their general skill, experience and memory in the service of others, secrecy may effectively be lost as soon as the first employee who helped write the secret program moves on to another job. Finally, as was the case with patent and copyright, the developer has the difficult problem of determining if his program has been misappropriated and then of proving misappropriation in court. Because he has none of the presumptions of copyright registration or letters patent working in his favor, his burden is especially heavy. He would fail even after proving that the defendant actually copied his program verbatim, if the defendant convinced the court that the plaintiff did not take adequate measures to guard the program's secrecy.

VI. Recommendation

Legal protection for software must provide adequate rewards for the software developer as well as benefits to the public. To merely repeat that the purpose of copyright and patent is "to promote the progress of science and useful arts" does little to resolve the complex issues involved in software protection. It is equally simplistic to say that the Constitution demands that patent and copyright look first to the public interest, for that interest is often difficult to identify and is also inextricably related to the welfare of industry. If no significant financial rewards follow from creation of new ideas and inventions, then technological progress will stagnate and the public will necessarily be the poorer.

Moreover, one cannot merely consider only the public interest versus the interest of the computer industry. The interests of the hardware manufacturers compete with those of the software developer. The client of the computer industry has his own needs. The impact that any form of protection may have on the courts and administrative agencies must also be taken into account.

The CONTU report recommends that copyright protection be extended to programs under the Copyright Act of 1976, and the hardware producers, anxious to avoid any form of protection that would significantly impede sales of their machines, agree. David Bender proposes patent protection be available for programs, and the software houses, anxious to gain monopolies on their own programs, concur. Others conclude that the form of protection most in use now in the software industry, trade secrecy, is the best. Still others suggest federal trade secrecy legislation or a compulsory licensing scheme such as that adopted for phonograph records. Who is right? Is any new legislation in this area really needed? This question must be answered by considering the arguments of those proposing and opposing such legislation.

Software houses argue that patent protection should be available for software because such protection has long been available for hardware, and hardware and software are essentially interchangeable. Such an argument, however, is easily answered. An invention is not patentable until it is presented in patentable form. Until then, the courts may consider it to be too abstract, too close to being a mere idea. An analogous situation exists in copyright law: a work is not entitled to a copyright until it is fixed in a tangible medium of expression, even though it may be fully developed in the mind of its author.

Many argue that protection other than secrecy is needed to encourage an open transfer of information and to enable the technology to develop more efficiently. Given the unprecedented rapidity with which the computer industry has grown, it is difficult to believe that secrecy has really restrained the industry. Nevertheless, trade secrecy does discourage a free exchange of ideas in the private sector. There is, moreover, an interchange of ideas through academic research, publications in journals, and the movement of computer personnel from one employer to another. From the evidence presented to CONTU, the availability of copyright would not change the emphasis on secrecy where it currently exists. Patents require open publication. It is questionable whether program developers would seek them because of the ease with which patented programs could be obtained by potential infringers, the difficulty of detecting and proving infringements, the high risk associated with patent litigation, and the length of time and the expense initially associated with obtaining a patent. Moreover, the availability of patent or copyright protection might have the paradoxical effect of intensifying secrecy by those who wish to avoid potential suits for infringement, particularly if the availability of copyright or patent protection was held to preempt trade secret law.

Patent or copyright protection for programs might mean lower costs to the consumer. Trade secrecy incurs enterprise costs by making manufacture of software less efficient. Because of secrecy, many programmers must spend time repeating work others have done. However, aside from the fact that the availability of copyright and patent "protection" might increase secrecy and add to whatever costs secrecy might entail, such availability might also escalate the legal expenses of the computer industry. Moreover, fees for use of a copyrighted or patented program might be higher than if the program were merely under a contract prohibiting disclosure. A program protected only by secrecy becomes available to the general public once that secrecy is lost, but fees for programs protected by copyright or patent could continue until the copyright or patent expires; it is doubtful that any program could possibly remain secret that long.

Some argue that copyright or patent protection is necessary for the growth of the software industry. But this industry is growing by leaps and bounds without it. It is doubtful that the industry could absorb more work than it has due to a shortage of trained personnel.

Most software development is custom-tailored to particular users. Even software packages are often modified to include features needed by an individual client, or to run on a different machine. Clients are often willing to pay licensing fees, not because the licenser has a stranglehold on the program, but because it makes sense economically. Many small firms do not have the expertise to write their own software, or even to run someone else's without outside help. The software house not only provides a program at a price much lower than what it would cost the client to write it himself, but also it installs the program in the client's computer, and maintains, updates and warrants the program as well. The client is buying expertise and service as much as he is buying a particular piece of software. The practice of marketing hardware without a discreet charge for the included software is no longer prevalent. Software houses can compete with hardware manufacturers for the software market.

If copyright protection were available for programs, there would probably be few additional problems for either the courts or the Copyright Office. This, of course, stems from the fact that the software industry has shown almost complete indifference toward copyrights. The administrative problems associated with patentability of software, however, was one of the principal reasons that led the President's Commission on the Patent System to recommend against it:

> The Patent Office now cannot examine applications for programs because of a lack of a classification technique and the requisite search files. Even if these were available, reliable searches would not be feasible or economic because of the tremendous volume of prior art being generated. Without this search, the patenting of programs would be tantamount to mere registration and the presumption of validity would be all but nonexistent.

Should software patents be allowed then, the courts' current problems with the exotic technology and novel questions raised by computer-related suits would be intensified beyond toleration by the proliferation of infringement suits.

Much of value to the computer industry can already be protected by patent or copyright. Hardware has been patented. Data compilations and directories, instruction manuals, program documentation, warranties and other important documents all may clearly be copyrighted under the new Copyright Law. Because most complex programs have significantly less value without supporting documentation and such documentation can be copyrighted, copyright protection may now be obtained indirectly even if the copyrightability of the program itself is open to question.

But it is not enough to look to both the past and the present. What legislation is called for is in part determined by what the future holds for the computer industry. What are the directions in computing?

First, the use of computers will increase and touch virtually every segment of society. Small computers of considerable power and versatility are now available at prices affordable by even the smallest of firms and by families for household use and entertainment. Computers of astounding power and speed are available at higher prices for industry and government, but still at a remarkably low cost per operation. This increased computer usage will create a demand for more software that software houses are likely to satisfy in large part, particularly for the smaller computer users, who cannot afford to hire their own computer staffs. The market for software packages for home use may also grow substantially in the next few years. These trends are likely to create a healthy competition among software developers. Patent protection would stifle that competition whereas continuation of the *status quo* would encourage the software developers to constantly improve their products.

Second, more programs are likely to be converted to hardware and stored as a part of the computer itself. Such program modules should not be patentable if the underlying program itself is not, though the courts may decide otherwise. A lack of patent protection will encourage competition and drive the price for such program modules down.

Third, the increasing power of the machines, the more sophisticated hardware and increased size of the memory, will enable computers to handle programming languages which resemble ordinary speech. The more a program approximates ordinary speech, the harder it will be for a court to analyze the nature of a computer program. Computers themselves will be able to write complex programs and design improvements to their operating systems. This development would raise profound philosophical questions and may further confound the courts.

What about compulsory licensing? Compulsory licensing would suffer from most of the same defects as ordinary copyright protection and would be all but impossible to administer. What of a federal trade secret law? Such a law would have the advantage of providing uniformity throughout the United States, but it would also represent federal preemption in a form of protection that has traditionally been left to the states. The issues here extend far beyond computer programs.

Reliance on copyright protection remains the best alternative when protection is desired for work that would be protected without consideration of its use in a computer. Beyond this, no form of patent or copyright protection should be available for programs. Congress and the courts should state this rule clearly as soon as possible. Such a policy would resolve those issues which now cause unnecessary concern in the courts and undue speculation in the law reviews. It would allow the software industry to follow that path of trade secrecy which its practices indicate it prefers, and which it has thus far traveled with eminent success.

31. Diamond, Commissioner of Patents and Trademarks v. Diehr et al.

PATENT APPLICANT APPEALED from decision of Patent and Trademark Office Board of Appeals, Serial No. 602,463, rejecting claims for process for curing synthetic rubber. The Court of Customs and Patent Appeals, Rich, J., 602 F.2d 982, reversed. Certiorari was granted. The Supreme Court, Mr. Justice Rehnquist, held that: (1) although by itself a mathematical formula is not subject to patent protection, when a claim containing such formula implements or applies it in a structure or process which considered as a whole is performing a function designed to be protected by the patent laws the claim constitutes patentable subject matter; (2) subject process constituted patentable subject matter notwithstanding that in several of its steps it included use of a mathematical formula and a programmed digital computer, as process involved transformation of uncured synthetic rubber into a different state or thing and solved an industry problem of "undercure" and "overcure"; and (3) fact that by themselves one or more steps might not be novel or independently eligible for patent protection was irrelevant to issue of whether the claims as a whole recited subject matter eligible for patent protection.

Affirmed.

Justice Stevens filed a dissenting opinion, in which Justice Brennan, Justice Marshall and Justice Blackmun joined. . . .

Justice REHNQUIST delivered the opinion of the Court. . . .

I

The patent application at issue was filed by the respondents on August 6, 1975. The claimed invention is a process for molding raw, uncured synthetic rubber into cured precision products. The process uses a mold for precisely shaping the uncured material under heat and pressure and then curing the synthetic rubber in the mold so that the product will retain its shape and be functionally operative after the molding is completed.

Respondents claim that their process ensures the production of molded articles which are properly cured. Achieving the perfect cure depends upon several factors including the thickness of the article to be molded, the temperature of the molding process, and the amount of time that the article is allowed to remain in the press. It is possible using well-known time, temperature, and cure relationships to calculate by means of the Arrhenius equation when to open the press and remove the cured product. Nonetheless, according to the respondents, the industry has not been able to obtain uniformly accurate cures because the temperature of the molding press could not be precisely measured, thus making it difficult to do the necessary computations to determine cure time. Because the temperature *inside* the press has heretofore been viewed as an uncontrollable variable, the conventional industry practice has been to calculate the cure time as the shortest time in which

450 U.S. 1048–1073.

all parts of the product will definitely be cured, assuming a reasonable amount of mold-opening time during loading and unloading. But the shortcoming of this practice is that operating with an uncontrollable variable inevitably led in some instances to overestimating the mold-opening time and overcuring the rubber, and in other instances to underestimating that time and undercuring the product.

Respondents characterize their contribution to the art to reside in the process of constantly measuring the actual temperature inside the mold. These temperature measurements are then automatically fed into a computer which repeatedly recalculates the cure time by use of the Arrhenius equation. When the recalculated time equals the actual time that has elapsed since the press was closed, the computer signals a device to open the press. According to the respondents, the continuous measuring of the temperature inside the mold cavity, the feeding of this information to a digital computer which constantly recalculates the cure time, and the signaling by the computer to open the press, are all new in the art.

The patent examiner rejected the respondents' claims on the sole ground that they were drawn to nonstatutory subject matter under 35 U.S.C. § 101. He determined that those steps in respondents' claims that are carried out by a computer under control of a stored program constituted nonstatutory subject matter under this Court's decision in *Gottschalk v. Benson,* 409 U.S. 63, 93 S.Ct. 253, 34 L.Ed.2d 273 (1972). The remaining steps—installing rubber in the press and the subsequent closing of the press—were "conventional and necessary to the process and cannot be the basis of patentability." The examiner concluded that respondents' claims defined and sought protection of a computer program for operating a rubber-molding press.

The Patent and Trademark Office Board of Appeals agreed with the examiner, but the Court of Customs and Patent Appeals reversed. *In re Diehr,* 602 F.2d 982 (1979). The court noted that a claim drawn to subject matter otherwise statutory does not become nonstatutory because a computer is involved. The respondents' claims were not directed to a mathematical algorithm or an improved method of calculation but rather recited an improved process for molding rubber articles by solving a practical problem which had risen in the molding of rubber products.

The Commission of Patents and Trademarks sought certiorari arguing that the decision of the Court of Customs and Patent Appeals was inconsistent with prior decisions of this Court. Because of the importance of the question presented, we granted the writ. 445 U.S. 926, 100 S.Ct. 1311, 63 L.Ed.2d 758 (1980).

II

Last Term in *Diamond v. Chakrabarty,* 447 U.S. 303, 100 S.Ct. 2204, 65 L.Ed.2d 144 (1980), this Court discussed the historical purposes of the patent laws and in particular 35 U.S.C. § 101. As in *Chakrabarty,* we must here construe 35 U.S.C. § 101 which provides:

> Whoever, invents or discovers any new and useful process, machine manufacture, or composition of matter, or any new and useful improvement thereof, may obtain a patent therefor, subject to the conditions and requirements of this title.

In cases of statutory construction, we begin with the language of the statute. Unless otherwise defined, "words will be interpreted as taking their ordinary, contemporary, common meaning," *Perrin v. United States,* 444 U.S. 37, 42, 100 S.Ct. 311, 314, 62 L.Ed.2d 199 (1979), and, in dealing with the patent laws, we have more than once cautioned that "courts 'should not read into the patent laws limitations and conditions which the legislature has not expressed.'" *Diamond v. Chakrabarty, supra,* at 308, 100 S.Ct., at 2207 quoting *United States v. Dubilier Condenser Corp.,* 289 U.S. 178, 199, 53 S.Ct. 554, 561, 77 L.Ed. 1114 (1933).

[1] The Patent Act of 1793 defined statutory subject matter as "any new and useful art, machine, manufacture or composition of matter, or any new or useful improvement [thereof]." Act of Feb. 21, 1793, ch. 11, § 1, 1 Stat. 318. Not until the patent laws were recodified in 1952 did Congress replace the word "art" with the word "process." It is that latter word which we confront today, and in order to determine its meaning we may not be unmindful of the Committee Reports accompanying the 1952 Act which inform us that Congress intended statutory subject matter to "include anything under the sun that is made by man." S.Rep.No.1979, 82d Cong., 2d Sess., 5 (1952); H.R.Rep.No.1923, 82d Cong., 2d Sess., 6 (1952), U.S. Code Cong. & Admin.News 1952, pp. 2394, 2399.

[2, 3] Although the term "process" was not added to 35 U.S.C. § 101 until 1952 a process has historically enjoyed patent protection because it was considered a form of "art" as that term was used in the 1793 Act. In defining the nature of a patentable process, the Court stated:

> That a process may be patentable, irrespective of the particular form of the instrumentalities used, cannot be disputed. . . . A process is a mode of treatment of certain materials to produce a given result. It is an act, or a series of acts, performed upon the subject-matter to be transformed and reduced to a different state or thing. If new and useful, it is just as patentable as is a piece of machinery. In the language of the patent law, it is an art. The machinery pointed out as suitable to perform the process may or may not be new or patentable; whilst the process itself may be altogether new, and produce an entirely new result. The process requires that certain things should be done with certain substances, and in a certain order; but the tools to be used in doing this may be of secondary consequence. *Cochrane v. Deener,* 94 U.S. 780, 787–788, 24 L.Ed. 139 (1877).

Analysis of the eligibility of a claim of patent protection for a "process" did not change with the addition of that term to § 101. Recently, in *Gottschalk v. Benson,* 409 U.S. 63, 93 S.Ct. 253, 34 L.Ed.2d 273 (1972), we repeated the above definition recited in *Cochrane v. Deener,* adding: "Transformation and reduction of an article 'to a different state or thing' is the clue to the patentability of a process claim that does not include particular machines." 409 U.S., at 70, 93 S.Ct., at 256.

Analyzing respondents' claims according to the above statements from our cases, we think that a physical and chemical process for molding precision synthetic rubber products falls within the § 101 categories of possibly patentable subject matter. That respondents' claims involve the transformation of an article, in this case raw, uncured synthetic rubber, into a different state or thing cannot be disputed. The respondents' claims describe in detail a step-by-step method for accomplishing such, beginning with the loading of a mold with raw, uncured rubber and ending with the eventual opening of the press at the conclusion of the cure. Industrial processes such as this are the types which have historically been eligible to receive the protection of our patent laws.

III

Our conclusion regarding respondents' claims is not altered by the fact that in several steps of the process a mathematical equation and a programmed digital computer are used. This Court has undoubtedly recognized limits to § 101 and every discovery is not embraced within the statutory terms. Excluded from such patent protection are laws of nature, natural phenomena, and abstract ideas. See *Parker v. Flook,* 437 U.S. 584, 98 S.Ct. 2522, 57 L.Ed.2d 451 (1978); *Gottschalk v. Benson, supra,* at 67, 93 S.Ct., at 255; *Funk Bros. Seed Co. v. Kalo Inoculant Co.,* 333 U.S. 127, 130, 68 S.Ct. 440, 441, 92 L.Ed. 588 (1948). "An idea of itself is not patentable," *Rubber-Tip Pencil Co. v. Howard,* 20 Wall. 498, 507, 22 L.Ed. 410 (1874). "A principle, in the abstract, is a fundamental truth; an original cause; a motive; these cannot be patented, as no one can claim in either of them an exclusive right." *Le Roy v. Tatham,* 14 How. 156, 175, 14 L.Ed. 367 (1853). Only last Term, we explained:

> [A] new mineral discovered in the earth or a new plant found in the wild is not patentable subject matter. Likewise, Einstein could not patent his celebrated law that $E = mc^2$; nor could Newton have patented the law of gravity. Such discoveries are "manifestations of . . . nature, free to all men and reserved exclusively to none." *Diamond v. Chakrabarty,* 447 U.S., at 309, 100 S.Ct., at 2208, quoting *Funk Bros. Seed Co. v. Kalo Inoculant Co., supra,* at 130, 68 S.Ct., at 441.

Our recent holdings in *Gottschalk v. Benson, supra,* and *Parker v. Flook, supra,* both of which are computer-related, stand for no more than these long-established principles. In *Benson,* we held unpatentable claims for an algorithm used to convert binary code decimal numbers to equivalent pure binary numbers. The sole practical application of the algorithm was in connection with the programming of a general purpose digital computer. We defined "algorithm" as a "procedure for solving a given type of mathematical problem," and we concluded that such an algorithm, or mathematical formula, is like a law of nature, which cannot be the subject of a patent.

Parker v. Flook, supra, presented a similar situation. The claims were drawn to a method for computing an "alarm limit." An "alarm limit" is simply a number and the Court concluded that the application sought to protect a formula for computing this number. Using this formula, the updated alarm limit could be calculated if several other variables were known. The application, however, did not purport to explain how these other variables were to be determined, nor did it purport "to contain any disclosure relating to the chemical processes at work, the monitoring of process variables, or the means of setting off an alarm or adjusting an alarm system. All that it provides is a formula for computing an updated alarm limit." 437 U.S., at 586, 98 S.Ct., at 2523.

In contrast, the respondents here do not seek to patent a mathematical formula. Instead, they seek patent protection for a process of curing synthetic rubber. Their process admittedly employs a well-known mathematical equation, but they do not seek to pre-empt the use of that equation. Rather, they seek only to foreclose from others the use of that equation in conjunction with all of the other steps in their claimed process. These include installing rubber in a press, closing the mold, constantly determining the temperature of the mold, constantly recalculating the appropriate cure time through the use of the formula and a digital computer, and automatically opening the press at the proper time. Obviously, one does not need a "computer" to cure natural or synthetic rubber, but if the computer use incorporated in the process patent significantly lessens the possibility of "overcuring" or "undercuring," the process as a whole does not thereby become unpatentable subject matter.

Our earlier opinions lend support to our present conclusion that a claim drawn to subject matter otherwise statutory does not become nonstatutory simply because it uses a mathematical formula, computer program, or digital computer. In *Gottschalk v. Benson,* we noted: "It is said that the decision precludes a patent for any program servicing a computer. We do not so hold." 409 U.S., at 71, 93 S.Ct., at 257. Similarly, in *Parker v. Flook,* we stated that "a process is not unpatentable simply because it contains a law of nature or a mathematical algorithm." 437 U.S., at 590, 98 S.Ct., at 2526. It is now commonplace that an *application* of a law of nature or mathematical formula to a known structure or process may well be deserving of patent protection. As Justice Stone explained four decades ago:

> While a scientific truth, or the mathematical expression of it, is not a patentable invention, a novel and useful structure created with the aid of knowledge of scientific truth may be. *Mackay Radio & Telegraph Co. v. Radio of America,* 306 U.S. 86, 94, 59 S.Ct. 427, 431, 83 L.Ed. 506 (1939).

We think this statement in *Mackay* takes us a long way toward the correct answer in this case. Arrhenius' equation is not patentable in isolation, but when a process for curing rubber is devised which incorporates in it a more efficient solution of the equation, that process is at the very least not barred at the threshold by § 101.

In determining the eligibility of respondents' claimed process for patent protection under § 101, their claims must be considered as a whole. It is inappropriate to dissect the claims into old and new elements and then to ignore the presence of the old elements in the analysis. This is particularly true in a process claim because a new combination of steps in a process may be patentable even though all the constituents of the combination were well known and in common use before the combination was made. The "novelty" of any element or steps in a process, or even of the process itself, is of no relevance in determining whether the subject matter of a claim falls within the § 101 categories of possibly patentable subject matter.

It has been urged that novelty is an appropriate consideration under § 101. Presumably, this argument results from the language in § 101 referring to any "new and useful" process, machine, etc. Section 101, however, is a general statement of the type of subject matter that is eligible for patent protection "subject to the conditions and requirements of this title." Specific conditions for patentability follow and § 102 covers in detail the conditions relating to novelty. The question therefore of whether a particular invention is novel is "wholly apart from whether the invention falls into a category of statutory subject matter." *In re Bergy,* 596 F.2d 952, 961 (Cust. & Pat. App., 1979) (emphasis deleted). . . . The legislative history of the 1952 Patent Act is in accord with this reasoning. The Senate Report stated:

Section 101 sets forth the subject matter that can be patented, "subject to the conditions and requirements of this title." The conditions under which a patent may be obtained follow, and *Section 102 covers the conditions relating to novelty.* S.Rep.No.1979, 82d Cong., 2d Sess., 5 (1952), U.S. Code Cong. & Admin. News, 1952, p. 2399 (emphasis supplied).

It is later stated in the same Report:

> Section 102, in general, may be said to describe the statutory novelty required for patentability, and includes, in effect, an amplification and definition of "new" in section 101. *Id.,* at 6, U.S. Code Cong. & Admin. News, 1952, p. 2399.

Finally, it is stated in the "Revision Notes":

> The corresponding section of [the] existing statute is split into two sections, section 101 relating to the subject matter for which patents may be obtained, and section 102 defining statutory novelty and stating other conditions for patentability. *Id.,* at 17, U.S. Code Cong. & Admin. News, 1952, p. 2409. . . .

In this case, it may later be determined that the respondents' process is not deserving of patent protection because it fails to satisfy the statutory conditions of novelty under § 102 or nonobviousness under § 103. A rejection on either of these grounds does not affect the determination that respondents' claims recited subject matter which was eligible for patent protection under § 101.

IV

We have before us today only the question of whether respondents' claims fall within the § 101 categories of possibly patentable subject matter. We view respondents' claims as nothing more than a process for molding rubber products and not as an attempt to patent a mathematical formula. We recognize, of course, that when a claim recites a mathematical formula (or scientific principle or phenomenon of nature), an inquiry must be made into whether the claim is seeking patent protection for that formula in the abstract. A mathematical formula as such is not accorded the protection of our patent laws, *Gottschalk v. Benson,* 409 U.S. 63, 93 S.Ct. 253, 34 L.Ed.2d 273 (1972), and this principle cannot be circumvented by attempting to limit the use of the formula to a particular technological environment. *Parker v. Flook,* 437 U.S. 584, 98 S.Ct. 2522, 57 L.Ed.2d 451 (1978). Similarly, insignificant post-solution activity will not transform an unpatentable principle into a patentable process. *Ibid.* To hold otherwise would allow a competent draftsman to evade the recognized limitations on the type of subject matter eligible for patent protection. On the other hand, when a claim containing a mathematical formula implements or applies that formula in a structure or process which, when considered as a whole, is performing a function which the patent laws were designed to protect (*e.g.,* transforming or reducing an article to a different state or thing), then the claim satisfies the requirements of § 101. Because we do not view respondents' claims as an attempt to patent a mathematical formula, but rather to be drawn to an industrial process for the molding of rubber products, we affirm the judgment of the Court of Customs and Patent Appeals.

It is so ordered.

Justice STEVENS, with whom Justice BRENNAN, Justice MARSHALL, and Justice BLACKMUN join, dissenting.

The starting point in the proper adjudication of patent litigation is an understanding of what the inventor claims to have discovered. The Court's decision in this case rests on a misreading of the Diehr and Lutton patent application. Moreover, the Court has compounded its error by ignoring the critical distinction between the character of the subject matter that the inventor claims to be novel—the § 101 issue—and the question whether that subject matter is in fact novel—the § 102 issue.

I

Before discussing the major flaws in the Court's opinion, a word of history may be helpful. As the Court recognized in *Parker v. Flook,* 437 U.S. 584, 595, 98 S.Ct. 2522, 2528, 57 L.Ed.2d 451 (1978), the computer industry is relatively young. Although computer technology seems commonplace today, the first digital computer capable of utilizing stored programs was developed less than 30 years ago. Patent law developments in response to this new technology are of even more recent vintage. The subject of legal protection for computer programs did not begin to receive serious consideration until over a decade after completion of the first programmable digital computer. It was 1968 before the federal courts squarely addressed the subject, and 1972 before this Court announced its first decision in the area.

Prior to 1968, well-established principles of patent law probably would have prevented the issuance of a valid patent on almost any conceivable computer program. Under the "mental steps" doctrine, processes involving mental operations were considered unpatentable. . . . The mental-steps doctrine was based upon the familiar principle that a scientific concept or mere idea cannot be the subject of a valid patent. . . . The doctrine was regularly invoked to deny patents to inventions consisting primarily of mathematical formulae or methods of computation. It was also applied against patent claims in which a mental operation or mathematical computation was the sole novel element or inventive contribution; it was clear that patentability could not be predicated upon a mental step. Under the "function of a machine" doctrine, a process which amounted to nothing more than a description of the function of a machine was unpatentable. This doctrine had its origin in several 19th-century decisions of this Court, and it had been consistently followed thereafter by the lower federal courts. Finally, the definition of "process" announced by this Court in *Cochrane v. Deener,* 94 U.S. 780, 787–788, 24 L.Ed. 139 (1877), seemed to indicate that a patentable process must cause a physical transformation in the materials to which the process is applied. See *ante,* at 1054–1055.

Concern with the patent system's ability to deal with rapidly changing technology in the computer and other fields led to the formation in 1965 of the President's Commission on the Patent System. After studying the question of computer program patentability, the Commission recommended that computer programs be expressly excluded from the coverage of the patent laws; this recommendation was based primarily upon the Patent Office's inability to deal with the administrative burden of examining program applications. At approximately the time that the Commission issued its report, the Patent Office published notice of its intention to prescribe guidelines for the examination of applications for patents on computer programs. See 829 Off.Gaz.Pat.Off. 865 (Aug. 16, 1966). Under the proposed guidelines, a computer program, whether claimed as an apparatus or as a process, was unpatentable. The Patent Office indicated, however, that a programmed computer could be a component of a patentable process if combined with unobvious elements to produce a physical result. The Patent Office formally adopted the guidelines in 1968. See 33 Fed. Reg. 15609 (1968).

The new guidelines were to have a short life. Beginning with two decisions in 1968, a dramatic change in the law as understood by the Court of Customs and Patent Appeals took place. By repudiating the well-settled "function of a machine" and "mental steps" doctrines, that court reinterpreted § 101 of the Patent Code to enlarge drastically the categories of patentable subject matter. This reinterpretation would lead to the conclusion that computer programs were within the categories of inventions to which Congress intended to extend patent protection.

In *In re Tarczy-Hornoch,* 397 F.2d.856, 55 CCPA (Pat.) 1441 (1968), a divided Court of Customs and Patent Appeals overruled the line of cases developing and applying the "function of a machine" doctrine. The majority acknowledged that the doctrine had originated with decisions of this Court and that the lower federal courts, including the Court of Customs and Patent Appeals, had consistently adhered to it during the preceding 70 years. Nonetheless, the court concluded that the doctrine rested on a misinterpretation of the precedents and that it was contrary to "the basic purposes of the patent system and productive of a range of undesirable results from the harshly inequitable to the silly." *Id.,* at 867, 55 CCPA (Pat.), at 1454. Shortly thereafter, a similar fate befell the "mental steps" doctrine. In *In re Prater,* 415 F.2d 1378, 56 CCPA (Pat.) 1360 (1968), modified on rehearing, 415 F.2d 1393, 56 CCPA (Pat.) 1381 (1969), the court found that the precedents on which that doctrine was based either were poorly reasoned or had been misinterpreted over the years. 415 F.2d, at 1382–1387, 56 CCPA (Pat.), at 1366–1372. The court concluded that the fact that a process may be performed mentally should not foreclose patentability if the claims reveal that the process also may be performed without mental operations. *Id.,* at 1389, 56 CCPA (Pat.), at 1374–1375. This aspect of the original *Prater* opinion was substantially undisturbed by the opinion issued after rehearing. However, the second *Prater* opinion clearly indicated that patent claims broad enough to encompass the operation of a programmed computer would not be rejected for lack of patentable subject matter. 415 F.2d, at 1403, n. 29, 56 CCPA (Pat.), at 1394, n. 29.

The Court of Customs and Patent Appeals soon replaced the overruled doctrines with more expansive principles formulated with computer technology in mind. In *In re Bernhart,* 417 F.2d 1395, 57 CCPA (Pat.) 737 (1969), the court reaffirmed *Prater,* and indicated that all that remained of the mental-steps doctrine was a prohibition on the granting of a patent that would confer a monopoly on all uses of a scientific principle or mathematical equation. *Id.,* at 1399, 57 CCPA (Pat.), at 743. The court also announced that a computer programmed with a new and unobvious program was physically different from the same computer without that program; the programmed computer was a new machine or at least a new improvement over the unprogrammed computer. *Id.,* at 1400, 57 CCPA (Pat.), at 744. Therefore, patent protection could be obtained for new computer programs if the patent claims were drafted in apparatus form.

The Court of Customs and Patent Appeals turned its attention to process claims encompassing computer programs in *In re Musgrave,* 431 F.2d 882, 57 CCPA (Pat.) 1352 (1970). In that case, the court emphasized the fact that *Prater* had done away with the mental-steps doctrine; in particular, the court rejected the Patent Office's continued reliance upon the "point of novelty" approach to claim analysis. *Id.,* at 889, 57 CCPA (Pat.), at 1362. The court also announced a new standard for evaluating process claims under § 101: any sequence of operational steps was a patentable process under § 101 as long as it was within the "technological arts." *Id.,* at 893, 57 CCPA (Pat.), at 1366–1367. This standard effectively disposed of any vestiges of the mental-steps doctrine remaining after *Prater* and *Bernhart.* The "technological arts" standard was refined in *In re Benson,* 441 F.2d 682, 58 CCPA (Pat.) 1134 (1971), in which the court held that computers, regardless of the uses to which they are put, are within the technological arts for purposes of § 101. *Id.,* at 688, 58 CCPA (Pat.), at 1142.

In re Benson, of course, was reversed by this Court in *Gottschalk v. Benson,* 409 U.S. 63, 93 S.Ct. 253, 34 L.Ed.2d 273 (1972). Justice Douglas' opinion for a unanimous Court made no reference to the lower court's rejection of the mental-steps doctrine or to the new technological-arts standard. Rather, the Court clearly held that new mathematical procedures that can be conducted in old computers, like mental processes and abstract intellectual concepts, see *id.,* at 67, 93 S.Ct., at 255, are not patentable processes within the meaning of § 101.

The Court of Customs and Patent Appeals had its first opportunity to interpret *Benson* in *In re Christensen,* 478 F.2d 1392 (1973). In *Christensen,* the claimed invention was a method in which the only novel element was a mathematical formula. The court resurrected the point-of-novelty approach abandoned in *Musgrave* and held that a process claim in which the point of novelty was a mathematical equation to be solved as the final step of the process did not define patentable subject matter after *Benson.* 478 F.2d, at 1394. Accordingly, the court affirmed the Patent Office Board of Appeals' rejection of the claims under § 101.

The Court of Customs and Patent Appeals in subsequent cases began to narrow its interpretation of *Benson.* In *In re Johnston,* 502 F.2d 765 (1974), the court held that a recordkeeping machine system which comprised a programmed digital computer was patentable subject matter under § 101. *Id.,* at 771. The majority dismissed *Benson* with the observation that *Benson* involved only process, not apparatus claims. 502 F.2d, at 771. Judge Rich dissented, arguing that to limit *Benson* only to process claims would make patentability turn upon the form in which a program invention was claimed. 502 F.2d, at 773–774. The court again construed *Benson* as limited only to process claims in *In re Noll,* 545 F.2d 141 (1976), . . . apparatus claims were governed by the court's pre-*Benson* conclusion that a programmed computer was structurally different from the same computer without that particular program. 545 F.2d, at 148. In dissent, Judge Lane, joined by Judge Rich, argued that *Benson* should be read as a general proscription of the patenting of computer programs regardless of the form of the claims. 545 F.2d, at 151–152. Judge Lane's interpretation of *Benson* was rejected by the majority in *In re Chatfield,* 545 F.2d 152 (1976), . . . decided on the same day as *Noll.* In that case, the court construed *Benson* to preclude the patenting of program inventions claimed as processes only where the claims would pre-empt all uses of an algorithm or mathematical formula. 545 F.2d, at 156, 158–159. The dissenting judges argued, as they had in *Noll,* that *Benson* held that programs for general-purpose digital computers are not patentable subject matter. 545 F.2d, at 161.

Following *Noll* and *Chatfield,* the Court of Customs and Patent Appeals consistently interpreted *Benson* to preclude the patenting of a program-related process invention only when the claims, if allowed, would wholly pre-empt the algorithm itself. One of the cases adopting this view was *In re Flook,* 559 F.2d 21 (1977), which was reversed in *Parker v. Flook,* 437 U.S. 584, 98 S.Ct. 2522, 57 L.Ed.2d 451 (1978). Before this Court decided *Flook,* however, the lower court developed a two-step procedure for analyzing program-related inventions in light of *Benson.* In *In re Freeman,* 573 F.2d 1237 (1978), the court held that such inventions must first be examined to determine whether a mathematical algorithm is directly or indirectly claimed; if an algorithm is recited, the court must then determine whether the claim would wholly pre-empt that algorithm. Only if a claim satisfied both inquiries was *Benson* considered applicable. 573 F.2d, at 1245. . . .

In *Flook,* this Court clarified *Benson* in three significant respects. First, *Flook* held that the *Benson* rule of unpatentable subject matter was not limited, as the lower court believed, to claims which wholly pre-empted an algorithm or amounted to a patent on the algorithm itself. 437 U.S., at 589–590, 98 S.Ct., at 2525–2526. Second, the Court made it clear that an improved method of calculation, even when employed as part of a physical process, is not patentable subject matter under § 101. *Id.,* at 595, n. 18, 98 S.Ct., at 2528. Finally, the Court explained the correct procedure for analyzing a patient claim employing a mathematical algorithm. Under this procedure, the algorithm is treated for § 101 purposes as though it were a familiar part of the prior art; the claim is then examined to determine whether it discloses "some other inventive concept." *Id.,* at 591–595, 98 S.Ct., at 2526–2528.

Although the Court of Customs and Patent Appeals in several post-*Flook* decisions held that program-related inventions were not patentable subject matter under § 101, . . . in general *Flook* was not enthusiastically received by that court. In *In re Bergy,* 596 F.2d 952 (1979), the majority engaged in an extensive critique of *Flook,* concluding that this Court had erroneously commingled "distinct statutory provisions which are conceptually unrelated." 596 F.2d, at 959. In subsequent cases, the court construed *Flook* as resting on nothing more than the way in which the patent claims had been drafted, and it expressly declined to use the method of claim analysis spelled out in that decision. The Court of Customs and Patent Appeals has taken the position that, if an application is drafted in a way that discloses an entire process as novel, it defines patentable subject matter even if the only novel element that the inventor claims to have discovered is a new computer program. The court interpreted *Flook* in this manner in its opinion in this case. See *In re Diehr,* 602 F.2d 982, 986–989 (1979). In my judgment, this reading of *Flook*—although entirely consistent with the lower court's expansive approach to § 101 during the past 12 years—trivializes the holding in *Flook,* the principle that underlies *Benson,* and the settled line of authority reviewed in those opinions.

II

As I stated at the outset, the starting point in the proper adjudication of patent litigation is an understanding of what the inventor claims to have discovered. Indeed, the outcome of such litigation is often determined by the judge's understanding of the patent application. This is such a case.

In the first sentence of its opinion, the Court states the question presented as "whether a process for curing synthetic rubber . . . is patentable subject matter." *Ante,* at 1051. Of course, that question was effectively answered many years ago when Charles Goodyear obtained his patent on the vulcanization process. The patent application filed by Diehr and Lutton, however, teaches nothing about the chemistry of the synthetic rubber-curing process, nothing about the raw materials to be used in curing synthetic rubber, nothing about the equipment to be used in the process, and nothing about the significance or effect of any process variable such as temperature, curing time, particular compositions of material, or mold configurations. In short, Diehr and Lutton do not claim to have discovered anything new about the process for curing synthetic rubber.

As the Court reads the claims in the Diehr and Lutton patent application, the inventors' discovery is a method of constantly measuring the actual temperature inside a rubber molding press. As I read the claims, their discovery is an improved method of calculating the time that the mold should remain closed during the curing process. If the Court's reading of the claims were correct, I would agree that they disclose patentable subject matter. On the other hand, if the Court accepted my reading, I feel confident that the case would be decided differently.

There are three reasons why I cannot accept the Court's conclusion that Diehr and Lutton claim to have discovered a new method of constantly measuring the temperature inside a mold. First, there is not a word in the patent application that suggests that there is anything unusual about the temperature-reading devices used in this process—or indeed that any particular species of temperature-reading device should be used in it. Second, since devices for constantly measuring actual temperatures—on a back porch, for example— have been familiar articles for quite some time, I find it difficult to believe that a patent application filed in 1975 was premised on the notion that a "process of constantly measuring the actual temperature" had just been discovered. Finally, the Patent and Trademark Office Board of Appeals expressly found that "the only difference between the conventional methods of operating a molding press and that claimed in [the] application rests in those steps of the claims which relate to the calculation incident to the solution of the mathematical problem or formula used to control the mold heater and the automatic opening of the press." This finding was not disturbed by the Court of Customs and Patent Appeals and is clearly correct.

A fair reading of the entire patent application, as well as the specific claims, makes it perfectly clear that what Diehr and Lutton claim to have discovered is a method of using a digital computer to determine the amount of time that a rubber molding press should remain closed during the synthetic rubber-curing process. There is no suggestion that there is anything novel in the instrumentation of the mold, in actuating a timer when the press is closed, or in automatically opening the press when the computed time expires. Nor does the application suggest that Diehr and Lutton have discovered anything about the temperatures in the mold or the amount of curing time that will produce the best cure. What they claim to have discovered, in essence, is a method of updating the original estimated curing time by repetitively recalculating that time pursuant to a well-known mathematical formula in response to variations in temperature within the mold. Their method of updating the curing time calculation is strikingly reminiscent of the method of updating alarm limits that Dale Flook sought to patent.

Parker v. Flook, 437 U.S. 584, 98 S.Ct. 2522, 57 L.Ed.2d 451 (1978), involved the use of a digital computer in connection with a catalytic conversion process. During the conversion process, variables such as temperature, pressure, and flow rates were constantly monitored and fed into the computer; in this case, temperature in the mold is the variable that is monitored and fed into the computer. In *Flook,* the digital computer repetitively recalculated the "alarm limit"—a number that might signal the need to terminate or modify the catalytic conversion process; in this case, the digital computer repetitively recalculates the correct curing time—a number that signals the time when the synthetic rubber molding press should open.

The essence of the claimed discovery in both cases was an algorithm that could be programmed on a digital computer. In *Flook,* the algorithm made use of multiple process variables; in this case, it makes use of only one. In *Flook,* the algorithm was expressed in a newly developed mathematical formula; in this case, the algorithm makes use of a well-known mathematical formula. Manifestly, neither of these differences can explain today's holding. What I believe does explain today's holding is a misunderstanding of the applicants' claimed invention and a failure to recognize the critical difference between the "discovery" requirement in § 101 and the "novelty" requirement in § 102.

III

The Court misapplies *Parker v. Flook* because, like the Court of Customs and Patent Appeals, it fails to understand or completely disregards the distinction between the subject matter of what the inventor *claims* to have discovered—the § 101 issue—and the question whether that claimed discovery is in fact novel—the § 102 issue. If there is not even a claim that anything constituting patentable subject matter has been discovered, there is no occasion to address the novelty issue. Or, as was true in *Flook,* if the only concept that the inventor claims to have discovered is not patentable subject matter, § 101 requires that the application be rejected without reaching any issue under § 102; for it is irrelevant that unpatentable subject matter—in that case a formula for updating alarm limits—may in fact be novel.

Proper analysis, therefore, must start with an understanding of what the inventor claims to have discovered—or phrased somewhat differently—what he considers his inventive concept to be. It seems clear to me that Diehr and Lutton claim to have developed a new method of programming a digital computer in order to calculate—promptly and repeatedly—the correct curing time in a familiar process. In the § 101 analysis, we must assume that the sequence of steps in this programming method is novel, unobvious, and useful. The threshold question of whether such a method is patentable subject matter remains.

If that method is regarded as an "algorithm" as that term was used in *Gottschalk v. Benson,* 409 U.S. 63, 93 S.Ct. 253, 34 L.Ed.2d 273 (1972), and in *Parker v. Flook,* 437 U.S. 584, 98 S.Ct. 2522, 57 L.Ed.2d 451 (1978), and if no other inventive concept is disclosed in the patent application, the question must be answered in the negative. In both *Benson* and *Flook,* the parties apparently agreed that the inventor's discovery was properly regarded as an algorithm; the holding that an algorithm was a "law of nature" that could not be patented therefore determined that those discoveries were not patentable processes within the meaning of § 101.

As the Court recognizes today, *Flook* also rejected the argument that patent protection was available if the inventor did not claim a monopoly on every conceivable use of the algorithm but instead limited his claims by describing a specific postsolution activity—in that case setting off an alarm in a catalytic conversion process. In its effort to distinguish

Flook from the instant case, the Court characterizes that postsolution activity as "insignificant," *ante,* at 1059, or as merely "token" activity, *ante,* at 1059, n. 14. As a practical matter however, the postsolution activity described in the *Flook* application was no less significant than the automatic opening of the curing mold involved in this case. For setting off an alarm limit at the appropriate time is surely as important to the safe and efficient operation of a catalytic conversion process as is actuating the mold-opening device in a synthetic rubber-curing process. In both cases, the post-solution activity is a significant part of the industrial process. But in neither case should that activity have any *legal* significance because it does not constitute a part of the inventive concept that the applicants claimed to have discovered.

In *Gottschalk v. Benson,* we held that a program for the solution by a digital computer of a mathematical problem was not a patentable process within the meaning of § 101. In *Parker v. Flook,* we further held that such a computer program could not be transformed into a patentable process by the addition of postsolution activity that was not claimed to be novel. That holding plainly requires the rejection of Claims 1 and 2 of the Diehr and Lutton application quoted in the Court's opinion. *Ante,* at 1052–1053, n. 5. In my opinion, it equally requires rejection of Claim 11 because the presolution activity described in that claim is admittedly a familiar part of the prior art.

Even the Court does not suggest that the computer program developed by Diehr and Lutton is a patentable discovery. Accordingly, if we treat the program as though it were a familiar part of the prior art—as well-established precedent requires—it is absolutely clear that their application contains no claim of patentable invention. Their application was therefore properly rejected under § 101 by the Patent Office and the Board of Appeals.

IV

The broad question whether computer programs should be given patent protection involves policy considerations that this Court is not authorized to address. . . . As the numerous briefs *amicus curiae* filed in *Gottschalk v. Benson, supra* . . . and this case demonstrate, that question is not only difficult and important, but apparently also one that may be affected by institutional bias. In each of those cases, the spokesmen for the organized patent bar have uniformly favored patentability and industry representatives have taken positions properly motivated by their economic self-interest. Notwithstanding fervent argument that patent protection is essential for the growth of the software industry, commentators have noted that "this industry is growing by leaps and bounds without it." In addition, even some commentators who believe that legal protection for computer programs is desirable have expressed doubts that the present patent system can provide the needed protection.

Within the Federal Government, patterns of decision have also emerged. Gottschalk, Dann, Parker, and Diamond were not ordinary litigants—each was serving as Commissioner of Patents and Trademarks when he opposed the availability of patent protection for a program-related invention. No doubt each may have been motivated by a concern about the ability of the Patent Office to process effectively the flood of applications that would inevitably flow from a decision that computer programs are patentable. The consistent concern evidenced by the Commissioner of Patents and Trademarks and by the Board of Appeals of the Patent and Trademark Office has not been shared by the Court of Customs and Patent Appeals, which reversed the Board in *Benson, Johnston,* and *Flook,* and was in turn reversed by this Court in each of those cases.

Scholars have been critical of the work of both tribunals. Some of that criticism may stem from a conviction about the merits of the broad underlying policy question; such criticism may be put to one side. Other criticism, however, identifies two concerns to which federal judges have a duty to respond. First, the cases considering the patentability of program-related inventions do not establish rules that enable a conscientious patent lawyer to determine with a fair degree of accuracy which, if any, program-related inventions will be patentable. Second, the inclusion of the ambiguous concept of an "algorithm" within the "law of nature" category of unpatentable subject matter has given rise to the concern that almost any process might be so described and therefore held unpatentable.

In my judgment, today's decision will aggravate the first concern and will not adequately allay the second. I believe both concerns would be better addressed by (1) an unequivocal holding that no program-related invention is a patentable process under § 101 unless it makes a contribution to the art that is not dependent entirely on the utilization of a computer, and (2) an unequivocal explanation that the term "algorithm" as used in this case, as in *Benson* and *Flook,* is synonymous with the term "computer program." Because the invention claimed in the patent application at issue in this case makes no contribution to the art that is not entirely dependent upon the utilization of a computer in a familiar process, I would reverse the decision of the Court of Customs and Patent Appeals.

---

32. Apple Computer, Inc. v. Franklin Computer Corporation

Introduction

APPLE COMPUTER, INC. appeals from the district court's denial of a motion to preliminarily enjoin Franklin Computer Corp. from infringing the copyrights Apple holds on fourteen computer programs. . . .

In this case the district court denied the preliminary injunction, *inter alia*, because it had "some doubt as to the copyrightability of the programs." *Apple Computer, Inc. v. Franklin Computer Corp.*, 545 F. Supp. 812, 812 (E.D. Pa. 1982). This legal ruling is fundamental to all future proceedings in this action and, as the parties and amici curiae seem to agree, has considerable significance to the computer services industry. Because we con-

---

U.S. Court of Appeals, Third Circuit, No. 82-1582.

clude that the district court proceeded under an erroneous view of the applicable law, we reverse the denial of the preliminary injunction and remand.

Facts and Procedural History

Apple, one of the computer industry leaders, manufactures and markets personal computers (microcomputers), related peripheral equipment such as disk drives (peripherals), and computer programs (software). It presently manufactures Apple II computers and distributes over 150 programs. Apple has sold over 400,000 Apple II computers, employs approximately 3,000 people, and had annual sales of $335,000,000 for fiscal year 1981. One of the by-products of Apple's success is the independent development by third parties of numerous computer programs which are designed to run on the Apple II computer.

Franklin, the defendant below, manufactures and sells the ACE 100 personal computer and at the time of the hearing employed about 75 people and had sold fewer than 1,000 computers. The ACE 100 was designed to be "Apple compatible," so that peripheral equipment and software developed for use with the Apple II computer could be used in conjunction with the ACE 100. Franklin's copying of Apple's operating system computer programs in an effort to achieve such compatibility precipitated this suit.

Like all computers both the Apple II and ACE 100 have a central processing unit (CPU) which is the integrated circuit that executes programs. In lay terms, the CPU does the work it is instructed to do. Those instructions are contained on computer programs.

There are three levels of computer language in which computer programs may be written. High level language, such as the commonly used BASIC or FORTRAN, uses English words and symbols, and is relatively easy to learn and understand (e.g., "GO TO 40" tells the computer to skip intervening steps and go to the step at line 40). A somewhat lower level language is assembly language, which consists of alphanumeric labels (e.g., "ADC" means "add with carry"). Statements in high level language, and apparently also statements in assembly language, are referred to as written in "source code." The third, or lowest level computer language, is machine language, a binary language using two symbols, 0 and 1, to indicate an open or closed switch (e.g., "01101001" means, to the Apple, add two numbers and save the result). Statements in machine language are referred to as written in "object code."

The CPU can only follow instructions written in object code. However, programs are usually written in source code which is more intelligible to humans. Programs written in source code can be converted or translated by a "compiler" program into object code for use by the computer. Programs are generally distributed only in their object code version stored on a memory device.

A computer program can be stored or fixed on a variety of memory devices, two of which are of particular relevance for this case. The ROM (Read Only Memory) is an internal permanent memory device consisting of a semi-conductor "chip" which is incorporated into the circuitry of the computer. A program in object code is embedded on a ROM before it is incorporated in the computer. Information stored on a ROM can only be read, not erased or rewritten. The ACE 100 apparently contains EPROMS (Erasable Programmable Read Only Memory) on which the stored information can be erased and the chip reprogrammed, but the district court found that for purposes of this proceeding, the difference between ROMs and EPROMs is inconsequential. 545 F. Supp. at 813 n.3. The other device used for storing the programs at issue is a diskette or "floppy disk," an auxiliary memory device consisting of a flexible magnetic disk resembling a phonograph record, which can be inserted into the computer and from which data or instructions can be read.

Computer programs can be categorized by function as either application programs or operating system programs. Application programs usually perform a specific task for the computer user, such as word processing, checkbook balancing, or playing a game. In contrast, operating system programs generally manage the internal functions of the computer or facilitate use of application programs. The parties agree that the fourteen computer programs at issue in this suit are operating system programs.[1]

Apple filed suit in the United States District Court for the Eastern District of Pennsylvania pursuant to 28 U.S.C. §1338 on May 12, 1982, alleging that Franklin was liable for copyright infringement of the fourteen computer programs, patent infringement, unfair competition, and misappropriation. Franklin's answer in respect to the copyright counts included the affirmative defense that the programs contained no copyrightable subject matter. Franklin counterclaimed for declaratory judgment that the copyright registrations were invalid and unenforceable, and sought affirmative relief on the basis of Apple's alleged misuse. Franklin also moved to dismiss eleven of the fourteen copyright infringement counts on the ground that Apple failed to comply with the procedural requirements for suit under 17 U.S.C. §§410, 411.

After expedited discovery, Apple moved for a preliminary injunction to restrain Franklin from using, copying, selling, or infringing Apple's copyrights. The district court held a three day evidentiary hearing limited to the copyright infringement claims. Apple produced evidence at the hearing in the form of affidavits and testimony that programs sold by Franklin in conjunction with its ACE 100 computer were virtually identical with those covered by the fourteen Apple copyrights. The variations that did exist were minor, consisting merely of such things as deletion of reference to Apple or its copyright notice. James Huston, an Apple systems programmer, concluded that the Franklin programs were "unquestionably copied from Apple and could not have been independently created." He reached this conclusion not only because it is "almost impossible for so many lines of code" to be identically written, but also because his name, which he had embedded in one program (Master Create), and the word "Applesoft," which was embedded in another (DOS 3.3), appeared on the Franklin master disk. Apple estimated the "works in suit" took 46 man-months to produce at a cost of over $740,000, not including the time or cost of creating or acquiring earlier versions of the programs or the expense of marketing the programs.

Franklin did not dispute that it copied the Apple programs. Its witness admitted copying each of the works in suit from the Apple programs. Its factual defense was directed to its contention that it was not feasible for Franklin to write its own operating system programs. David McWherter, now Franklin's vice-president of engineering, testified he spent 30–40 hours in November 1981 making a study to determine if it was feasible for Franklin to write its own Autostart ROM program and concluded it was not because "there were just too many entry points in relationship to the number of instructions in the program." Entry points at specific locations in the program can be used by programmers to mesh their application programs with the operating system program. McWherter concluded that use of the identical signals was necessary in order to ensure 100% compatibility with application programs created to run on the Apple computer. He admitted that he never attempted to rewrite Autostart ROM and conceded that some of the works in suit (*i.e.* Copy, Copy A, Master Create, and Hello) probably could have been rewritten by Franklin. Franklin made no attempt to rewrite any of the programs prior to the lawsuit except for Copy, although McWherter testified that Franklin was "in the process of redesigning" some of the Apple programs and that "[w]e had a fair degree of certainty that that would probably work." Apple introduced evidence that Franklin could have rewritten programs, including the Autostart ROM program, and that there are in existence operating programs written by third parties which are compatible with Apple II.

Franklin's principal defense at the preliminary injunction hearing and before us is primarily a legal one, directed to its contention that the Apple operating system programs are not capable of copyright protection. . . .

The District Court Opinion

In its opinion, the district court referred to the four factors to be considered on request for a preliminary injunction: a reasonable probability of success on the merits; irreparable injury; the improbability of harm to other interested persons; and the public interest. . . . The court stated it based its denial of the motion on the first two factors. The court held Apple had not made the requisite showing of likelihood of success on the merits because it "concluded that there is some doubt as to the copyrightability of the programs described in this litigation." 545 F. Supp. at 812. It also stated that "Apple is better suited to withstand whatever injury it might sustain during litigation than is Franklin to withstand the effects of a preliminary injunction" because an injunction would have a "devastating effect" on Franklin's business, *id.* at 825, apparently concluding on that basis that Apple had failed to show irreparable harm.

It is difficult to discern precisely why the district court questioned the copyrightability of the programs at issue since there is no finding, statement, or holding on which we can focus which clearly sets forth the district court's view. Throughout the opinion the district court referred to the "complexity of the question presented by the present case," 545 F. Supp. at 824, and the "baffling" problem at issue. *Id.* at 822.

The opinion expresses a series of generalized concerns which may have led the court to its ultimate conclusion, and which the parties and amici treat as holdings. The district court referred to the requirement under the Copyright Act of finding "original works of authorship," 17 U.S.C. §102(a), and seems to have found that there was a sufficient "modicum of creativity" to satisfy the statutory requirement of an "original work." 545 F. Supp. at 820–21. The court was less clear as to whether the creation of a computer program by a programmer satisfied the requirement of "works of authorship," *id.*, and whether an operating system program in "binary code or one represented either in a ROM or by micro-switches" was an "expression" which could be copyrighted as distinguished from an "idea" which could not be. *Id.* at 821.

Again, although we cannot point to a specific holding, running throughout the district court opinion is the suggestion that programs in object code and ROMs may not be copy-rightable. Thus, for example, in a series of discursive footnotes, the district court stated that it found "persuasive" a district court opinion "holding that object code in ROM is not copyright protected," 545 F. Supp. at 818 n.8 . . . described an opinion reaching a contrary conclusion as containing "rather terse analysis [which] provides little guidance" 545 F. Supp. at 818 n.8 . . . ; and stated that "Congressional intent regarding the copyrightability of object codes and ROMs is not clear," 545 F. Supp. at 819 n.9, and that even among members of the industry it was not clear that the copyright law protects works "like those in suit that are ROM-based," *id.* at 819 n.10.

We read the district court opinion as presenting the following legal issues: (1) whether copyright can exist in a computer program expressed in object code, (2) whether copyright can exist in a computer program embedded on a ROM, (3) whether copyright can exist in an operating system program, and (4) whether independent irreparable harm must be shown for a preliminary injunction in copyright infringement actions.

Discussion

Copyrightability of a Computer Program Expressed in Object Code

Certain statements by the district court suggest that programs expressed in object code, as distinguished from source code, may not be the proper subject of copyright. We find no basis in the statute for any such concern. Furthermore, our decision in *Williams Electronics, Inc. v. Artic International, Inc., supra*, laid to rest many of the doubts expressed by the district court.

In 1976, after considerable study, Congress enacted a new copyright law to replace that which had governed since 1909. Act of October 19, 1976, Pub. L. No. 94-553. 90 Stat. 2541 (*codified at* 17 U.S.C. §§101 *et seq.*). Under the law, two primary requirements must be satisfied in order for a work to constitute copyrightable subject matter—it must be an "original wor[k] of authorship" and must be "fixed in [a] tangible medium of expression." 17 U.S.C. §102(a). The statute provides:

> Copyright protection subsists, in accordance with this title, in original works of authorship fixed in any tangible medium of expression, now known or later developed, from which they can be perceived, reproduced, or otherwise communicated, either directly or with the aid of a machine or device.

Id. The statute enumerates seven categories under "works of authorship" including "literary works," defined as follows:

> "Literary works" are works, other than audiovisual works, expressed in words, numbers, or other verbal or numerical symbols or indicia, regardless of the nature of the material objects, such as books, periodicals, manuscripts, phonorecords, film, tapes, disks, or cards, in which they are embodied.

17 U.S.C. §101. A work is "fixed" in a tangible medium of expression when:

> its embodiment in a copy or phonorecord, by or under the authority of the author, is sufficiently permanent or stable to permit it to be perceived, reproduced, or otherwise communicated for a period of more than transitory duration. A work consisting of sounds, images, or both, that are being transmitted, is "fixed" for purposes of this title if a fixation of the work is being made simultaneously with its transmission.

Id. Although section 102(a) does not expressly list computer programs as works of authorship, the legislative history suggests that programs were considered copyrightable as literary works. . . . Because a Commission on New Technological Uses ("CONTU") had been created by Congress to study, *inter alia*, computer uses of copyrighted works, Pub. L. No. 93-573, §201, 88 Stat. 1873 (1974), Congress enacted a status quo provision, section 117, in the 1976 Act concerning such computer uses pending the CONTU report and recommendations.

The CONTU Final Report recommended that the copyright law be amended, *inter alia*, "to make it explicit that computer programs, to the extent that they embody an author's original creation, are proper subject matter of copyright." National Commission on New Technological Uses of Copyrighted Works, *Final Report* 1 (1979) [hereinafter CONTU Report]. CONTU recommended two changes relevant here: that section 117, the status quo provision, be repealed and replaced with a section limiting exclusive rights in computer programs so as "to ensure that rightful possessors of copies of computer programs may use or adapt these copies for their use," *id.*; and that a definition of computer program be added to section 101. *Id.* at 12. Congress adopted both changes. Act of Dec. 12, 1980, Pub. L. No. 96-517, §10. 94 Stat. 3015, 3028. The revisions embodied CONTU's recommendations to clarify the law of copyright of computer software. H.R. Rep. No. 1307, 96th Cong., 2d Sess. 23, *reprinted in* 1980 U.S. Code Cong. & Ad. News 6460, 6482.

The 1980 amendments added a definition of a computer program:

> A "computer program" is a set of statements or instructions to be used directly or indirectly in a computer in order to bring about a certain result.

17 U.S.C. §101. The amendments also substituted a new section 117 which provides that "it is not an infringement for the owner of a copy of a computer program to make or authorize the making of another copy or adaptation of that computer program" when necessary to "the utilization of the computer program" or "for archival purposes only." 17 U.S.C. §117. The parties agree that this section is not implicated in the instant lawsuit. The language of the provision, however, by carving out an exception to the normal proscriptions against copying, clearly indicates that programs are copyrightable and are otherwise afforded copyright protection.

We considered the issue of copyright protection for a computer program in *Williams Electronics, Inc. v. Artic International, Inc.*, and concluded that "the copyrightability of computer programs is firmly established after the 1980 amendment to the Copyright Act." 685.F.2d at 875. At issue in *Williams* were not only two audiovisual copyrights to the "attract" and "play"modes of a video game, but also the computer program which was expressed in object code embodied in ROM and which controlled the sights and sounds of the game. Defendant there had argued "that when the issue is the copyright on a computer program, a distinction must be drawn between the 'source code' version of a computer program, which . . . can be afforded copyright protection, and the "object code" stage, which . . . cannot be so protected," an argument we rejected. *Id.* at 876.

The district court here questioned whether copyright was to be limited to works "designed to be 'read' by a human reader [as distinguished from] read by an expert with a microscope and patience," 545 F. Supp. at 821. The suggestion that copyrightability depends on a communicative function to individuals stems from the early decision of *White-Smith Music Publishing Co. v. Apollo Co.*, 209 U.S. 1 (1908), which held a piano roll was not a copy of the musical composition because it was not in a form others, except perhaps for a very expert few, could perceive. . . . However, it is clear from the language of the 1976 Act and its legislative history that it was intended to obliterate distinctions engendered by *White-Smith*. . . .

Under the statute, copyright extends to works in any tangible means of expression "*from which they can be perceived*, reproduced, or otherwise communicated, either directly or *with the aid of a machine or device*." 17 U.S.C. §102(a) (emphasis added). Further, the definition of "computer program" adopted by Congress in the 1980 amendments is "sets of statements or instructions to be used *directly or indirectly* in a computer in order to bring about a certain result." 17 U.S.C. §101 (emphasis added). As source code instructions must be translated into object code before the computer can act upon them, only instructions expressed in object code can be used "directly" by the computer. . . . This definition was adopted following the CONTU Report in which the majority clearly took the position that object codes are proper subjects of copyright. *See* CONTU Report at 21. The majority's conclusion was reached although confronted by a dissent based upon the theory that the "machine-control phase" of a program is not directed at a human audience. *See* CONTU Report at 28–30 (dissent of Commissioner Hersey).

The defendant in *Williams* had also argued that a copyrightable work "must be intelligible to human beings and must be intended as a medium of communication to human beings," *id.* at 876–77. We reiterate the statement we made in *Williams* when we rejected that argument: "[t]he answer to defendant's contention is in the words of the statute itself." 685 F.2d at 877.

The district court also expressed uncertainty as to whether a computer program in object code could be classified as a "literary work." However, the category of "literary works," one of the seven copyrightable categories, is not confined to literature in the nature of Hemingway's *For Whom the Bell Tolls*. The definition of "literary works" in section 101 includes expression not only in words but also "numbers or other . . . numerical symbols or indicia," thereby expanding the common usage of "literary works. . . . Thus a computer program, whether in object code or source code, is a "literary work" and is protected from unauthorized copying, whether from its object or source code version. . . .

Copyrightability of a Computer Program Embedded on a ROM

Just as the district court's suggestion of a distinction between source code and object code was rejected by our opinion in *Williams* issued three days after the district court opinion, so also was its suggestion that embodiment of a computer program on a ROM, as distinguished from in a traditional writing, detracts from its copyrightability. In *Williams* we rejected the argument that "a computer program is not infringed when the program is loaded into electronic memory devices (ROMs) and used to control the activity of machines." 685 F.2d at 876. Defendant there had argued that there can be no copyright protection for the ROMs because they are utilitarian objects or machine parts. We held that the statutory requirement of "fixation," the manner in which the issue arises, is satisfied through the embodiment of the expression in the ROM devices. *Id.* at 874, 876. . . . Therefore we reaffirm that a computer program in object code embedded in a ROM chip is an appropriate subject of copyright. . . .

Copyrightability of Computer Operating System Programs

We turn to the heart of Franklin's position on appeal which is that computer operating system programs, as distinguished from application programs, are not the proper subject of copyright "regardless of the language or medium in which they are fixed." Brief of Appellee at 15 (emphasis deleted). Apple suggests that this issue too is foreclosed by our *Williams* decision because some portion of the program at issue there was in effect an operating system program. Franklin is correct that this was not an issue raised by the parties in *Williams* and it was not considered by the court. Thus we consider it as a matter of first impression.

Franklin contends that operating system programs are *per se* excluded from copyright protection under the express terms of section 102(b) of the Copyright Act and under the precedent and underlying principles of *Baker v. Selden*, 101 U.S. 99 (1879). These separate grounds have substantial analytic overlap.

In *Baker v. Selden*, plaintiff's testator held a copyright on a book explaining a book-keeping system which included blank forms with ruled lines and headings designed for use with that system. Plaintiff sued for copyright infringement on the basis of defendant's publication of a book containing a different arrangement of the columns and different headings, but which used a similar plan so far as results were concerned. The Court, in reversing the decree for the plaintiff, concluded that blank account-books were not the subject of copyright and that "the mere copyright of Selden's book did not confer upon him the exclusive right to make and use account-books, ruled and arranged as designed by him and described and illustrated in said book." *Id.* at 107. The Court stated that copyright of the books did not give the plaintiff the exclusive right to use the system explained in the books, noting, for example, that "copyright of a work on mathematical science cannot give to the author an exclusive right to the methods of operation which he propounds." *Id.* at 103.

Franklin reads *Baker v. Selden* as "stand[ing] for several fundamental principles, each presenting . . . an insuperable obstacle to the copyrightability of Apple's operating systems." It states:

> *First, Baker* teaches that use of a system itself does not infringe a copyright on the description of the system. *Second, Baker* enunciates the rule that copyright does not extend to purely utilitarian works. *Finally, Baker* emphasizes that the copyright laws may not be used to obtain and hold a monopoly over an idea. In so doing, *Baker* highlights the principal difference between the copyright and patent laws—a difference that is highly pertinent in this case.

Brief of Appellee at 22.

Section 102(b) of the Copyright Act, the other ground on which Franklin relies, appeared first in the 1976 version, long after the decision in *Baker v. Selden*. It provides:

In no case does copyright protection for an original work of authorship extend to any idea, procedure, process, system, method of operation, concept, principle, or discovery, regardless of the form in which it is described, explained, illustrated, or embodied in such work.

It is apparent that section 102(b) codifies a substantial part of the holding and dictum of *Baker v. Selden. See* 1 *Nimmer on Copyright* §2.18[D]. at 2-207.

We turn to consider the two principal points of Franklin's argument.

"Process," "System" or "Method of Operation"

Franklin argues that an operating system program is either a "process," "system," or "method of operation" and hence uncopyrightable. Franklin correctly notes that underlying section 102(b) and many of the statements for which *Baker v. Selden* is cited is the distinction which must be made between property subject to the patent law, which protects discoveries, and that subject to copyright law, which protects the writings describing such discoveries. However, Franklin's argument misapplies that distinction in this case. Apple does not seek to copyright the method which instructs the computer to perform its operating functions but only the instructions themselves. The method would be protected, if at all, by the patent law, an issue as yet unresolved. *See Diamond v. Diehr*, 450 U.S. 175 (1981).

Franklin's attack on operating system programs as "methods" or "processes" seems inconsistent with its concession that application programs are an appropriate subject of copyright. Both types of programs instruct the computer to do something. Therefore, it should make no difference for purposes of section 102(b) whether these instructions tell the computer to help prepare an income tax return (the task of an application program) or to translate a high level language program from source code into its binary language object code form (the task of an operating system program such as "Applesoft," *see* note 4 *supra*). Since it is only the instructions which are protected, a "process" is no more involved because the instructions in an operating system program may be used to activate the operation of the computer than it would be if instructions were written in ordinary English in a manual which described the necessary steps to activate an intricate complicated machine. There is, therefore, no reason to afford any less copyright protection to the instructions in an operating system program than to the instructions in an application program.

Franklin's argument, receptively treated by the district court, that an operating system program is part of a machine mistakenly focuses on the physical characteristics of the instructions. But the medium is not the message. We have already considered and rejected aspects of this contention in the discussion of object code and ROM. The mere fact that the operating system program may be etched on a ROM does not make the program either a machine, part of a machine or its equivalent. Furthermore, as one of Franklin's witnesses testified, an operating system does not have to be permanently in the machine in ROM, but it may be on some other medium, such as a diskette or magnetic tape, where it could be readily transferred into the temprary memory space of the computer. In fact, some of the operating systems at issue were on diskette. As the CONTU majority stated,

Programs should no more be considered machine parts than videotapes should be considered parts of projectors or phonorecords parts of sound reproduction equipment. . . . That the words of a program are used ultimately in the implementation of a process should in no way affect their copyrightability.

CONTU Report at 21.

Franklin also argues that the operating systems cannot be copyrighted because they are "purely utilitarian works" and that Apple is seeking to block the use of the art embodied in its operating systems. This argument stems from the following dictum in *Baker v. Selden*:

> The very object of publishing a book on science or the useful arts is to communicate to the world the useful knowledge which it contains. But this object would be frustrated if the knowledge could not be used without incurring the guilt of piracy of the book. And where the art it teaches cannot be used without employing the methods and diagrams used to illustrate the book, or such as are similar to them, such methods and diagrams are to be considered as necessary incidents to the art, and given therewith to the public; not given for the purpose of publication in other works explanatory of the art, but for the purpose of practical application.

101 U.S. at 103. We cannot accept the expansive reading given to this language by some courts. . . .

Although a literal construction of this language could support Franklin's reading that precludes copyrightability if the copyright work is put to a utilitarian use, that interpretation has been rejected by a later Supreme Court decision. In *Mazer v. Stein*, 347 U.S. 201, 218 (1954), the Court stated: "We find nothing in the copyright statute to support the argument that the intended use or use in industry of an article eligible for copyright bars or invalidates its registration. We do not read such a limitation into the copyright law." *Id.* at 218. The CONTU majority also rejected the expansive view some courts have given *Baker v. Selden*, and stated "That the words of a program are used ultimately in the implementation of a process should in no way affect their copyrightability." *Id.* at 21. It referred to "copyright practice past and present, which recognizes copyright protection for a work of authorship regardless of the uses to which it may be put." *Id.* The Commission continued: "The copyright status of the written rules for a game *or a system for the operation of a machine* is unaffected by the fact that those rules direct the actions of those who play the game or *carry out the process.*" *Id.* (emphasis added). As we previously noted, we can consider the CONTU Report as accepted by Congress since Congress wrote into the law the majority's recommendations almost verbatim. . . .

Perhaps the most convincing item leading us to reject Franklin's argument is that the statutory definition of a computer program as a set of instructions to be used in a computer in order to bring about a certain result, 17 U.S.C. §101, makes no distinction between application programs and operating programs. Franklin can point to no decision which adopts the distinction it seeks to make. In the one other reported case to have considered it, *Apple Computer, Inc. v. Formula International, Inc.*, 562 F. Supp. 775 (C.D. Cal. 1983), the court reached the same conclusion which we do, *i.e.*, that an operating system program is not *per se* precluded from copyright. It stated, "There is nothing in any of the statutory terms which suggest a different result for different types of computer programs based upon the function they serve within the machine." *Id.* at 780. Other courts have also upheld the copyrightability of operating programs without discussion of this issue. *See Tandy Corp. v. Personal Micro Computers, Inc.*, 524 F. Supp. at 173 (input-output routine stored in ROM which translated input into machine language in a similar fashion as Applesoft and Apple Integer Basic proper subject of copyright); *GCA Corp. v. Chance*, 217 U.S.P.Q. at 719–20 (object code version of registered source code version of operating programs is the same work and protected).

Idea/Expression Dichotomy

Franklin's other challenge to copyright of operating system programs relies on the line which is drawn between ideas and their expression. *Baker v. Selden* remains a benchmark in the law of copyright for the reading given it in *Mazer v. Stein, supra*, where the Court stated, "Unlike a patent, a copyright gives no exclusive right to the art disclosed; protection is given only to the expression of the idea—not the idea itself." 347 U.S. at 217 (footnote omitted).

The expression/idea dichotomy is now expressly recognized in section 102(b) which precludes copyright for "any idea." This provision was not intended to enlarge or contract the scope of copyright protection but "to restate . . . that the basic dichotomy between expression and idea remains unchanged." H.R. Rep. No. 1476, *supra* at 57 *reprinted in* 1976 U.S. Code Cong. & Ad. News at 5676. The legislative history indicates that section 102(b) was intended "to make clear that the expression adopted by the programmer is the copyrightable element in a computer program, and that the actual processes or methods embodied in the program are not within the scope of the copyright law." *Id.*

Many of the courts which have sought to draw the line between an idea and expression have found difficulty in articulating where it falls. *See, e.g., Nichols v. Universal Pictures Corp.*, 45 F.2d 119, 121 (2d Cir. 1930) (L. Hand J); see discussion in *3 Nimmer on Copyright* §13.03[A]. We believe that in the context before us, a program for an operating system, the line must be a pragmatic one, which also keeps in consideration "the preservation of the balance between competition and protection reflected in the patent and copyright laws." *Herbert Rosenthal Jewelry Corp. v. Kalpakian*, 446 F.2d 738, 742 (9th Cir. 1971). As we stated in *Franklin Mint Corp. v. National Wildlife Art Exchange, Inc.*, 575 F.2d 62, 64 (3d Cir.), *cert. denied*, 439 U.S. 880 (1978). "Unlike a patent, a copyright protects originality rather than novelty or invention." In that opinion, we quoted approvingly the following passage from *Dymow v. Bolton*, 11 F.2d 690, 691 (2d Cir. 1926):

> Just as a patent affords protection only to the means of reducing an inventive idea to practice, so the copyright law protects the means of expressing an idea; and it is as near the whole truth as generalization can usually reach that, *if the same idea can be expressed in a plurality of totally different manners, a plurality of copyrights may result*, and no infringement will exist.

(emphasis added).

We adopt the suggestion in the above language and thus focus on whether the idea is capable of various modes of expression. If other programs can be written or created which perform the same function as an Apple's operating system program, then that program is an expression of the idea and hence copyrightable. In essence, this inquiry is no different than that made to determine whether the expression and idea have merged, which has been stated to occur where there are no or few other ways of expressing a particular idea. *See, e.g., Morrissey v. Procter & Gamble Co.*, 379 F.2d 675, 678–79 (1st Cir. 1967); *Freedman v. Grolier Enterprises, Inc.*, 179 U.S.P.Q. 476, 478 (S.D.N.Y. 1973) ("[c]opyright protection will not be given to a form of expression necessarily dictated by the underlying subject matter"). CONTU Report at 20.

The district court made no findings as to whether some or all of Apple's operating programs represent the only means of expression of the idea underlying them. Although there seems to be a concession by Franklin that at least some of the programs can be rewritten, we do not believe that the record on that issue is so clear that it can be decided at the appellate level. Therefore, if the issue is pressed on remand, the necessary finding can be made at that time.

Franklin claims that whether or not the programs can be rewritten, there are a limited "number of ways to arrange operating systems to enable a computer to run the vast body of Apple-compatible software," Brief of Appellee at 20. This claim has no pertinence to either the idea/expression dichotomy or merger. The idea which may merge with the expression, thus making the copyright unavailable, is the idea which is the subject of the expression. The idea of one of the operating system programs is, for example, how to translate source code into object code. If other methods of expressing that idea are not foreclosed as a practical matter, then there is no merger. Franklin may wish to achieve total compatibility with independently developed application programs written for the Apple II, but that is a commercial and competitive objective which does not enter into the somewhat metaphysical issue of whether particular ideas and expressions have merged.

In summary, Franklin's contentions that operating system programs are *per se* not copyrightable is unpersuasive. The other courts before whom this issue has been raised have rejected the distinction. Neither the CONTU majority nor Congress made a distinction between operating and application programs. We believe that the 1980 amendments reflect Congress' receptivity to new technology and its desire to encourage, through the copyright laws, continued imagination and creativity in computer programming. Since we believe that the district court's decision on the preliminary injunction was, to a large part, influenced by an erroneous view of the availability of copyright for operating system programs and unnecessary concerns about object code and ROMs, we must reverse the denial of the preliminary injunction and remand for reconsideration.

Irreparable Harm

The district court, without any extended discussion, found that Apple had not made the requisite showing of irreparable harm, stating "Apple is better suited to withstand whatever injury it might sustain during litigation than is Franklin to withstand the effects of a preliminary injunction." 545 F. Supp. at 812, 825. In so ruling, the district court failed to consider the prevailing view that a showing of a prima facie case of copyright infringement or reasonable likelihood of success on the merits raises a presumption of irreparable harm. . . .

The CONTU Final Report recognized that "[t]he cost of developing computer programs is far greater than the cost of their duplication." CONTU Report at 11. Apple introduced substantial evidence of the considerable time and money it had invested in the development of the computer programs in suit. Thus even without the presumption of irreparable harm generally applied in copyright infringement cases, the jeopardy to Apple's investment and competitive position caused by Franklin's wholesale copying of many of its key operating programs would satisfy the requirement of irreparable harm needed to support a preliminary injunction. . . .

In *Kontes Glass Co. v. Lab Glass, Inc.*, 373 F.2d 319, 320–21 (3d Cir. 1967), this court appeared to adopt an inverse relationship approach to the irreparable harm issue, suggesting that the strength of the required showing of irreparable injury varies inversely with the strength of plaintiff's showing of a likelihood of success on the merits. *See Midway Mfg. Co. v. Bandai-America, Inc.*, 546 F. Supp. 125, 141–42 (D.N.J. 1982). In *Kontes*, we were not presented with a case in which copyrighted material central to the essence of plaintiff's operations was concededly copied, as we are here. We believe the *Kontes* approach is best suited to those cases where the injury from copying can be fairly considered minimal, limited or conjectural. In those circumstances it provides flexibility in applying the equitable remedy of preliminary injunctions through evaluation of the irreparable harm factor. Normally, however, the public interest underlying the copyright law requires a presumption of irreparable harm, as long as there is, as here, adequate evidence of the expenditure of significant time, effort and money directed to the production of the copyrighted material. Otherwise, the rationale for protecting copyright, that of encouraging creativity, would be undermined. As Judge Broderick stated in *Klitzner Industries, Inc. v. H. K. James & Co.*, 535 F. Supp. at 1259–60:

> Since Congress has elected to grant certain exclusive rights to the owner of a copyright in a protected work, it is virtually axiomatic that the public interest can only be served by upholding copyright protections and, correspondingly, preventing the misappropriation of the skills, creative energies, and resources which are invested in the protected work.

Nor can we accept the district court's explanation which stressed the "devastating effect" of a preliminary injunction on Franklin's business. If that were the correct standard, then a knowing infringer would be permitted to construct its business around its infringement, a result we cannot condone. . . . The size of the infringer should not be determinative of the copyright holder's ability to get prompt judicial redress. . . .

For the reasons set forth in this opinion, we will reverse the denial of the preliminary injunction and remand to the district court for further proceedings in accordance herewith.

Notes

1. The fourteen programs at issue, briefly described . . .
   (1) *Autostart ROM* is sold as part of the Apple Computer and is embedded on a ROM chip. The program has also been published in source code as part of a copyrighted book, the Apple II manual. When the computer's power is turned on, Autostart ROM performs internal routines that turn on the circuits in the computer and make its physical parts (e.g., input/output devices, screen, and memory) ready for use.
   (2) *Applesoft* is Apple's version of the Beginner's All-purpose Symbolic Instruction Code (BASIC) language. The program is stored in ROM and is sold as part of the computer. Applesoft translates instructions written in the higher-level BASIC language into the lower-level machine code that the computer understands.

(3) *Floating-Point BASIC* is the same program as Applesoft but is stored on disks rather than on ROMs. It is used in earlier versions of the Apple II computer that did not have the Applesoft program in ROM.

(4) *Apple Integer BASIC*, another translator program, is stored on the DOS 3.3 Master Disk. This program used Apple's first version of BASIC for the Apple II computer. It implements a simpler version of the Applesoft program.

(5) *DOS 3.3*, the disk operating system program, provides the instructions necessary to control the operation between the disk system (disk drive) and the computer itself. It controls the reading and writing functions of the disks and includes other routines which put all the data transfers in sequence. The DOS 3.3 Master Disk is sold separately from the computer, and includes several of the other operating programs referred to in this note.

(6) *Master Create* is stored on a disk. When the disk is prepared for use, the DOS 3.3 program is placed on that disk in a form that is dependent on the amount of Random Access Memory (RAM) available. The Master Create program replaces the DOS 3.3 on the disk with a version that is independent of the amount of RAM available.

(7) *Copy*, which is stored on a disk, enables the user to copy programs written in Apple Integer BASIC from one disk to another.

(8) *Copy A*, also stored on a disk, enables the user to copy programs written in Applesoft from one disk to another.

(9) *Copy OBJO* contains a file of subroutines used by the Copy and Copy A programs.

(10) *Chain*, another disk stored program, allows data to be passed between different parts of a program when only one part of the program is in RAM at a given time. Thus, Chain preserves data already stored in RAM while another part of the program is being loaded into RAM.

(11) *Hello*, also disk stored, is the first program executed after the power is turned on and a disk is ready for use. It determines how much RAM is in the computer and which version of BASIC needs to be loaded into the computer.

(12) *Boot 13* is stored on a disk and sold on a Master Disk. It allows the user having a disk controller card that contains the Apple 16-Sector Boot ROM to use older versions of the Apple disk operating system.

(13) *Apple 13-Sector Boot ROM* is stored in a ROM located on the disk controller card plugged into the Mother Board. By turning on numerous circuits on the card and in the Apple II computer, this program causes other parts of the disk operating system used for 13-Sector format disks to load.

(14) *Apple 16-Sector Boot ROM*, stored in a ROM located on the disk controller card, turns on numerous circuits on the card and in the Apple II computer and causes other parts of the disk operating system used for 16-Sector format disks to load. It therefore enables the user to start or permit the running of another program or to prepare the computer to receive a program.

The above descriptions represent an effort to translate the language used by computer experts into language reasonably intelligible to lay persons. They differ in some respects from the descriptions in the district court's opinion, 545 F. Supp at 815–16, which were taken from the complaint.

33. Computer Software and Unfair Methods of Competition

Joseph Scafetta, Jr.

Unfair Competition in the Traditional Sense

WHEN THE COMMON law term "unfair competition" is bandied around in legal circles in discussions of wrongful actions by others in the computer industry, the term itself is not appropriate because it traditionally refers only to the practice of attempting to pass off one's own goods, by imitation of general appearance, as the goods of a competitor who enjoys immediate favorable public recognition. The phrase that should be used is the more general term "unfair methods of competition" which is, unfortunately, quite nebulous itself and, not unexpectedly, appears undefined in Federal Trade Commission Act section 5. Although not defined therein, this term has generally become known to embrace any unfair trade practice which dishonestly negates a competitor's opportunity for fair play in the market-place, such as false advertising, palming off, misappropriation of trade secrets, etc.

Common law unfair competition and false advertising are exemplary of unfair methods of competition that either do not occur or are not special problems in the computer industry. However, because of the nature of software and the meager extent of legal protection available to the industry, there is one unfair method of competition that stands out as a matter of deep and anxious concern—misappropriation of trade secrets. This article will attempt to explore why both present laws and software itself have led to this problem, what are the major aspects of the problem, and, finally, what those in the industry can do to protect themselves against its occurrence.

The Preferred Choice of Legal Protection for Computer Software

There are three routes by which one may protect intellectual property. Usually, the most favored protection for property of a utilitarian nature is patenting. However, this route has been generally shunned by the computer industry because of the present uncertainty over the extent, if any, of protection available for software. In *Gottschalk v. Benson* the Supreme Court denied a patent on a process for use in programming a digital computer but specifically refused to preclude a patent for all programs servicing a computer. Later, in *Dann v. Johnston* the Supreme Court denied a patent on a computer-programmed system for automatic record keeping on the grounds that the invention was obvious to one of reasonable skill in the data processing art. However, in so ruling the Court again deliberately

From *John Marshall Journal of Practice and Procedure* 10 (1977): 447–464. © 1977 by The John Marshall Law School. Reprinted by permission of *The John Marshall Law Review*. Footnotes omitted except where indicated.

sidestepped the threshold issue of the general patentability of computer programs. Thus, the continuing refusal of the Supreme Court to decide the basic issue has resulted in a concomitant reluctance on the part of the computer industry to seek patent protection.

The most favored route for protection of property of a written nature is usually copyrighting but this likewise has been generally shunned by the computer industry. The reason is twofold. First, a copyright provides protection only against a taking by substantial copying of the expressed form in the written program. To find infringement, there must be some actual appropriation of language. A skilled programmer can easily avoid infringement by restating any routine in analogous machine-readable language that would produce the identical end result of the program sought to be appropriated. Second, a copyright does not provide protection to the owner against another's use of the concept, idea, or algorithm embodied in the software. Also, there is a prerequisite of "publication" before a written program can be registered for a federal statutory copyright. At the point of publication, the contribution made by the concept, idea, or algorithm passes into the public domain for free use by everyone. Because the value of software to its owner lies in the contribution of the concept, idea, or algorithm to the data processing art, copyright protection of only a particular written expression of a program is too narrow and totally inadequate in the eyes of the computer industry.

Because of the uncertainty of the extent of protection available via the usually favored routes of patenting and copyrighting, the preferred choice of legal protection for computer software has been to maintain them as trade secrets. Now that state laws for the protection of trade secrets have been recognized as generally constitutional by the Supreme Court, the trade secret route has become the rule for the industry. Concomitantly, the industry considers computer software programs to be clearly trade secret subject matter.[1]

Another reason the trade secret route is preferred over patenting and copyrighting is that, unlike the statutorily limited terms for patents and copyrights, state protection for trade secrets lasts as long as the software program is kept secret, which conceivably may be forever. Secrecy, an essential element,[2] must be proven in order to establish a trade secret. Indeed, the value of a trade secret resides in its secrecy, not in its disclosure. However, a problem for owners lies in obtaining restitution and possibly even retribution against those who would unfairly compete in the industry by misappropriating trade secrets.

A New Look at Unfair Methods of Competition in View of a New Technology

Unfair methods of competition involving misappropriation of trade secrets have traditionally required a taking or copying of tangible property. Analog computers—which by their very nature do not utilize software—and the hardware parts of digital computers constitute tangible property. Consequently, their misappropriation would easily meet the traditional common law requirement of a "taking."

However, the digital computer requires the use of software. This technological innovation led to the creation of basic legal problems for those who wanted to protect their software against the unscrupulous by traditional tort and criminal law concepts.

Software As Property

The first and most basic problem facing owners was whether or not software was indeed property. Because of its nature as input in the form of holes in paper cards and magnetized areas on magnetic tape, software was questioned initially in the courts as to whether it was property capable of being taken in the traditional, legal sense. A reexamination of the basic concept of property as a tangible was required. The question was answered affirmatively when the criminal law was viewed through the magnifying glass of computer programs in *Hancock v. State*.

The defendant, a computer programmer employed by Texas Instruments (TI) in Dallas, worked with approximately 100 secret programs that related to seismic and other geophysical applications. He printed out and photocopied fifty-nine of these programs, valued by his employer at two and one-half million dollars, and attempted to sell them to Texaco Oil for five million dollars. Texaco representatives alerted TI to the offer and they jointly hired an investigator who, upon being shown the programs by the defendant's accomplice, confiscated the photocopies and turned them over to the state prosecutor in Dallas. Criminal charges for theft of property worth more than fifty dollars were brought. Defendant contended that the programs were not "corporeal personal property" within the meaning of the state penal code, that if the programs were property they were valueless in Dallas because there was no market for them, and that, if the programs were valuable property, he had stolen at most thirty-five dollars worth of tangible paper.

These defenses were unavailing and defendant was convicted. On appeal, the Court of Criminal Appeals of Texas found that the computer programs were property subject to theft because the state statute enumerated "all writings of every description, provided such property possess any ascertainable value." The court also found that, although the programs were used in Dallas only by TI employees, they had a market value in excess of fifty dollars because they were used for a price by others, albeit outside Dallas.

The defendant's petition for a writ of habeas corpus in the federal district court was denied, and on appeal to the fifth circuit, the appellate court felt bound by the statutory interpretation of the state court that the papers containing the photocopied computer programs were corporeal property. Consequently, the appellate court affirmed the denial of the request for a writ of habeas corpus on the grounds that the state law, as so construed, did not violate due process.

Although the case was decided on the basis of a liberal interpretation of a state statute, the *Hancock* opinions show a clear willingness to extend the definition of property to include a valuable intangible, such as a computer program.

Intangible Property Capable of Being Taken

A second basic problem confronting those who wished to protect their software by traditional tort and criminal law concepts was whether or not software, as intangible property, was capable of being "taken." It appears that, after the *Hancock* cases cleared the hurdle of finding that software was property, the decision-makers concluded *sub silentio* that software—like any other property—was indeed capable of being taken. Because the *Hancock* cases did not analyze the issue of whether or not there was a taking in the traditional legal sense by trespass and asportation, the issue is still wide open for a detailed analysis that may result in a contrary conclusion. Clearly, if any court is to decide that software can be the subject of trespass and asportation, it must do so by making a constructive finding to include situations where a disloyal person enters upon the employer's premises and carries off valuable software information in his mind.

In any event, unsatisfied with this singular legal victory in the *Hancock* cases, representatives of the computer industry have actively petitioned state legislatures for enactment of broadly worded criminal laws specifically punishing those who would take intangible property such as computer programs.

Although a "taking" is often broadly defined in criminal statutes, the concomitant strict construction of penal codes by the courts may not provide a sufficient deterrent effect in some future cases, and consequently it may be necessary to pursue money damages in a tort action against any apprehended, solvent culprit—individual, corporate, or otherwise—with resort to the broader concept in the Restatement of a taking as any "improper means of discovery."[3]

The Prime Method of Unfair Competition in the Computer Industry—Misappropriation of Trade Secrets

The most common method of unfair competition in the computer industry is the misappropriation of trade secrets. Liability for this type of interference with business relations is expounded in the Restatement of Torts section 757[4] which has been noted as "widely relied upon" by the Supreme Court.[5] Damages will be levied by state courts in tort cases whenever trade secrets are discovered by improper means.[6] Although incapable of precise definitions, improper means of discovery do include "means which fall below the generally accepted standards of commercial morality and reasonable conduct." However, known incidences of such improper means are not too numerous. Perhaps this is so because the intellectual sophistication of those involved in such activity and the nature of the offense as a nonviolent, inconspicuous commission have combined to prevent widespread detection. On the other hand, the sparsity of cases may be due to a level of honesty among those in the industry that is higher than that of the general population. In either event, the quarter century since the commercial advent of computer technology has not been long enough to produce abundant examples of improper means. Nevertheless, there are some cases that merit attention.

The Disloyal Employee

Although "equity has no power to compel a man who changes employers to wipe clean the slate of his memory," this maxim applies only as long as there is no breach of confidence by the former employee. However, a breach may occur in several ways. An employee may be disloyal at heart and commit larceny of tangible computer hardware by his own hand.

In *Sperry Rand Corp. v. Pentronix, Inc.*, Sperry Rand began research and development in 1954 on a process for making magnetic memory cores for use in computers. By 1962, commercial production began at its UNIVAC plant in suburban Philadelphia. During the development, Sperry Rand had its project employees sign a confidential agreement not to disclose any trade secrets or other proprietary information learned during the course of the employment. In late 1966 and early 1967, officers of a small competitor, Pentronix, met with and offered three of Sperry Rand's top employees a higher salary and a profit-sharing plan that amounted to approximately four times their present salary. The trio accepted Pentronix's offer and tendered their resignations to Sperry Rand. Before leaving, however, they photocopied 668 pages of progress and technical reports and 420 pages of engineering bulletins. They also took a certain circuit diagram design and a set of model cores. Finally, other employees observed them toting out briefcases and cardboard boxes full of undetermined documents. Five months after the resignations were effective, Pentronix began commercial sales of sixteen different magnetic memory cores substantially identical to those cores that Sperry Rand had taken eight years to develop. Sperry Rand sued the three former employees for breach of contract and Pentronix for unfair competition. Citing the Restatement of Torts section 757, the court found that the former employees had misappropriated trade secrets, that the competitor was engaging in a conspiracy with the individual defendants, and that, as a result thereof, Sperry Rand had been irreparably harmed. A permanent injunction was issued against Pentronix's manufacture of the cores and damages for lost profits were awarded to Sperry Rand.

An employee may also be disloyal at heart and commit larceny of intangible computer technology by carrying out trade secret information in his mind. In *Sperry Rand Corp. v. Rothlein*, Rothlein approached Sperry Rand in 1953 about going into the business of manufacturing semiconductors for use in computers. Sperry Rand agreed and hired Rothlein to head a research and development division on Long Island, New York. In 1956, the division was moved to Norwalk, Connecticut, and commercial production began. In the meantime, Rothlein, as did each new employee, signed an agreement not to divulge any trade secret to any unauthorized person during or after his term of employment.

Early in 1959, Sperry Rand reorganized the semiconductor division and appointed Sittner as Rothlein's superior. Because this appointment was made without prior consultation with Rothlein, and because of other difficulties with Sperry Rand's management over equipment and production performance, Rothlein decided to form his own company, National Semiconductor Corporation. For another five months, Rothlein worked for Sperry Rand while he obtained financial backing and recruited other Sperry Rand employees for the new firm. After all arrangements were completed for the establishment of National Semiconductor, Rothlein and his recruits resigned en masse from Sperry Rand and the new company went into direct competition, severely cutting into Sperry Rand's share of the market.

One month after the resignations, Sperry Rand sued Rothlein and seven of the twenty-seven other former employees who went to work for National Semiconductor, charging breach of contract and misappropriation of trade secrets. The court found that the defendants had breached their fiduciary duty to their former employer by suppressing corporate opportunities for their own advantage, inducing fellow employees to quit in order to staff their own operation, and taking and using trade secrets learned while in Sperry Rand's employ for the purpose of furthering National Semiconductor's business; all in violation of their employment contracts. Citing the Restatement of Torts section 757, the court also found that the defendants had physically taken a copy of specifications for a silicon alloy junction transistor, various drawings, and other confidential documents. The defendants vigorously contested this point. The court's statement was most interesting on the issue of mental misappropriation:

> The defendants claim that the drawings used by their company, National Semiconductor Corporation, most of which were the same as and interchangeable with Sperry's drawings, were constructed, not by copying from Sperry's, but from memory. It may be and if so, it was a remarkable display of memory, for numerous measurements were in thousandths of an inch. But it does not matter whether a copy of a Sperry drawing came out in a defendant's hand or in his head. His duty of fidelity to his employer remains the same.

Also, regarding employees, an employer must guard against not only the disloyal at heart but also those vulnerable to bribery and coercion through threats of harm by third parties or through blackmail because of an employee's present or past matters of personal sensitivity. Finally, simply because an employer has information that it regards as a trade secret is no assurance that a court will hold a disloyal employee accountable for any unauthorized use of such information after terminating his or her employment. An employer must take reasonable safeguards to maintain the confidentiality of a trade secret. Information cannot be a trade secret one day for purposes of muting an employee and not be a trade secret another day for purposes of obtaining new business. Confidentiality must be maintained at all times. Although it is not absolutely necessary to have employment agreements prohibiting disclosure of confidential information as in the two *Sperry Rand* cases, an employer should be advised to have such written agreements. A failure to safeguard purported trade secrets and to have nondisclosure employment agreements can have disastrous consequences on an employer's business.

In *Republic Systems & Programming, Inc. v. Computer Assistance, Inc.*, a computer software business had a branch office managed by Vignola who, like the rest of its employees, had no written employment contract. Disenchanted with financial conditions and supervision by the home office, Vignola consulted his top assistants and his lawyer about forming his own company and discussed subsequent merger plans with his employer's chief competitor. As soon as the incorporation papers of the new company were prepared, Vignola mailed a letter of resignation to the home office. The resignation, sent on a Friday, was to be effective immediately. During the weekend Vignola contacted his former co-workers and offered them jobs with his new company at slightly higher salaries than they were being paid at that time. When the employer's branch office opened Monday morning, only five of the twenty-five employees arrived. On that Monday, Vignola started soliciting business from his former employer's customers, and most switched their business to him.

Four days after receiving Vignola's letter of resignation in the mail, the former employer sued Vignola for breach of fiduciary duty and for misappropriation of trade secrets, i.e., customer lists. The district court dismissed the employer's action. The court ruled that the fiduciary duty ended when the employment ended and that, since there was no written contract between the parties, each employee was "entitled to terminate the employment relationship at will at any time with or without cause." Citing the Restatement of Torts section 757, comment b, the court also ruled that customer lists did not qualify as trade secrets because many of the clients were openly listed in advertising brochures as "representative clients" and "efforts to keep the names of the remainder secret were meager at best." The court of appeals affirmed the district court's opinion with one judge dissenting.

Customers

Secrecy in the industry is ordinarily maintained by software owners through nondisclosure clauses in leases with customers for the computer programs. These written agreements allow owners to seek money damages in court through breach of contract actions for any unauthorized disclosures made by lessees of the trade secret.

For example, in *Data General Corp. v. Digital Computer Controls, Inc.*, a manufacturer sold small general-purpose digital computers. Ordinarily, the logic or design drawings of the machine were not included in the sale; however, if a customer wanted to make its own repairs rather than wait for the manufacturer's maintenance personnel to do so, the drawings would be made available at no extra cost upon signing an agreement not to disclose them to third parties. All drawings were marked with a legend that they were proprietary information and not to be used for manufacturing purposes. One customer sold everything, including the design drawings, to one of the competitors of the computer manufacturer. The competitor used the drawings as the basic design for a new model.

The manufacturer sought a preliminary injunction against the use of its drawings and the competitor filed a motion for summary judgment. The state chancery court denied both motions. Apparently, because the manufacturer sold the computer, making it generally available to the public for reverse engineering purposes, the court denied the motion for a preliminary injunction. The court considered the manufacturer entitled to an injunction only for that period of time determined to be necessary for the competitor to reverse engineer the computer without the drawings. Since the term of the injunction during the court proceedings might extend beyond that period needed for successful reverse engineering, the court decided not to grant any injunction. However, because the manufacturer had taken some precautions to protect the design drawings as trade secrets, the court denied the competitor's motion for summary judgment. The conclusion was that the adequacy of the precautions was a factual dispute preventing summary judgment. Ten months later, the state supreme court affirmed the chancery court, citing the Restatement of Torts section 757.

Also, an owner must guard against not only those customers who obtain the trade secret legally and later sell it for their own monetary gain when the opportunity comes, but also customers who approach the owner and initially misrepresent their intentions for the sole purpose of obtaining the trade secret to sell or otherwise dispose of it for their own gain. Such activity suggests criminal acts of deceit and taking property under false pretenses.

Competitors

In protecting its trade secrets, a software owner should design safeguards mainly against discovery by direct competitors. However, as indicated above, those safeguards can be breached by a competitor via the instrumentality of employees and customers. In an industry where high intellect and low capital are the only requirements to enter the marketplace, it is no surprise that the competition is fierce and occasionally sinks to the most unscrupulous level. The unfair methods of competition practiced in the software industry by competitors today have taken an interesting twist from those of unfair competition in the traditional sense. In the latter type of practices, a competitor sold its own goods as those of another—commonly known as "palming off."

Today in the software industry, a competitor, as a result of a misappropriation of a trade secret, sells or leases another's goods or information as its own. However, since most software arrangements are leases and most of these are made in confidence, it is difficult for one to learn when a competitor has misappropriated one's trade secrets. This is true even if both approach the same prospective customer. Unless the customer has the highest moral standards, the customer will usually stand mute when the same computer program at substantially different prices is offered confidentially by two competitors, because it is in the financial interest of the customer to remain silent and accept the lower offer.

Although there is a constant fear in the software industry about espionage, conspiracies, burglaries, malicious destruction of property, and other types of sabotage by competitors, the number of cases exposed is far less than one would expect for an industry that fluctuates so widely at times in its number of market participants. However, there is one leading case that is significant because of the amount of money involved. The owner survived simply because it was big enough to absorb the losses.

In *Telex Corp. v. IBM Corp.*, Telex sued IBM for violating the Sherman Antitrust Act by monopolizing the market in plug compatible peripheral products attachable to central processing units for IBM computers. IBM counterclaimed for misappropriation of trade secrets relating to the pertinent technology. In the manufacture of plug compatible peripheral products, IBM had about thirty-five percent of the market and earned about 1.14 billion dollars in 1970. All its combined competitors earned slightly less than 100 million dollars. About this time, one competitor in this computer products sub-market, Telex, embarked upon a systemic plan to lure away key employees of IBM. In 1970, only one of its fifty engineers had worked for IBM but, by 1973, 152 of its 1,929 employees were ex-IBM personnel. The recruits were offered substantially higher salaries, stock options, and bonuses, in one case up to one-half million dollars and were encouraged to take out all the confidential information and trade secrets they could before they left IBM's employment. As a result of this piratical activity, Telex was able to reduce significantly its development time on many projects, in one case from five to one and one-half years. Also, it was able to save significantly on costs, as much as ten million dollars on the same project and seven and one-half million dollars on another project. On the counterclaim, the trial court awarded 20.9 million dollars actual damages and assessed one million dollars punitive damages. The court of appeals affirmed the decision but reduced the amount of actual damages to seventeen and one-half million dollars.

Joint Venturers

A common practice, an outgrowth of the highly competitive nature of the computer software industry, is the joint venture in which several small competitors pool resources and assist each other in carrying out their separate services. However, when one company gets desperate, financially or otherwise, as sometimes happens, there is a falling out between the parties. Such disagreements often lead persons to commit acts which they would not have considered in better times and, as has been the case from the time of Caesar, a stab in the back has been known to be delivered by a former friendly hand. Consider the following two cases.

In *Com-Share, Inc. v. Computer Complex, Inc.*, two financially struggling software development companies entered into a technical exchange agreement in 1967. After differences arose between the parties, the agreement was prematurely terminated in 1970. The agreement had provided that neither party could disclose the exchanged trade secrets to third parties without prior written consent of the other for a period of twenty-four months after its expiration. However, nine months after the termination, Computer Complex announced that it was selling out substantially all of its assets to a larger competitor of Com-Share. The former joint venturer sued for an injunction against the sale of its exchanged trade secrets. The defendant contended that the duty not to disclose ended when the agreement was terminated by mutual consent and that the injunction would be an idle gesture because the transfer of the software trade secrets had begun and "the omelet cannot be unscrambled." The court was "not persuaded that modern technology has withered the strong right arm of equity" and ruled that the disposition of the assets would unjustly enrich the defendant at the expense of Com-Share. A preliminary injunction was issued and affirmed by the court of appeals.

A more complicated fact situation involving joint venturers and a disloyal employee arose in *University Computing Co. v. Lykes-Youngstown Corp.* In 1969, a small computer service company, University Computing Co. (hereinafter UCC), and a large holding company, Lykes-Youngstown Corp. (hereinafter LYC), entered into a joint venture agreement whereby a new company, Lykes/UCC, was formed to open new markets for computer systems. UCC was to provide management and LYC was to post capital. A UCC officer, Shinn, became president of Lykes/UCC, but advised LYC that, if it formed its own wholly-owned subsidiary, chances for commercial success would be substantially the same but at a better rate of return on its capital. Consequently, LYC terminated the joint venture agreement after only two months existence and established a subsidiary, Lykes-Youngstown Computer Services Corp. (hereinafter LYCSC), with Shinn as its president. Shortly thereafter, LYCSC bribed an employee of a UCC customer in order to steal the computer tapes and materials incident to a computerized retail inventory control system leased by UCC subject to a restrictive use agreement. LYCSC then began marketing the system in direct competition with UCC. UCC sued LYC, LYCSC, and Shinn for misappropriation of the computerized system. Citing the Restatement of Torts section 757, the court of appeals affirmed the jury verdict for UCC that the computerized system was a trade secret wrongfully appropriated by the three co-defendants.

Suggestions for Protecting Computer Software Against Methods of Unfair Competition

Although there is no assured way to protect one's computer software against a determined enemy, a number of routine security precautions should substantially decrease the chance of inadvertent damage or losses and increase the likelihood of detection and apprehension of any ill-meaning culprits.

First, access to the computer and its material storage areas should be well controlled.

Casually parading business visitors and members of the general public on good will tours may result in the loss of a seemingly inconspicuous piece of hardware or software as a surreptitiously taken souvenir. Duplicate or even triplicate files of all card decks, tapes, and other tangible material should be maintained in separate storage areas, preferably remotely located from each other in individual fireproof safes or vaults. These are inadvertent losses that may be easily avoided by simple safety measures.

It is more difficult to protect one's computer software against deliberate abuse. However, a number of safeguards may be invoked particularly directed toward monitoring the activities of employees who, as was pointed out above, are the major perpetrators of trade secret misappropriations. The safeguarding process should begin before the potential employee is hired by conducting an extensive screening of the person's background. Nothing less than a check with the FBI for past criminal activity may be satisfactory. At the moment of hiring, an employment contract with a clause forbidding the disclosure of trade secrets should be presented for the prospective employee's signature. The clause should be carefully and forcefully explained in order to impress upon the person the seriousness of any violation and the resulting civil and criminal penalties. After the employee is hired, one way to keep him or her honest is to pay a high salary with generous bonuses and merit raises for good work. Since most employees that have become disloyal did so for more money, this practice, although applicable to any industry, takes on added significance in the computer field where the detection of misappropriation of trade secrets is quite difficult.

It is advisable that a password be developed for allowing direct access to the computer by only those employees who need to have such access. This password should be changed periodically so that former employees who no longer need access cannot obtain it at their pleasure or relay an effective password to the unscrupulous. A rewards policy for any employee who reports suspicious activity or unusual operating procedures by a co-employee that turns out to be justified creates an effective internal system of checks and balances. Finally, a periodic and unannounced random accounting and/or run of computer software by selected employees would also serve as an internal security procedure.

Some employees may object to such strict security measures on grounds that they create a work atmosphere of fear and suspicion. The natural answer to the objection is that only employees who have anything to fear are those who have something to hide. After all, the employer is in a high risk business and must be vigilant with such an intangible as computer software. Likewise, the employer's attorney must not be ignorant of the pitfalls facing the client before and during its venture into the dark and treacherous business world of computer software technology.

Notes

1. Restatement of Torts §757, Comment b (1939) states:
   Definition of trade secret. A trade secret may consist of any formula, pattern, device or compilation of information which is used in one's business and which gives him an opportunity to obtain an advantage over competitors who do not know or use it. . . . A trade secret is a process or device for continuous use in the operation of the business. Generally it relates to the production of goods as, for example, a machine or formula for the production of an article. It may, however, relate to the sale of goods or to other operations in the business. . . .

2. Restatement of Torts §757, Comment b (1939) states:
   Secrecy. The subject matter of a trade secret must be secret. . . . [A] substantial element of secrecy must exist, so that, except by the use of improper means, there would be difficulty in acquiring the information. An exact definition of a trade secret is not possible. Some factors to be considered in determining whether given information is one's trade secret are: (1) the extent to which the information is known outside of his business; (2) the extent to which it is known by employees and others involved in his business; (3) the extent of measures taken by him to guard the secrecy of the information; (4) the value of the information to him and to his competitors; (5) the amount of effort or money expended by him in developing the information; (6) the ease or difficulty with which the information could be properly acquired or duplicated by others.

3. Restatement of Torts §757, Comment f (1939) states:
   Improper means of discovery. The discovery of another's trade secret by improper means subjects the actor to liability independently of the harm to the interest in the secret. . . . Examples of such means are fraudulent misrepresentations to induce disclosure, tapping of telephone wires, eavesdropping or other espionage. A complete catalogue of improper means is not possible. In general they are means which fall below the generally accepted standards of commercial morality and reasonable conduct.

4. Liability for Disclosure or Use of Another's Trade Secret—General Principle.
   One who discloses or uses another's trade secret, without a privilege to do so, is liable to the other if (a) he discovered the secret by improper means, or (b) his disclosure or use constitutes a breach of confidence reposed in him by the other in disclosing the secret to him, or (c) he learned the secret from a third person with notice of the facts that it was a secret and that the third person discovered it by improper means or that the third person's disclosure of it was otherwise a breach of his duty to the other, or (d) he learned the secret with notice of the facts that it was a secret and that its disclosure was made to him by mistake. Restatement of Torts §757 (1939).

5. In ruling that state laws for the protection of trade secrets are not preempted by the federal patent law, the Supreme Court cited this Restatement section in *Kewanee Oil Co. v. Bicron Corp.*, 416 U.S. 470, 474–76 (1974).

6. Restatement of Torts §757 (1939) states: "One who, for the purpose of advancing a rival business interest, procures by improper means information about another's business is liable to the other for the harm caused by his possession, disclosure or use of the information."